W9-CMA-380

The Borzoi Book of Modern Dance

THE
BORZOI
BOOK
OF
MODERN
DANCE

by Margaret Lloyd

a republication
by Dance Horizons

Copyright 1949 by Margaret Lloyd

A Dance Horizons Book
Princeton Book Company, Publishers
P.O. Box 109
Princeton, New Jersey 08542

This is an unabridged republication of the original
edition published in 1949 by Alfred A. Knopf, Inc.,
New York.

All rights reserved. No part of this book may be reproduced
or utilized in any form or by any means, electronic or
mechanical, including photocopying, recording or by any
information storage and retrieval system, without
permission in writing from the Publisher.

ISBN 87127-023-4
Library of Congress Catalog Card Number 78-77181
Printed in the United States of America

Third printing 1987

"*To dance means to be new, to be fresh at every moment, as though one had just issued from the hand of God.*"

JACOB WASSERMANN: *The World's Illusion*

PREFACE

This book is written for those who want to know about the development of modern dance in the United States, by a layman who has followed it with affection for nearly twenty years. It is intended as an over-all picture, and not as a definitive history, and is written, of course, from one point of view. For other points of view, and greater enlightenment, I suggest the appended Bibliography as a reading list.

There are many more interesting people in the American modern dance than could be included in this volume. I have written about those who seem to me to have made the most marked individual creative contributions to it, and, so far as possible, those who have come within my experience.

To the young moderns just coming up, whose work I do not know, to the many modern dancers herein anonymous, whose work I have enjoyed, to all dancers of every kind, and to all workers in the field of dance, I am grateful.

MARGARET LLOYD

Brookline, Massachusetts
August 21, 1948

ACKNOWLEDGEMENTS

I am indebted to a great many people for this book. To all the dancers in it, most of whom have talked with me for or before it, and many of whom have tabulated for me the chronological data of their careers and supplied photographs; to Thomas Bouchard and John Lindquist, who supplied other photographs; to Pauline Lawrence, who dug up facts and memories of the early Humphrey-Weidman days; to Pauline Chellis, who also reminisced about those days, and of her long experience in the educational dance; to Judith Delman, who outlined the history of the New Dance Group, Aileen Flaven Gardner, who wrote from Los Angeles about Lester Horton's new Dance Theater, Dorothy Adlow, who told me her impressions of Hanya Holm's 1947 production at Colorado College, Sally Kamin, who made suggestions for the Bibliography; and to the dance magazines—*The American Dancer, Dance,* and *Dance Observer*—for informative material.

Most of all I am indebted to my editor, Herbert Weinstock, for inviting me to write the book, and for his wise and patient counsel and criticism in reading the first draft; and to John Martin, for recommending me for the job, and for his leadership in the field of dance criticism.

MARGARET LLOYD

CONTENTS

MODERN DANCE ON THE WEST COAST

ILLUSTRATIONS

INTRODUCTION

What is *Modern Dance?*

Modern dance is what modern painting and modern music are—a new development of an old art—a creative manifestation of our time. It is an outgrowth of all that has gone before, and is subject to constant new growth and change. It is, specifically, the continuous opening of new paths for the expression of the human spirit through the human body.

It is not always so understood. Some people dismiss it as the latest in ballroom steps; others regard it as a willful negation of grace and beauty, a cult of ugliness comprehensible only to the initiated.

"These angular abstractions are grotesque," they say. "They are without meaning, or if they have a meaning, it is too esoteric for me."

And of course the hard-shell balletomane is sure the whole thing is a plot, an aggressive anti-ballet movement.

Against these popular misconceptions, against the inevitable undertow of apathy or animosity toward anything new or different, in the midst of a general resurgence of dance of all kinds, especially in the United States, the kind of dance called modern has managed to build first a following and then a public. There must be something in it, something for plain people as well as for experts.

Since its inception over twenty years ago, there has been a certain amount of dissatisfaction with the term itself. But it is a term that cannot be evaded. Contemporary dance is not just right, because that term covers all forms extant today. Expressional dance won't do, either, for all dance is expression of one sort or another.

The need of expression, together with the common instincts of rhythm and of religion, is the basis of dance. Primitive man expressed in the most direct way possible, that is, through rhythmic bodily movement, his reverential awe at the world of mystery and wonder around him. The modern dancer, with less awe, perhaps, and a more intelligent sense of wonder, expresses, as directly, his reaction to the more complex modern world.

The dances of antiquity had their origin in the expression of religious faith, even if some of them went extremely secular in due course. The gods the ancients worshipped or propitiated were heathen gods, but their belief in them gave validity to their dance rituals and ceremonies. Folk dances of all nations are a communal expression, a devout togetherness (though the participants might not name it so) in veneration for their peasant earth. And what if the courtiers of Italy and France, in their first ballet steps, were only trying to improve their manners? It was a looking up, an endeavor to give form to an ideal of something better than they had known.

Throughout dance history the religious impulse has been the motive power of dance. It is not always formal religion, clothed in churchly vestments. It is not to be confused with sanctimony or necessarily with the moral virtues. It is what is deeply felt, often inexplicable and unavowed, what is otherwise unutterable, man's hidden treasure, that comes out in his dancing.

No, modern dance is not alone in expressivity. The departure is in the why and what and how of its expression. Where other forms are content to imitate nature, modern dance discloses nature, particularly human nature—the inner nature of man. Where primitive forms are semiconscious expressions of the conscious and the unconscious through the body, modern dance consciously uses the body to express states of consciousness, and more recently, of the unconscious. Modern dance is fantasy, a palimpsest of unreality, through which the underlying realities are brought to life more sharply than in every-day life.

And why is the body the means of expression? Not only because the body is what the dancer dances with, but because what is said cannot be said in words or music, paint or stone. There are other reasons. Much of what we are is shown in the way we move. We frequently express our innermost feelings (and sometimes give ourselves away) in involuntary movements. Modern dance puts these common involuntary movements (of which there are many more than we are normally aware) into voluntary rhythmic movement. Taking the natural motor impulse as a springboard, it distorts, diminishes, augments, expands, and adds to the instinctive gesture or motion, gives it artistic shape, so that by the sympathetic response of metakinesis a straight line of communication is established.

It is not anything so literal as pantomime, which, by spelling everything out, affords no griphold for the spectator's imagination. It is rather intimation, suggestion, the planting of posts of recognition, allowing space between for the spectator to fill in; and also introducing new movement values that go beyond the spectator's former level. Modern dance is organic. It models not from but out of life. What distinguishes it from other forms is that it has learned to use the body to a fuller capacity, to relate dance movement to life movement, to a greater degree than has ever been done before.

Technically, the chief difference is in the torso, a stress and strain in the muscles of the trunk, a more minute, more complicated flexibility than that seen in the ordinary side, forward, or back bend. The muscular control is centered from the pelvic girdle, at once supporting and freeing the action. There is no arbitrarily turned out thigh, as in the classic ballet. And while there are resemblances to the classic school, the *danse d'école,* in the occasional *coupé, glissade, cabriole,* and so on, done in bare feet on a larger, freer scale, in attitudes and arabesques that are distortions of the conventional, and in other ways, there is nothing strictly according to Petipa, or ballet-master, rule.

A modern leg extension can be something like a ballet *développé*. The famous Martha Graham leg extension in second position is an extension *à la seconde,* with more push and pull to it. And in the high jumps and leaps (for, contrary to general opinion, modern dance has levitation as well as gravitation) the legs are held at odd angles in the air, feet stuck up or out instead of pointed down. Falls are done in succession movements flowing through the body from part to part, instead of all in one piece. But one should not be too definite on these points. Modern dance is individually creative, and each artist conceives and masters his technique in his own way.

One feature, however, is explicit. Modern dance is a matter of dynamic volume rather than of presentation solely on the frontal plane, of mass more than of line. Being more concerned with the abstraction of things felt than with the pictorial representation of things seen, it chooses broken rhythms, off-balances, the casual appearance, the imperfect cadence, in preference to what is smooth and formal and regular. And if this would seem to make it jangle like sweet bells out of tune, it makes its own tune. It is free but not formless, rugged but polished, for it is governed by a discipline of its own.

Dance (with the allied art of acting) is the one art that employs the body as a unit. The hand paints, or plays the musical instrument; in dance the body *is* the instrument. The hand writes words or music, molds the sculpture, designs the architectural plan; the whole body dances. Yet it is not the body that speaks. Not a muscle moves of itself. The hand does not do the painting, the fingers do not bring forth the music or set down the words, themselves. It is not the larynx that sings, it is not the actor's limping leg that tells us a character is old or lame. It is in each case the mind of the artist.

So modern dance, though exercising the entire musculature, the very articulating bones of the dancer, is not primarily muscular or anatomical. It is a thing of the spirit. If you come away from a modern dance performance as one who walks on air, chest lifted, head held high, a sense of renewal pervading your being, it is not because by sensory perception muscle has spoken to muscle, but be cause through controlled muscular action, spirit has spoken to spirit, something ineffable has been conveyed. It is a spiritual elation.

If you don't come away in any such exalted state, but rather the reverse (and fairly angry about it), try again. Those annoying dissonances and deformations, those sharp accents and irregular rhythms, will eventually come clear as having something to do with you. You will find that the accents are on life, the rhythms of an awakening subtlety, the dissonances an illumination of many disturbing undercurrents you have denied or resisted or didn't know existed at all.

If it were not for our need of dancing there would be no public, hence no professional dancers. The dancer dances for us who have been deprived of dancing, to vent for us our need of rhythmic movement, so that we may share vicariously the refreshment of the dance experience. The modern dance goes further and reveals us to ourselves. But elation of the spirit is within the power of all dance to give. It can be imparted by a fine performance of a classical *pas de deux,* a spirited folk dance, a vigorous hopak or czardas. It can be enkindled by the Spanish dance as done by great artists like the Argentina and Argentinita of memory; by the Hindu dance as Shan-Kar and others have shown it to us; and even by the once lowly tap step as glorified 'in Ray Bolger's wonderful solo, "The Old Soft Shoe." Our rhythmic natures cannot help responding to rhythmic movement.

Dance is one, as art is one, as humanity is one, however platitudinous it may be to say so. The more we sample its infinite variety, the more we know this oneness. Modern dance, sensitive to the ideal of unity, conceived if not yet demonstrated in our age, is increasingly drawing on other forms, not by absorption but by adaptation. Indeed, the two dominant art forms—ballet and modern dance—are, without loss of identity, slowly mingling in idea and technic. Each has influenced the other, and both have influenced the musical comedy dance, and to a lesser extent the screen and other processed forms. Both have influenced modern music and stage design.

The special impact of modern dance lies in its correlation with humanity. Despite its contemporaneity, it does not hesitate to look backward for the fundamental links between other ages and ours. It looks forward with prophetic discernment; inward to what is going on in human consciousness; it embraces the thoughts and activities of mankind. Modern dance is world conscious, concerned with social, national, and international problems, as well as with those of personal relationships. Not that it is always serious, or without humor, lightness, vivacity. An art that so closely reflects life could hardly leave humor out. Its source is a deep and penetrating, an inclusive intelligence. However much the attempt is made to separate modern dance from intellect, the creative modern dancer *is* intellectual. Modern dance is intellectually conceived and projected, and requires something more than the basic motor instinct, namely, at least a modicum of intellect, to be fully perceived. It is not, after all, an art of shallow minds.

This does not mean that the leading artists are dry academicians. It refers, of course, to modern dance in its highest estate—something one does not always see. The carved-out clichés of the imitators are but so many still-lifes of genuine movement; the weak dilutions of the uninspired are hardly more than calisthenics. Nor is modern dance at its best always as eloquent as it intends to be. There are limits to what the body can say as well as to what the body can do. So much are these limitations currently felt that modern choreographers are increasingly resorting to words. Where movement fails them, they expect words will not. It is not wholly that, either, for the use of words has increased with the trend of modern dance away from concert into theater.

The art dance has always leaned upon words more, perhaps, than it has apprehended. It depends on the printed title to establish the mood; on printed program notes to provide clues to the action; on the printed review to tell the public about it. What more natural than that it should go a step further and introduce spoken, sung, or chanted words into the dance itself? The whole man speaks and sings as well as moves. Let him speak, then, in the dance, if he can make himself heard.

But the modern use of words is still in the experimental stage.

Fusion is seldom attained. The struggle to hear what the words are saying, while watching to see what the movement is saying, distracts attention from the real substance of dance, which is movement. Two separate channels of communication are set up, weakening the communicative power of each. There are notable exceptions, as in Martha Graham's *Letter to the World,* in which fragments of Emily Dickinson's verses are successfully interpolated by a dancer who speaks well and moves comparatively little; in Doris Humphrey's *Lament for Ignacio Sánchez Mejías,* in which a skilled actress speaks translated portions of the poem by García Lorca, and also moves but slightly; and in Charles Weidman's *On My Mother's Side,* in which verses especially written for that dance are recited, like spoken program notes, by a chorus standing at one side, before each dance interlude. In the modern ballets, *Facsimile* and *On Stage!* colloquial ejaculations are used with startling effect.

Poetry written for the dance (as music so often is nowadays) instead of being adapted to it, is one solution of the word problem that is gaining favor. It must be spaced and timed in relation to the movement it accompanies and is supposed to elucidate; and, when words are given to dancers, with due regard for their breathing. With due regard for the audience, too, one might add, in having the words made clearly audible without the aid of a loud speaker.

On the whole, modern dance is most satisfactory as rhythmic movement unadorned, except for the propulsion of its music and the necessities of its costume and décor, sheer, unadulterated movement, exhilarating, infectious, something beyond the realm of words, that cannot be felt or described in words. However, if words must be, they no doubt will be guided into their proper place, as they already have been in some instances.

Modern dance has not reached a blessed state of set perfection, wherein to dwell happily ever after. It is merely the progressive part, the new growth, of an art that is as old as man, as universal as the smile. It is no more finished than any growing thing. But it is, like every growing thing, very much alive.

The Borzoi Book of Modern Dance

FORERUNNERS

Duncan—Wigman—Denishawn

ANGELA ISADORA DUNCAN

What Beethoven is to modern music, what Walt Whitman is to modern poetry, Isadora Duncan is to modern dance —the first great romanticist, the first apostle of freedom and democracy in her art, the liberator from sterile conventions. The first free-verse dancer was, of course, the modern dancer of her day. When as a child of six she assembled a small impromptu class of neighborhood babies on the living-room floor, and taught them to wave their arms, she started, all unwittingly, the movement now known as modern. It was not our modern dance, or anything like it. It was a seed whose later flowering would have astonished Isadora herself. It was that instinctive turning to nature, drawing on the natural resources within and without, that marks all dance expression. But it had in it that extra something that was Isadora, and it is that extra something as unfolded in Isadora's life experience that places her first in the spiritual ancestry of today's modern dance. She was a natural dancer, a lover of nature, and a rebel from childhood. Her first idea of movement, she says in her autobiography, came from the rhythm of the waves.

Isadora, whose magnificent arms were so often extended in the outgiving or upsoaring gesture, began with arms—the members the modern dancers were slowest to develop. She held them naturally, never in a fixed, formalized style, the hands easy, the fingers not artificially curved, though the fists could be clenched in passion or palms spread open in beneficence. Her face and neck were mobile and expressive, and these factors, too, today's modern dance, in its early stages, overlooked. But her movements were simple compared with what we have now. The feet, which she was first (professionally) to bare, were not played as separate keys of eloquence, were not as tensile as those of modern dance. The torso, which she was first to free, did not turn and twist and writhe as modern torsos do. There was no extreme distortion, if any. The movements were round without softness, there was more symmetry than asymmetry, more melody than counterpoint.

Everything Isadora did was on the heroic scale. She reclined rather than fell; she kneeled to rise again; her movements were mainly upspringing. Although she revitalized the dance, gave it new weight and force, and although her dancing was of a dynamism that blazoned across a stage, it did not have the dynamic range or accent of today's. It was more a harmonious plasticity, an inspired fluidity, or swinging, swaying, flowing rhythms, with no marked dissonances, no small planes, no little vibratory motions, no littleness of any kind. These positive statements are based solely on conjecture, from a study of her innumerable pictures, and of verbal descriptions of her dancing. I never saw her dance.

One sees in these pictures no evidence of very high or very wide leg extensions, just a moderate lifting of the leg forward, knee bent, head thrown back, Bacchante-like, or a low kick backward, and now and then a flying leap of no very great elevation. Speaking comparatively, she used the natural means of locomotion only slightly intensified. One sees in modern dance studios similar motor patterns, the pupils running, skipping, prancing, galloping diagonally over the floor, contorting their bodies in the wide leap or high jump, and holding their legs in a manner Isadora would probably have called ungainly. Not that her dancing was pretty, or unduly graceful. One gathers from many sources that strength as well as simplicity characterized her movements, and that they were considered as baffling and remote, as revolutionary and wild, by the recalcitrants of her day, as modern dance is by contemporary objectors.

To conclude the comparison, Isadora, statuesque, majestic, in robe or tunic, opaque or sheer, long or short, as the need might be, with no décor but the famous blue draperies, held the stage alone, was more powerful alone. She has said that she always tried to be the Chorus, meaning the tragic Chorus of the Greeks, that she "never once danced a solo." Nevertheless, she danced alone, and better so, and her six "Isadorables," when they did appear, were hardly more than vain repetitions of her.

Today in modern dance the solo recital is all but obsolete. The genius of the modern dance solo, when it does occur, is its implication of the life around it, which is no doubt what Isadora intended. Modern dance requires the group or company for full expression, and this group is the chorus. It is made up of individuals of assorted shapes and sizes, each with a different office to fill. With few exceptions, it participates in the action, instead of standing aside and commenting upon it. There are great soloists among us still, and these soloists can, like Isadora, be, on occasion, the chorus in themselves. But the full purport of modern dance lies in its employment of the group, or actual chorus.

Modern dance is not based on Isadora's technique, except as that technique is "innerly," as her brother, Augustin, the actor, once described it to me in an interview. He assured me that she had a very definite technique of her own; that she had, to his knowledge, studied ballet with Marie Bonfanti and with Katti Lanner, two celebrities of the time; that she had studied other kinds of dancing, and from childhood had used certain exercises to train the body for expression. Her technique, the mastery of the means of expression, was so submerged in the expression, he said, that some people mistakenly inferred she hadn't any. It is this "innerliness" of expression, and not the outward form, that modern dancers draw upon. They do not attempt literally to copy her any more than she attempted literally to copy the figures on Greek vases. However, Isadora's technical approach has been preserved in a measure by the band of sincere followers who are the true believers of the Duncan faith. They are the perpetuators of the Duncan technic, what there was of it, and if an art so personal, so individual, as Augustin said, that it can never be duplicated, can be continued in the persons of others. Two of the "Isadorables"—Maria Theresa, with a group called the Helioconodes—and Irma, the faithful disciple of the Russian days—carried on in New York for many years; and Irma wrote a slim textbook, *The Technique of Isadora Duncan,* which gives in twelve lessons the fundamentals of Duncan dancing as she learned it.

In May 1946 the Duncan Dance Guild published its first issue of the *Duncan Dance Bulletin,* with the idea of further promoting and preserving the Duncan art intact. Some of the younger members of the league, pupils of Isadora's pupils, have swerved sufficiently to introduce new movements into their work. Julia Levien, who was an awestruck little girl when she picked up the beads the boorish Essenin (Isadora's young husband) had broken at a party in her house, has appeared with modern dance groups from time to time. Anita Zahn and Kathleen Hinni are bringing their interpretive dances closer to their own day and age.

Isadora was the product of her period if well in advance of it. She was a nineteenth century romanticist, who would be out of place in the middle of the twentieth century. One has only to read Carl Van Vechten's early reviews (1909–11–17) as reprinted in the book *Isadora Duncan,* edited by Paul Magriel, to wonder if the *Marseillaise* and the *Marche Slave* wouldn't look like ham-dancing today. They sound terribly overwrought and self-expressional, in spite of their impersonal radiations. They were really propaganda in pantomime. The *Marseillaise* was danced in the same spirit that Sarah Bernhardt, then lame and old, delivered her oratorical plea, *"Ne les pardonnez-point car ils savent ce qu'ils font!"* during the first world war. The *Marche Slave* was a thought for the Russian moujik. Shackles were shaken from torn wrists and patriotism glorified in dance recitals for years afterwards. Such dances belong to the past. History had better be careful about repeating itself here.

It was not until after the American modern dance was well established that Isadora became its figure-head, symbol of its philosophic origin. Her philosophy was not particularly intellectual. It was based less on reason than instinct, a desire for self-expression, albeit an expression of the self in relation to the rest of humanity. Much has been made of her quest for the soul or center of movement and final locating of it in the solar plexus. A hungry man will tell you that the soul is in the stomach and it amounts to the same thing. More has been made of her analysis of "first movements," the source movements of emotional dance. John Martin, in his profound if somewhat fanciful article, "Isadora and Basic Dance," reprinted from the first issue of *Dance Index* in the Magriel book, likens these first movements to Stanislavsky's principles of memory-acting, and invites some scholarly unknown to search the Duncan scriptures and therefrom produce a system in what he thinks might probably be "the greatest textbook of the dance ever written."

Isadora had no system. She was not a scholar. She was an artist, as slightly mad—or volatile, erratic, impulsive—as most artists are. She skimmed the cream of culture. She took exactly what pleased her and left all that was drab and drear and studious to the erudite. Her ideas were fragmentary, often as extravagant as, in print, they are inspiring. She no doubt had certain rudiments of movement she used and taught after her fashion. But the creative dancers who have followed her have been able to find their own first movements, their own centers of operation. The legacy she left the modern dance was a spiritual legacy. Why not leave it at that? The startling innovator of her time was the precursor of more startling innovations. She was also the legatee of other innovators.

The American dance, like most Americans, was born of European ancestry. Its forefathers came with the immigrant and the political refugee, with the dancing masters from France and Italy, the ballroom and country dances from Great Britain, the exponents of nature dancing and gymnastic dancing from Germany. Before Isadora's career had begun, Genevieve Stebbins was lecturing on François Delsarte's life-studies of dramatic expression through movement and gesture; and the music-and-movement theories of Dalcroze Eurythmics were becoming known in this country. As an example of her youthful interpretive abilities, Augustin told me how Isadora as a girl used to do "I Shot an Arrow in the Air" with appropriate gestures, forgetting, perhaps, that that little recitation piece was right out of the Delsarte book. Isadora may never have seen it, but not long after the first baby class, which she announced to her surprised mother was the beginning of her school of dance, she and her sister Elizabeth were teaching "fancy" dancing to the little girls of San Francisco for payment, and helping to support the family.

The fancy, natural, aesthetic, and interpretive dancing that flooded the country in the twenties cannot entirely be attributed to her. All these influences were permeating physical education, then called physical culture, and drifting into the dance schools. Out of the French and Italian ballet was evolved the simplified or modified ballet taught in the colleges, where Delsarte gestures were sometimes done in Greek draperies, and the bare foot was not altogether unknown. This was the background of Isadora's dance. These were the prevailing elements in the atmosphere out of which she brought to a peak her highly magnetic, personal style.

The whole story of modern dance is a story of interrelated influences, of growth and change. And so it was with Isadora, who is said never to have done any one dance twice alike. The obscure "artiste" who danced on Mrs. Astor's lawn at Newport, in the drawing-rooms of New York and London (and sometimes wore slippers and a lace dress), who crossed the Atlantic with her devoted family in a cattle-boat, and after many hardships, at last had Europe at her bare feet, went through many transformations. Young and impressionable, she imbibed ideas from every springhead, learned to see truth glistening from a myriad facets. In the stolid British Museum she worshipped at the shrine of Greek culture with her brother Raymond, and again, in Paris, at the Louvre. She made her recital debut in Budapest, and found her first lover there. But in Paris, at the height of her youth and beauty, she was the goddess of dance, object of panegyrics, inspiration of painter, sculptor, and poet. She queened it in a perpetual salon of adulation, stimulated by that *apéritif* and by the brilliance of ideas surrounding her. She basked in the glitter and took what she needed for herself and her dance. The little Scotch-Irish American with the California accent became a citizen as well as a woman of the world. Her dance changed with her.

After the period of stony grief that followed the tragic drowning of her children in the Seine, her dancing changed again. There were those who found in it new qualities, ugly and repellent. Just as it is today with those who expect the modern dancer to remain in a stencil they have come to admire, once they have become accustomed to it. Isadora had always loved children, and longed to teach as many of them as possible to move with spontaneous ease and freedom, less as professional dancers than as happy, useful human beings. She was, as in all her undertakings, most impractical about it. Her efforts to establish the school in Russia, on the scale and of the caliber she had visualized, were constantly frustrated; and she received no encouragement whatever in her own country. But in ways she never dreamed her vision of America dancing is partially realized today.

According to the Puritan code, Isadora lived amorally, but she had a religious reverence for all that pertained to art. She was a pagan with a streak of divinity that came out in dancing. Dance was a sacrament to her. It came of life experience and so became of universal import. She danced to the music of Beethoven, Wagner, Tchaikovsky, Gluck, Chopin, Schubert, and Bach—music big enough for her bigness. She did not try to interpret or visualize the music. It merely provided her with an afflatus of sound that enveloped her and coursed through her and carried her on its momentum. And all the while she foresaw a future when music would be composed for dance.

Isadora was a Dionysian dancer, opposed to all things Apollonian. There was nothing Greek or classic about her dancing, except that which was universally human. She was the most audacious idealist in dance history—a Personality, who lived and danced like a Free Spirit, and wrote like a Noble Soul. Her idolizing contemporaries, remembering her through mists of moonbeams, have canonized her in the Legend of Isadora, which a few realists have spattered with detracting comments. They recall the aging nymphomaniac with dyed hair and body bloated from sensual indulgences where others see the slender girl with pansy eyes, in love with Art and Love. It is best here to think of her only as the great dancer and great mother, the matrix of modern dance.

Two of her American contemporaries, Loie Fuller and Maud Allan, lived also abroad, having won success there, but had some indirect influence on the development of American dance. A third, Gertrude Hoffman, was active mainly in ballet and vaudeville.

Loie Fuller came from Chicago, and was hailed by all Paris as "La Loié." One suspects that she cultivated a French accent for her American visits. Her contribution was unique. It consisted of the wielding of draperies under colored lights. She worked in movement of materials more than in movement of the body. She could swirl yards of tulle or gauze into the color and form of flame or flower. The *Serpentine Dance* and *Ballet of Light* were two of her most famous compositions. There were imitators in the United States, on the Keith vaudeville circuit, and some of them did it with mirrors as well as with lights. The skirt dance also ensued, and Ruth St. Denis may have been mildly infected. The young Isadora was thrilled at the spectacle, but felt no compulsion to incorporate the practice into her own dance. She tells, however, with delicate innuendo, in *My Life,* of her encounter with this *originale* and her entourage of beautiful but over-affectionate girls. Isadora preferred gentlemen-admirers.

The Canadian-born Maud Allan, less conspicuous for novelty, danced in the free, plastic mode to the lighter classics of music— Mendelssohn's *Spring Song,* Rubinstein's *Melody in F,* Grieg's *Peer Gynt* Suite, and so on. A sensation of her career was *The Vision of Salome,* a subject controversially popular at the time in the play of Oscar Wilde and the music drama of Richard Strauss. Miss Allan at first upset London (in 1907) with *Salome,* and thereafter danced it nightly for over a year. Although highly praised as a beautiful woman and a graceful dancer, she seems to have served chiefly as a counter-irritant to ballet in ballet-loving England. The level of quality and distinction she maintained proved that other forms could also be enjoyable. In America, too, she helped to free the public from its prejudices against the free dance.

In this, Isadora's period, began the art of dance photography (with the portraits by Arnold Genthe and Edward Steichen), so fruitfully developed today. Isadora's career indirectly affected the Russian Ballet, not by imitation, but by strengthening the purpose of the revolutionary Michel Fokine in his then radical reforms. It affected to a lesser degree and a greater extent the young Nijinsky, with whom she danced in Paris. Fokine's choreography remained within the realm of ballet. Nijinsky, in his choreography, foreshadowed certain angularities and broken rhythms of modern movement; and, whether by instinct or impress, held his body, in his own dance posture, more as a modern than as a ballet dancer does. It was not the same thing, either as Isadora's dance, for it was not based on natural movement; or as modern dance, for it was more two-dimensional than three-dimensional; but it branched beyond Fokine's conception into even freer forms.

In a similar but not identical way, Isadora's dance indirectly affected the German modern dance. The country that had produced nature dancing and gymnastic dancing was ready for her free movement, maybe owing to a longing for freedom that dared not otherwise show itself. When Mary Wigman as a music student saw a dance performance by Grete Wiesenthal, who had come under Isadora's influence, she knew that dance, not music, was to be her career.

MARY WIGMAN

Mary Wigman's dance was born in one war and blighted by another, yet she emerges from the terrible *mise en scène* a world figure as important in her individual contribution to dance as Isadora herself. Because of the obscuration that befell her art during the Nazi reign of terror, because there is little hope, if some slight possibility, that she will return to the United States to dance for us again, it seems advisable here to refer to her career in the past tense—since what she has achieved is known, and what she may achieve is not.

Wigman caught only a remote reflection of Isadora's dance, and is only by inspiration of the breath of freedom beholden to it. Everything in her nature—her cultural and historical background, her geographical and mental environment—was different. Whereas Isadora was a creature of light, Wigman was dark and somber. Where Isadora was ecstatic, exaltée, dancing an ennoblement of tragic grief when she must, Wigman's was largely an ecstasy of gloom, stressing the demonic and macabre, as if to exorcise through movement the secret evils in man's nature. She lived among such evils, in an atmosphere seething with the demoniacal intent that forced two wars upon the world. The first one touched and stirred Isadora in France, smote and saddened Wigman in Switzerland and Germany. The second engulfed the German dancer.

Wigman's dance was as essentially German as Isadora's (for all the time she spent in Europe) was essentially American. Isadora had the quick Celtic humor, in private life; Wigman must have had some humor, if only the heavy Teutonic kind. But there appears to be no record of humor in the dances of either, and in those I saw of Wigman's there was none. Certain things they had in common, apart from their artistic stature. One was their physical stature. Both were large, womanly women, and if in the early days there was girlishness in Isadora's dance and a streak of masculinity in Wigman's, the dance of their latter years was a dance of womanhood. Wigman, like Isadora, was more impressive alone than with a group. It was as if each, in her majestic singleness, her capacious womanliness, contained humanity within herself. Both drew in from humanity and went out to humanity, even if their exhalations were of entirely divergent character. Both were concerned with the dance of the future, the generations of the future. And both danced religiously the faith that was in them, a faith in the dignity and worth of individual man.

Wigman, understandably, was engrossed with man and his fate; the light of man and his hope shot through the fabric of her dance but sparingly. Her movements were not all in the lower registers, but they were predominantly low-keyed. Kneeling, crouching, crawling, creeping, falling—she often just lay down on the stage floor at the end of a dance, bringing the expenditure of energy into its natural cadence, rest—all in closeness to earth, rather than, like Isadora, touching earth only to spring away from it. The sloping shoulder line, the downcast head, the arms only half raised, seldom joyously upflung, these were the attributes of Wigman's dance. Earthy, strong, stark, ugly and powerful, distressingly costumed, dismaying, but altogether electrifying, this was Mary Wigman's dance as I saw it in Boston in the early thirties. Her first programs consisted of excerpts from full-length works that had been produced as dance cycles in Germany. At that time Hanns Hasting was her composer-accompanist and Meta Menz the percussionist.

Her Boston debut was made in Symphony Hall (where in October 1922 Isadora had so sensationally danced on her last visit to the United States) on January 22, 1931. It was a major event, sensational in another way, for her reputation, from both Europe and New York, had preceded her. It was attended by the usual sprinkling of dance lovers, more music lovers, and critics mainly of music and drama. The strideful opening dance, *Invocation,* was forceful and direct, establishing a mood of virile strength. This was Mary Wigman's dance, and there was to be no compromise. This was the celebrated Mary Wigman, stocky, muscular, a not very young or very attractive woman, alone on the stage, without scenery, sometimes without music other than that made by the beat and swish of her bare, pulsatile feet.

There were quiet dances: *Face of the Night,* crepuscular, mysterious; the paired *Pastoral* and *Summer Dance,* each against a different thin, reiterated treble theme; the *Pastoral* in a clumsy, square-cut dress of harsh blue, with white godets at the hem, over a red lining or petticoat, making delicate, almost lyrical figurations in space; the *Summer Dance* in a more satisfying yellow velvet, earth-close, as if the dancer were reposing in a field of buttercups and meadow grasses, listening to the hum of insects, watching their minutial activity, watching the green blades turn and lift in the sun, feeling the vibrations of earth, letting them surge up through her, inundating her being. The *Witch Dance,* also done from a sitting posture, crawled and crept, the body dragging forward on the haunches, the face masked, the effect eerie. No broomstick-witch this, but a Teutonic earth-gnome, sister to Mime and Alberich.

Then there were the swirling dances: the *Storm Song,* in a flame-colored robe, its folds undulating with her arms, enwrapping her wild dervish spins, the insistent drumbeats keeping pace, till the audience went mad with her, and actually, in Boston, took to stamping and shouting its excitement. Even the anticipated *Monotony Whirl* brought no such response, though like a swimmer, resting by change of stroke and shift of base, of plane, of tempo, she won a stunning championship. This marvel of balance and velocity seemed to go on endlessly, yet it was too soon over. The program closed with two maenadic *Gypsy Moods,* in a costume of crazy patchwork, denoting the volatile gypsy temperament, dances of step more than of movement, skipping in abandon, whether of gayety or despair. The artist received an ovation at the end.

At her second appearance in Symphony Hall, in March of the same year, she received another ovation, and corsages were thrown upon the stage. Slight variations were discernible in her repetitions of various numbers from the previous concert. Added were "Dream Image" and "Dance of Sorrow" from the cycle, *Visions,* the latter in tribute to Pavlova, who had just died. Also new to Boston was the "Allegro Arioso" from the *Suite Based on Spanish Songs and Rhythms,* a paraphrasing of the Spanish idiom, and not a literal translation, that presaged something of what was later to be done with these rhythms by the younger generation of American modern dancers.

A third visit in December brought the then new dance cycle, *Sacrifice,* the first complete dance cycle to be presented in Boston; and an improvement in costuming wrought by a new designer. The opening movement, "Song of the Sword," sharp, energetic, was a mighty thrust into the emotions; the gentler "Dance for the Sun," a paean of homage in cloth-of-gold. The grotesque "Dance for the Earth" evoked titters mixed with torrential applause; but the eloquent "Lament" that followed was received in silence, as the dancer's recumbent body, in its clinging cloth-of-silver garment, slowly folded upon itself, enclosing itself, as a flower encloses itself in its petals, at the end. The tense "Death Call," in a black robe, and the frenetic "Dance into Death," in ghastly green, with its diagonal dashes across the stage, brought the cycle to a close—and left the audience gasping.

What was all this about? I don't know. It was something primordial, something that dug deep into forgotten roots, an almost atavistic approach to man in relation to his universe, a return to the primitive through layers of civilization. It was something that stirred distant reverberations of things long past, something inexplicable, truly unutterable in words.

In late February 1933 Wigman brought her group of twelve stalwart girls to Symphony Hall, and by so much diminished her glory. Four movements from the eight-movement cycle, *The Way* (man's tortured way through life), showed a more complicated choreography, with Wigman always seeming to stand apart, an imposing solitary figure outside the happenings within the group. She *was* a being apart. Her ample presence required no reinforcement; so that these Teutonic Amazons seemed extraneous. We could more easily imagine the group action intimated in Wigman's solo passages than accept it as conveyed through these healthy, hearty, and quite uninspired young women.

"You would not expect every member of an orchestra to be a Toscanini, would you?" she asked in an interview next day. And I gathered from her remarks that she regarded the group as a complementary unit of expression or comment, somewhat in the nature of the Greek chorus, not wholly apart from the action, nor wholly of it. But this was in 1933. Judging from illustrations in her book, *Deutsche Tanzkunst* (it is in German and I have never been able to read it), and from other sources, she may have made more telling use of the group as a participating element (as, by report, she did with her first group), in later works. She went back to Germany that year, the year Hitler came to power, and she did not return to the United States.

Her voice, by the way, was low and cultivated. There was no trace of German stress in her very English speech. She wore a black hostess gown with dull red accents at waist and throat that set off her fine, green-gray eyes and luxuriant reddish brown hair. She was, indeed, much better looking at close view than she appeared to be upon the stage. She was extremely intellectual, quiet, composed. In her presence one felt in touch with greatness.

The four movements of *The Way* given in Boston were "Dreams," of disturbing, dissolving patterns; "Shadows," in grisly white robes, all dark in feeling; "Hymnus," hard, metallic, with its Roman helmets, clashing cymbals and primitive pipes; and the contrastingly softer "Pastorale" in variegated high colors that almost reverted to prettiness. Whatever magic the full cycle may have had, it was lost in this truncated version; and the cumulative effect of Wigman's solo appearances was dissipated by the appearance of her group. Wherever she took her band of husky German girls, the result was disappointment. It is unfortunate that this was her last American tour.

Nevertheless, Wigman's contribution to the progress of the art dance is threefold. With her came new ideas of the dancer's relation to space and the dance's relation to music, of movement evolved out of its own meaning, of dance self-governing and self-contained. She advanced movement in scale, direction, range, and quality by her amplification of spatial values and choice of material. She separated dance from pre-composed music, causing new music to be written for each dance, relying only occasionally on a folk air or lighter musical piece, or dispensing with music altogether. She may (half reluctantly) be said to have advanced costuming, for in spite of the rather dismal array seen in the American seasons between 1930 and 1933, later reports and pictures show an increased use of interesting textiles, rich brocades, flowing robes, masks, and headdresses that attained a stark sort of sumptuousness, and, sometimes, beauty.

That space consciousness is inherent in the German modern dance and is its chief contributing factor, may be owing to the nation's eternal yearning for *Lebensraum,* may be an offshoot of that seeking of compensation in art for lacks in life which is one of the impulsions of art. In any case, space, whether considered as an enemy to be grappled with and overcome, or as the dancer's special life-giving atmosphere, is a tangible substance incorporate in the German modern dance. The idea began to take shape in the work of

Rudolf von Laban, a Hungarian dancer, who experimented with a crystal icosahedron to find the potential movement directions and movement qualities of man. How he expected to find them in a many-sided geometric object big enough for a man to enter instead of in the body of man himself in unrestricted space, some more sympathetic person will have to explain. One might as well look for the source of human movement in the atom bomb (and, as a study of energy, perhaps there is more in that than first appears). However, each must create according to his nature, and Laban's nature was evidently of scientific bent.

From the icosahedron (whose twenty faces provide a basis for mathematical permutations, according to Webster's Dictionary), Laban worked out a system of laws, involving scales of movement, dividing and subdividing his system with characteristic thoroughness. Under the heading of Eukinetics he placed centrifugal movement—from the center of the body, as in modern dance; and peripheral movement—of the extremities, as in traditional ballet. Choreutics was the study of spatial values. And the purpose of all this apparently cold research, mixed with psychological exploration, was to find a means of interpreting life in a new kind of dance for the theater.

Laban, who has been called the father of the German modern dance, is also the inventor of a dance script as elaborate and difficult as his icosahedron theory. It, too, appears to have a geometric approach. The one sample of it I have seen disclosed a red upright rectangle, blobs of black, with several lines riding off in all directions, and discouraged all further attempts on my part to understand it. Whether, given sufficient patience to master it, Laban's script is viable for the recording of other forms than the German modern dance, is problematical. At all events, the search for a universally applicable dance script continues.

These mechanics of dancing did not hold Mary Wigman's attention long. After studying with Laban in Ascona, Switzerland, during the first world war, and teaching for a while in the school he established at Zurich, she was soon off on tangents of her own. Her first recitals in Switzerland, and, more especially, those at the close of the war, divulged an entirely new approach to dance. From then on she was a law unto herself, in obedience only to the unwritten law of growth and change.

Wigman had her derogators and traducers, as does any innovator, but hungry, (temporarily) war-weary Germany, which, prior to the first world war, had received the different new dance ideas of both Isadora and Ruth St. Denis with a mixture of intellectual curiosity and appreciation, was ready ground for the development of a new and distinctly German dance. The thought of strength through muscularity, if not yet of strength through joy, was in the air. The German nature was looking for restoration of the depleted body through gymnastic movement and dance as recreational movement, as an aid to national reconstruction. Germany had never made ballet so much its own as had other European countries. It was, therefore, by these several reasons, more or less prepared for the new German dance when it arrived.

By 1926, the year the American modern dance began its entirely separate career, Wigman had formed her first dance group and founded schools in Central Europe. In subsequent years, young Americans (not the leaders of the new American dance) began their trek to the main Wigman School in Dresden, and returned to spread her doctrine at home. One of the first group members, Hanya Holm, came to the United States to conduct the New York Wigman School, and remained to work independently as an American citizen. Yvonne Georgi and Harald Kreutzberg, later Kreutzberg alone, are distinguished Wigman disciples who visited the United States frequently in the years before the second world war, and may have had some influence on the growing American art among its less creative exponents. Kurt Jooss, Wigman's associate teacher at the Laban School in Zurich, made his company, with its repertory of original ballets, well known in the Americas. But of all these, more later.

Wigman's first step in preparing herself as a dancer had been the study of Dalcroze Eurythmics at Hellerau. This system, evolved by the Swiss composer, Émile Jaques-Dalcroze, as a study of music through body rhythms, has been immensely serviceable to dance students as a study of movement through music rhythms. But Wigman did not go far in this study. The novice, who a little later was told by Laban that she would never become a dancer, was laughed at by her classmates at Hellerau for awkwardness.

As she developed her own dance, Wigman sought music that would be integral with, but subservient to, this dance, not calling undue notice to itself, but acting merely as a sustaining agent or rhythmic support to the movement. The repetitive flute or flute-sounding themes in the early *Pastoral* and *Summer Dance,* the beat of drums in *Storm Song,* offer simple illustrations of her theory. In practice, or at least on first hearing, the theory was contradicted, as the extraordinary effect made by the piercing monotony of sound, the exciting drumbeats, attracted a great deal of notice and caused no end of speculation. However that may have worked out in later years, Wigman also experimented with silent dances. When the movement did not, for her, seem to require music, whether in single passages or in whole works, she omitted music, after some testing to verify her first reaction. From the beginning she had recognized the classic symphonies and music dramas as artistic entities in themselves, to which nothing could properly be added, and which had nothing to add to her dance.

An Oriental vein is evident in her choice of instruments— Hindu drums, Balinese gongs, archaic woodwinds—as in her movements, so often from the seated posture, using torso, arms and hands, not in the Oriental manner but with something of the Oriental feeling. Not that her movement was restricted to the seated form, any more than the Oriental's is. There can hardly be a completely legless dancing. And there can be no isolationism in art, no "pure Nordic" nonsense about the German dance, because it was a blend of many strains, as the foregoing example proves. A multiplicity of influences went into the making of Wigman the creative dancer, among them her early association with the painter, Emil Nolde, in Rome, and her study of the dances of primitive peoples.

There seems to have been a good deal of demonology in Wigman's dance, of German mysticism and philosophy; much of it was morbid, coming as it did out of a land depressed by war, suffering, as it was, from its own evils. Yet for her, singing and dancing went hand in hand, the song was in the dance, the dance in the song.

There was an undercurrent of singing in her nature, however plaintive it might be; and sometimes it could be joyous. Strangely enough, her dance was without sentimentality.

In 1936 in Germany, with Hitler in power, Wigman's creative star was still in ascendance, according to Dr. Artur Michel, the first Continental dance critic to devote himself to modern dance. He watched her progress in Germany until he was obliged to retreat from the monstrous, impending evil, swelling like the great red dragon of the Apocalypse with desire to consume the world, and ending, like the dragon, by destroying itself. Dr. Michel came to the United States in 1941 or thereabouts, after a sojourn in Cuba, where he had first fled. Here he happily watched the progress of the American dance, wrote for the German-language weekly, *Aufbau*, and for various dance magazines, and worked on a history of the dance which was all but finished when he died. His last article, "Mary Wigman—On Her Sixtieth Birthday," was published in *Dance Observer* on November 13, 1946, the day of his death. In that article, he notes among Wigman's important works up to the outbreak of war, the suite of *Women Dances* (1936), the cycle, *Autumnal Dances* (1937), and the two contrasting dances, *Bright Queen* and *Dark Queen* of her last recitals early in 1939.

After that came the black-out. Friends tried to communicate with her and failed. Rumors fled hither and yon. "Mary Wigman was a Nazi sympathizer." "Mary Wigman was imprisoned by the Nazis." Whether she chose or was forced to stay in Germany, she is reported at one time to have said that Germany was her fatherland and she must share her country's fate. Not till the late fall of 1946 did the news come through that Mary Wigman, having suffered more crushingly than ever before, was picking up the threads of her war-wracked career and starting over again. She was conducting her work on a reduced scale in Leipzig, where she had been living since 1942.

Late in March 1947 she produced Gluck's *Orpheus* as a dance drama, with considerable satisfaction to herself and to the Leipzig public. It had been prepared during a hard winter under many handicaps. Shortage of materials for costumes troubled her more than cold and hunger, she wrote in an uncomplaining letter to a friend, but the work kept her spirit alive. The same year there appeared in *Dance Observer* a letter from one of her followers asking that food and clothing be sent to Mary. A can of soup might make all the difference, the letter said.

Europe's ravaged soil has stunted the growth of the German dance. Three of its exponents returned in the 1946 and 1947 seasons in the same state of development they were in before the war. Indeed, two of them had stood so still they had retrogressed. Trudi Schoop's Switzerland Funny Page was more obvious and less funny than her first edition, *Fridolin on the Road.* Kurt Jooss, whose anti-war ballet, *The Green Table,* won top prize at the International Dance Congress in Paris in 1932, has never since said anything of equal importance in dance. Time was when some of us looked to his combination of modified ballet and Laban techniques as the beginning of a happy and fruitful union. But by his last American tour *The Green Table* had become a masquerade, the tender and wistful *The Big City* dated, and the new works offered, by himself and others, verged on the puerile. The tour ended in a fiasco, and the company disbanded soon afterwards.

When the duly whitewashed Harald Kreutzberg came to New York in the fall of 1947, he was dancing just as he had nine years before. He lavished punctilio of execution on dances of charming filigree, and won a great popular success. His delighted audiences were as ready as he to pick up where he had left off, as if nothing had happened in the interim.

That the American modern dance has shot way past the Central European may be partly imputed to America's escape from war's effect on its own territory. More is it ascribable to the bright land of its birth—a land where freedom and democracy are ideals at least; where traditions of human decency (in spite of arrant violations), of good will if not always of good manners, prevail; a land where all races (again in promissory note) are learning to work out their destiny together; a land of great spaces and mighty projects that still leave room for the need of compensatory values in art.

RUTH ST. DENIS AND TED SHAWN
AMERICAN PIONEERS

The American dancers who did their visiting to instead of from England and the Continent, and later the Orient, who did the most for American Dance, were, indeed, the founders of it, are Ruth St. Denis and Ted Shawn. They were the pioneers who established the Denishawn School and the Denishawn Company in a wilderness of dance art and dance appreciation. Before that school and that company, dance as a generally recognized American art was nowhere to be found amid the hoofers and skirt dancers, the acrobatic dancers and other vaudevillians who populated the American stage. Art was something that arrived from Europe, even when the attraction was originally American.

Without that school and that company the American modern dance could not have come into being, for there would have been no base of departure for the so-called rebels who founded it. It was out of a broad dance culture that the new explorations and discoveries were made. If Martha Graham, Doris Humphrey, and Charles Weidman had not been conversant with all sorts and conditions of dancing, if they had not been surfeited with the exotica they came to regard as foreign to their natures, they might never have become dissatisfied enough to project into the future, to search for a more basically American, a more basically human dance. Whatever has unfolded in their separate careers, their roots are in the Denishawn family tree, and they owe more than has been openly acknowledged to their artistic forbears. Whatever the limitations of the Denishawn dance, it gave the public all and a little more than it was then prepared to receive. For both partners were artists more than sufficient unto their time. Nor have they, in the intervening years, been standing still.

Ruth St. Denis and Ted Shawn began their remarkable careers independently and are continuing them independently today. The meeting and marriage that produced Denishawn cost them all the sacrifices of normal parenthood. Each surrendered for the time a portion of his own artistic development and suffered years of incompletion, unfulfillment. They suffered, too, the privations and harassments of domesticity. As Anita Loos's Blonde said long ago, "Family life is for those who can stand it," and artists are rarely among them.

The school was not continuous, Shawn has told me. There were lapses and lapovers, interruptions by company tours and individual tours. Sometimes Ruth, always the prima donna, would retire from the scene and it would become the Ted Shawn School of Dance. Then Ruth would come back and it would be Denishawn again; or Ted, not without an ego of his own, would go off by himself, and the sign would read the Ruth St. Denis School. Sometimes the sign would be taken down altogether and there would be no school. Nevertheless, from 1915 to 1932, first in Los Angeles and last in New York, with a period of branch schools between, Denishawn existed with some sort of actuality as a place where dreams bigger than its billfold sometimes came true. Both school and company exerted a tremendous influence on the youth of America, and made as many converts to Denishawn dance as Pavlova did to ballet.

What was this Denishawn dance? It was the most eclectic system imaginable. The basic technique was modified ballet in bare feet. It included turns, beats, elevation, practically everything but *pointes.* Shawn was the chief organizer and teacher. With antennæ alert to all impressions, he proceeded on one of his favorite theories, namely that the dance-educated person should know all forms of dance. If he came across a Japanese sword dancer in Los Angeles, he must perforce bring him to the school to give instruction in his art. Later Michio Ito taught there, and one of the distinguished offspring of the latter-day Denishawn is the modern Japanese dancer, Yeichi Nimura. Without overstressing this thin thread of Japanese culture, which is only one of many threads, but remembering the impact of the Japanese dramatic dancer, Sadi Yaco, on the young St. Denis, her later lessons with an ex-geisha girl in Los Angeles, and her own Japanese dance drama, *O-Mika,* it is worth pondering for a moment whether Martha Graham's current addiction to the stage designs of Isamu Noguchi and her use of the little Japanese-American dancer, Yuriko, in her present company, may be indefinably traceable to these early impressions.

But to go back to Denishawn in its early years, the Hawaiian hula was taught by a native teacher, and whether or not that was the source, more than an occasional bit of hip-swinging can be seen in modern dance today. The history of costume and treatment of fabrics was the basic training of one of the most original of modern costume designers, Pauline Lawrence, who went to Denishawn as a pianist and remained to sing and to dance. Guest teachers were often invited, among them exponents of Dalcroze and Delsarte. The aim was to foster individuality, to turn out completely rounded individuals. If the school had been endowed, academic and industrial courses would have been added to this end.

As it was, the school appears to have hit in its haphazard way upon some of the elements of progressive education. The California set-up was a little like a country day school. One old house the school family occupied had a tennis court surrounded by eucalyptus trees, a rose arbor, and a swimming pool. A platform was built over the court, with the railing for practice bar, and much of the class work was done out of doors. There were pets of all kinds, including a parrakeet in the parlor and a peacock in the backyard; there were meals in the arbor, swims in the pool. Denishawn was a way of life in itself. It cannot have failed to leave its mark on the most insurgent of pupils—if, and it seems unlikely, there was any insurgency in those days.

Although Ted was the prime mover and shaker, Ruth taught what could be taught from her "Oriental Impressions," and here again one stops to wonder, this time if her classes in Yogi were in any way responsible for that sense of "inner stillness" so vibrant in Martha Graham. The point is, there is no telling what may have seeped into the thoughts of the budding geniuses at Denishawn who were later to revolutionize the American Dance. Ruth was a personality and an influence even if, as she herself admits, she was not a very good teacher. She was essentially a solo performer, with a personal career behind her and ahead of her, when Shawn came to her as a prospective dancing partner (ballroom dancing—the maxixe, the tango—was then the rage, and she had intended to introduce it into her programs) and the Denishawn idea was born.

While loving the trappings of theater, having a theatrical background, she was innately a searcher for the truth, as eclectic in sampling religions as Shawn in sampling dance. For a candid analysis of this search, a record of spiritual growth through the tumults and triumphs of her long career, it is important to read her autobiography, *An Unfinished Life,* which was put into shape from her own writings, notes, and journals by Henrietta Buckmaster, and speaks in terms of her own lively humor and groping idealism. Today a charming woman in her seventies, working in Los Angeles toward the realization of her ideal "Temple of the Spiritual Arts," she is still the same old Ruth—a priestess with a twinkle in one eye.

It is interesting to observe that while Miss St. Denis pursues her inspirational idea of religious expression, the three revolutionary descendants of Denishawn are, without public avowal of religious impulses, expressing them or their equivalents in more specific ways—Martha Graham by a terrific exposure of the evils in the recesses of the human heart, Doris Humphrey by social criticism and exaltation of the human spirit, and Charles Weidman by spearing with wit and humor the social and separate frailties of mankind.

From the beginning the religious impulse was the animus of Ruth St. Denis's dance. As Ruthie Dennis, the long-legged, dancing child on a New Jersey farm, a nature-loving, fun-loving girl, both sweet and saucy, devoted to her father and mother and brother "Buzz," she was always looking for the meaning of things. Somehow, after dabs of dance instruction here and there, and a number of preparatory experiences, she got a small part in Mrs. Leslie Carter's company, then playing *Zaza* and later *Madame DuBarry,* under the management of David Belasco. She did a little dancing, a little acting when called upon, for Ruthie, who had already modeled cloaks and won sixth prize in a six-day bicycle race, could improvise her way through anything. Like Isadora, she was not so strong on technique as on inspiration.

From what I remember of her dancing, it was largely a matter of plastiques and poses, of manipulation of scarves and draperies, in decorative costumes, all very pictorial, and all done with an air.

Her tall figure was slim and girlish, her small head luminous with its white hair framing the now pert and pretty, now extraordinarily lovely face. Except for her "Oriental Impressions," there was a touch of vaudeville in the way she, and Shawn, too, flirted with an audience now and again. But that was in the late twenties and early thirties, after years of intermittent appearances in vaudeville to pay for their concert and school work. It was after the Oriental tour, and long after the epochal confrontation by the cigarette poster, the incident that was the starting point of her career.

To most people a cigarette poster in a drugstore window a cigarette poster is, and it is nothing more—unless perhaps a reminder to buy a pack of one's favorite rather than the advertised brand. To the ardent, inquiring young mind of Ruthie Dennis it was a revelation. She was not the least interested in Egyptian Deities for smoking purposes, but as a symbol of supernal calm the pictured deity, Isis, fired her imagination. It ignited sparks from memories of various Egyptian-type spectacles she had seen, and the whole blazed into a mighty bonfire of a conception—a wonderful ballet to be called *Egypta*.

Followed a period of avid research in libraries and museums across the country, as the *DuBarry* company toured from New York to California and back. In San Francisco she had her picture taken in a makeshift Egyptian costume with a short, black wig, and this picture, reproduced in her book, shows a tense and earnest young Isis who resembles the goddess even less than the commercial poster did. She came home with *Egypta* all planned, nothing lacking but the finances, which were, as usual, incredibly distant of realization. Before that plan was achieved other impressions crept in. East again mixed with West in the inimitable American way. A glimpse of Nautch dancers, snake charmers, and holy men in an East Indian village on exhibition at Coney Island, and Mother India supplanted Ancient Egypt in the mind of the impressionable girl. Further research brought her to the temple dancers and Radha, information that was amplified by talks with Oriental merchants, and eventually the new American *Radha* and the new American dancer, Ruth St. Denis, emerged together.

The history-making *Radha* was auditioned for a group of

vaudeville managers and first engaged as a Hindu dancing act for a Sunday night Smoking Concert at the New York Theater, but it soon attained the dignity of a socially sponsored matinee performance at the Hudson Theater, New York. Ruth, never one to miss an effect, rigged up pseudo-Oriental costumes for the ushers and had incense burning in the auditorium. There were two shorter pieces on the program—*Incense* and *Cobra*—and all three are fully described in *An Unfinished Life*. These dances, with the bared diaphragm, the rippling arms and shoulders, the exotic subject matter and theatrical presentation, were something entirely new to the Western world. They were the first of a long line of beguiling stage pictures whose metaphysical overtones probably passed over many an enchanted spectator's head. The *Yogi, Green Nautch, Black and Gold Sari, White Jade, Invocation to the Buddha,* and other Oriental titles long familiar to the American public, were slowly succeeded (though not replaced) by *White Madonna, Gold Madonna,* the *Masque of Mary,* (a church service) and other titles of Biblical origin as the dancer increasingly turned to the Christian religion as a source of expression.

Ruth St. Denis's "Oriental Impressions" were plastic compositions, selective, arbitrary as any painter's, in which she chose color, form, movement, to express what she had gleaned from Oriental culture and philosophy that she felt to be of universal import. As everybody knows, she had an immense success with them at home and abroad. When she returned from Europe, a transcontinental tour of the United States put the final flourish to that glorious phase. For when Ted Shawn walked and talked into her life he changed the course of her career, and together they changed the entire American dance scene.

In the early years the young Shawn, scarcely older than some of his pupils, was (as he is now) a prodigious worker and overcomer of difficulties. During his third year as a theological student at the University of Denver, he had become paralyzed from the hips down as the result of a serum treatment for diphtheria. Refusing to submit to any such stricture on activity, he recovered the use of his muscles by sheer determination to use them. He would wriggle first a toe, then an instep, gradually manipulating the larger muscles, until he finally forced himself out of bed. Naturally he turned to dancing as soon as he was able, to further his muscular release. He first studied with Hazel Walleck, a former member of the Metropolitan Opera Ballet, doing odd jobs, studying stenography and ultimately landing a good clerical position, to finance himself the while. Before very long he had a studio of his own (in Los Angeles), and with his partner, Norma Gould, made a film, *The Dance of the Ages* (a subject he later used for his men's group), tracing the development of dance from primitive rhythms to the latest ballroom steps.

Shawn's was always the big all-over concept, and he voraciously studied every kind of dance that came to his attention. When the partners worked their way East on a concert tour, he was already equipped to produce a *Grecian Suite,* a *Hungarian Mazurka,* and an *Oriental Suite* in a program that ended with the tango and the hesitation waltz—incidentally, the most popular numbers. In New York he studied both Russian and Italian ballet, after spending some time at New Canaan, Connecticut, working with Mary Perry King and Bliss Carman, who together had contrived a working combination of her dance ideas with his poetry. From the beginning Shawn regarded dance as a manly art and fought valiantly to establish the essential masculinity and worth of men's dancing. And, after the amicable separation of Mr. and Mrs. Shawn, he did establish, in 1933, the famous ensemble of men dancers that toured America for seven years (punctuated by a season in England) with mounting success.

For his forthcoming book of memoirs, *One Thousand and One Night Stands,* Shawn, the writingest of dancers, first set down over six hundred thousand words. Of the several other books he has written, a few are now out of print. At Denishawn he published the *Denishawn Magazine,* which was high-minded, but, for lack of funds, short-lived. He always was, and still is, brimming with ideas.

Denishawn was the scene of constant experiment and innovation. They had dance to spoken poetry, dance without music, dance to percussion only, motion choirs, and when they could afford it they had music composed for dance. Two notable features were the "music visualizations" inaugurated by Ruth St. Denis, admittedly under the influence of Isadora, and the "synchoric orchestras," by roundabout descendance from Dalcroze, in which the congregation of instruments was matched by a congregation of dancers, each dancer representing a single instrument. In later years, Margarete Wallman, an assistant to Mary Wigman, came to teach. But probably the most far-reaching instruction was that brought by one of the first of the guest teachers, Mrs. Richard Hovey, a disciple of François Delsarte, the noted French explorer of human movement.

Delsarte spent his life studying the movements of people under stress. He even visited morgues, and mines, after an explosion, to watch rather ruthlessly it seems how the bereaved betrayed their grief. From behind bushes in parks he studied children at play, and cynically analyzed the differences in movement behavior between the attendants who loved children and those who did not. With cold, scientific detachment, he peered at humanity unconsciously registering its emotions, and made copious notes. From his observations he devised a system of dramatic expression, and some of his pupils were the great actors of the day.

In his book of compiled lectures, *Dance We Must,* Shawn gives a more complete (and more sympathetic) idea of Delsarte's life work. Especially interesting in his account is the use of three of the key words of modern dance—"oppositions," "parallelisms," and "successions," which appear in Delsarte's teaching; and also his reference to Delsarte's discovery of the laws governing what modern dancers call "tension and relaxation" or "contraction and expansion." Shawn believes that Delsarte was the actual source of the German modern dance, of which (he believes) the American modern dance is a by-product.

It is true that the American modern dancers were not starting from scratch but from Denishawn (including the three other D's of dance development—Duncan, Dalcroze and Delsarte) in their initial efforts toward a freer and fuller expression. But they did learn to move from their own impulses, not from prescribed movement patterns catalogued by another student of movement; they found the source of movement values in their own bodies (each creative dancer moves differently, runs his own gamut with individual diversity); even if something of the foundational training of their formative years did linger to guide them in their search. To follow movement laws laid down by others would lead to a mechanical formalization of movement, as in Angna Enters's satirization of the Delsarte system in one of her early "episodes in dance form."

For example, when grief is expressed so variously, how could a dancer use a formula for grief? I asked Shawn about this in an interview.

"Of course he could not," Shawn replied. "The important thing is for the dancer to grasp the principle and make an individual demonstration of it.

"You can do the same pelvic contraction," he said, illustrating by drawing in the abdominal muscles, tightening the shoulders, with face screwed up, arms pulled down, hands clasped as if in pain, "for 'Oh dear, I *wish* I hadn't eaten that salmon!' as for 'Oh *God*, I can't stand this separation!' " But, I gathered, the belly-ache would be differentiated from the heart-ache by the emotional coloring put into it.

I do not believe that Delsarte captured and bound into a system all possible human movements, but that he discovered certain universal laws in the realm of movement, which still contains laws yet to be discovered. Until some dancer finds the way for us to flap our arms and fly under our own power, we cannot say that the movement potentialities of the human body have been exhausted; and even then new movement potentialities we cannot now envision will doubtless vaguely outline themselves on some distant horizon.

Shawn's own dancing seems smooth and rounded, his clean-cut choreography square-cut, compared with the irregularities of modern dance. It is excellent of its kind, and where there are no pet standards to provoke invidious comparisons, relishable. If his range of territory is greater than his range of movement, he certainly put dance on a global plane in the American consciousness before the word "global" was driven into it. His popular suite of *Flamenco Dances* acquainted American audiences with *zapateado* before native Spanish dancers had begun to visit the country in large number. His *Cosmic Dance of Siva,* in forty-five pounds of costume made for him by silversmiths during his stay in India, came before

Shan-Kar; and, like Ruth St. Denis's "Oriental Impressions," helped pave the way for receptivity to the Hindu dancer's art. In dance and in actuality Shawn has roamed the world. But he has not overlooked the American Indian, the American folk themes, the Negro spiritual, the simple, homely dances of labor and of play. His delight in spectacle, in resplendent costume (or next to none at all), his Lisztian love of the grandiose, his faults and his virtues, are an intransic part of the American dance scene.

Perhaps the crowning achievement of his career is the founding of the Jacob's Pillow Dance Festival and University of the Dance in the Berkshire Hills of Massachusetts. The school, by no means a full-fledged university yet, may be the embryo of one. It includes in its curriculum, as the festival (a summer-long affair) exhibits in its weekend concerts, as many kinds of dance as feasible—an extension of the Denishawn idea. The project began in 1930 when Shawn bought the farmstead called "Jacob's Pillow" for a retreat and soon turned it into a summer headquarters and training camp for his men's group. Their weekly concerts in the converted barn brought hordes of visitors. In 1942 (when the men had already left for war service—as Shawn had done a quarter century before) it was incorporated under the administration of a board of directors, with Shawn as managing director; and a fine new dance theater in old-barn style was built. In 1947 he took Sabbatical leave to go to Australia on a dance and lecture tour, and was at the time I talked with him planning to fly over continent and ocean to one of the few lands he had never visited.

At this time, when his thoughts were full of preparations for the Australian journey, he kindly consented to reminisce for me about the early Denishawn days. With energy unabated, he was then taking three ballet lessons a week with the Italian teacher, Madame Toscanini, and keeping up a strenuous course with his physical trainer, Joseph Pilates. Slimmed down from an arduous season at Jacob's Pillow the previous summer, he was looking more handsome and distinguished than ever. In public or private, he is a delightful conversationalist, with a keen sense of humor. His whole mentality was bent toward the new and untried field before him. I thought it particularly gracious of him to stop and look backward a bit over what must have seemed to him an old and outworn story. It is a story that only he, on his part, can fully tell in print.

"I never decided to become a dancer," he said. "I just walked into it and kept going. Then, the first time I saw Ruth dance, before I had met her personally, I knew that I was not giving up religion for dance but finding it in dance."

He is, like Ruth St. Denis, fundamentally religious, and like her, and sometimes with her, has danced whole religious ceremonies in various liberal churches. He has also choreographed stage works on religious themes. He felt strongly about his position as the father of the American art dance; and still a little hurt (in spite of the outward reconciliation) at the apparent waywardness of his artistic offspring, and what he regards as unfortunate comparisons of his work with theirs.

"You don't expect an oak to turn into a chestnut tree, or that the trunk must stop growing because the tree puts forth new branches or the branches new leaves. I don't like this 'going beyond' you keep saying. The new dance may be different but it is not necessarily 'going beyond.' Does Schönberg's music make Bach's less good? Each has his place in the scheme of music, and so it is in dance. Modern dance is only a transitional stage. It may ultimately unify all forms, but that remains to be seen.

"I have believed in pure dance from the beginning. If you can't make a dance in the studio that stands independently of costume, that dance has not earned a costume, I have always said. But, mind you, it is not necessary, or possible, for every dancer to be able to make a dance."

Denishawn sent many dancers into the entertainment world (Lillian and Dorothy Gish, Ina Claire, Lenore Ulric, Ruth Chatterton, Grace Hartman, and Myrna Loy are among the stars who had some training there); it sent many dancers into the concert field; but among them all there were only three creative revolutionists. Whether Shawn's memories of them have been faded or heightened by the years, here they are:

"Martha came in 1916, a plain, awkward, abnormally shy girl. She'd hover at the back of the stage, timorous, inhibited. Ruth wasn't interested in her at all. I told her I'd work with her but that she had no dance talent and would never make a dancer. One day I noticed her in a dance of barbaric intensity. For the first time she seemed to be really letting go, really dancing."

From that start Shawn prepared her for the role of the maiden in his ballet, *Xochitl*, based on a Mexican legend. "It was the first use of an Aztec theme on the American stage. A Mexican artist, Francisco Cornéjo, did the décor, and Homer Grunn did the music." Ted danced the emperor who carried off the maiden with dishonorable intentions but was induced by her love for him to make her his bride. *Xochitl* was toured as a vaudeville presentation and Martha Graham won her first success in it. When she left Denishawn in 1923, it was not as a rebel, but to go into the *Greenwich Village Follies*. John Murray Anderson had seen her in *Xochitl* and wanted her for his show.

Martha later substantiated this, saying: "I did no creative work at Denishawn. I was content with what I was doing there. It was not until I began to teach at the Eastman School that I realized I was going to leave all that behind. I never thought of myself as a creative dancer. And do not now. I have never called myself a choreographer. I am merely an instrument of the creative principle."

Doris Humphrey came to Denishawn in 1915 as a student and returned in 1917 as a teacher and company member. Shawn remembers her as a small, trim, somewhat severe looking young woman in a tweedy suit and toque, who regarded the voluptuous beauty of one of the older girls with some disapproval. "She was always a lovely, lyrical dancer," Shawn said. "She worked mainly with Ruth." She did most of the work on the music visualizations, having a keener ear, brought up in music as she was, than Ruth, who was more concerned with visual effectiveness.

In 1920 arrived Charles Weidman, a raw youth from Nebraska, showing distinctly romantic tendencies in his "diagnosis audition." He had made a little dance about an eleventh century Japanese poet who wanted to write a poem to the moon, but overcome by the ineffable beauty of the moon itself, was unable to write the poem.

Shawn saw the comedy potential in Charles long before

Charles did. "He looked like a Charles Ray character then popular in the movies. His suits were always too tight for him, short in the sleeves and trousers. He was a crow for collecting. On tour he'd rush into a railway station—his suitcase stuffed, arms bulging with bundles—as if the train were steaming out before his eyes."

Shawn wanted to turn this unconscious comedy into a dance, but the serious, romantic youth resisted. Shawn eventually did compose a dance for him, costumed in a quick-fitting russet brown suit, with a little brown derby hat and shiny tan shoes, and called it *The Crapshooter*—using the music of Eastwood Lane. It took, and that was the beginning of the famous modern dance comedian.

"As a teacher I have always worked to release and fulfill what is in a person," Shawn said. "What is the divine design? Let that come forth."

And Ruth St. Denis in *An Unfinished Life*: "What I gave Denishawn and what I shall give to pupils as long as I am able, is an artistic stimulus and an incentive to go and do something—anything—that is a release and a joy to the young artist." *

The threefold release ensuing was more than they had bargained for.

* Reprinted by permission of Harper & Brothers, New York.

THE THREE CREATIVE REVOLUTIONISTS

"Martha"—*"Doris"*—*"Charles"*

MARTHA GRAHAM

In the public mind today, Martha Graham is the archetype of the American modern dance. She is a prophetess not without honor in her own country. She even rates a snide "Profile" in the *New Yorker*. Pictorial weeklies bow before her as a "highbrow," indicating in the cutlines under their photographs of her unusual dances that she is far removed from the level of their readers. Her name, though not exactly a household word, is a known quantity, like that of a famous musician. But her dance is not for the masses, and there is no good pretending it is. In its latest phase, it sometimes seems more esoteric than ever.

Nevertheless, "Martha," as she is called in the expanding world outside the popular taste in entertainment, has built, in her twenty odd years of growing, a steadily expanding public. If it is not the cult audience of earlier years, it *is* a special audience. And part of this audience has helped to build and support her success. In 1932 she was the first dancer to receive a Guggenheim Fellowship. From 1935 to 1941 the Bennington School of the Dance at Bennington, Vermont, made many of her larger productions possible. In the spring of 1944 a group of New York actors and artists subsidized her first full-week Broadway engagement; and since the fall of that year commissions from the Elizabeth Sprague Coolidge Foundation and the Alice M. Ditson Fund have afforded further production opportunities.

Whether or not commissioned work is always inspired work, Martha has earned her success without compromise. She has hewn to the line of what she felt was right for her, take it or leave it, and a continuously increasing portion of the public is learning to take it. Her work is respected by dancers of other persuasions. She is recognized as an artist of dance who has something important to say to artists in other fields. Those who are accustomed to terms of imagery, of movement, of rhythm, in any medium, are equipped for response to that strange art that is so often baffling even to them. Those who are not so equipped find it more difficult. There is a point of contact in the basic laws of the physical universe—the laws of gravity, of expansion and contraction, the pulse of breathing, the atmosphere in which the human spirit moves—that is not wholly a matter of sensory appeal; it is an externalization of what goes on inside. Anyone interested enough to attend a Graham performance is pretty sure to catch at least the overtones of these inner experiences as related to himself and the rest of humankind. To make the audience share the experience is the artist's responsibility. If, in return, the audience makes no effort to share it, there is no emotional exchange, and the work does not come alive. Martha at once makes demands upon and depends upon her audience.

An illustration of this essential rapport between artist and spectator was given in a climactic Sunday evening performance (March 2, 1947) at the Ziegfeld Theater, New York, concluding a week's engagement (later extended) by Miss Graham and her company. Dancers, actors, painters, and other men and women of distinction, together with youthful students and devotees, filled the house. It was an enlargement of her old audiences at the Guild Theater, the special audience, surcharged with electrical expectancy and response, that ignites Martha to her most exciting best. The program consisted of her three then newest works, each a kind of ritual: the first, *Errand into the Maze,* a ritual of fear; the second, *Cave of the Heart,* a ritual of hate; and the last, *Dark Meadow,* a modern fertility ritual. The works mounted in tension, carrying the audience along with them. The performances were fused and burnished. The audience paid them the tribute of rapt and silent attention followed by audible enthusiasm, the clapter and cheers, the stampings and "Bravo-Bravas!" that have always put the final seal of success on a Graham concert.

One cannot describe a modern dance, made up as it is of disjointed movement phrases that in themselves project, or are supposed to project, states and stages of consciousness, as one would a ballet, with its established diction of steps and chains of steps, pantomime and plot. A sustained position in balance, body bent forward, may look something like a *penché* arabesque, but it is not one. However balanced it may be, it is sure to swerve away from the classic line, as when Martha bends or leans forward till her face meets the floor. There are no words for the conjunctions and disjunctions that take place. One cannot make a diagram of a dream, a blueprint of what Martha calls "a graph of the heart." Some patient person who saw a work over and over again, and supplemented his observations with specific details from the choreographer, might eventually be able to indicate floor and spatial designs and directions. But that would be only the shell of the work. The substance of it is intangible and cannot be analyzed. It is the total impression of what is seen through the eye, heard through the ear, felt through the body and grasped through the mind. Modern dance is as subjective in its coming in as in its going out. Therefore the following layman's-eye-views of Martha's works cannot be considered definitive.

To return to the Sunday night performance in discussion: *Errand into the Maze,* which had had its *première* during the week, was Martha's second consecutive essay in tapping the vein of Greek mythology without literally exploiting it. That is, the two characters, though not so named in the program, suggested Theseus and the

Minotaur; the white ribbon of Isamu Noguchi's setting, unwinding from a central staple into an irregular pattern on the floor, suggested the thread into the labyrinth; the action suggested, with the aid of the program note, the Theseus figure (Martha) representing any one of us, making an "errand-journey into the maze of the heart," there "to face and do battle" with the Minotaur figure (Mark Ryder) representing the Creature of Fear, familiar, in one form or another, to all of us. On the other hand, Noguchi's white bare-bone structure in the shape of a tree-fork, half branch, half crutch, at stage right, and at stage left his semi-bird design in air, reminiscent of Alexander Calder's "mobiles," made no obvious reference to the myth; and the poem by Ben Belitt, whose first line contributes the title, is apparently disassociated from it altogether. The poem, "Dance Piece (For Martha Graham)," published in *The Nation* in 1940, deals obliquely with the drama of conflict and resolution in the heart that is the essence of Martha's current dance theater. Vividly underscoring the work was the theatrical music Gian-Carlo Menotti had composed for it.

The combatants were dressed "twinly," after the fashion of those matching brother-and-sister sets shown in the advertisements, Martha in a white frock girdled with black rickrack braid, Mr. Ryder wearing the braid vertically on his white trousers, and in addition, a bull's head. This latter item of children's entertainment was far from awesome. In fact, the Creature of Fear was so entirely papier-maché, so gropingly inactive, one had to believe, if one was to believe at all, that he existed only in the mind of the fearer. And that may have been Martha's intention. Cautiously the traveler picks her way into the Maze. Her cringing shoulders and shuddering body say that she senses the approach of the Creature before he appears. When at last the thing she greatly fears has sneaked up on her, she opens her mouth in a silent crying out, is still with terror, and with much effort slowly summons courage to turn and face the monster. He, surprisingly, fails to put up much of a fight as she grapples with him until she sends him rolling over and over into the wings. The victory is not final. Another, fiercer struggle is required. This time, after minute nervous motions throughout the body, followed by a temporary paralysis when the Creature actually

clutches her from behind, she faces and surmounts him in a spectacular lift requiring great strength and balance on both parts,
forcing him backward to the floor. She has "deaded" him, as the
children say, and the conquest is complete. The victor takes up the
white ribbon from the floor, goes to the forked tree, and stands in
its crotch with an air of triumph.

The chief difficulty posed by this work was the ability to take
it seriously. The somewhat static monster of make-believe bordered
upon the comic. His presence emphasized physical, elemental fear
at the expense of the subtleties of mental fear. In view of the advanced psychology of Martha's recent works, one would expect her
to handle the psychopathic and pathological aspects, the manifold
complexities of fear. Perhaps she meant to reduce fear to "the fear
of fear itself." In the form presented, fear was over-simplified and
too easily dismissed. But it was not presented in that form again.
Martha is remorselessly self-critical, and also susceptible to audience
criticism. Having tested *Errand into the Maze* before an audience,
she was bound to feel its defects and correct them. In her Broadway
season of February 1948, at the Maxine Elliott Theater, the work
was purged of its follies (including the bull's head) and many of its
weaknesses, according to report. I give the version I saw because it
is the one I can best describe, and to show that Martha is not afraid
to make mistakes or reluctant to make over.

A more impressive work, and a further example of her proclivities for revision, is *Cave of the Heart,* with score by Samuel Barber,
commissioned in both choreography and music by the Alice M.
Ditson Fund, and first presented under the title of *Serpent Heart*
at the second annual Festival of Contemporary Music at Columbia
University in May 1946. At that time the four characters were
named "One Like Medea," "One Like Jason," "Daughter of the
King," and "Chorus." Martha as the Medea figure wore a Medusa-
like headdress of snarled serpents. When the revised work arrived
at the Ziegfeld the hairdo was changed to a long, bedeviled strand
hanging at one side, and Martha was simply the Sorceress. The cast
was the same, but Erick Hawkins was now the Adventurer, Yuriko
the Victim, and May O'Donnell still the Chorus. The choreography
had been altered for the better. The setting is by Isamu Noguchi

and the costumes are by Edythe Gilfond, following a pattern of stage design that is in danger of becoming a formula. This is not to decry the wonderful imaginativeness and appropriate weirdness of Noguchi's sculptural units, or the ingenuity of Mrs. Gilfond's use of line and color. Everything in a Graham production, including the professional lighting by Jean Rosenthal, comes under the choreographer's supervision, and so the final unifying stamp is hers. But change is the constant in Martha's work. She changes things when you wish she wouldn't. So it is fair enough to wish that once in a way she would change her artistic collaborators, as she used to do.

Cave of the Heart, Martha's first venture (by remote association) into Greek myth, is described in the program note as "a dance of possessive and destroying love, a love which feeds upon itself and when it is overthrown, is fulfilled only in revenge." This love is made manifest in a perfect hysteria of hate. Its altar is a cave-like structure with low, irregular turrets having holes through them that are remindful of the sculptures of Henry Moore. At stage left a marvelous golden-branched young tree stands like a solidified fountain by a marble basin. The Sorceress wears a stunning dress of basic black with gold outline trimming; the Victim a short white tunic; and the Adventurer, divided as he is between the two, gallantly repeats in his costume the colors of both. The Chorus makes her series of entrances and exits, like short verses of comment on the action, in a grayish robe. Now and again she resorts to the central structure for a moment of movement conversation with the Sorceress. The Adventurer shows all too plainly that he is attracted to the Victim. It is clear that she likes him, too. But all are virtually background figures to the leading lady, as jealous hate, mingled with desire, suppurates within her until it bursts with the destruction of the lovers.

The tension is terrific. There are spastic jerks and tremblings throughout the body. Tight, nervous, jiggling motions continue relentlessly in telegraphic dots and dashes. Now the body curves forward in a surge of movement from the spinal base, now, in a kneeling position, the thighs wobble in a frenetic tremolo. She walks about on her knees, folding in the lower half of her leg as she progresses. Ceremoniously she goes to the basin where stands the coppery-golden tree, to pick up the death-wreath for her rival; and to place in her bosom the symbol of the serpent heart, the red strip she is later to unroll for a fetish dance in an ecstasy of vengeance. A quieter passage is her stately entrance, dragging the dead body of the Victim in the folds of a black funeral cloth. Then when the Adventurer falls upon the body of his beloved, and they lie together, limbs entwined in the death embrace, the Sorceress stands upright, still, all the tremors of palpitation concentrated in one upraised hand. As in a trance she goes again to the golden tree, encages herself in its ray-like branches, moves thus to the altar, plants the stems in its turrets, and swings there, a petrified image of introverted hate and accomplished revenge.

There is a good deal of walking about on the knees, or on the toes with the body held in a crouched position, among the other dancers. There are erratic manipulations of the arms and legs by the Adventurer and the Victim that sometimes smack more of invention than of inspiration. The irreverent, who never seem to get into a Graham performance, could laugh. But for the spectator once caught in the spell there is no retrieve. Martha, especially in her long solo incantation, forces him through a shattering experience. The Medea legend is only barely touched upon. The work, for me, did not have the depurative effect of Greek tragedy in any case. It was an enthrallment of the senses and a violent assault upon the nerves.

Martha lays great stress on nerves. She believes that motor memory inhabits the nervous system. (Some people call it nervous system—others call it consciousness.) In a talk following the program under discussion, she told me the reason for her present predilection for Greek myth. Something she read in Plato led her to the conclusion that mythology was the psychology of another age. She wanted to go back through motor memory to the ancestral moods to find an explanation of what we are today. She uses the symbols of mythology as ancestors of present-day moods. In this spirit of tracing the ancestral, before she began her Greek trilogy, she composed *Dark Meadow,* a work of somber grandeur, without mythological connotations, under the working title, *Ancestral Footsteps.*

It was originally commissioned in dance and music for the Coolidge Festival of Chamber Music held in Washington in 1944, but Carlos Chávez was late with his score, and it did not reach production until January 1946, when Martha, supported by her company, played her first two-week season on Broadway at the Plymouth Theater, under management of S. Hurok.

The music, said to be a retake of an old string quartet of the composer's, tones in well with the movement, whatever its value as music per se. The setting is by Noguchi, the costumes are by Edythe Gilfond, and both also are in tune. The cast at the Ziegfeld Theater performance still in discussion consisted of:

SHE OF THE GROUND	*May O'Donnell*
HE WHO SUMMONS	*Erick Hawkins*
THEY WHO DANCE TOGETHER	*Pearl Lang, Yuriko, Ethel Winter, Helen McGehee, Natanya Neumann, Mark Ryder, Robert Cohan, Graham Black, Stuart Gescheidt*
ONE WHO SEEKS	*Martha Graham*

According to the program note, the action is concerned with the adventure of seeking and the mysteries which attend that adventure. Its four parts are:

REMEMBRANCE OF ANCESTRAL FOOTSTEPS
TERROR OF LOSS
CEASELESSNESS OF LOVE
RECURRING ECSTASY OF THE FLOWERING BRANCH

All of which translates into the recurring mystery of sex. The stage is a field of phallic symbols of heroic size, and some of the ritualistic performances are extremely uncomfortable to watch—as when She of the Ground slowly envelops one of the phalluses in a long, flowing cape of bright green—or when the One Who Seeks languishes, half-reclining, against an ovalescent triangular object, which later becomes a target for dart and feather symbols—or in the sextet of men and girls in such close-knit union that each pair moves as one. There is nothing pornographic about any of this, though if censors understood plastic as they do verbal values the work would be deleted out of existence in short order. In art dance as in art music, frankly erotic passages often escape notice, partly because they are not expected, and partly because they are not understood.

But eroticism is not the main purpose of *Dark Meadow*, which is intended to express faith in recurrence, in the continuous line of life. Procreation is treated as a fundamental earth mystery. A red cloth in a formally transported bowl signifies the menses. There are ceremonial decorations of the phalluses. A symmetrical, stylized, flowering tree is planted in one; another, the towering central phallus, snaps out by a mechanical contrivance a painted green-leafed branch at the end.

Martha's crimson costume with black and gold line ornamentation, pale gold bands woven into her dark hair, stands out above all the others. She is always the central figure and always gives herself the most remarkable things to do. It is doubtful if anybody else could do everything she does with her amazingly supple body. Her play with the elongated black mat she wears as mantle, rolling herself up into it and unrolling out of it, in her quest of the ancestral footsteps, is one of these remarkable feats.

In *Dark Meadow* evidently began the grotesqueries of squatting locomotion seen in *Cave of the Heart*, though it has none of the neurotic jigglings of that work. The movements are on the whole broader, more sustained. The group dynamics are wonderful, reminiscent of the beautiful early work, *Primitive Mysteries*. In their warm earth-colors the dancers bound from and return to the earth-base, as if drawing from its undercurrents the force that flows into their design. The work has dignity and form. It is not entirely sensual. Nor is it at all spiritual. It is, rather, psychological, psychiatrical.

Dark Meadow is suffused with a pale light of mysticism, a primordial feeling, like the dawn of creation. It is to me a materialistic mysticism, offering little or no promise of spiritual progress in the reiterated round of physical reproduction. But Martha says it is based on "the deep promise that it is possible for every person to be reborn." She sees this promise in the turn of the earth, the return of the seasons, and believes the re-creation of the individual to be as inevitable as the recurring spring.

"In a way, it is tracing the lineage, the genealogy of the soul of man, like a graph," she said. "It stems back to our remote ancestry, going into the barbaric, the primitive, the roots of life, coming out of racial memory," which, remember, she considers as motor memory, existing in the nerves and bloodstream. "It is concerned with the psychological background of mankind."

It is, perhaps, her way of recording "the collective unconscious." She has read Jung but not Freud. At any rate, what drew her to the primal was psychology, psychiatry. It is not surprising, then, that this seeker into the psyche should hit upon the source of the "Oedipus-complex" for her third venture with Greek myth.

Night Journey, with score by William Schuman, was commissioned in choreography and music by the Elizabeth Sprague Coolidge Foundation, and first presented on a dance program with *Dark Meadow* at the concluding concert of the Harvard Symposium on Music Criticism in Cambridge, Massachusetts, on May 3, 1947. Unlike its predecessors in the trilogy, the work based on the Oedipus legend used the actual names of the characters. Martha was the Jocasta, Erick Hawkins the Oedipus, Mark Ryder the Seer, and as Daughters of Night, Pearl Lang, Yuriko, Ethel Winter, Helen McGehee, Natanya Neumann, and Joan Skinner functioned as Chorus. "The action takes place in Jocasta's heart at the instant when she recognizes the ultimate terms of her destiny," in other words, when she realizes that she is the mother as well as the wife of the king. The others "pursue themselves across her heart in that instant of agony," as secondary characters.

Noguchi's set consisted of a series of wooden pedestals, each a different size and shape, mounting, as if they might be palace stairs, to Jocasta's chamber, where a white-bone structure placed flat on the highest pedestals, indicated in distorted male and female properties the incestuous marriage bed. (This is all reading from left to right as seen from out front, and is in the past tense because none of it happened in precisely the same way again.) Beyond the bed an illumined length of transparent white material twisted down from the flies to suggest a dressing table or window. The props were a rope of symbolical significance and artistic leanings, which held the doomed pair in some astounding intertwinings before it fulfilled its lethal mission; and a large, surrealistic pasteboard eye with heavily fringed lids, a blue pupil on one side, a red on the reverse, which Oedipus carried about at the end to tell us what we all knew —that he had put out his eyes after Jocasta had hanged herself.

It is not that one had been drained of emotional response by previous more powerful impact of the legend, but that artiness prevailed over "pity and terror." The work was technically interesting, interestingly costumed by Mrs. Gilfond. Oedipus looked handsome in unconventional scarlet shorts with diagonal straps across his bare torso; Jocasta wore a becoming beige gown with scarlet touches in the bodice; the Seer in a Greek-style robe of golden brown had a fine solo of troubled prescience; and the Chorus, in black, was effectively used. In little runs and darts of anguish, in small, vibratory motions and large extensions, Martha sought, unavailing, to tell us of Jocasta's suffering. Only in the curious duet with Oedipus, insinuating in its contrasts between maternal affection and marital love, was the horror of the situation brought home.

With changes in décor, omitting The Eye, and clarification of the choreography, *Night Journey* shaped up better than it began by the 1948 Broadway season (so it is said)—another Graham work that refused to be a failure.

Martha's morbid dissection of the darker reaches of the mind seems to have begun with *Deaths and Entrances*, produced at the Forty-Sixth Street Theater, New York, on December 26, 1943, and revived at the Ziegfeld in the 1947 season with the following cast:

THE THREE SISTERS	*Martha Graham, May O'Don-nell, Pearl Lang*
THE THREE REMEMBERED CHILDREN	*Ethel Winter, Yuriko, Helen McGehee*
THE DARK BELOVED	*Erick Hawkins*
THE POETIC BELOVED	*John Butler*
THE CAVALIERS	*Mark Ryder, Robert Cohan*

Arch Lauterer was the designer of this production, which has costumes by Edythe Gilfond and music by Hunter Johnson.

Deaths and Entrances deals with the inner life of the Brontë sisters in the same detached way the newest works touch upon, without absorbing, the Greek myths. Like most of Martha's major works, it dawns slowly upon the consciousness and only after repeated viewings is begun to be comprehended. The title, taken from a poem by Dylan Thomas, refers to the hopes, fears, dreams, desires, and memories that throng and press, torture or bless, as they come and go.

A new feature was the introduction of small, portable objects —a vase, a goblet, a shell—the sight or touch of which summons remembrances so vivid they blot out the present moment. This allusion to the intensification of memory experience through sensory contact, as common as the sensation "this has all happened before," is a definite link to reality that affords considerable aid in our uneasy progress through the fantasy. Just what the purport of each object is, and the wherefor of its removal from place to place, is not so clear. But the blue glass goblet, handled as reverently as if it were the Holy Grail itself, seems to be associated with the cup of happiness in love, since its peculiar magic results in the presence of the Dark Beloved; and the two chess pieces, red and white, as if enclosing the action between the first and last moves of a game of chess, have an ironic logic at the end. What precisely is the significance of the large conch shell and the pair of white vases, I have yet, after repeated viewings, to learn.

These emblems of intensified experience are extensions of the abstracted architectural forms used to denote a house that tenuously suggests "the house on the moors," but is not that house. It is any house where three sequestered sisters dwell in too close confinement and get on one another's nerves, where remembered loves and disappointments and hates and rivalries abound, and there is little display of sisterly affection. It is a house where the ingrown protagonist, feeding upon her dreams and visions and memories, turns in upon herself until she reaches the point of madness. And in this terrifying mad scene, which Martha begins with a minute quivering in the upper chest and shoulder and odd displacement of neck and head that instantly proclaim madness, she so extracts the essence of that state that Ophelia's mummery with the flowers, Giselle's balletic deformations, are merely pictorial in comparison. She moves with dislocated step, distorted body, the mental aberrations reflected in the physical, and all echoed in the music with its piercing cries of woodwind, wild murmurings in the bass, fierce drumbeats, and percussive piano tones. It is as repellent as the yawning "snakepit." One stands with this eldest sister at the brink of hell. Great is our gratitude for the resolution showing her, erect in her black, satin-striped dress, poised at the moment of "ultimate vision," which we hope means a saner outlook upon life.

Although Martha is, as usual, the central figure, in whose heart and mind occurs the phantasmagorial action, it is by no means a solo performance. The two other sisters, one protective, one peevish, are important characterizations. The remembered children are visualized recollections of childhood. The two beloveds have a proper fight, and the four men together a plangent dance of assertive masculinity. They remain, however, in the past. The three women are left loveless, alone. Martha is not making Hollywood movies.

Modern dance has casting trouble that ballet escapes. Any number of ballerinas can dance *Swan Lake* adequately. We may have our preferences, but part of the fun of ballet is comparing the different details of execution and interpretation. In modern works, including certain modern ballets, substitutions are more difficult. The characters are more like people. Thus with the two other sisters of *Deaths and Entrances.* Jane Dudley and Sophie Maslow created the roles and so they *are* the sisters, and those who come after them seem like interlopers. The problem comes up repeatedly in Martha's works.

Deaths and Entrances, with its light foothold in literary legend, is a kind of disunited sequel to the work immediately preceding it, a work which many consider Martha Graham's masterpiece. *Letter to the World* is based upon the life, as legend, of Emily Dickinson, the inner life of the New England poet in relation to her environment, as imagined by Martha. But before going into this great work, or other revivals of the 1947 season, it would perhaps be helpful to trace the growth of "America's great dancer" from the beginning.

Variable and unpredictable as she is, taking, as she says she does, a new point of departure for each work, the line of her development is distinctly traceable, and embryos of what became fully formed in later works are often discernible in early ones. Before she was psychologically studious Martha was psychologically aware.

"I agree with Picasso that a portrait should not be a physical or a spiritual likeness, but rather a psychological likeness," she said in New York in 1947.

Long before that she was delving below surfaces, looking for "the why underneath," as the bright little ballerina, Ruthanna Boris, puts it. Martha has always been One Who Seeks. Dance has always been an inner emotional experience to her.

The story is told that as a child of two or three she danced down the church aisle during the playing of the offertory (much to the discomfiture of her mother) in an involuntary response to the music and the atmosphere of religious worship, that later she entertained her nurse and the cook in the kitchen, and her father's patients in the ante-room, with her little action dramas. Her father, a physician and alienist, told her he could tell by the way she moved rather than by what she said whether or not she was telling a lie. The child was movement-conscious. She lisped in movement for the movement came, and movement came to speak truth for her.

It was a family of Presbyterian faith and Puritan tradition, stemming back to Miles Standish on her mother's side. There is also a mixture of Scotch-Irish and Dutch in her ancestry. Although Martha was born in a suburb of Pittsburgh, the family moved to California while she was still a child. She does not remember the time when she did not want to be a dancer, but the desire was brought to a head when, as a high-school girl in Santa Barbara, she first saw Ruth St. Denis dance. This was in 1914. By 1916 she had sufficiently overcome parental opposition to begin her studies at Denishawn. In 1922 she went to England with the company. In addition to her work with Shawn, she studied Oriental forms with "Miss Ruth" (as she was called at Denishawn), and Ruth's metaphysical approach strongly appealed to her. Then, while she was touring in *Xochitl,* she saw the six original Duncan Dancers, and they, too, had their effect.

"I saw something there that was of a natural quality, yet had a certain formalism. It spoke to me emotionally. It did not excite the senses, it spoke deeper than that."

A little later, she read an article in a new American magazine about Mary Wigman (long before Wigman came to the United States), but she does not recall that anything she read or heard of Wigman made any particular impression on her. Shawn, who believes that the American modern dance is an outgrowth of the German, said he saw Martha and Louis Horst, then a pianist at Denishawn, later her musical director, poring over Wigman pictures that he had brought back from Europe. But memories can be short at long distances. Louis went to Vienna to pursue his musical studies in 1925, when the Denishawn Company was starting its Oriental tour, and Martha, teaching at the Eastman School of Music in Rochester, gave her first New York recital in 1926, with Louis as her pianist. Certainly that recital reflected her Denishawn training more than anything else, for she had then hardly begun to find herself. At any rate, she disavows any debt to Wigman.

The very rhythm and tempo and psychological constitution of our countries are so unlike, she has said in effect, it would be impossible for us to think or dance alike. For example, we think of "frontier" as an opening up, a vista into something new. Mary Wigman, hearing the word for the first time, thought it meant a barrier. Modern dance, both German and American, comes out of individual be-ing, and none can dispute that be-ing in Germany and be-ing in the United States, are, and always have been, two very different things.

When Martha left Denishawn (or *Xochitl*) in 1923, to go into the *Greenwich Village Follies*, she knew vaguely, without rancor or malcontent, that she was at the end of that kind of dance. When, after two seasons in the *Follies*, she took up her teaching at the Eastman School, she knew she was at the beginning of "the adventure of seeking."

"The first morning I went into class I thought, I won't teach anything I know. I was through with character dancing. I wanted to begin, not with characters, or ideas, but with movement. So I started with the simplest—walking, running, skipping, leaping—

and went on from there. By correcting what looked false, I soon began creating. I wanted significant movement. I did not want it to be beautiful or fluid. I wanted it to be fraught with inner meaning, with excitement and surge. I wanted to lose the facile quality. I did not want it to *leak* out, so I concentrated in a small space. Gradually, as I was able to force out the old, little new things began to grow."

Martha worked with music and drama students, and used three of the most promising girls among them for composing. They appeared with her on her debut program as a concert dancer at the Forty-Eighth Street Theater, New York, April 18, 1926. The music was from recognized composers—César Franck, Schumann, Schubert, Debussy, Scriabin, Ravel, Rachmaninoff, Satie, and Cyril Scott. There was no décor, just the usual plain curtains. The titles were romantic, the short dances mostly pictures of types or moods: *A Florentine Madonna, A Study in Lacquer, Danse Languide, Danse Rococo, Gypsy Portrait, Désir, Deux Valses Sentimentales, Intermezzo,* and *Novelette.* One of her solos was *Maid with the Flaxen Hair,* in a long blonde wig; another, *Tanagra,* in Greek headdress and flowing draperies. Martha's first solos were axial. In her attempt to simplify movement to its core, she scarcely moved at all.

For the next three years she continuously added new pieces to her repertory, and presented them in about two New York recitals a year. As early as the second recital of the first year she began, in her *Three Poems of the East,* the use of music especially composed for the dance that has had such far-reaching effect. The score was by Louis Horst, her pianist (and at that time choreographical adviser), who thus opened the new art of the composer-accompanist in this country. In 1927 she turned from romanticism to *Revolt* (Honegger), which Fannie Brice blithely rode on her burlesquing broomstick, *Rewolt,* in a subsequent *Ziegfeld Follies* number. The following year brought further social comment in the two-part *Immigrant*: "Steerage," "Strike" (Slavenski), and *Poems of 1917*: "Song Behind the Lines," "Dance of Death" (Ornstein); and a second work with music by Louis Horst, *Fragments*: "Tragedy," "Comedy." These were all solo dances. In 1929 came the solo suite, *Four*

Insincerities: "Petulance," "Remorse," "Politeness," "Vivacity" (Prokofiev), in which, with the solos, *Unbalanced* (Harsanyi) and *Adolescence* (Hindemith), she began to hold inner qualities to the light. In the *Four Insincerities* she wore shoes for the first time, leaning lightly on a pair of giddy high-heeled slippers, and on pantomime, for her portrayal, not of a person but of personal attributes.

On April 14, 1929, at the Booth Theater, New York, she presented her first large group work, *Vision of the Apocalypse* (Reutter); and appeared with the group in her first outstanding work, *Heretic,* a landmark of her career and of the American modern dance. *Heretic,* to reiterated bars from an old Breton air, poses the progressive solo figure against massed intolerance, the lone radical against reaction. The implications are not necessarily political. It is the essence of the eternal struggle of the individual with something new to offer, coming up against the blank wall of conservatism in any field—religion, art, science, or private life. The striving figure in white circles the black-robed inquisitorial opponents, tries to break through the adamant, and fails. The new idea continues to be opposed by those who are comfortably set in their traditions, who do not want to make the effort to grasp anything new. No doubt Martha had her personal reasons for making this dance, but she transformed them into something impersonal, of general appeal.

The idea of intolerance was later expanded in her *American Provincials*: "Act of Piety," a solo, and "Act of Judgment," with group, which, with an excellent score by Louis Horst, was presented at the Guild Theater, New York, November 11, 1934. This was a mighty knifing of the prurient prudery of fanatical puritanism, a subject she returns to again and again. It hinges, in her usual tenuous fashion, on Hawthorne's *The Scarlet Letter,* and other writings not unaware of the scourge of self-righteousness and scornful disapproval of others, the holier-than-thou attitude that obtains in many religious sects.

Martha's development of movement began with concentration, with squeezing out the juice and discarding the pulp; with integration, the tying together of the body and soul of man into a close-knit, co-ordinated unit; with finding the intrinsic meaning of movement as movement. One of her departures was in what she calls percussive movement, movement of sharp accent and rebound, as of the downbeat of bare feet at the moment of shifting weight; of the offbeat, as of the accented leaning of the body in different directions; of short, broken movements that look unfinished, yet complete themselves in space. An early theory used to be that Martha's famous angles were really segments of invisible curves. A later theory (advanced by Marjorie Gowie, a New York sculptor who has done many figurines of her) is that Martha's angles come within the measurements of the "Divine Proportion" or "Golden Section" used by painters and sculptors since the time of Giotto, and by architects since the building of the pyramids, and so have classical truth in them. At all events, she has consistently extended the range of movement, year after year, adding new oscillations, large and small, new extensions and suspensions, new ways of attack and release, and just when you think she must have come to the end of the gamut, she comes up with some new deviation instead.

The second landmark of her career was *Primitive Mysteries*: "Hymn to the Virgin," "Crucifixus," "Hosanna," presented at the Craig Theater, New York, February 2, 1931. This, with its beautiful score by Louis Horst, based on American Indian themes, and adding the flute and oboe to piano and percussion, is one of Martha's loveliest works, a timeless masterpiece of shining simplicity. It is a naïve-primitive on the Spanish-Indian religious attitude of the American Southwest. The white-clad Madonna of the "Hymn to the Virgin" epitomizes the native concept of a Virgin Mother whose tender compassion embraces them; the "Crucifixus" depicts the anguish of the Passion as felt by the Mother, in their minds; and the "Hosanna" is that glorification which amounts to deification of the Queen of Heaven in simple hearts. The movement progresses with an air of ritual, the atmosphere of an early miracle play, for the most part in broad, sustained harmonies, distortion without extreme dissonance, except in the "Crucifixus." Here, as in any Graham work, it is impossible to describe the movement from beginning to end.

One remembers only the total impression, a few highlights.

Memorable are the Virgin's archaic hands, held in stiff folded angles throughout; the long sweep of her white dress in the processional entrance, the maidens in their stark blue, almost uniform attire, setting off the virginal white; the thumping footbeats of the maidens as they weave their primitive patterns; or, as they stand in silent adoration, the effect of their widespread fingers, like rays of light received from the sacred presence; and then the crowning of the Virgin with a halo made of spread and shining fingers. In this work the dance detail of hands and feet is in itself remarkable. The arms, too, are eloquent. The group design is always striking, the dynamics stirring. And always the Virgin is a being apart, with arms and hands that bless, bestow, invoke, in stylized angularity, a cherishable figure of the primitive imagination.

Primitive Mysteries had a notable performance at the Guild Theater on December 20, 1936, when Jane Dudley, Sophie Maslow, Anna Sokolow, May O'Donnell, Gertrude Shurr, Anita Alvarez, Dorothy Bird, Ethel Butler, Frieda Flier, Marie Marchowsky, and Marjorie Mazia were regular members of the concert group, and imparted the virility, or "guttiness," the work demands. They have all gone on to independent careers, save Miss O'Donnell, who has returned from one, and Miss Mazia, who seems to be half in and half out of the company half of the time.

When the work was revived during the extension of the Broadway season of 1947, it was nowhere near so well performed, not only because rehearsal time was short and extra girls had to be called in, but because the girls of the present company are "thin" in more ways than one. They are young and attractive; they are so light they could be mistaken for ballet dancers; they serve well in the mixed company in pieces composed around them and perhaps modulated to them. But they lack the full-blooded vigor of the concert group of the mid-thirties seen in the rousing concert dances that marked the end of a period. Excepted are May O'Donnell, of course, and Yuriko, perhaps.

In the solo, *Dance* (Honegger) of 1929, Martha used her first hint of participant décor. It was a low platform or wooden construction that later appeared in various forms—as in the dais of *Adolescence* and the mourning bench of *Lamentation,* her first great solo and one that remained long in her repertory. *Lamentation* (Kodaly) (1930) was done wholly in a seated position on the bench. The figure of grief (whose shroud-like robe shared the tortured movement) stretched and writhed in every direction, farther off balance than it could go—though it did go. The bare feet, gnarled with bracing the wracked and twisted body, the hands, knotted in agony, bespoke the dagger in the heart. It was superb emotional dancing, restrained enough to draw the spectator in.

Contrasted with it on the same program was *Harlequinade* (Toch), Martha's first shot at really obvious humor. The self-pitying Pessimist, magnifying minor troubles, weeps into a large polka-dotted kerchief, which becomes a sack weighted with mock-sorrow that she carries off on bowed shoulders; while the light-headed Optimist, making an ornament of the kerchief, capers about with open arms and flying legs, in careless disregard of trouble. These contrasted concert pieces seemed marvelous until they were overshadowed by the greater theater pieces. They were shown in a few major cities of the Middle West and the Pacific Coast during Martha's first transcontinental tour (a solo expedition in 1936), and thereafter often reflected.

There were many subtler and more difficult solos in the first fecund decade, as the *Dithyrambic* of 1931, a set of movement variations of mounting intensity, on a Dionysiac theme, to Aaron Copland's Piano Variations; *Ekstasis* (1933), a dance of sensuous delight, to music composed for it by Lehman Engel; and, in 1934, the suite, *Transitions,* with special score also by Engel, in which she used voice for the first time. Martha's works are chronologically listed, as are her many extra-concert activities, in Barbara Morgan's beautiful book of dance photographs, *Martha Graham.* The book carries through to 1940, and some of the outstanding works are described. Unfortunately, the ground cannot be covered so microscopically here. There is space only for landmarks on the explorer's path.

One of these was the epochal *Frontier—An American Perspective of the Plains,* with a notable score by Louis Horst and décor by Isamu Noguchi, presented in a Sunday night concert at the Guild Theater, April 28, 1935. This eventful solo marked Martha's first use of actual décor (a word she once rejected, used here in the sense of sketchy but significant setting). It consisted of a fragment of rail fence and two lines of thick white rope extending diagonally upward, right and left. *Frontier* is a radiant dance of the American pioneer woman, strong, courageous, young and free. It is a dance full of space, in which any momentary sense of wilderness or loneliness is quickly overcome by the sense of opening vista and the fullness of the woman's life. The action centers on the log stile, or fence. The torso lies horizontally across it; one leg is lifted like a banner vertically above it; the pioneer figure sits in a prayerful attitude before it; and from it and toward it she walks or runs in little happy steps with high back kicks. It is a jubilant, sunlit dance, in certain respects a forecast of *Appalachian Spring*.

Frontier was Martha's second out-and-out handling of the American theme, following as it did *American Provincials* by about six months. She protests that she has always danced as an American, the American rhythms, the American tempi, the American psyche. But there were some pretty fancy titles on her early programs, and I believe that as she grew as an artist and as a woman, the awareness of America steadily grew upon her; and that as the inner vision deepened, the means of its externalization grew as inevitably.

Martha had one foot in the theater from the beginning. In 1929 she danced at the Manhattan Opera House, with Charles Weidman as partner, in a production of Richard Strauss's *Ein Heldenleben*, directed by Irene Lewisohn and presented by the Neighborhood Playhouse with the Cleveland Symphony Orchestra, Nikolai Sokoloff conducting; in 1930, at the Mecca Auditorium (now the New York City Center of Music and Drama) with Weidman again, in Charles Martin Loeffler's *Pagan Poem*, under the same auspices, with the same orchestra and conductor; and at the Metropolitan Opera House in Philadelphia and the Metropolitan in New York, as the Chosen One in Stravinsky's *Le Sacre du Printemps*, choreographed by Léonide Massine, with the Philadelphia Orchestra, Leopold Stokowski conducting. In that year she joined the first modern dance co-operative, the Dance Repertory Theatre founded by Helen Tamiris, a well-intentioned but short-lived attempt to demonstrate the brotherhood of dancers, of which Doris Humphrey and Charles Weidman were also members.

Between 1931 and 1935 she toured with Blanche Yurka in *Electra;* used her Guggenheim Fellowship for research among the Indians of the Southwest; assisted Katharine Cornell and Guthrie McClintic in their production of André Obey's *Lucrece;* produced six miracle plays for Stage Alliance; and directed the movement for Archibald MacLeish's play, *Panic.*

Meanwhile she was developing her concert group and presenting group works of growing importance, widening and deepening the channels of movement, of interest and point of view, touching often upon themes she was later to expand. She was experimenting with new music, and, very tentatively, with that unique, abbreviated, evocative type of setting she does not like to have called "décor." Subject-springboards into movement, to which she returned from time to time, to handle with freshness and variety each time, are: the theater of ancient Greece; the barbaric primitive; the pagan-Christian primitive; puritanism; the adaptation of pre-classic dance forms to contemporary comment; the American idea; the social scene; the complex nature of woman (so magnificently diagnosed in *Herodiade*); the general faulty, thrilling aliveness of humankind. Never taking anything at surface value, she dug deeper and deeper into "the why underneath," until she came upon that secret mental and emotional life that now engrosses her and brings out an even newer dance telegraphy. A long path of development had yet to be traversed, however, before she arrived at this point of using movement as a divining-rod to discover the deep wells of feeling below thought.

In the middle thirties, when Martha was still an ugly duckling in the provinces, she was nothing short of a divinity, a modern Swan Queen, in New York. Her Sunday night concerts at the Guild Theater summoned a cult of worshippers who packed the house— exuberant young people cheering, stamping, shouting—mixed with their quieter elders, who at every turn of a profile proved to be celebrities. There would be Jane Cowl in a sport hat, Katharine Cornell in a turban, painters, sculptors, musicians, writers, and of course all the other dancers in the city. Graham stretches, Graham extensions, were analyzed by Marthatomanes in the lobby as minutely as any ballerina's *fouettés* by balletomanes at the Metropolitan. At this time Martha's dance was movement for movement's sake. She eschewed all literary entanglements, all drama save what was movement's own. The face was rapt, immobile; the hands were stiff, the costumes stark. Martha was the priestess, the girls a group of vestal virgins. The surge and swell, the run and charge, ebb and flow, of movement was the thing; and there were devotees who regretted the change when it came. It was not what the dance was about but what it did to you that mattered.

One such unliterary group dance was *Course,* with a score composed for it by George Antheil, presented at the Guild Theater on February 10, 1935. It was an embodiment of rhythmic energy—running, leaping, jumping—that left the spectator breathless. It was simply the coursing across the stage of vigorous young bodies at varied speed, accent, volume, and tempi, that stirred the blood and animated the spectator with a new sense of vigor, a new feeling of strength and dominion within himself. Notable here were the bars of rest, used as in music, not only as a temporary cessation of activity, but as an emphasis of the activity that had proceeded and was to come. This dynamic stillness, the stillness of life, not death, vibrating with a myriad small pulsations, minute radiations of aliveness, has always marked Martha's dance. In herself it is felt as inner repose, the source of an energy that makes no unnecessary expenditure. In her dances it may appear as punctuation, interludes of immobility, or it may appear as tranquility, the calm of self-possession in the midst of action. Like *Course, Celebration* (Horst) of the year before, was a vital, exhilarating, dance. But the two were soon dropped from the repertory. Martha was striding toward her so different future, though she had yet several paces to go.

With the solo suite, *Dance in Four Parts*: "Quest," "Derision," "Dream," "Sportive Tragedy," to a set of Preludes by George Antheil, already composed, Martha ended her reliance upon music not composed especially for her dance. Up to then Louis Horst, Lehman Engel, and Wallingford Riegger had composed occasional scores for her. With Antheil's score for *Course,* and Paul Nordoff's score for the solo *Praeludium* (on the same program), began that steady employ of American composers which, supplemented by Doris Humphrey, Charles Weidman, and other modern dancers, and more recently by choreographers in the ballet field, has so strongly influenced American music, with the result that much of the best music composed in the United States today is that composed for dance.

Panorama, with music by Norman Lloyd, the first workshop production of the Bennington School of the Dance, was presented in the Vermont State Armory, in the town, on August 14, 1935. It was performed by a nucleus of Graham dancers, headed by Martha, and selected students from the workshop group who had trained with her during the summer. The large floor space was reserved for the dancers, the spectators looking down from built-up bleachers and a balcony, a seating arrangement not without precedent in ancient times. Arch Lauterer, the stage designer, used varied levels and screens to space the action. The work had three subtitles: "Theme of Dedication," "Imperial Theme," and "Popular Theme;" and the program note referred rather vaguely to American traditions and background. It was important less for its texture or substance than for its experimentation with functional stage design.

Another experiment in décor came the following winter in a concert at the Guild Theater on February 23, 1936, with the introduction of "mobiles" by Alexander Calder for the new work, *Horizons* (Horst). These mobiles were small, colored geometric objects swinging or sliding from wires (miniatures of his more elaborate designs shown at the Museum of Modern Art some years ago), intended as "visual preludes to the dances." They were supposed also "to enlarge the sense of horizon," but all they succeeded in doing was to keep the audience puzzling over them. Martha has not reverted to mobiles since, though she may at any time discover a more fruitful use for these interesting items of modern art. Like *Panorama, Horizons* touched vaguely upon the American background, as indicated in its four subtitles: "Migration (New Trails);" "Dominion (Sanctified Power);" "Building Motif (Homesteading);" and "Dance of Rejoicing."

The same year brought a more significant experiment in the

full-length group work, *Chronicle,* with score by Wallingford Riegger and décor by Noguchi, first presented at the Guild Theater on
December 20, 1936, and revised in substance and costume a week
later. This was a dance that sensed the seething world atmosphere
of the time, that remembered the war not long past and discerned
the war even then looming much larger than a man's hand (and
that hand Hitler's). This was a dance that, like the nation, felt a
war coming on and failed to prevent it. But the dance called attention, the dance gave a warning; only too few people saw and heard.
Some who did were annoyed at what they considered a premature
handling of the theme, just as other people were annoyed at any
similar far-visioned expression in the press.

Chronicle was in three sections; the first:

DANCES BEFORE CATASTROPHE

(a) *Spectre—1914* (Drums—Red Shroud—Lament)

(b) *Masque* (Idolatry of Tradition)

In the "Spectre" solo, Martha, in a flowing black dress, wielded a
voluminous red garment that served as cape or overskirt, weaving
its folds into the movement design, and reminding us that red is
the color of blood. The group "Masque" was a ritual of no great
intensity. But in

DANCES AFTER CATASTROPHE

(a) *Steps in the Street* (Devastation—Exile)

(b) *Tragic Holiday* (In Memoriam)

"Steps in the Street" was a dance of terrible urgency. The bare feet
of the girls whipping across the stage reverberated like drumbeats
in the heart. This is a sound effect, this use of shaded footbeats, advancing, receding, echoing, this audible breathing of bare feet in
concert as they stroke or brush the floor in delicate or dynamic
percussion, that belongs distinctly to modern dance, and that
Martha makes telling use of.

In "Tragic Holiday" her black gauze flag becomes a mourning
veil, worn as an insigne of the grief the world had borne and was
again to bear, and some of us felt it then. Noguchi's setting, more
carpenter-ish than sculptural, was nothing like those he designs today, but its units were participants of the action, even so. The
formal setting of the opening section, a series of circular, silver-

colored pedestals, surrounded by variegated pennants, was re-arranged into a flight of steps for the second section, which closed with a tragic processional. The dance might well have ended here. For the third section,

PRELUDE TO ACTION (Unity—Pledge to the Future)

with red and white coming cheerfully into the costuming, fell something short. Perhaps because we surmised more than we could then see, the Prelude was more of foreboding than of promise, the Unity was of armies yet to march, the Pledge to the Future was yet to be redeemed.

Martha took *Chronicle* on her second transcontinental tour in 1937 (this time with the group), but it did not remain long in the repertory. Much of what she tried to say of her faith in America through these three works—*Panorama, Horizons* and *Chronicle*—came out more definitely in *American Document,* produced at the Bennington Festival of 1938. In this work she introduced her first male partner (since the early appearances with Charles Weidman) in Erick Hawkins, and her first costume designer (other than herself) in Edythe Gilfond. She made her first protracted use of spoken words, and her first presentation in an established entertainment form—with her usual divagations from the norm. This was the beginning of Martha Graham's Dance Company, the transitional step between concert and theater.

The year before she had done two splendid solos, *Immediate Tragedy* and *Deep Song,* both inspired by the war in Spain. The music was by Henry Cowell. *Immediate Tragedy* was a sweeping indictment, in Martha's own dance metaphor, of the torch that set the world aflame; and *Deep Song* was earth-stricken and floor-bound in pity of it. In these solos and in *Chronicle,* Martha's heart had gone out to the world in compassion for its anguish. She turned from world-suffering to find comfort in the American ideal, to affirm that ideal in *American Document.* The work marked a pause for refreshment of the creative spirit, wherein to find an object of fortifying faith in the circumambient distress. Martha looked to America, as the world looked, for strength and leadership. But not with astigmatic eyes.

American Document is set in a nebulous framework of the old-time minstrel show, part and parcel of American entertainment traditions, without being very much like one. It is not in blackface, it does not go in for "darky" or other popular comedy. It is, to borrow from the films, a dance documentary, and its score, by Ray Green, has the color and disjointed continuity of film music. It does have two End Figures (minus oral badinage), and an Interlocutor who binds together with dignified phrases excerpts from the classical prose of certain American writings—among them the Declaration of Independence, a letter from Red Jacket of the Seneca Indians, Jonathan Edwards's sermons, the Bible, Walt Whitman's poems, Lincoln's Gettysburg Address and Emancipation Proclamation.

The performance begins with the Walk-Around, a processional entrance of the characters, which recurs between the episodes, and at the end. "Declaration" interprets our great state paper in terms of individual independence. In "Indian Episode," Martha has a lovely solo as the "Native Figure," and the group ("Lament for the Land"), taking up the heel thrusts of her solo, falls into exciting patterns, all without obvious reliance on the authentic Indian steps, but, *with the words,* giving us a rather hang-dog feeling for our wicked dispossession of the race. The "Puritan Episode" is a duet by Martha and Erick, with love and love's desires rhetorically frowned upon by our Puritan forefathers, while the "Song of Songs," in figurative language, defends them. The "Emancipation Episode" pertains to individual freedom everywhere. "The After Piece" is a round-table conference on what it means to be an American, and how best to fulfill America's high synonym, Democracy. The "Finale and Exit" is the closing Walk-Around.

American Document was composed and rehearsed during the six-week session of the Bennington School of the Dance, and produced in the State Armory August 6, 1938. Housely Stevens, Jr., a young actor who stood, moved and spoke his lines well, was the Interlocutor. The work was revised and considerably tightened up, in Martha's inevitable way, before its first New York showing in Carnegie Hall in October, and was taken on the third transcontinental tour, in 1939. Its devout patriotism won the country. It was easily understood, therefore easily appreciated, for this was one

Graham work that was not a Graham mystery. It was almost too explicit. The stripped, clean, poetic words said all there was to say, so that the movement phrases served chiefly as illustrations.

A second work in entertainment form, the full-length tragicomedy, *Every Soul is a Circus,* marked Martha's entrance into theater. It was presented in a Holiday Festival series (organized by Frances Hawkins, her manager at the time) at the St. James Theater, New York, on December 27, 1939, and was an immediate success. The score is by Paul Nordoff; the costumes are by Edythe Gilfond; and the first of the décors elaborate enough to be called a setting is by Philip Stapp. The allusion of the title, and the motto of the piece, is from Vachel Lindsay's poem, beginning:

> Every soul is a circus
> Every mind is a tent
> Every heart is a sawdust ring
> Where the circling race is spent.

As the elliptical setting hints, and the quizzical action proves, this is a circus that never was, in tent or arena, but might be, in your heart or mine. Analogies are provided in the small set of draperies upstage that suggest an entrance to the dressing rooms, in the spectators' gallery beside it, in the circular pedestal center stage that becomes a sitting place or a performance spot, in the long diagonal ropes pulled with pretense of great effort to denote the lifting of an imaginary front curtain, and in the couch at stage left, to which the Empress of the Arena resorts the better to brood upon her troubles. Here is the woman of *Four Insincerities,* the Pessimist and Optimist of *Harlequinade,* in fuller portraiture. Here is vain, silly, shallow woman, with all her egosyncracies, trying to give herself a build-up on a basic inferiority complex, and remaining frustrated, incomplete. The portrait is not actually of woman, but of certain womanish characteristics that have inhabited the female mind since Eve, or possibly Lilith. Pity is mixed with laughter as we watch the antics of self-love. The comedy note is struck at once as the Empress, indulging a mood of self-pity on the couch, flings herself laterally across it and literally paws the ground in mock grief. When she turns her head to watch the separate performance of her feet, as a corner of one's self is inclined to watch such emotional orgies, the effect is hilariously funny.

The Empress's big ideas for herself are constantly being thwarted by the Ring Master (Erick Hawkins), whose whiphand holds a real whip. He is the epitome of the masterful man, and the Empress rather likes it. But when the Acrobat enters, she wants to do a little conquesting herself. The acquisitive gleam in her eye, the whole yearning, forward slant of her body, betray her. And the Ring Master is not slow to notice the signs. Just as things begin to look interesting in the new courtship, he picks her up bodily, as is, legs and arms flung wide apart in air, or body curled for a jump, and conclusively removes her from any success in temptation. There is a good deal of dance dialogism among the three, with the Empress now near-triumphant, now defeated, in her amorous pursuit. The by-play between the would-be lovers, with a large, long-stemmed rose, the moments of mock contrition when the Empress, linked in the Ring Master's arm, walks in humble deep knee-bends beside him, are all made transparent by a new element in Martha's dance, a kind of mimesis that is neither actual pantomime nor the traditional pantomime of the classic ballet, but a wayward deploy of instinctive gesture.

A lot goes on outside the triangle in this multi-ringed circus, where every soul is the center of his own ring. Each of the men has an opportunity to show off a bit by himself. The Ideal Spectator not only makes an entrance but changes her headgear and strikes attitudes as she spectates. The other performers take great relish in their own performances. There is a Garland Entry by four girls and the Acrobat, and another satirical sequence called Poses and Plastiques by the same ensemble. The music (since re-scored) makes sly comment on the action, as the action makes sly comment on the world of the circus and the circus of the world. Now it sighfully recalls a familiar sentimental tune, now it sends forth drum rolls, as in the Empress's Star Turn, in which Martha burlesques her own easy leg extension by using a long strip of red cloth for a pulley. The costumes are gayer, more theatrical than formerly, Martha's white, accordion-pleated dress lending itself with wonderful viability to the variegations of mood and movement. The piece ends with a recapitulation (like that in music, not an exact repetition) of the Empress's first theme of self-pity on the couch.

With *Every Soul is a Circus* began The Theater of Martha Graham. The phrase, now in general use, is a paraphrase of The Theater of Angna Enters. But the two theaters are in nowise alike. In Miss Enters's one-woman theater the movement is not the organic movement of modern dance, and dance is an incident in mime. In Martha's full-company theater, movement is still paramount, in spite of remote literary, mythological, or pantomimic references. The work introduced Martha's second male partner, Merce Cunningham, as the Acrobat. Like Erick Hawkins, he came to her from Lincoln Kirstein's Ballet Caravan. The advent of these ballet-trained men brought a more active adaptation of ballet *pas* into the Graham technic—another proof that the living material a choreographer has to work with is bound to influence the use he makes of that material. This is seen also in *Letter to the World,* which added two more men to the company; and firmly established the strange, unrealistic theater that holds a magnifying glass to human nature, revealing sometimes what is glorious, sometimes what is monstrous therein.

In *Letter to the World,* the new innerliness came out in poetic imagery. But, like several of Martha's major works, this one did not hit the mark at first. When produced at the Bennington Festival on August 11, 1940 (on the small stage of the college theater in the Commons Building), it was stamped by certain critics as a letter not worth mailing, among other derisive comments, whereas the little miracle play, *El Penitente,* on the same program, was an instantaneous success.

El Penitente, with a most companionate score by Louis Horst, setting by Arch Lauterer, and costumes by Edythe Gilfond, derives from the Penitentes, that religious sect of Old and New Mexico, whose beliefs mingle flagellation with the supreme sacrifice of the Crucifixion. The three characters are the Penitent (Erick Hawkins), the Christ Figure (created by Merce Cunningham), and the Mary Figure in three aspects—Virgin, Magdalen, and Mother—(created by Martha). The trio makes its processional entrance (note the frequency of this processional entrance in Martha's work) as three strolling players. They carry their properties, and publicly affix the fragments of costume that will transform them into the characters of the miracle. This they solemnly enact, and when it is over, burst into a joyous festival dance that sets the miracle apart, and unites the players with the imaginary audience of naïve people who have witnessed it.

The Penitent has a solo of self-flagellation lashing a heavy rope (another Graham frequency) across his bare, writhing torso. In the vision following his frenzy, "the Virgin pleads, the Christ blesses." Then the Magdalen tempts him. In this sequence, Martha dons a fancy headdress and a seductive air, and with steps of slightly Spanish flavor, artfully entices her prey. He looks on, increasingly bewitched, and when he picks up the steps, at first insecurely but finally dancing them in unison with her, you know that he is indeed undone. The Christ Figure, with magnificent gesture, condemns the sinners. Now the Penitent, roped to the Death Cart (symbol for sin, according to the program note), painfully drags it forward, while the Mary Figure, in hooded black, wearily pushes it from behind. A symbolic bearing of the cross by the Penitent, accompanied by the bowed, sorrowing figure of Mary the Mother, leads to the climax and the resultant promise of redemption.

Such matter-of-fact description of the action is ruinous to the delicate mood of a dance that is as rapt and tender as a prayer. It can give only the outline of what is in performance a miracle of movement values, whose mimetic intrigue of design is the outward sign of all it emanates. Nor can the music, with its primitive woodwind tones, its low, vibrant drumbeats, be properly appraised in words. As for the costumes, there is no good whatever in describing them, for they are, like all things Martha, subject to change. The Christ Figure first wore what looked like a crown of thorns and a papal robe. In Barbara Morgan's priceless book of photographs, he wears a sunburst headdress of Mongolian effect. And I have seen him in a triangular mask that boxed in the face, in line, perhaps, with the tradition that the face of the Christ should not be shown upon the stage.

In the revival at the Ziegfeld Theater (February 28, 1947), the piece was re-set by Isamu Noguchi, John Butler was the Christ Figure, and Pearl Lang the Mary Figure—the first dancer to be given a role of Martha's. The new production offered no valid excuse for the substitutions. One preferred Arch Lauterer's original rough-hewn concepts of the players' paraphernalia. Miss Lang, however winsome and technically proficient, was handicapped by the fact that youth continues to be wasted upon the young. The loss of Merce Cunningham could not be helped, because he had joined the new Ballet Society, of which his former director, Lincoln Kirstein, is the chief animator; and Mr. Butler did have stature and dignity for the role. The constant turnover in modern dance personnel is most annoying to the un-ideal spectator, who wants to see the status quo preserved, when it is satisfactory, instead of rejoicing in the progress of young dancers. Long ago Martha accepted it as right that her dancers should leave her whenever they felt ready. Erick, without leaving, Merce at Ballet Society, Jean Erdman, and Nina Fonaroff on their own, are among the younger Graham dancers who are developing as choreographers.

So Graham dancers come and go, and Graham dances fluctuate in performance quality—which obtains not always in the personnel, but sometimes in the spectator's state of receptivity. A case in point is *Letter to the World,* revised into a masterpiece that is never twice the same. Its score by Hunter Johnson is constantly popping up with relevancies overlooked at previous hearings, just as details of action come to light anew on repeated viewings. In a Graham work, you are never sure whether a detail is something Martha has just added or something you have only just seen, whether Martha is wearing a new dress, or you had forgotten the costume. In *Letter* her wardrobe (designed by Mrs. Gilfond) changes with the mood. Arch Lauterer's setting (also revised) limns by white wrought-iron gates and shutters, upstage left as on a rise of ground, a breath, not a replica, of what might be the famous house at Amherst; and by a white settle, downstage right, the garden. And all takes place, not in that house, not in that garden, but in the mind and heart of a woman whose prototype is the New England poet.

The actuality of Emily appears only in the spoken quotations from those spontaneous little verses that erupted out of her inner life. The rest is fantasy, built on the revelation by those verses of that life, wherein the poetic imagery of movement substantiates the poetic imagery of words. The words are used sparingly, choicely. The One Who Speaks represents the circumspect outer Emily, dressing quietly, moving gently, taming her wild-rushing thoughts into the subdual of poetic form. The One Who Dances (Martha) vents the emotional life in dress and behavior. All the other characters are extensions of this dual self.

Now she is the radiant young girl, seeing gladly within the limits of her traditions, "Because I see New Englandly." Now she plays with two neighbor children, now with other young people at a party, where the skittering footbeats of the dancers—approaching, vanishing—have the haunting eeriness of memory or dream. The young men, pale forerunners of the lover concept, elude her. Now dark forebodings gather, fear, and thoughts of death. "It is coming—the postponeless creature," and the tall, imperious figure of the Ancestress in a sweeping black gown, bears down upon her, prostrating her, as, pondering the death of a neighbor, she goes through the death-experience in imagination. In the sequence "Gay Ghastly Holiday," the party theme is inverted in music and group dancing, the music intoning solemnly while four men bear the corpse-like form on their shoulders, and the girls kneel in mourning. It is all elusive, evanescent, and one cannot really pin it down in words.

Love awakens the sufferer from her frightening daydream. The Lover (Erick Hawkins) helps her to her feet, to regain balance, restores her to the sweetness of life. The shadow of the Ancestress parts them temporarily. But Emily is intoxicated with her new-found happiness, "The little tippler, leaning against the sun." She is riotously gay in her garden, inviting new experience. "Dear March, come in," and March, the spirit of spring, of joy in love, bounds on. They innocently disport themselves around the garden settle, turn it over, rock in it in its new position, until the Ancestress (" 'Tis conscience, childhood's nurse") comes to set it right again. There is delectable comedy here, in the Ancestress's disapproving mien, and the way Emily runs off like a naughty child who has been reprimanded.

Light and shade play through the piece, as sunlight or skylight plays through leaves—first the full-leafed tree, each leaf clearly defined in morning light, then the clouding of the leaves into a dark mass at dusk. After the morning play of limpid youth, the noon of love, the dark shape forms, the "Leaf at love turned back." It is as the embodiment of Puritan tradition, not as the figure of death, that the Ancestress separates the lovers.

The separation is followed by the most tragic scene in Martha's repertory. In comparison, *Lamentation* was a plastic monument of grief, a grief depersonalized, ennobled, as in an exalted sculpture. The immediacy of Emily's grief is hardly to be borne. "There is a pain so utter it swallows being up." This is that pain. This is an agony that possesses every fiber of being, that makes itself felt and shared; as do "the leaden days" that come after, the days of dragging about the business of daily living, weighted with a heart-load heavier than death. The dance comes to a luminous conclusion, with thwarted wifehood and motherhood transfigured in the crucible of suffering. Emily, in a dress of the white that contains all colors, sits resigned on the white settle, serene in the gift that burns the colors of emotion into the white prism of poetry. "This is my letter to the world."

The work was revived during the 1947 spring season at the Ziegfeld, and again one must deplore certain cast changes, however unavoidable. Jane Dudley, who created the role of the Ancestress, was, in her tall, majestic carriage, her indefinable emanations, the very spirit of the stern, unwritten law that rules the hearts of most New Englanders, and of the fear and awe of death that held sway in Emily's heart—the combination that inheres in this powerful role. May O'Donnell moves beautifully, is beautiful, unmatchable in certain roles she has created, but she is not the Ancestress and never will be, to this intransigent observer, simply because Jane Dudley is. On the other hand, Jean Erdman, who did not create the role of the One Who Speaks, seems today irreplaceable. When *Letter* was first produced at Bennington, an actress, Margaret Meredith, was ineffectual with the spoken lines and made very little use of her body. When the revised version had its first New York showing at the Mansfield Theater on January 20, 1941, at Bennington the following summer, and in subsequent performances of that period, Jean Erdman, then a member of the company, spoke movingly, moving as she spoke, with just the right inflections in both speech and movement. Angela Kennedy, an actress, who later took it on, has an artificial, theatrical manner in carriage and delivery that is not in accord with the poetic atmosphere of the whole. Nor has Mark Ryder, good as he is in his own type of thing, the deft aeriality and elfin other-worldliness of Merce Cunningham, the original March.

However, *Letter* is strong enough to withstand such handicaps, and others. Erick has always been a stiff and distant Lover. Martha, who can be superlative, and tear your heartstrings out one by one, can also dance it as if she were tired of the whole thing. A bill consisting of *El Penitente, Letter to the World,* and *Every Soul is a Circus,* in their pristine states, was given on tour under WGN Concerts management, with high success, publishing the new Theater of Martha Graham from one end of the country to the other.

The next production was *Punch and The Judy,* a scintillating comedy of "squabble and scuffle" that made an instantaneous hit at the Bennington Festival of 1941. The setting, by Arch Lauterer, placed a library chair and large globe at stage right, a narrow doorway behind them, a stretch of black and white linoleum, a couch, chimney piece, and window (or curtain of clouds) upstage—all the comforts of home in harlequinade—and all taking a strenuous part in the action. The costumes by Charlotte Trowbridge, the score by Robert McBride, were apt and clever. As done at Bennington:

The *aria da capo* begins with the Three Fates (Jane Dudley, Jean Erdman, Ethel Butler) clustered like maiden aunts or village gossips in elegant long gowns, around the library globe. Miss Erdman, book in hand, reads aloud from time to time what prove to be sardonic comments on the action, from Gordon Craig's "Tom Fool." Punch (Erick Hawkins in the best role of his career) reclines peacefully on the couch. The Judy (Martha, fussily dressed) daydreams at her fantastic window-piece. She casts a baleful glance at her sleeping spouse and with a flick of the wrist expresses her opinion of him. With the entrance of the Child (Nina Fonaroff), a brat who has to be coaxed and scolded, rocked and spanked, the first round of the fighting starts. The Judy, bored with domesticity, seeks refuge in an interlude with Pegasus (Merce Cunningham), a figment of romance whose means of ingress and egress is the dream window. But Punch goes her one better. He gets Pretty Polly (Pearl Lang), a more tangible expression of romance, and there's a pretty howdy-do over that. The Three Fates, like a trio of puritanical umpires, indulge their barren pleasure in other people's affairs; and the music laughs at the lot of them.

Once again The Judy tries escape by the romantic route, this time in Three Heroes: the Soldier (David Campbell), the Scout (David Zellmer), and the Pony Express Rider (Sasha Liebich—now Mark Ryder). Attentive as they are, she returns to Pegasus, who, naturally, is not very satisfactory, either. The pay-off comes when Punch, ever the hearty extrovert, and now particularly well pleased with himself, enters with great braggadocio to clasp each rival warmly by the hand. Somehow the handclasps get mixed up with back-slaps and face-slaps and another row ensues. Finally, in an irrational game of blind-man's-buff, The Judy finds herself stuck with her legal partner; and by the pointed finger of one Fate, the sarcastic question of the reader, "Shall we begin again?" and the ironical answer from the orchestra, we are led to believe that the game of "squabble and scuffle" will go on ad infinitum.

Punch and The Judy, whose only tie to the Punch and Judy show is in the theme of connubial combat, is, to date, Martha's last dance in entertainment form, or rather, to approximate an entertainment form in its own amorphous way. At that time she seemed to have plumbed as deep into the reservoir of feeling, as deep into the reservoir of feeling's physical expression, as it was possible to go. There was no psychosis in the underlying psychology of these first dance dramas, and now they seem warm and human and healthy in comparison with some of her later works. But in her very next piece, *Deaths and Entrances,* as has been recorded here, she began the psychiatric probing that in *Cave of the Heart* appears to have brought up the last remnant of bile in the human system. God help us if she probes farther and finds worse (if there is anything worse than lustful, murderous hate) to expose in this age of raw nerves and jittery unrest. One might say in extenuation that Martha's dance psychoanalysis is a reflection of the age, with its scientific explorations into the mental as well as into technological realms.

The trouble is that movement, her kind of movement, in its latest developments, gives inner diabolism such preposterous reality that her Medea of remote association is less remote than the actual Medea of Greek tragedy, and twice as shocking to the sensibilities.

Before Martha embarked on her psycho-mythological cycle, she produced two transcendent works—*Appalachian Spring,* with score by Aaron Copland, and *Mirror Before Me,* which has now resumed the original title, *Herodiade,* given it by its composer, Paul Hindemith. These were commissioned in both choreography and music by the Elizabeth Sprague Coolidge Foundation, and, first presented at the closing concert of the Coolidge Chamber Music Festival in the Library of Congress, Washington, D. C., on October 30, 1944, were repeated by request the following night. Before that, on the same program with the first *Deaths and Entrances,* was the lovely solo, *Salem Shore,* then contemporary and sympathetic in its feeling of women waiting all over the world, waiting and wondering if their men would ever come home. Martha's very middle-agedness is an asset to her. Just as no actress can play Juliet until she is long past Juliet's age, so Martha's women, springing from the fount of experienced womanhood, can be as young as she wants them to be, and more expressive than youth knows how to make them.

In *Salem Shore,* lifted into timelessness by the program note, "a ballad of a woman's longing for her beloved's return from the sea," she looked gloriously young, a glamorous concentrate of all the young war-wives and sweethearts, as she danced with the lilt and poignancy of deepfelt song, a condensation of their longing, of all the longing of women who wait and have waited the world over. Her versatile dark hair was youngly dressed. Her wide-skirted, floating gown of soft gray and white, was youthful. In Arch Lauterer's setting, a pale blue backcloth became a vast stretch of sea beyond its sandy border; small pieces denoted the "widow's walk" of an old Salem house, the weathered prow of a wrecked ship. A coil of seadrift, round like a wedding ring, rough like a thorny crown, a black lace parasol with shell-pink lining, played their parts as memory links in emotional event. Paul Nordoff's music recalled old ballads, spoke of the cruel blue brightness and gray melancholy of the sea, spoke of the woman's longing, in accord with the dance. This lyrical solo was marred at the first two performances by the projection of spoken verse in the offstage voice of Martha's actress sister, Georgia Sargeant. At the *première* the words were barely audible. At the repetition the voice, metallicized by a public address system, broke harshly into the mood.

Again the implicative setting in *Appalachian Spring*, this time by Noguchi, but in architectural rather than sculptural form. We see the framework of a new house, with its front porch and rocking chair to make it home, the adjoining shed and side bench that says it is a farmhouse, the bit of fence that announces the wide fields and wooded hills of the Pennsylvania frontier beyond. Again the processional entrance, as the members of the little community one by one take their stands: The Pioneering Woman, representing faith in the Promised Land, the future of America; the Revivalist with his four young Followers, betokening the freedom of religious worship on which the country was founded; and finally the Husbandman and his Wife, symbols of the family unit, the basis of national stability. In the first production the costumes were of earth colors (except the faded-blue of the Followers), shading from the deep brown of the Revivalist's frock coat and preacher's hat to the wheat-colored gown of the Wife. At the 1947 revival, Martha wore a new red and white pin-striped dress, and Erick's neat work-clothes were in tones of green. May O'Donnell, as before, wore the Pioneering Woman's long house-dress and large sunbonnet.

The groupings constantly change as those who are not dancing assume poses of restful but alert immobility. The motherly Pioneering Woman is all beneficence, and quite athletic for a woman of her supposed age. The Revivalist combines zeal and showmanship in his exhortation. He wrestles with sin in violent contortions of his long, lean body, denounces it, stamps upon it, in wild leaps and bounds. But his hand blesses the house, congratulates the bridal couple at the end. With a not entirely impersonal reverence, the young Followers surround him, praise him in unusual measures. Now they have a passage in unison, now each turns and jumps separately, making patterns like the opening petals of some improbable flower. Among them the motif of clapping hands recurs, and this natural sound effect, as primitive in source as the shaded foot-beats, is also heard frequently in Martha's work.

The Husbandman asserts his pride in the land, in his bride, by the wide stance of masculinity, the big, virile gesture. The Wife teems with fertility. She posits her joy in ecstatic little whirls and runs, blows phantom kisses, holds within gently rocking arms her vision of the child to come, bends as if to caress other future children, pretends to play with them, goes to her husband and stands demure beside him. They have a quiet duet, then joy mounts in her again, she springs into the air, supported by his strong hand, and the odd lifts that follow (like ballet lifts, with Graham adjustments) proclaim their happiness together.

There is a darker passage. While the others stand upstage, backs to the audience, as if in church, heads bowed as if in prayer, she kneels alone downstage in a dance of doubt and questioning. Fears of the unknown, of childbirth pangs, of family responsibility —all the fears attendant upon girlhood's initiation into womanhood —crowd into that moment. We feel her praying for courage to be the good wife and mother she wants to be. Then, with neighborly good will, one by one as they entered, the Pioneering Woman, the Revivalist, and his Followers, leave the Husbandman and his Wife to take possession of their house alone. She sits in the rocking chair, he stands behind her, extending one arm lightly over her shoulder to clasp her hand. On the tender note of idealization with which most marriages begin, ends this modern ballet of springtime in the heart and in the land.

Indispensable to the buoyancy and sunny spaciousness of the work is Aaron Copland's music of fountainous freshness and transparency, only mildly acerb, just enough to spice its sweetness. The score, which he first called simply "Ballet," though it is filled with folk flavor and the lyric spirit, won the Pulitzer Prize in music in 1945, and has since been played as a suite (under the title *Appalachian Spring*) by major symphony orchestras. Unlike the early accompaniments to modern dance, it is music that stands alone, makes no attempt to negate its own identity. And this has proved to be, not detrimental as previously thought, but actually beneficial to modern composition in both dance and music.

In the days of its bareness and gauntness, strings were considered too luscious for modern dance. The violins in *Appalachian Spring* contribute to its radiance, and enrich the chamber ensemble of wind and percussion that Louis Horst developed from the early piano and percussion accompaniment. Now tested and approved, there is no telling where they may lead—possibly to the full orchestra in time. At present, however, the chamber orchestra seems more in keeping with the abbreviated décor, the concentrated intensity, the intimating of the whole and saying the smallest part, that characterize Martha's unique dance dramas.

Louis Horst, who has always believed in keeping music subservient to dance, has himself composed distinguished music for Martha's works, as in *Primitive Mysteries, Frontier,* and *El Penitente.* Other modern composers have done good work, some in what is called "utility music," some in scores of individual worth. Many important composers have done scores for both ballet and modern dance. Aaron Copland's *Billy the Kid* and *Rodeo* scores came before *Appalachian Spring;* William Schuman's *Undertow* before *Night Journey;* and Paul Hindemith's *Nobilissime Visione* (for Massine's *Saint Francis*) is one of the most impressive scores in ballet.

Hindemith composed *Herodiade* after the poem by Stephen Mallarmé, and its igneous currents are as suited to Martha's conception as to the original. Nor are the two as disparate as might appear. In Martha's manner of remote association, Herodias is at least a distant relative of Eve, hence of Everywoman, and so the woman who waits in Noguchi's strange ante-room, and knows not for what she is waiting, becomes the prototype of any woman who knows when a time for self-searching has arrived. As usual with the later Noguchi, there are three sculptural units: at stage right the glass-less mirror, frame and stand, in bleached-bone articulation; at stage left the skeletal clothes-tree; in the center the white stool and head-rest against a stark screen. It is a dismal place in which to wait for one knows not what, to find in one's looking-glass something even more appalling than signs of encroaching age, to scrutinize one's self-deceptions, inhibitions, motives, aims, until finally one issues forth anew, purged of all hypocrisy, ready to meet squarely one's unknown destiny.

As I first saw it in Boston, where it was given after the Coolidge Festival but before it reached New York, it was deeply evocative, a stream of consciousness palpably unrolling in movement. Certain details in setting, action, and the costumes (by Edythe Gilfond) have been changed since then, notably a bizarre yoke taken by the Attendant from the clothes-tree and suspended from the Woman's neck like a symbolic burden of expiation, which did not appear at the revival. Martha's garments were more ceremonial, as befits the slow, ceremonial duo-dance that *Herodiade* is; and when the regal purple robe was removed to reveal the glistering white of sacrifice and of victory, it was a lustrous moment. The Attendant, beautifully done by May O'Donnell, clad in the soft bronze gown and ribboned cap of an upper servant, is little more than foil to the agonizing of the Woman, but an essential one. The quiet of the waiting-woman accentuates the turmoil of the woman who waits. It reinforces the majestic calm of the resolution.

The foregoing descriptions are not the gospel according to Saint Martha. They are only one person's reaction. Another person's reaction might be entirely different, and Martha's intention different still. The best way to get to the heart of Martha Graham's dance is to get in direct line of communication and don't let words get in your eyes. Lean back, and let the Theater of Martha Graham take its course. One idea will germinate others, rising out of your own background and experience, until you have something that is yours and yours alone. If the word "creative" were not so overworked, one might call this process of spontaneous ingestion creative looking and creative listening. It is, at any rate, the only means of capturing creative dancing on the wing, and making it one's own.

However disconcerting, however actually unlikable, Martha's dances seem at first, they are generally rewarding in the end. What looks like willful "uglification" turns out to be a new kind of beauty. What appears to be irrational proves its own fundamental logic. Martha's works have form, design, conciseness. They are wrought with strict economy of means, with that restraint that proffers the emotional prerogative to the beholder. They are strong, fibrous, sinewy, virile. Above all, they are stirring of impact, and never leave you where they found you.

With the artist's power of divination, Martha pierces beneath surfaces, and tells us what she sees. We may not like all she sees. We may find some of it unpleasant, even abhorrent. But excavations are perhaps as necessary as explorations to the advancement of art and civilization, and it is the province of genius to lead the way. Martha is not a freak, a phenomenon, or a veritable iconoclast. She comes from a long line of tradition, she says, and has merely developed her dance out of that tradition in the only way that was possible for her.

DORIS HUMPHREY AND CHARLES WEIDMAN

As a dance artist Doris Humphrey is second to none. As a choreographer she is first of all. To the general public she has never been the prodigy that Martha Graham has. But she, and Charles Weidman, her partner for many years, are equally important as creators of the American modern dance. Since her retirement as a dancer she has composed three of her greatest works: *Lament for Ignacio Sánchez Mejías* (after the poem by Federico García Lorca), a dance elegy of surpassing beauty; *The Story of Mankind* (after a *New Yorker* cartoon by Carl Rose), a dance satire with a terrific and timely bite; and the shimmering idyll, *Day on Earth*. Soon after their professional separation Charles formed a small company and produced two notable works: *A House Divided—*, based on Abraham Lincoln's efforts to unite the nation; and *David and Goliath*, making an innocent funny page out of Bible pages. In the spring of 1947 he received a Guggenheim Fellowship for the project of transcribing a selection of James Thurber's *Fables For Our Time* into dance, which he did with signal success. A third artist in the Humphrey-Weidman picture is Pauline Lawrence—costume designer, pianist, singer, publicity agent, business manager, and several-other-useful-things-plenipotentiary throughout the long joint career.

The three ex-Denishawners were the founders of the wonderful modern dance company whose influence on American dance has been as immeasurable as it is ineradicable. It was the first modern dance company to have men and women dancers from the beginning, the first to present a full-length or ballet-sized work, the first to make an extended tour. That they began with a mixed company is not surprising, since the group stepped directly out of Denishawn, where men and women dancing together was a matter of course. That they succeeded in maintaining the mixture, however uneven, for it cannot be said that males were ever in preponderance, is astounding. In those early days modern dance was hardly known, having only just begun to exist in the United States, and dancing for men was largely considered effeminate. The story goes that in order to induce men to come to the studio, the girls were asked to invite their boy friends and relatives to the classes for free instruction, the boys to pay only when they were absent from the roll call. This practice, which insured at least a modicum of masculine attendance, was gradually dispensed with as the men thus wooed were won by the virility of the technique and human interest of the dances, and either themselves took the work seriously or were supplanted by others of more professional inclination.

The first dance program, "Presented by Doris Humphrey, With Charles Weidman, and Students of the Denishawn School," was given in the Brooklyn Little Theater on March 24, 1928, and less than a month later at the John Golden Theater in New York. The pianists were Louis Horst, Clifford Vaughn, and Pauline Lawrence. Among the charter members later heard from were Gertrude Shurr, Sylvia Manning, Katherine Manning, and Eleanor King.

The dances were almost as Denishawn as the dancers. But not wholly so. Doris's group work, *Color Harmony,* was a distinct try-out of new ideas. The choreography was absolutely new and different at the time. The music was composed for it (by Clifford Vaughn) after the dance was made. The work was then supposed to have its basis in scientific theories of light and color. Looking back upon it Doris now sees it as a memento of her early concern with social problems. The merging of the prismatic colors into white, each color having a dance alone, the finale dominated by a single white-clad

figure, she says, dramatized the ultimate harmonization of conflicting interests and emotions within and among people—an idea that
was to come out full strength in her *New Dance* seven years later.
The young Doris was an incipient humanist then, and a
thinker always. She thought her way through every innovation. She
thought in group terms, going back to the primitive communal
dances, tracing their development from the circular rituals (as
around the camp fire), the file, or flowing line, to the processional
that led to the dance performed for spectators. The solo was never
a vehicle for the artist, but an intrinsic part of group expression.

On the first program, the Scriabin duet, *Pathetic Study,* composed and danced by Doris and Charles together, also contained
inklings of modern movement. Her *Air for the G String* (Bach),
done by four dancers, she likened, when directing it, to a long,
golden ray of light moving from place to place. Charles's trio,
Minstrels (Debussy), in rather obvious comedy vein, showed three
troubadors serenading beneath a window with that wide-mouthed
silent vocalism he has so often put to comic use, and getting doused
for their pains; while his solo, *Scherzo* (Borodin), a pantomimic
juggling of invisible objects including such elusive items as feathers,
presaged the more subtle comedy to come. His *Cathédrale Engloutie*
(Debussy), cumbered with much robing, and frankly descriptive in
its ascending and descending line, had a touch of sweetness in its
youthful romanticism, but little that was new.

Doris, Charles, and Pauline had all made the eighteen-month
tour of the Orient (Japan, China, Malaysia, India, and Java) with
the Denishawn Company in 1925–26. In 1927, while Ruth and Ted
were touring in the *Ziegfeld Follies* to earn money for the proposed
new Denishawn House in New York, Doris, with Charles and Pauline assisting, was left in charge of the newly organized New York
branch of the school. Soon after the travelers returned, and before
the edifice was completed, the trio departed more or less in a state
of dudgeon. There had been great plans for Denishawn House. It
was, on paper, to be as all-embracing as the still incompletely realized University of the Dance Shawn later founded in Massachusetts.
Doris, who had done a lot of thinking on the Oriental tour, was disturbed by this tremendous catholicity. Ruth and Ted, on the other

hand, were disturbed by her radical ideas. The result was that she was voted off the faculty, a post she had occupied since 1917. Thus, she did not initiate the break with Denishawn, though such a break was inevitable, as was the collapse of Denishawn House from other causes a few years later.

Doris was happy at Denishawn, she has told me. She found the work dramatically rich and exciting. In the Orient they all studied with native teachers and observed native performances. As she gained an insight into the genuine Oriental dance she became increasingly conscious of the discrepancies between the authentic forms and Ruth's "Oriental Impressions." She began to feel that native movement was inborn, fostered by long traditions, and that native dances could not truthfully be performed by other races. She might be (and was) able to move *like* a Hindu, Javanese, or Chinese girl, making lateral motions with her neck, curving her fingers in a semblance of the *mudras* (Hindu hand gestures), but it was not the real thing because she was an American girl and a different stream of traditions flowed through her. She wanted to dance as an American, to make dances out of American life. And, when the time came, the firm young woman with the long tawny hair had enough red-headed Irishness mixed with tough-fibered Englishness in her make-up to fight for what she wanted. That both her grandfathers were Congregational clergymen, that she is a descendant of Elder Brewster, and that her father's step-mother was Elizabeth Emerson, daughter of Ralph Waldo Emerson, may have little to do with the case; but this high heredity and collateral heredity are worth mentioning in passing.

Doris had always composed. She grew up in dance and music in Oak Park (a suburb of Chicago), where she was born. Her father, a photographer, sang in the Chicago Apollo Club; her mother was a pianist—and a good one, too, Doris says—and both encouraged her to dance; her mother, in fact, urged her to. She had her first lessons with Mary Wood Hinman of Chicago, a pioneer importer of national folk dances, whose many books on the subject contain somewhere a little Greek ball dance composed by her young pupil.

Miss Hinman, the youngest child of a large family, had begun as a girl giving ballroom lessons at home, while her mother played the piano. It was the Big House of the neighborhood and it soon became open house as the neighborhood children flocked to the dance school that was always like a party. One day John Dewey, the educator, stood in the doorway watching, and said: "I thought I'd see what's going on here. I can't keep my children away and it's the first time they've taken to any sort of study." He told Mary Wood that she had hit upon a big thing in education, and offered her a more professional teaching post. After that she went to Europe every summer, bringing home armfuls of folk dances, costumes and costume designs, notations of steps and music. Folk dance, she learned, was a felt experience, a ceremonial of man's being. It was harvest and planting time, courtship and betrothal, mourning and festival. It was the fullness of daily living running over into ritual. It came from the deep heart of the people, and though it was often blithe and gay, it was more than surface entertainment, for all that the people felt and were went into it.

Something of this reverence for people and love of dance must have been imparted to the young Doris by the tall, blue-eyed gentlewoman who was her first teacher; but innate in the child herself must have been the qualities that later developed the underlying philanthropy of her work. Her mastery of many forms prepared her for the discovery of new forms. Her acquaintance with international dance culture led her home to the source of an intrinsic native dance. Doris studied tap, clog, and the interpretive dancing of the day, as well as folk and ballroom, and then, at Miss Hinman's suggestion, went on to the classical ballet. After a period with Madame Josephine Hatlanek, a retired and corpulent Viennese dancer who supported her traditions with a large admonitory stick and believed that eating gooseberries somehow sustained talent, she continued her ballet training at the popular Pavley-Oukrainsky School. She was already teaching in her own school when, in 1915, and again at Miss Hinman's suggestion, she went to Denishawn (then in California), where Ruth St. Denis told her she had the makings of an artist and wanted her to join the faculty and company. Two years later she did, leaving her devoted mother, who had played the piano and business-managed for her, in charge of what became the Humphrey-Moulton School.

The first dance Doris created at Denishawn was called *Soaring*, to Schumann's *"Aufschwung,"* and the title was typically Doris. Typically Denishawn were the titles *Hoop Dance* and *Scarf Dance*, which she also contributed to the repertory. Significant was the *Sonata Tragica*, composed to MacDowell's music and later (on the decision of Ruth, under Wigman influence) done without music. These and other dances by her, soon a featured dancer of the company, together with the music visualizations for which she was largely responsible, were all performed on tour.

When in 1920 Charles Weidman came to Denishawn from Lincoln, Nebraska, Doris was his first teacher there. His actual first teacher, in his home town, was Eleanor Frampton, who later turned about and studied with him and taught Humphrey-Weidman techniques in Cleveland. Who his progenitors were and what they were like has been so delightfully published in his dance biographies, *On My Mother's Side* and *And Daddy Was a Fireman,* that this information is reserved for the description of those dances. There is English, Dutch, and German in his ancestry, but how it got there he does not know. Charles began his career with those home theatricals to which parents of gifted (and/or ungifted) offspring are so often subjected. The twig was bent in the direction of gods and grandeur when he came across photographs of Ruth St. Denis and Isadora Duncan, Sarah Bernhardt and Grand Opera, in old magazines. One touch of Denishawn in performance made his whole being kin, and when, soon after his arrival, he got by accident a chance to play the Emperor in *Xochitl* (opposite Martha Graham), he was a confirmed dancer and nothing could be done about it.

His father had hoped he would become a cartoonist (a hope based on his drawing abilities at school) and he did in an unexpected way, as the dance cartoon, *Ringside,* proved some years later. There is no record of his doing any creative work while dancing with the Denishawn company. The pantomimic *Danse Americaine* of 1923 may have become famous because of his performance, and he may have added his mite to it, but it was choreographed for him by Shawn—an expansion of the earlier *Crapshooter*, with a little baseball, promenading, and girl interest thrown in. The program of the first Humphrey-Weidman concert, prepared at the New York

Denishawn School, with Denishawn students, contained his first original compositions of professional status; but among the numbers, the beloved *Pierrot,* which he had made popular, was also a left-over from Denishawn, choreographed for him by Shawn. Charles was eventually to work out new technical devices and rhythmic combinations especially adapted to men, to cast new light on the differentiation between masculine and feminine movement, and here, too, his initial indebtedness to one of Shawn's pet theories must be taken into account. He was ultimately to develop ideas all his own and to become the master dance comic of his day. It does not detract from his individual achievement to recognize his dance paternity.

Pauline Lawrence, a Californian born and bred, went to Denishawn straight from the Los Angeles High School in 1917. She had first gone down to play the piano for Ted, in military training at San Diego, and then she came up and played for Ruth, studying some dancing and more costuming, the latter with Pearl Wheeler. She traces one branch of her lineage to the Duke of Wellington, and had an uncle who was mayor of Nome, Alaska. Small, dark, reserved, and mistress of many talents, she has done much to publicize and promote the Humphrey-Weidman Company, while keeping herself well in the background.

The Unholy Trio, as they were playfully called, opened their first New York studio in the fall of 1928. They promptly invested in a set of ten gilt screens (later painted gray), eighteen feet high and five feet wide, that could be made into flats and double flats, wings, towers, or cyclorama; and a shallow platform. They soon added a set of large boxes, like children's playing blocks many times magnified. The boxes came in cubes and double cubes, half and quarter cubes, and were also painted gray. Any number of combinations could be made with them—a flight of steps or a rocky mountain, a castle rampart or a plateau, a bush or a settee. They were designed by Erika Klein, an artist of the Dalton School, though the total idea probably stemmed from the then electrifying stage designs of Gordon Craig. This décor became the trademark of Humphrey-Weidman productions. Together with an occasional drapery and Pauline's intelligent lighting, carefully rehearsed in close connection with the costumes, they provided a changeful flow of vivid if unrealistic dance settings.

There may have been an impromptu air about some of the early endeavors, as when Charles, who always designed and often made his own costumes, hacked up a crimson couch cover that had been given him for a present, to clothe a solo called *Passion*. Pauline's costumes were brewed into life. She would stroll through the yard goods section of a department store, humming the music of a dance, until the right material called out to her, "I am it." With the material popped ideas for cutting. Hems were left unfinished, not only because there was no time to finish them, but because they moved better so. Movement and music, lighting, make-up, and dance idea were active ingredients in the costuming, which came out in unusual, sometimes ravishing, color combinations.

The partners complemented each other beautifully. Doris, whose ribbon-bound hair with its tawny waterfall set a fashion, was lyrical and lovely in her delicate, steely strength against the asseverative line of the tall, dark-haired Charles. The Humphrey-Weidman dance was good to look at from the beginning. The bloom of charm lay upon it. Everything was fresh and novel and attractive in this new theater of the imagination. But movement was the core of it, and here we must stop to consider what movement meant to Doris, what it meant to Charles.

Doris's discoveries came of her desire to bring dance closer to people and what happens to them. Out of the fullness of her dance experience she felt it was time for a fuller range of human experience to be expressed in dance. The other arts, especially literature and painting, were coming to closer grip with life, getting away from the classic or idealized beauty, nearer to humanity as it is than as we wish it were. Why should not dance step from its airy pedestal and come down to earth? Fokine had a similar idea in his search for greater verisimilitude in ballet. Isadora, St. Denis, Shawn, had striven in their several ways for a deeper expression of the human spirit. And all had stopped short of what she was after.

She was looking for something more fundamental. She wanted to abandon completely the fictitious and get to the root of the matter, the actual state of being human, specifically of being human in no other language than her own. She knew she could create truthfully only out of her own experience, and effectually only as she made that experience touch or illumine the experience of others. She felt no necessity for digging into the dregs of human nature. Her vision mainly precluded the debased. Hers was a concept of humanbeingness that kept to the level of decency, standing squarely in its normal condition of struggle, resisting evil and reaching for the good.

She had yet to find the way this human being moved when not pretending to be something or somebody else. To do this she must look to her own body. Conducting her research before a mirror, she found a physical expression of the essence of struggle at once. While seeming to stand still her body swayed ever so slightly, making minute motions just to maintain balance. Letting go to see what would happen, she began to fall, more and more rapidly as she went down. In an involuntary effort to save herself she saw that the resultant movement made a design, and with the finish of the fall came an accent. The recovery brought a new design, with new accents. Thus in the simple process of fall and its natural corollary, recovery, she found three elements of dance: *design,* made by changing positions in space; *rhythm,* or accents occurring at definite intervals; *dynamics,* or varying degrees of tension; plus a fourth element, *emotion* or *drama*—what she felt as she went down and as she came up. This was a brand new point of view (or action), a motivation entirely different from that of any other dancer, modern or otherwise. It was a re-application of certain laws of physics to dance.

Nor was that all. She further discovered that by the exercise of her own volition the drop could be arrested. Before she gave in to the pull of gravity, or let go completely, the reflex resistance to falling was enforced by a determination not to fall. One leg advanced to break the fall, the arms extending themselves for balance. This resulted in two sharp movements, down-up, with a suspension between. By contrasting this with a smooth movement, like carrying the body forward in a long, easy stride, and repeating the sequence, she arrived at sequential dance form. It was form generated by human impulses, not by a decision to change weight or to follow a prescribed series of steps. It was here a form that expressed the con-

tinuous conflict in the individual between inertia, the desire to relax, give in to lassitude, repose; and exertia, the spirit of making
effort, the will to achieve.

Doris found other significant reactions in the complicated organization of the body, such as the tense hold or leap when movement seems to stop but does not, because movement never stops in
life. From her basic discoveries gradually unfolded a myriad impel-
lent variations, so that each new dance created new forms (not without certain Humphrey mannerisms—Doris is, after all, a *human*
being herself). At first the idea evolved out of the substance of movement. Eventually idea came first, shaping the movement, its timing
and direction. Sometimes even now, she told me, the movement has
to be started arbitrarily. She strikes off a sharp accent and gets a
rebound, and the dance opens up from there. But in general, idea
is the source of movement, not movement of idea.

It will readily be seen that this kind of choreography, based
on the movement impulses of people, their proclivities for rise and
fall, for suspended action and reaction, for off-balance and re-
balance, in constant process of equalization, of adjustment to self,
to surroundings, to other people, is very different from the choreography that consists of a formal combination of steps and patterns.
Yet it is formal in its own way, made up of formalized movement,
of which the basic human movements are only the raw material. We
may move in natural rhythm; we do not naturally move in rhythmic
form. Nor do we go about with arms held high or out at chest level,
distorting our locomotion with partial falls or sudden sidewise
bends. If we tried moving the modern dance way on the sidewalk
we would no doubt be looked upon as sorely afflicted or locked up
for disorderly conduct. If modern dancers moved in a perfectly natural way upon the stage, it would not be dance.

Doris is an artist, therefore she works in form. She was a dancer
to her finger tips, so her new forms included a new *port de bras*. Her
arm positions are more than angulated versions of ballet arm positions. The angled elbows have a reason. The hands confess knuckles;
the fingers articulate instead of curving decoratively. "Even fingers
fall," she once said in a lecture-demonstration illustrating the correlation of all the members of the body. No, Doris did not overlook

arms and hands. She made them more resilient, brought out their sinewy strength. It was in the reflective maturity of nearly twenty years later, in the spring of 1947, that she spoke to me of the significance of hands, the importance of gesture in dance.

"We have a tremendous heritage of gesture," she said, "that goes back to primitive man. An endless number of movements began in the early days, just with hands. These lie deep in the subconscious, and we draw upon them for dramatic expression. Dancers have always used them, but modern dancers use them differently. The palm of the hand is the most sensitive, the most expressive part of the most expressive member of the body. It says offering, greeting, tenderness, compassion. It says these things because for centuries people have instinctively used the palms of their hands to say them. For centuries the palms have been used to hold, to soothe, to comfort, to give and to receive. The back of the hand denies. It lacks the beneficence of the palm."

But gesture is not confined to hands, she pointed out. The nodding head, the stamping foot, the shrugging shoulders, are other types of gesture that can be stylized and rhythmized into dance. Nor can gesture be used too elaborately in a large group. The more people, the less gesture, is the general rule. Gesture, in her sense of it, is as different from pantomime as modern movement is from steps. It is not routine. It comes spontaneously of emotion. It adds color and drama to dance. "Movement expresses the all-over psychic reaction to environment, to circumstance, to atmosphere. Gesture makes movement more specific. And words are more specific than gesture.

"All finite things demand words." Like time: "At five in the afternoon," a recurring phrase in *Lament for Ignacio Sánchez Mejías*. Or objects, as in "A child brought a white sheet," from the same work. Movement alone does not bring the meaning home to the spectator. But the spoken words illumine the moment of movement. They shoot straight into consciousness and make a picture there. The phrase "A child brought a white sheet" summons the sheet and all its implications before us. The phrase "At five in the afternoon" establishes the degree of light, the crepuscular feeling of foreboding in that hour of death for the Spanish bullfighter, more forcibly than movement or lighting could do. Of course the words chosen must be words of color and imagery. Prosaic words would be out of key, just as words that indicate mood would be redundant. "The language of dance *is* mood. Mood is where dance lives."

In her desire to get to the living source Doris turned to nature rhythms as she turned to natural movement. An early landmark of her career is the *Water Study* of 1927, created while she and Charles were in charge of the New York Denishawn School. It started with human feeling, she told me, with body movement and its momentum in relation to the psyche and to gravity, and as it developed the movements took on the form and tempo of moving water. It was done by a group of girls in flesh-colored leotards that under blue lights and seen from a distance gave an effect of modest nudity. It was a silent dance, so that the breathing of the dancers could be heard, and this breathing, with the pound of their bare feet and rustle of their movements, was the breath and pulse and rustle of the waves their arching backs and plunging bodies resembled. Their bodies, stretched prone on the floor in rows, mounted through succession movement into the cresting wave, with leaps and high flung arms to denote the spray, then slowly receded as another wave mounted and broke. It was a novelty of its time, and a delight to see.

While *Water Study* was built on rise and fall, in angled curve, in up-and-down, *Life of the Bee* (Guild Theater, New York, April 1929) was built on the horizontal spread of bees' wings, the diagonal of combat between the rival queens. And here again was a new accompaniment or sound effect for modern dance in the chorus of human voices humming through combs and tissue paper to suggest the insect buzz. It was the only accompaniment, and in its shaded dynamics and changing tempi, a fitting and musical one. Doris had read Maeterlinck's *Life of the Bee* and studied the life of the bee herself, noting the geometric exactness of their building, the intricate mechanism of their bodies, observing that the wings were the center of bee activity. All of this helped to shape her dance. The pattern of hive and honeycomb went into it, as the gold and black of bee color went into the costuming. For drama there was the conflict between the newborn queen, fanned into life by the worker bees, and the old queen who must give place to the new.

In these early works Doris intuitively struck theater while striving to reach autonomous, abstract dance. In the tripartite *Drama of Motion,* which had no accompaniment whatever, she came as close to her goal as it is possible to come with the human material of dance; for dance, using human movement and human gesture, cannot actually be abstract, and emotional overtones made themselves felt above the staff of movement themes and development that constituted the work. It was presented during the first season of the Dance Repertory Theatre (1930), and was the first step in the symphonic form she was later to expand in greater works. Other products of that season were the solo, *Descent into a Dangerous Place,* which, springing into action from a crouched position on a height of blocks, presented another aspect of the fall and recovery theme; the duo, *Air on a Ground Bass,* to Purcell's music, with Doris taking the air, Charles the accompaniment; and a group work to Ravel's *La Valse,* called *Choreographic Waltz,* in contrapuntal form. This was later revised and produced with a full symphony orchestra in Philadelphia and New York in the summer of 1933.

Her first masterwork was produced during the second season of the Dance Repertory Theatre (1931) in *Dance of the Chosen,* now called *The Shakers,* and become a living classic. It was based on the religious attitude of the Shaker sect and their belief in literally shaking off their sins; and danced in the long, full brown skirts and bodices and white bonnets of the women, the broad-brimmed hats and preacher-like garb of the men, to another novel accompaniment—Doris's own arrangement of drum, accordion, and the intermitten wordless tones of a high soprano voice. The movement was derived but not literally copied from the Shaker behavior in their pewless meeting-houses, the men and women divided into the separate groups of celibacy on either side of a rectangular floor plan. The intimation of sex repression beneath the religious frenzy distressed some observers at the time. They found the work too neurotic for their taste. But the abandon could be counted in measures, the impression of a spontaneous crescendo of fervor came through ordered thematic development. The calm, clear-eyed Doris, of the cool intellect and logical reasoning power, is always at the helm of a composition. What the heart knows is well tempered by what the head commands for the purpose of form, restraint, and clarity. She never goes off the deep end. And when sex is a conspicuous factor in the experience she is presenting, she handles it with care and not with a capital letter.

The design of *The Shakers* was wrought of small quiverings and tremblings that increased to violent shakings and twistings of the whole body; of running half-falls, the forward or backward thrust of the supporting leg keeping the body in a constant state of off-balance, never lost; of single wild jumps into the air. Brief ebbs in the action, allowing for the descent of the Holy Spirit, replenished the communicants for an even more vigorous declamation of fiery faith, expressed partially in words. At the end, the men kneeling on one side, women on the other, encircled the leader, their vibrating palms held high in ecstasy. Doris, her wide skirt swirling in emphasis of the circular pattern, her face alight, her arms and hands outspread, was a radiant figure. The white of her fichu and headdress, of the other women's bonnets, of the men's collars and socks, against the severe dark garments, contributed a striking pictorial effect to a dance of outward brilliance and inward grace.

In these early years Charles, as co-dancer, colleague, and collaborator, was also experimenting with new ideas. He had worked independently for a time. Both artists preserved a certain amount of separateness throughout their joint career. It was a potent partnership. Charles has changed since it ended. As dancer and choreographer he was always more limited than Doris. But what he did do he did without waste, with clear-cut, pointed immediacy. He delighted in incongruities, in fragmentary, mercurial movement, ringing abrupt changes of tempo, rhythm, and dynamics in the broken pieces he let the spectator put together as he would. His comic sense developed on altogether original lines. He jested in stroke and curlicue, lampooning right and left with his pencil-slim body, making jokes with his fingers and witty observations with his bare toes. And his mouth, which could compete with Joe E. Brown's, but was used far more subtly, was a cave of comedy in itself. He could always be counted on to do the unexpected thing. The movement was choppy on the surface, but underneath flowed the current of human feeling; sometimes the surface, too, was smooth with serious intent.

Charles is still absolutely one of a kind. His funnybone is still in the right place. Only now it sometimes gets a little out of joint. He goes out more for gags. He disavows all desire to be elevated (in spite of his beautiful characterization of Abraham Lincoln). It is possible that he has not put into his works all that has seemed to come out of them, that his mordant comments on a defective world have been more intuitive than calculated. He is not verbally articulate. He cannot explain how he does a dance, or why.

Some of Charles's first dances lingered in Denishawn Orientalism, as the *Japanese Actor* and *Singhalese Drum Dance;* others clung to the romantic streak. In *Ringside,* the boxing-match cartoon (music by Winthrop Sargent), he began that communicated sense of muscular effort, that linking with an audience by snatches of familiar behavior patterns, which he was later to develop into his own brand of pantomime, brought to term and statement in the solo, *Kinetic Pantomime,* of 1934. *Ringside* was composed as a duo, but Charles introduced a referee, danced by himself, when he did it for the Roxy Theater some time afterwards, and this heightened both action and design. In similar vein were the *Dance of Work* and *Dance of Sport,* to music of Henry Cowell, rhythmizing the motions of labor and of sports, not as a ballet or an interpretive dancer might, but as Charles, the modern dancer, must; that is, by letting the essence mold the form. Form is what he was working for primarily in those days. There were experiments with Scriabin's music for putting emotion into form; with abstract form, as *Studies in Conflict,* the theme of which—the various kinds of conflict within and without one's self—he was to treat more emotionally in the larger *Quest;* and there was *Marionette Theater,* crossing human movement with puppet movement and getting fun effects.

His first major work, *The Happy Hypocrite,* after Max Beerbohm's "Fairy Tale For Tired Men," with music by Herbert Elwell, who suggested the ballet, came in the second Dance Repertory season; and, like *The Shakers* of that season, became a classic of the Humphrey-Weidman repertory. This was probably the first modern dance to be done in narrative technique; and certainly the first to expatiate successfully in movement on a theme that had already had a masterly presentation in words. Without relying on oral delivery, it followed the story practically gesture by syllable, with Weidman embellishments. The discourse was pantomimic in the same inimitable manner, dance and pantomime flowing logically, the one out of the other, and the whole high comedy of the most delectable flavor.

To see Charles switching the mask of Lord Hell for that of Lord Heaven, and by this artful expedient winning the artless country maiden, Jenny Mere, to watch them picking invisible daisies together in a field that wasn't there, to witness his conversion as the countenance of Lord Heaven becomes a permanent fixture and Jenny acquires "the husband with the face of a saint" she had always wanted, only added to the relish of the written story. For the opening Banquet Hall the blocks, arranged to form a long refectory table, set the scene of revelry. The other scenes, In a Park and In a Forest, were as sketchily evoked. The masks were by Nura, and the gay and motley costumes by Charles.

The work was tightened up and seasoned by further performances. One at the Guild Theater during the winter of 1938 is memorable for its distinguished cast. Katherine Litz was the Jenny Mere; José Limón, Mr. Aeneas the Mask-Maker; Sybil Shearer the Señora Gambogi; and Edith Orcutt the Merry Dwarf Who Was a Cupid, Too. William Bales was Cyclops; George Bockman, Apollo; and Katherine Manning, Beatrice Seckler, Joan Levy, Harriet Anne Gray, Eva Desca, and Lee Sherman were guests and other characters. Most of these names stand for some achievement in the modern dance field, and some of them stand for leadership.

A Humphrey-Weidman concert was first of all a good show. It was full of *joie de danse*. Its dress and décor were neither stark nor lush. The movement was in indicative (not representative) mood, but was not therefore inaccessible. The costumes were nonrepresentational, like the movement, like the assorted boxes that could be transformed into so many varieties of setting. A man might wear a top-hat, tights, and a jerkin for evening attire. A woman might top the typical modern dance skirt, split at front or side for free-wheeling, with basque or blouse, scarf or headdress, that betokened her place or character. Such combinations were amusing in themselves, and helped to keep the dance in the unrealistic realm wherein it belonged. In Charles's work there was an atmosphere of nonchalance, a deceptive appearance of improvisation, that gave it a touch of *commedia dell' arte.* It was he who set the pace and kept the comedy effervescing. Most of his things are unimaginable without him, just as some of Doris's can never be the same without her. But any substitution alters the nuance of a characterization, shifts an emphasis here and there, and in minor parts, let us be thankful, occasionally for the better.

In this prolific period of the early thirties Doris's group work, *Dionysiaques,* based on the pagan ritual involving the sacrifice of a virgin, and set to music of Florent Schmitt, was produced. Its magnificent swirling patterns were enhanced by the migration of its colors under migratory lights. The broad, horizontal stripes of the chorus dress marched with the group formations, shading from blue and green to blue and purple, to green and black, two blues. two purples, greens, and so on. If this seems an exterior aspect of a dance founded in basic, emotional movement, it was none the less an inseparable part of its impact. The duet, *Rudepoema* (Heitor Villa-Lobos), a highly stylized dance of courtship, also went to the primitive. The solo, *Two Ecstatic Themes: Circular Descent, Pointed Ascent,* was an essay in circular and spiral forms.

Doris and Charles were the first modern dancers to transplant ensemble concert pieces bodily into a revue, and the revue, J. P. McEvoy's *Americana* (1931), was the first musical to embrace modern dance in concert form. *Water Study, The Shakers,* and *Ringside,* together with one old and two new comedy numbers by Charles, were presented unspoiled. Their freshness and originality were just what the producers, and evidently the public, were looking for, and they were such a success that other Broadway opportunities soon followed. The sapient Doris, however, could see beyond the temporary boost in finances. She sensed, or experience had taught her, the complications that would set in. She foresaw the steady deterioration in quality—a little bit lopped off here, a little extra put in there—the insistent cheapening for effect. So she rejected most of the overtures.

She did stage the Negro dances for Hall Johnson's *Run Lil Chillun,* and choreographed and danced with Charles in the Theater Guild's production of Molière's *School for Husbands,* a clever creation that added to both their reputations. In the spring of 1930 she had collaborated with Charles in the dances for the Norman Bel Geddes production of *Lysistrata.* But this was the extent of her Broadway ventures for the time being. Charles, who had the flair, and possibly less conscience about it, went cheerfully ahead, contributing "Heat Wave," "Revolt in Cuba," and "The Lonely Hearts' Column" to *As Thousands Cheer,* staging dances for *Flying Colors, Hold Your Horses, Life Begins at 8.40,* and other passing shows. Finally, pleasant as it was to earn an income of folding money, and buy a farm and indulge his taste for antiques, he got enough of compromise, and returned to the concert fold. He had made one great advance in his creative work in a production of Voltaire's *Candide* (1933), a political satire with a soupçon of bawdiness that was just his forte, and was all but ruined by the Broadway attitude. It was later revised, with a new score by Wallingford Riegger, for the Federal Theater.

Meanwhile, in 1932, Doris had married Charles F. Woodford, and in 1933 borne a son. As if in prelude to that experience, she had composed her *Dances of Women,* a modern fertility ritual impressed with the thought of burgeoning life and its antithesis, death. For this she had studied a book of pictures on plant life and watched growing things. The work was full of plant and flower formations, of large leaves unfolding from stem and stamen in the group patterns; of delicate unfurling of fingers like tendrils and petal-like opening and closing of hands, in the single figure. It depicted the physical life-process, with spiritual overtones. The music was composed for it by Dane Rudhyar.

While she was carrying her child she composed her *Orestes,* to Darius Milhaud's incidental music to the *Orestes* trilogy of Aeschylus, a splendid work that has never had a formal presentation for lack of an orchestra, chorus, an enterprising conductor, and funds. It was made and shown in the studio only, with José Limón as Orestes and Eleanor King as Electra, and all who saw it found it exhilarating indeed. She choreographed it to a recording that used the chorus and solo voices in a *Sprecht-Gesang* technique (but in French), and an unusual orchestration. It is significant that Doris was *simpática* with the music of the modern master thus early in her career. Significant it is, too, that the rebels return periodically to traditional sources, and continue to find inspiration in the deep wellspring of Greek drama.

By 1934 the partners were together again, and, with Martha Graham and Hanya Holm, joined the faculty of the Bennington School of the Dance. In many ways the Bennington years were the ripest of their joint career. But Bennington was a summer activity, and only partially responsible. The company was at its peak. The artists were in command of a viable system of techniques, and in possession of a wealth of ideas. Their large classes offered a wide variety of human material for orchestration. They had everything in fact but money, an inconvenience that failed to hold them back. It did, however, cause the expensive Sunday night concerts at the Guild Theater, which tied with Martha Graham concerts in favor, to be sufficiently infrequent to be events. There were other New York concerts, under the Federal Theater project, in the Students Dance Recitals and the Y. M. H. A. Dance Theatre series, which with the Bennington school and festival, were largely instrumental in keeping modern dance alive through its most difficult years. But the less charitably inclined Guild Theater concerts had more glamour and prestige.

The summer of 1935 Doris presented her *New Dance* in the College Theater at Bennington. This was the first that became last in the great *New Dance Trilogy*. It was more than a landmark, it was a mountain that towered above the entire modern dance landscape. Revised and expanded in New York the following October, it came to the Guild Theater with the *première* of *Theatre Piece,* the first part of the *Trilogy,* on January 19, 1936. The same year brought the middle section, *With My Red Fires,* first at Bennington, and later in New York. Each is a long work, and all together would take about three hours to perform, actually no longer than the regular double-feature movie bill, or most operas. Art, it seems, must be dispensed in smaller portions. No attempt to present the *Trilogy* as a unit was ever made. It would, of course, be too taxing for the dancers.

The first and last sections on one program gave converse sides of the social picture, *Theatre Piece* of the competitive real, *New Dance* of the co-operative ideal. The whole concept began in the affirmative. *New Dance* was an affirmation of faith in a possible democratic society, in which the individual could develop his own capabilities in harmonious relationship with, and to the benefit of, his fellows. *Theatre Piece* showed the negative side, the ruthless self-seeking in civic and commercial relationships that hinders the realization of this desirable state. *With My Red Fires* dealt with another hindrance, the destructive selfishness of possessive love in personal relationships. The music for the entire work was composed by Wallingford Riegger in concurrence with its energy and spirit. The score called for piano, percussion, clarinet, trumpet and English horn, and, with the usual Humphrey-Weidman penchant for unusual sound effects, the strings of a dismantled upright piano struck with tympani sticks in *Theatre Piece,* and the plucked strings of a grand piano in *With My Red Fires.* The costumes were simple, impersonal, identifying types when necessary without being too explicit.

New Dance was the first modern dance work of extended length. It marked the transition from modern dance divertissements to modern ballets. It was a true symphonic ballet (the symphony in the choreographic structure) and a masterpiece in itself, unlike Léonide Massine's so-called symphonic ballets of the period, which consisted of choreography *to* symphonic masterpieces. In the "Prelude" a Man and Woman of good will each make a movement statement of his identity and convictions, as a separate individual and in relation to each other. At either side of the stage, a group of men and women observe these declarations. In the "First Theme," the Woman, strong, assured in her own integration, tries to draw the other women into her plan for the betterment of society. It takes the "Second Theme" to achieve her aim, for she has their prejudices and pettinesses to overcome before she can get them working together, without spite or rivalry, as happy integers in the plan. Here any resemblance to a woman's club is completely accidental.

A third step required is to find a like working relationship for the men. The "Third Theme," composed by Charles for himself and three others, brings the men into the requisite pattern of variety within unity. In the following "Processional" the two groups, headed by their leaders, come together for the first time, and gradually get adjusted to one another and to the whole. The sixth part, "Celebration," is a joyous commemoration of their new-found singleness of purpose. The "Variations and Conclusion" is a triumphal dance of the ideal state in operation.

The leaders, after their solos, retire to a subsidiary place within the group, lest they be mistaken for a pair of dictators, while one individual after another steps out from the group to proclaim himself and what he stands for in a solo, then merges with the group again. Doris made this assertion of individuality practical by inviting the group members to create their own solos. (It was a smallish group, comprised of Grade A dancers.) The gray boxes, which under lights could take on a platinum or silvery sheen, were arranged at the edge of the stage like a row of spectators at the beginning; and at the end symbolically piled together in the center, serving as a nucleus of action, providing pedestals at various levels for the dancers to leap from and remount. Charles's "Dance for the Men" (Third Theme), with its percussion accompaniment, was extremely popular; but the "Variations and Conclusion," whether performed as climax, or as detached number, always brought down the house.

In *Theatre Piece* Doris turned from the absolute to the concrete, from symphonic to program dance. Having proclaimed the ideal, she realized that she must show the obstacles to its fulfillment. She did it in terms of fantasy, presenting the modern world, in which competition is the life of trade and of everything else, not realistically, but surrealistically. The "Prologue" assigns the dancers to their roles as actors in the human comedy. "Behind Walls" is the home of good old free enterprise, where the profit motive reigns supreme, and one figure, probably the one who has amassed the most money, is a sort of boss-man over all the rest—humble creatures who antedate the yes-men of *The Hucksters*. Doris, in gauzy yellow, is the alert protestant to all she sees, throughout. "In the Open," sub-titled "Hunting Dance," like Agnes de Mille's *Tally-Ho!* of later years, "has nothing to do with fox hunting." Here the minions of Big Business, the office girls, put on their giddy little hats and go out in search of quarry, hoping to exchange one set of walls for another, not realizing, poor things, that the result is likely to be even more confining. The competition is stiff, even pugnacious, for all the nice men are married and there are never enough bachelors to go round.

All through the action the protesting figure explores, expostulates, and in dance apostrophes and asides expresses her horror of the various situations. "Interlude" is a longer statement of aversion, deploring the blind cruelty she sees on every side, yet holding firmly to the ideal of brotherhood she knows must take its place. The solo is based on a circular theme from *New Dance,* prophetic of the new world to come. "In the Stadium" spears the sports world, the vapidity of mob reaction, the game for championship's rather than for sportsmanship's sake, the same old greedy desire for fat success, and the mass worship of it. "In the Theater" was composed by Charles and is very funny. Here the boxes are mounted to make a small, irregular stage, on which the actors preen and disport themselves, open their mouths in silent speeches, steal each other's scenes, and fatuously take bows at the least hint of applause.

"The Race" sums it all up in a furious onslaught, as the puppets of greed tear over a blocked gap in a fence of blocks at breakneck speed. Here are the golf and football champions in their sweaters, the money-changers from the temples of business, the man-hunting women, the fame-and-favor-hunting actors, all running, running, like Alice's Red Queen, only to stay (figuratively) in the same place. One views the mad scramble with pity, while despairing of a world made up of such inane and futile people. But the protestant does not despair. In "Epilogue (The Return)," she rebels vociferously enough to arouse the competitors out of their hypnosis, and then directs their attention toward the new and better way of life. The dancers leave their play-acting and stand waiting in hushed expectancy, an ending which leads very nicely into the corrective *New Dance.*

Doris is poet, not preacher. She is not pressing sermons upon us. Dance is essentially religious expression, and religion is what one believes in, whether it be a golden calf or a higher humanhood. It is clear what Doris believes in. She may even be a trifle didactic about it at times. But *Theatre Piece* is entertaining, amusing, interesting, and astonishing as dance alone. Its variety in plane, dynamics, velocity, and tempo is enhanced by the active participation of the mobile boxes, which seem to become dislodged by invisible hands or to rearrange themselves, so that the traffic of the race, the hunt, the game, the business office, plunges or creeps or tears or slides in and out of the changing apertures, over the newly-formed levels, while apparently dismembered bodies and disjointed arms and legs disappear around corners, a headless trunk is glimpsed through one opening, as a trunkless head glides by at an odd angle above it. Doris leaped across the chasms, made sudden ascents and descents, clung perilously to the side of one block, or poised on the extreme edge of another, darted hither and yon like an inquisitive yellow butterfly (a comparison she would not like) on a flight of investigation, trying to find out what made these sammies run, trying to get at the heart of the matter so she could know what to do about it. Her skilled acrobacy belied the fragility of her appearance.

Whereas *Theatre Piece* was a program work, in the sense of program music, though it was also an abstraction, and *New Dance* was, in the musical sense, absolute dance in symphonic form, *With My Red Fires,* to continue the analogy, was choral drama, with the chief characters, the Matriarch and the Lovers, standing out as soloists. The title, and motto of the first part, was taken from William Blake's poem, *Jerusalem 11*—

> For the Divine appearance is Brotherhood, but I am Love
> Elevate into the Region of Brotherhood with my red fires.

It was produced at the Bennington Festival of 1936, when Doris and Charles were each in charge of a Workshop group. Arch Lauterer had a hand in the settings. At the State Armory, where the spectators looked down upon the dancing place, the action coursed from black screens forming wings, over the floor up on to the wide, stepped platform, and higher still to the architectural boxes as they formed house or tower.

The first part, RITUAL, consisted of "Hymn to Priapus," "Search and Betrothal," "Departure." The Hymn was choreographically gorgeous in its handling of the large group, now serried, now dispersed, in the sudden breaks of arrested action, in the broad sweep of its mass effect, like a collective surge of sexual desire. It was phallic worship without the genital symbols. It was the people's worship of the god of generation, demanding as for a sacrifice a pair of human lovers to represent, by actual consummation, the age-old ritual of mating. The atmosphere of impending drama haunted the meeting and departure of the nuptial celebrants, the Young Man and Young Woman, danced by Charles and Katherine Litz.

The second part, DRAMA, contained "Summons," "Coercion and Escape," "Alarm: Pursuit and Judgment." It introduced the Matriarch, grim figure of maternal possessiveness, vindictive in her envy of youthful happiness, her desire to consume the lovers and destroy their love. This was largely a mimed role for Doris, who did it superbly, without rant or raving, though one dance-magazine critic accused her of bringing ham acting to dance. With her bright hair dimmed down and drawn tightly into a knot, in her severe gray gown with its black sleeves and bodice trimming, her lovely face assuming a lined mask of scowl, she was more than a type of spinsterish matron or hateful mother-in-law. She was the symbol of possessive love in any guise, and of austere puritanism as well. Further lines from Blake set the key of this section:

THE GREAT SELFHOOD

Having a white Dot called a Center, from which branches out
A Circle in continual gyrations: this became a Heart
From which sprang numerous branches varying their motions
Producing many Heads, three or seven or ten, and hands and feet
Innumerable at will of the unfortunate contemplator
Who becomes his food: such is the way of the Devouring Power

Cryptic as these lines are, they were poetically borne out in the strange flashes of white hands from the black wings, of projecting feet, of fragmentary torsos and peering heads, as two red-robed figures, like angels of vengeance, made their awesome summons. In later versions it was the Matriarch, both as mother and as figurehead of her society, who called the Lovers to account. In RITUAL, they had obeyed a law of nature in accordance with primitive beliefs. In DRAMA, they seem to have come under the proprieties of modern civilization. With tearful entreaties and violent commands, in a dialogue of arms and facial play, the mother tries to regain possession of her child. The girl nearly succumbs, but longing overcomes filial affection, she rejoins her lover, and they escape. And, daring for Doris, they stop to lie down together on their way off stage. They evidently had not stopped to wed, for the Matriarch's angry alarm, sounded from the top of a high pillar, the collective pursuit of the Lovers and final judgment of society upon them, would indicate that she had the law, or at least public opinion, on her side. Yet the Matriarch does not win in the end. She makes her exit, a broken woman, the Lovers, unbeaten, facing the future with equanimity.

Again it must be repeated, what happens in dance cannot happen in words. This is dance drama, not realistic stage drama. It lives only in performance. In memory it is only half alive. Somehow, somewhere, the *New Dance Trilogy* should be restored to life. Whether Doris has it recorded in her dance script, I do not know.

For years she has been working on a system of dance notation that seems more sweetly reasonable than the Laban geometrics at least, and simpler than most of the fifteen odd systems abroad in the world since dance became an art. Some scripts are awkward, requiring the dancer to hold a book while working out the patterns. Others, like the Laban script, are pinned up poster fashion and have to be looked at piecemeal. Many are confined to ballet. Doris's script is in the form of a scroll to be unrolled on a mechanism, having something the effect of a motion picture screen. The dance unfolds as the screen unrolls and the dancers can follow it as they dance. No staff is used, but parallel vertical spaces are set out. In the first column the spatial pattern is outlined; in the second, numerals give the rhythmic count; in successive columns stick figures show the movement of arms, legs, middle body, etc. Unfortunately, the script has never been developed. Lack of time, of funds, of support, has kept it an unfinished project.

On January 15, 1937, *With My Red Fires* was performed with an augmented company at the Hippodrome, under the auspices of

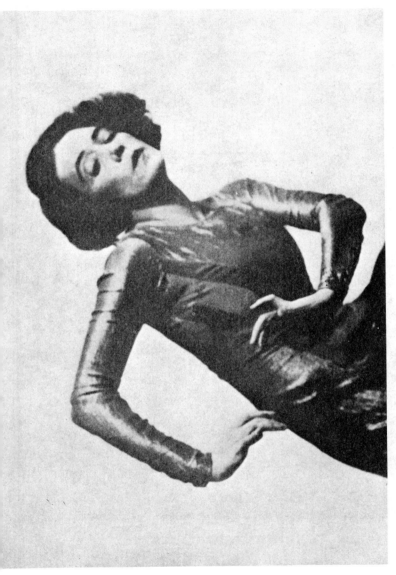

Mary Wigman in BALKAN DANCE

Ruth St. Denis

At Jacob's Pillow

Ted Shawn

Martha Graham at Mills College, California

Martha Graham and group in PRIMITIVE MYSTERIES
(*Jane Dudley second from left in standing row*)

The Martha Graham dance group of the middle thirties
(*Dorothy Bird, center; May O'Donnell second from right, rear*)

Arch Lauterer's set for PUNCH AND THE JUDY

Erick Hawkins, Jean Erdman, Ethel Butler, Jane Dudley, in PUNCH AND THE JUDY

Martha Graham
in CAVE OF THE HEART

Martha Graham and Erick Hawkins in EVERY SOUL IS A CIRCUS

Scene from Martha Graham's DARK MEADOW (*décor by Noguchi*)

Doris Humphrey in THEATRE PIECE

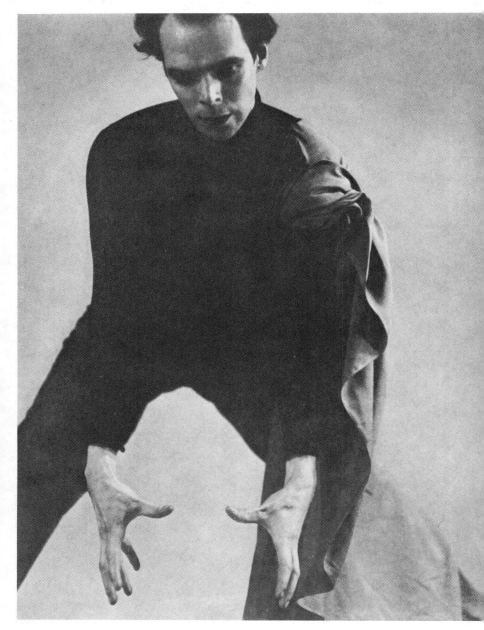

Charles Weidman

Doris Humphrey and group in DANCES OF WOMEN

Scene from PASSACAGLIA

*Doris Humphrey
as The Matriarch in*
WITH MY RED FIRES

*José Limón
and Doris Humphrey in*
CHORAL PRELUDE (*Bach*)

*Charles Weidman
and Doris Humphrey
in* AND DADDY WAS
A FIREMAN

*Doris Humphrey
and Charles Weidman
in* FLICKERS

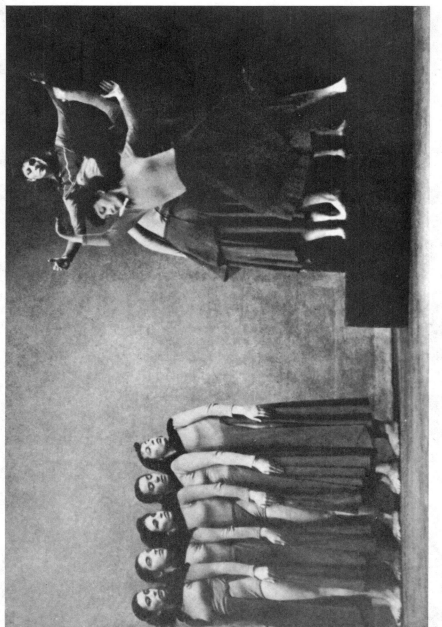

Helen Tamiris (top triangular formation) and early group

Helen Tamiris, Daniel Nagrin, Ida Soyer, in "Little David Play on Your Harp"
from suite of NEGRO SPIRITUALS

Hanya Holm in TREND

the International Labor Defense. The large stage, rising in a succession of levels, necessitated some changes in the action. The larger company, with its trainees, was cumbersome. At this performance the work temporarily lost its first glory. A dance changes with its milieu. It grows larger or smaller according to the stage to which it must be adapted. Its timbre is altered by the play of different audiences upon it. Then too, the self-critical artist is not easily satisfied (if ever) and sometimes spoils a work by fussing with it to make it better. In general, Doris knows objectively when she has achieved her aim. She does not make as many changes as Martha Graham does. A masterwork is not likely to look shoddy in any event, but it can on occasion be deprived of its full force and beauty by any number of mishaps.

On the bill with *With My Red Fires,* both at Bennington and at the Hippodrome, Charles's semi-autobiographical *Quest* was produced. Norman Lloyd's score for it gave strong and flexible rhythmic support without any great musical distinction. The costumes this time were by Pauline Lawrence, with perhaps a thread or two by Charles, the inveterate clothier of his own dances. *Quest* combined satirical spoofing with serious purpose in an Artist's Progress over the rough road to real fruition and the right kind of recognition. Charles danced the artist and Doris his alter ego, or inner spirit of comfort and guidance. The group was used to represent the obstacles to progress, the first of which (with due malice aforethought) was the critics. No sooner has the artist emerged from his trial by trivia (experiments with the inconsequential) than they are upon him, typewriters (imaginary) in hand. They are bored, supercilious, impercipient, and try to be clever at his expense. Wham! Then a group of society women takes him up. He quakes before their frightening efforts to spoil him by adulation yet govern his career, but finally succeeds in throwing off their bleak patronage.

In "Transition" (music by Clair Leonard) the men, led by José Limón, William Bales, and William Matons, express his mental state by falling, whirling, leaping, like so many tossing thoughts. This use of other dancers to express the principal dancer's emotions was new with Charles at the time. Another idea comes in the form of a woman (literally held up before him), but he will have none of her until he realizes that she stands as co-worker, for the platonic relationship, not romance. At home he is distressed by the literal-mindedness that would measure him by yardstick, weigh him in scales, and cut him to pattern with scissors. Abroad he finds only dissatisfaction in the response of a regimented culture. When war comes to his own country he tries to evade it, to live only in his art. But he is made to see that he must use his art to help expunge the evil. At last, in a grand finale of affirmation, the artist has found himself in finding the way to the understanding response of his fellows. This is not only Charles. It is any creative artist in any medium. It is the salt of the artist's experience condensed to Charles's special savor.

The movement was fascinating, with humor trickling over the sharper edges, and serious ideas hitting out from the midst of a laugh. So effective were some of the movement designs that they seeped into musical comedy without credit. The finale was transplanted bodily under another dance director's name. However, the joyous pronunciamento of the artist's mastery of his fate got somewhat denatured in the process. The arms aloft and widespread hands took on a routine aspect. Modern dance, having no copyrights, is subject to plagiarism. But also, individual modern dancers can have no facsimiles. Neither they nor their works can successfully be imitated (except in fun). And to those who have seen the original there is no danger of passing the counterfeit.

In a Humphrey-Weidman concert at the Guild Theater January 26, 1936, Charles produced a long work, *American Saga,* based on the legend of Paul Bunyan, with music by Jerome Moross; and a notable suite called *Atavisms,* with music by Lehman Engel. *American Saga* was not one of Charles's best, and though it had several smoothing-out performances, it never got a real foothold in the repertory. In his earlier *Prologue to Saga,* for men's group, he had sketched the work as it was then forming in his mind. The full work followed the story of the great logger's life to a considerable extent, but missed the magic of the tales. It was a case where movement did not prevail over words.

Atavisms, with its abrasive social criticism, was far more impressive. It began good-humoredly with "Bargain Counter," a bacchanalia of the bargain sale, and Charles, the perturbed floor-walker, at a loss how to handle the onrush of modern maenads. Each incited female, in feverish pursuit of her objective, was an opponent of all the others, let the eyes and hair fall where they might. This was a comedy of covetousness or lust for things. The décor consisted of a hint of counter and wire dressmaker forms.

The next reversion to type was "Stock Exchange," the wire frames representing stuffed shirts, or wealth by ticker-tape; the men's group, other pompous gentlemen. Charles was the modern tribal chief literally transported from place to place. Dressed by a valet, fed by a butler or footman, taken down town in a limousine, lifted to his office in an elevator, and in his office waited upon by obsequious clerks, he is utterly helpless without knowing it. Comes the crash and he knows it well. He strives to save himself at the expense of everybody else, leaving prostrate bodies in his wake, but unused to so much exertion, he collapses, sunk in his own helplessness. This ritual of money-lust was dropped as the stockmarket crash of 1929 became remote.

Timeless and still timely, alas, was "Lynch Town," the most formidable section of the three—performed by Charles's present company. The orgy of blood-lust is focused on an unseen jail, toward which a savage mob surges and eddies, while, as if to prove that these primitive barbarians are actually modern Americans, an American voice whistles the musical theme.

The *Kinetic Pantomime* of 1934 was a solo proclamation of Charles's artistic credo at the time, namely, the fusion and rhythmization of abstract and pantomimic elements into a new thing that was neither abstract dance nor straight pantomime, but consisted of a jumble of disconnected absurdities suggesting one idea and breaking off into another. Packaged in these iridescent bubbles of mirth were kernels for rumination. Part of the action was without music, part to music by Colin McPhee. It was something that nobody but Charles could ever have thought up, though it is said that John Martin, the eminent dance critic of the *New York Times,* coined the phrase that made the title. The idea was expanded in group form in the *Opus 51* that came later. In similar tone of purposeful high jinks was the *Traditions* of 1935 (music by Lehman

Engel), danced by Charles, José Limón, and William Matons. The trio depicted in crazy-quilt patterns man's tradition-embattled resistance to change, his slow acceptance of the new until the new in turn becomes tradition. In his stripped, laconic style, Charles made every digital exploit, every body accent, tell. The meaning could not be muffed.

Charles was not always the purposeful buffoon, nor did Doris confine herself to problem-dances. They made their comments as they came, because they were concerned with what was going on around them, and it was natural for them to speak their minds in dance. They could relax and have a good time when they chose. One of Doris's most engaging "little" works was the gay trio, *Exhibition Piece,* to music by Nicolas Slonimsky. It was racked by nothing stronger than gentle satire on styles in dancing—romantic, adagio, ballet, and modern—with the Humphrey-Weidman style for the cream of the jest. Another was the small group work, *To the Dance* (music by Clair Leonard and Norman Lloyd), which won the *Dance* (magazine) award for choreography in 1938, as an example of pure dance, unadulterated by drama or comedy, mime or pantomime, and was everywhere praised for its freshness and spontaneity.

Autonomous also was *Square Dances,* a set of country and couple dances to an original score by Lionel Nowak, based on folk and popular airs. These were done in exhibition style, that is, as sophisticated stage dances rather than as the simple recreation dances of their source. The four couples met periodically in the country dance that bound the piece together, then divided into pairs for the tango, schottische, or waltz. The multiple rhythms, sudden accents and pauses, unexpected changes in tempo, gave the steps a fillip. The movement was now languorous, suspenseful, now animated, and occasionally hearty. The costumes were as captivating as the dances, fluttery ankle-length party dresses for the girls, suits of Byronesque sobriety for the men.

In similar smile-hearted mood and dress was the early *Alcina Suite,* to music from Handel's opera, composed by Doris and Charles in collaboration. In three jocund sections: "Introduction, pomposa and allegro," "Pantomime," and "Menuet, musette, menuet," it translated the pre-classic or court dances into the medium of modern dance. Part of the *Alcina Suite* and all of the others made excellent opening dances. The artists knew the importance of a pleasant welcome.

In 1935 they took their concert group on the first extended tour to be made by a modern dance company, visiting some of the southern and western states and parts of Canada. They had much to learn about the audiences of the hinterland. In Dallas, for example, they inferred that the audience did not like them. because they received no recalls, until they were informed that the seeming lack of enthusiasm was merely a custom of the city. In other cities or towns people occasionally walked out on a performance, or newspaper reporters, reviewers pro tem, were smart at their expense. Then there were misadventures with luggage, hastily devised costumes when theirs did not arrive on time, all the usual trouper troubles.

The Humphrey-Weidman company approached its new public graciously, without unnecessary obfuscation, not by levelling down to a mean average, but by preparing the way for the best it had to give. The publicity consisted of clear, nontechnical descriptions of the dances instead of personal ballyhoo. These sometimes got into the local newspapers, and in any case appeared on the programs. In performance the dancers met an audience half way, projecting at least as much as they demanded. So, the nation's first taste of modern dance was palatable, however odd; and audiences were mostly cordial whether notices were or not. In college towns, where modern dance was included in the physical education departments, the response was ready-made. Here Doris and Charles would conduct master classes and technique demonstrations. The group members executed the techniques, unfolding in orderly progression from the simple to the complex, as Doris directed and explained them in her quiet, lucid way. On subsequent tours, which eventually took them to the West Coast, the technique demonstration reached a larger public.

The technique demonstration has always been an active agent in acquainting the public with modern dance. It helped to increase the understanding, and by so much the appreciation. As the

Humphrey-Weidman company was not long alone in the mission it was first to undertake, this knowledge soon spread across the continent. Instruction did not outweigh entertainment among the touring dancers, but through concert and demonstration the public, or a portion of it, found (1) that modern dance could be enjoyable and (2) that modern dance was not all alike. The European ballet was more popular in these early years, and that the American modern dance succeeded in endearing itself to a sizable quota of the American people outside New York is owing to the ministrations of its chief exponents.

It is impossible to cover here, or even note, all the Humphrey-Weidman works, most of which were notable. There were occasional lapses, a few experiments that did not quite come off. One of these was Doris's *American Holiday,* presented at the Guild Theater January 9 and 23, 1938. The music, an orchestral score composed for it by Morris Mamorsky, was played in a two-piano transcription at the *première.* There was also a text, both spoken and sung. Exclamations and some of the lines were given to the dancers while in motion (a dangerous device unless the phrase-length is very short), the majority to a narrator. The words, written by Doris, were forceful and direct. But the two mediums did not meet in an affecting synthesis. The first part, "Death of the Hero," was a funeral ceremonial for a soldier of the American Revolution. Around his coffin (one of the oblong boxes), Doris danced the spirit of his sacrifice "for justice and freedom." A visible resurrection of the hero symbolized the deathlessness of his ideals. His absorption into the crowd, typifying the assimilation of his influence by the people, constituted the second part, "Dance for the Living." As Doris has often said, not everything can be expressed in dance. She had planned a third part, "Fourth of July," which might have pointed up the work. It was to have combined marionettes and dancers with banners and bunting and pompous oration to show the hollow mockery, the rowdiness and revelry of "the modern celebration of the cause for which the hero died." But this did not materialize, and the work was soon dropped.

On the second program of this pair Charles's burlesque, *This Passion,* was produced. The first theme, "Tabloid," dealt with a sensational murder trial (the famous Snyder-Gray case); the second, "Air Raid," reduced acute militarism to absurdity by presenting a future country where gas masks were permanently affixed, and to remove one was tantamount to a strip-tease act. The third theme, "Interlude," turned from the sordid and oppressive to the contemplation of the good life. The three themes were each developed in three scenes, and the scenes were played tripartitely; that is, all the first scenes were played one after the other, then all the second scenes, etc. Charles had a social purpose here—to show that the evil-hearted when multiplied lead to the mass crime of war. Counter to this was the mounting sequence of harmony and peace. The music, by Norman Lloyd, was plainly functional, as much of his music for modern dance has been. He was later to show greater powers while remaining musically unobtrusive. All music for the Humphrey-Weidman dances was naturally done in consultation with the choreographers.

Race of Life, on the same program, was a hit, a palpable hit. It was Doris's first full-length comedy, a farce-fantasy based on James Thurber's cartoons in the *New Yorker.* It was more than that. It was a parable. You'd never catch Doris being funny just for the heck of it. That she was funny all Thurber fans agreed. As the odious woman of the drawings, she bulked out her slender figure under an apron, stragglified her hair and tried to uglify her face. Charles, looking very much like a man in child's clothing, was the son. José Limón, done likewise after the drawings, was the meek silent partner dragged by his wife up the mountain of boxes to her small-time conception of success. "Excelsior!" shouted the pennant the child carried like a toy. The predominating costume color was white. There was an interlude of Indians and Night Creatures in startling red, and another of the Beautiful Stranger (Katherine Litz) in seductive attire. Vivian Fine composed the score (using a Flexotone for the "Night Creatures" episode) in equivalent non-sense-verse vein. It was a case of laughter holding both its sides. But while the audience thought it was having fun it was actually being exposed to a little lecture on the futility of it all.

At the Bennington Festival of 1938, two major works, Doris's *Passacaglia,* and Charles's *Opus 51,* met their well deserved success.

The use, or mis-use, for dance, of Johann Sebastian Bach's great music, is a moot question. Some musicians, believing that music should be heard but not seen, object to tampering with a musical content already complete in itself. Others, reading by note and measure, perhaps, enjoy seeing an auditory form take visual form. On the ground that music means different things to different people, it may be acceptable; and Bach's music means so much to most creative dancers that sooner or later they are impelled to make dances to it. Another argument for the defense is that the passacaglia was originally a dance form. But, going over to the opponent's side again, Bach's *Passacaglia and Fugue in C minor* was not designed for dancing, and certainly the fugue, with its strictly musical form, is a matter of strictly musical interest.

Whatever the arguments, Doris made a serene and noble work of it. She had her own reasons for using the music, which she told me some time after the performance. She simply needed music of lofty serenity for what she wanted to express, and felt that no modern composer could give it to her. In *New Dance* she had proclaimed her ideal of the perfect introactive state of human brotherhood. That done, she realized that the perfection demanded in youth becomes in maturity a goal, but that a measure of happiness could still be found in working toward the goal. This was the thinking that inlaid her composition. She could not reconcile the dissonances of modern music with it. She found the music of peaceful grandeur and ordered complexity she needed in the *Passacaglia*. In harmonizing her choreography to the music of the master, she also pitted herself against it, and came off second best. It was a grand second, however. Whether it was the pealing music that bore the choreography aloft to its ringing note of quiet joy at the end, or the movement counterpoint and abstract design *with* the music, the two together made a double entry into the emotions. The effect was deeply impressive at the event and left a lambent afterglow.

Doris had worked out the *Fugue* with musicianly understanding of its structure. The reiterated theme of the *Passacaglia* that becomes the subject of the *Fugue,* was to her man's reiteration of faith in his ideals, despite the struggle of attaining them, the stretto passages of the *Fugue* constituted the struggle, mounting in the resolution to a majestic paean of faith. The costumes and formations were beautifully appropriate. In graceful brown and parchment garments, shod with brown half-sandals, the dancers stood motionless in symmetrical tiers against the background screens; then with great dignity flowed into harmonious rearrangements in conformance with the music's architectonic plan. The whole movement tone was elevated, ending, with the music, on the exalted note of joy.

Diametrically opposite was the mirthful and zany *Opus 51*. The Bennington audience, which had come from all over the nation and beyond, included two of Grant Wood's Daughters of the American Revolution. Their faces remained fixed throughout, just as he had painted them. A grumpy paterfamilias and a few other recalcitrants also remained obdurate. But for the main part it was *the* Bennington audience, wise in the ways of modern dance, itself its own *apéritif* for what was to be dished out. And an ollapodrida of a dish it was. Idiom and bromidiom, it was Charles all over. The subtitles were "Opening Dance," "March," "Comedia," "Solo," "Duet," and "Spectacle." The work began with deceptive formality but soon burst into the maddest, merriest prank of all the Weidman years. Expanding the idea of *Kinetic Pantomime,* it tossed about queer, disconnected oddments of motion or gesture that almost told you something and then darted off on another tangent— with a few private jokes on the side. For example, when Charles started to scratch his head, all Bennington (faculty and students) knew he was referring to an idiosyncrasy of one of its members who made decisions by such aid. The scratching had hardly begun when it was carried forward in air on a fluttering theme of the fingers. And that gave the outsiders something novel.

By thus transposing his wisps of suggestion from one place in space to another, and by leaping from wisp to wisp, he kept the audience on the jump and in a state of risibles. Anything went. That is, anything within his own experience. There was hoeing and weeding at the farm, sewing costumes, stumbling over an obstacle that wasn't there, taking a shower, sweeping a floor, and a bit of hair-pulling that could have been anybody's quarrel but wasn't. Flashes of camp meeting, circus, gymnasium stunts, acrobatics, were jumbled in with the personal touches. But the dance was quicker than the eye and nobody could catch it all at once. Charles, with his quips of fingers and quirks of toes, was of course the chief figure, though the groups, both concert and workshop, dressed in shades of green, mingled actively in the phantasmagoria. The *première* audience laughed knowingly at the seeming-spontaneous mummery, and devoured every morsel with glee. In New York and on tour, *Opus 51* became a matter of heated controversy. To some it was arrant nonsense, signifying nothing. To others it was a brilliant kidding of everything but the kitchen sink, and maybe that, too.

One of the sweetest and quaintest genre pieces ever created is Charles's *On My Mother's Side*, a suite of solo dances right out of his own family album. In ordinary slacks and shirt of brown and tan, he stands up (or lies down when necessary) and tells us about his relatives. He sketches them, not as they looked to him as a child, but as a grown-up who understands them. Prefacing each solo, a group of dancers in street clothes enters one side of the stage or the other, and in non-elocutionary, sing-song unison, chants the crude but vivid verses that point out to us who's who. The words (written by William Archibald, a former dancer in the company) are phrased, held, repeated, shaded and punctuated with musical effect. The supporting piano score is by Lionel Nowak, musical director of the company at the time the piece was composed. Without properties or décor, Charles makes us feel the presence of these kinsfolk of his, founders of an American middle-class family who came from Europe and took roots in the Middle West.

The first was the lusty young pioneer who became Great Grandfather Wolcott:

> Great man when he wanted
> Nothing daunted when he wanted
>   Way back—
>
> Proud of his name, he staked no claim
> He staked no claim, but he staked his name
>   Way back—
>   Way back—
>   Way back—

Then Great Grandfather Hoffman:

> A kind calm man was Hoffman
> Kind and calm and dignified, pioneer
> He got what he got
> He cared little or not
> Where or what he got
> Was his lot—
> Dignified, he settled down.

And Charles settles down by peacefully reclining on the floor, curling up his toes in sublime content. There follows a big surprise as the tall, straight dancer, with his black hair and full dark eyes, makes us see his gentle little Grandmother Hoffman

> With a love of the fine in her fingers
> And the curve of her work through her spine.

In the rounded back, the busy revolving hands, the fingers delicately engaged in invisible needlework, in the occasional straightening up as if to receive a guest, Charles imprints upon us such a lifelike image of this

> Fine old woman
> Fine old woman, and blind

that we forget all about him and see only her.

The next episode causes conflicting reactions. The words seem to laugh in the wrong place and their facetiousness is not borne out in the action.

> Grandfather Hoffman—a builder by trade
> Put into three houses—all the money he made
> All his money—all his time
> Every single little dime—
> Put into three houses—all the money he made.
> When the houses were built—
> They all burned down.
> He gave the situation a whole lot of thinking
> And just at the point of taking to drinking,
> He hanged—
> Himself.

This is a short-short story of ambition and defeat. The tight little motions of scrimping and saving, the larger movements of building well and the satisfaction therein, then the overwhelming blight of the catastrophe. And finally, without rope or other accouterment, the slow swaying, swinging, that gives the dreadful illusion of the end.

But we move on to the bright little scherzo of Aunt Jessie, to music based on the strains of "Dear Little Buttercup." Charles minces daintily, capers vivaciously, bows coquettishly, blows the gay kiss audienceward. As the chorus recites with sardonic emphasis:

> On her little toes she danced
> *Dear* Aunt Jessie
> With her little hands she clapped
> *Sweet* Aunt Jessie.
> Little hands, little feet,
> She used to make her aims complete,
> She swept an audience away from its seat—
> *Dear, sweet* Aunt Jessie.

The vignette of Vesta, Charles's mother (who appears in the sequel to this work) was later dropped. As given at the earlier performances, there were snatches of "Darling Nellie Gray" in the music, while Charles acted out the verse:

> To a fireman she gave a home,
> Daughters and a son.
> To a fireman she gave a home,
> And a son.
> Being a woman, being a wife,
> She liked gay, good things in life,
> Dancing, skating
> And hearing a song.
> To a fireman she gave a home,
> Daughters and a son.

The dancing stops abruptly, the music goes minor and chromatic, as Vesta removes her wedding ring, gathers her children about her, and leaves.

> She left the fireman
> Left his home
> And raised her children
> On her own.

For end-piece Charles takes a laugh at himself, the Sonny of the family:

> Today a fellow likes to dance
> No one knows why.
> Maybe because he likes to dance
> No one knows why—

He takes us back to Denishawn, writhing Orientally, bending his knees in the *Gnossienne,* with musical quotations; then tries a toe at ballet. None of it will do. Business of thinking. Ah, he has hit upon it at last. He moves tentatively, then more freely, into reminiscences (both musical and dancical) from the Humphrey-Weidman repertory. As the chorus sums it up:

> Then the modern creed it got him
> And some think they
> Might have shot him
> As a leader
> Of the bare
> Foot and Soul.

The disarming naïveté of this work is one of the secrets of its appeal. In dancing what is heartfelt and real for him, Charles makes it real for the spectator. By lighting up his own family tree he sheds light on everybody else's. *On My Mother's Side* was produced at the Studio Theater in 1940. The sequel, *And Daddy Was a Fireman,* followed in 1943. Fortunately, both items of Weidmaniana are included in the current Weidman repertory. They are actually modern ballets, as most full-length modern dance works are and as they are increasingly called.

And Daddy Was a Fireman is done with such childlike simplicity that it is almost as if Charles were dressing up in his father's red shirt and playing fireman. Cut-out pieces for props and scenery heighten this impression. The boyish Daddy is the kind of man who would have been a perpetual spark if he had not become a professional firefighter. From time to time a group of townswomen, in the long skirts and leg o' mutton sleeves of the tintype era, cluster in a gossipy knot and read in busybody tones items from the local newspapers of the day that trace the various promotions leading to the climax of his career. They pronounce the name Weedman, by the way. Before long he is Captain C. E. Wiedman of the Lincoln, Nebraska, Fire Department, having vanquished the double-threat villain of the piece, Fire in flame-colored tights, and his rival, Chief Malone—both in the person of Peter Hamilton.

When the lovely Vesta, in her fashionable clothes, comes to town on a visit, Captain Wiedman is no less susceptible than any male. Their meeting and courtship is portrayed with tender humor. No sweeter tribute was ever paid a pair of parents. The cocky fireman proudly polishes the brass on his cut-out fire engine as he explains the parts to Vesta, who listens with that wide-eyed interest women know how to assume on such occasions. He timidly calls on her, and finally, in a parlor with a melodeon and Grandmother Hoffman herself in it (though she leaves the room in time), he awkwardly manages his proposal. But he does not forget his life work. From the opening scene at the State Fair, where he puts out a small fire in one of the booths, to the Lindell Hotel fire, where he heroically saves a clamorous woman in a long white nightgown, he is on the job. His fidelity wins him the call to the captaincy of the fire department of the Canal Zone (during the building of the Panama Canal); and, debonair in his straw sailor, cut-out suitcase in hand, he departs, symbolically preceded by the demon Fire.

The action is mainly pantomimic, with typical Weidman touches, as when the fight with Chief Malone is paced out like a duel. But briefly. A hint only and Charles is on to something else. The score by Herbert Haufrecht adapts popular airs from *On My Mother's Side* (including "Oh Susanna") in its own style. In recent years Nadine Gae, as guest artist, has frequently taken the part of Vesta, created by Doris. The highly original cut-outs were designed by Perkins Harnly, and the marvelous fire engine by Peter Hamilton, a featured dancer and sometimes guest artist, now developing as a choreographer. One of Charles's latest projects is his *Panamic*

Suite, based on his memories of the Canal Zone when the family joined Daddy there.

The opening of the Studio Theater in December 1940, marked a new period in the Humphrey-Weidman career. The artists had shown their theater dance throughout the land. Now they were setting up a dance theater of their own, where they could practice and rehearse, compose and perform, at less expense and with greater security. For this they took a remodelled one-story building that had once been part of a department store and later an artist's studio, in lower New York. Seats accommodating about 200 people were arranged like bleachers to look down upon the dancing floor. The curtain was made of dimming lights. From a humble doorway on a cluttered street, beside a Chinese laundry, one entered a different world, the festive world of dance. A small foyer hung with soft red draperies, with dance photographs on the walls, led to the auditorium. The room was too intimate for works of great sweep and power, for large groups in contrary motion or opposing masses. But here as well as anywhere the screens and boxes could set a scene and many pieces in the overflowing repertory could be performed. There was a constant flow of *premières* besides.

The first ten (or twelve) years had been the hardest. At the Bennington Festival of 1941 Doris produced *Decade,* a compendium of those years as shared by the partners. It was the story of Doris and Charles in Dance Land, or, From Loft to Studio Theater, quoting from both their works of that period. It was disappointing to some of us at the time because it went over old ground instead of breaking into new, and because some of the works quoted could not adequately be handled. But now that it is no more than an intaglio in memory it has become as cherishable as an heirloom. At the Bennington performance Arch Lauterer had set the stage of the College Theater with a pair of central doors, and permanent wings of vitaglass, and part of the action moved over steps from the proscenium apron. This of course had to be altered somewhat for the Studio Theater and elsewhere. Lionel Nowak's score combined Aaron Copland's *Music for the Theater* with interpolations of his own and musical quotations fitting the dance quotations. Pauline's and Charles's costumes likewise quoted from the past. The twenty-five episodes of the first production were later reduced to seventeen. In both cases the ascending line of decadal development was maintained. What downward jaggedness occurred was caused chiefly by the merciless portrayal of the unctuous Mr. Business (who might have been cut out for a radio announcer) and his attempts to exploit the dancers.

The Prologue, "Vision of a New Life," is a dance overture, stating or brushing over lightly the movement themes to be developed. The villain enters with the body of the work, "The Path of Realization," for it is necessary to come to terms with Mr. Business before obtaining the whitewashed brick loft that is to be their workshop. He is represented by an offstage voice and an onstage dancer, or mime. He evidently pockets his rent in advance for we soon see and hear the dancers settling in—hammering, measuring, making decisions—while their students rush about to help make the place ready. They gather the group together and try out new ideas. Doris has done her "Gigue" from the *First Partita* (Bach), Charles his *Cathédrale Engloutie,* when along comes Mr. Business again, jauntily wearing his profit motive up his sleeve. Profit for him, that is, and a part in a movie-advertising project for them. They, in their innocence, expect it will help them financially, and, eager to please, offer a supersweet rendition of the *Air for the G String.*

They have no sooner started working again (on a pair of Scriabin études) when up pops Mr. Business with another proposition. This time it is a chance to put on an opera ballet in a production of *Iphigenia*—by "G-luck," he mispronounces (he should of stood in radio); and that gives the audience a chance to see Charles's hilarious *Air Gai.* We see it both in rehearsal and at the opera house, with Doris, Charles, Beatrice Seckler, and others going to town in the grand manner, curtain calls and all. At the Bennington performance another manager or agent (still Mr. Business) looked over a brief montage of *The Shakers,* but being a man who not only didn't know a thing about art but knew he didn't like it if it looked like art, would have none of it. At Bennington, too, the first part of *Decade* ended on a note of disappointment, as engagements were canceled and things did not go right all the time. At the Studio Theater Part 1 ended with the cheerful *Air Gai.* It is probably clear by this time that a modern dance does not spring full-panoplied into life, but undergoes many changes before it begins to arrive and sometimes after it has arrived. Doris and Charles were no exception to the fact that good work is usually good because it has been worked over.

In the revised edition of *Decade,* Part 11, continuing "The Path of Realization," opens with the "Curtain Music" from Copland's *Music for the Theater,* after which Mr. Business has himself a monologue of self-justification. A "Kaleidoscope of the Theater" (excerpts from the repertory) is then run off by the full company. Following preparations for a dress rehearsal, with the dancers their own stage hands and dressers, we see *Circular Descent, Kinetic Pantomime, Water Study,* and *Ringside,* unabridged. A "Fugue of Confusion," choreographed by Charles to percussion accompaniment, another "Dialogue with Mr. Business," leads to the apotheosis, "Departure Toward a New Vision," the new life of the Studio Theater.

In some ways the original production was better than the curtailed version, especially for an audience familiar with the background. It was more satisfactory as autobiography in its anecdotal survey of years of great consequence to the development of the American modern dance. The quick shots from *Red Fires* and *Theatre Piece,* from *Happy Hypocrite* and *Opus 51* were maddening because of all they left out, though the "Celebration" from *New Dance,* signifying the attainment of one ideal, the founding of their own repertory theater, was happily worked in. On the whole the first was the fuller picture of the progress of modern dance as exemplified in the professional lives of two of its gallant pioneers. We saw them meeting discouragements bravely, triumphs graciously, and finally emerging, ready to face the future with courage and hope, as heads of an organization that was to be of communal benefit.

The new vision soon became a new path of realization. The weekend programs at the Studio Theater were so popular that people were turned away and extra performances given. In the fall of 1941 came two parts of Doris's *Song of the West:* "The Green Land" (Lionel Nowak), a solo by Doris; and "Desert Gods" for group, with music for four hands, voice and percussion composed for it by Roy Harris. The solo was an utterance of the individual's feeling of kinship with nature and delight in its greenness and growth. "Desert Gods," in costume colors of sand and sunset and stratified rock, evoked an aboriginal atmosphere, as if the earliest inhabitants of the dry lands had come out from hiding to perform their ancient ceremonies in worship of their ancient gods. A year later "Mountain Rivers," to a recorded piece by Roy Harris, was added as the opening number, the title later simplified to "Rivers." In this suite Doris praised the inspiring geography of her country in relation to its people—the broad green plains of life-giving vegetation, the high-colored mysterious deserts with the breath of forgotten rituals upon the air, the mighty rivers uniting and nourishing the land. It used to be said that American modern dance came out of the artificial life of the metropolis, that it was conditioned by a vertical existence in skyscrapers, the fierce pace and nervous energy of the big city. But all three of its creators early experienced the vastness of the continent. Although New York may have flavored some of their work, they were never bound by its restrictions or limited to its provincial outlook (or inlook) upon the rest of the world.

In 1942, after many delays, partly due to an engagement at the Rainbow Room for Charles, Katherine Litz, and Peter Hamilton, *Flickers* made its popular hit. Charles's travesty of the old silent movies was in four reels: "Hearts Aflame," based on the old mortgage plot; "Hearts Courageous," the time-honored Western; "Flowers of the Desert," with Charles in the white burnoose of a Valentino-type sheik coming between Beatrice Seckler and Lee Sherman as a pair of lovers; and "Wages of Sin," showing Doris slinking around in a rare impersonation of Theda Bara. The pantomime reflected the jerky technique of movie beginnings, and the score by Lionel Nowak was in early nickelodeon style. Charles has a genius for amusing little night-club pieces, and has been immensely successful with them. Many of these were given on special theatrical programs at the Studio Theater, together with his priceless caricatures of other dancers. The titles practically tell the story: *Penguins, War Dance for a Wooden Indian, Park Avenue Intrigue, The Pro-*

fessor Visits Harlem, Rumba to the Moon, and other trifles. At this time Lee Sherman made his debut as choreographer with such items as *Jazz Trio, Effervescent Blues, Second Story Story,* and *Peculiar Apache.*

In November 1942 Charles was called up for military service, held for a while, and finally released. That same year José Limón was out on the West Coast giving recitals in partnership with May O'Donnell. In the late fall he married Pauline Lawrence and returned to the Studio Theater as guest artist, taking part in a Sunday night all-Bach program that ran from December 27, 1942 into February 1943, by popular demand. The program consisted of *Passacaglia;* the *Chaconne in D minor,* choreographed and danced by José under Doris's direction; *Four Choral Preludes;* and the *Partita in G major.* The *Partita,* which introduced low stools into the action, had an added scenic and sound effect when Ralph Kirkpatrick played the harpsichord on stage for one performance; and the *Chaconne* was illumined by Roman Totenberg as guest violinist on a few occasions. These abstract dances, in what should be regarded as a misalliance of music and movement but turned out to be an agreeable synchronization, belied the notion that modern dance had to be dramatic to be successful.

In the first years of the Studio Theater there were post-season children's concerts and request programs. The company continued to tour (on a smaller scale) and to appear in the Students Dance Recitals and the Y. M. H. A. Dance Theatre series. With the war years disruption began. At the end of the third official season José Limón was inducted into the Army. In the fall of that year (1943) Charles, who had been returning intermittently between night-club and theater engagements, was off on a new Broadway assignment. What with one thing and another, it was not until March 5, 1944, that Doris's long-delayed masterwork, *Inquest,* was produced.

Inquest choreographed the passage from the chapter "Of Kings' Treasuries" from Ruskin's *Sesame and Lilies,* containing quotations from a coroner's report on the death in England in 1865 of a poor "translator" of boots from overwork and starvation. For a diet of bread and tea when they could afford it, and a wretched lodging, Michael Collins and his son, Cornelius, worked day and night making over old boots, which the wife and mother, Mary Collins, bought and resold "for what she could get." The father collapsed and died. "It seems to me deplorable that you did not go into the workhouse," the coroner said to Mary at the inquest. "We wanted the comforts of our little home," she replied. And when he wondered what the comforts could be, she "began to cry and said that they had a quilt and other little things." "I will print the paragraph in red," Ruskin wrote. And it *was* printed in red in the first edition.

Doris, whose indignation was no less than Ruskin's, choreographed and costumed her work in more somber colors, but made of it an even more impassioned outcry against such economic inequities. In this she was ably supported by Norman Lloyd's atmospheric score, by the narrator's (Dan Reed at the first performance) exposition, and by the quiet, sympathetic playing of father and son by Charles and Peter Hamilton. She herself was the fragile, self-effacing mother to the life. The rest of the company formed an anonymous chorus of the poor. The setting, the first to depart from the screens and boxes, showed the cramped room the family called home. A candle-end on the bare window sill, a pallet on the floor, with a ragged quilt thrown over it, represented the "little things" Mary loved and clung to.

Outside the room, in what under dim lighting became a dingy slum street, shadowy forms—shawled women in their long black dresses, shabby, work-bowed men—passed to and fro. The beat of their footsteps resounded, the pulse of their hearts pierced through, the soft-focused picture of poverty. In rhythmic mimesis, as far from straight pantomime as poetry is from common speech, the piteous story was enacted, drawing us, the spectators, in, detached yet a part of it, making us feel a destitution we had hitherto only read about. And when the father, in his cobbler's apron, keeled over from utter weakness, the distracted, half-blind son helping him to the heap of straw in the corner, and the mother, shriveled inside her shawl, went out in a last desperate attempt to sell the made-over boots so that she could buy food and medicine, we knew a compassion we had never known before.

In a street that was no street, where no doors were, Mary Collins (it was no longer Doris) knocked in vain. According to the coroner's report, she sold the two pair of boots she had for next to nothing. "We must have our profit," the shopkeeper had said. But this was not literally observed. The death of Michael Collins ended the personal tragedy. Like figures in an allegory the family unit stood aside, while the people rose in the streets in a swelling outbreak against the oppressors who caused such things to be. In stormy cross currents, their angry, twisted bodies and violent gestures bespoke their wrath and despair. That the prolonged, stabbing wail seeming to issue from their midst was the voice of an offstage singer nobody could have noticed at the time. For this was not stunning group choreography or theatrical hokum. This was suffering "out of the hurt heart" of humanity. It opened our hearts to the homeless, the cold, the hungry people everywhere.

Inquest drew crowds to the Studio Theater and was also given on tour. Its last performance, at Swarthmore College, Pennsylvania, marked Doris's last appearance as a dancer. It was the end of an era. The old days never returned. The Studio Theater was more frequently rented to other dancers, and Charles with his new company eventually took over. Like revenants waiting to be believed back to life, the costumes of the great Humphrey-Weidman ballets hover in patient rows in the large basement room under the auditorium. Like buried scriptures of a glorious career the programs and press-books lie there pending the day their full story shall be brought to light. No number of small companies can ever supplant the one big company that gave a new dance diction to the world, coining phrases that have become the common currency of dance.

It was not the end of Doris's career. She continues to create masterpieces, to lead and inspire younger dancers in her extremely individual teaching of choreography, to give friendly counsel and criticism to Charles in his independent work. In the fall of 1944 they staged together the dances for *Sing Out, Sweet Land,* a musical described as a cavalcade of American song; and replaced Martha Graham and Louis Horst as heads of the Y. M. H. A. Modern Dance School, of which she is now director. In the war years she worked at the Studio Theater with José Limón, directing the trio he had formed with Beatrice Seckler and Dorothy Bird during furloughs and weekend passes, and since then has choreographed for and directed his ensemble.

But in view of the circumstances at the time, when all was not yet clear, it was discomfiting to learn that Charles's first work for his new company was called *A House Divided—*. The meaning, however, was not ulterior. He was referring to the Civil War. In the midst of war he was making a conscious plea for unity, remembering the conflicting factions that arise after wars. It is a serious work, dominated by the figure of Abraham Lincoln, with the other characters sketched in as types, and the group choreography weak in spots. Charles gives a beautiful portrait of the tall and spare and lonely leader of his people, touching in its simplicity and strength. The use of an actor (a role created by Peter Harris) to speak his thoughts while following him around and approximating his miming detracts somewhat from the might of his presence. Charles's Lincoln is most impressive when he walks alone.

The piece opens as the funeral obsequies end. The mourned President steps down from the platform that supports his bier, to take a retrospective view of the war and its causes, to yearn over his countrymen in the throes of reconstruction, to look forward with hope toward the consummation of his ideals. Spirit or no, he wears the expected black frock coat, and bears himself with the expected dignity. The events do not proceed in orderly sequence, since this is an epitome of history and not an historical narration; nor are they always clear. An outstanding interlude is the rape of the slave girl, played with distinction by Saida Gerrard. We see her crawling after the proud Southern Lady (Nadine Gae) in the crouched gait of frightened servitude. In her slow progress, she is left behind. The overseers come upon her. When Lincoln finds her lying desolate on the ground, he lifts her up in his arms and tenderly carries her home. There are times when Charles the humorist looks very like a humanist, too.

He quickly resumed his Puckish impudence in the next work, *David and Goliath,* a modern version of the Bible tale in pseudo-archaic movement, to music by Johann Kuhnau, with costumes by George Bockman. Charles gives the giant full credit for clownish dumbness, while Peter Hamilton is sprightly as the wonder-boy of his age. The Israelites are depicted by a group of seemly-behaving maidens; the Philistines by a riotous, ill-behaved crowd. Whether done with tongue in cheek or tongue stuck out, it could offend only the unco guid. Another novelty of the first season (1945), *Dialogue,* is a comedy of manners, putting a modern country weekend into pre-classic forms, with sophisticated insinuations. The music is from Ernest Bloch. These, with revivals from the Weidman repertory and some of Peter's maiden efforts, constituted the bills presented at the Studio Theater, in the Students Dance Recitals and Y. M. H. A. Dance Theatre series, and on tour. Except for the top layers, the company was quite inferior at the start, and still has growing pains. It's the old story—good dancers leave for better opportunities—and the gaps are not easily filled.

In July 1946 José Limón and his ensemble appeared before a semi-private audience at Bennington College in Doris's poetic tragedy, *Lament for Ignacio Sánchez Mejías,* and her second full-length comedy, *The Story of Mankind.* Both works, which were prepared at Bennington, had an enormous success, with repercussions in periodicals and press, when they were formally presented at the Belasco Theater, New York, in January of the following year. But the productions were no more handsome or impressive when they were generally recognized than they were at the first performance. In fact the Bennington *Lament* had an advantage in the actress, Ellen Love, who as the Figure of a Woman shared the spoken verse with Letitia Ide, the Figure of Destiny. The actress role calls for a telling minimum of dramatic movement and gesture and a voice of range and resonance. At Bennington the words pealed and glittered and echoed and broke like shards of sound. Meg Mundy, who had the role at the first New York showing, lacked the peculiar vocal prowess required.

For the *Lament,* which follows the poem written by García Lorca on the death of his friend, the famous Spanish bullfighter, Doris selected and combined lines from various English translations. The verses quoted hereinafter are those used in her dance, and so cannot be credited to any one translator. The setting and lighting, designed by Michael Czaja, place a clean-lined construction (painted off-white, with gray and black planes), suggesting the railings of the bull-ring beyond and massing into the climax of a coffin, under fluctuations of light and shade that help to propel the action. The costumes (by Pauline Lawrence Limón) are of sumptuous black, all black for the mourning Figure of a Woman, black with jewel tones—red, yellow, purple, green—for the Figure of Destiny and for Ignacio. The work brought out Norman Lloyd's best score, composed for a small orchestra of violoncello, flute, trumpet, clarinet, and guitar with piano, but played in a piano version at Bennington.

José Limón, attesting his racial heritage in face and bearing, is the ideal Ignacio. Letitia Ide, his feminine counterpart in beauty of movement, endows her role with the necessary cool repose, and speaks in a clear, trained voice of delicate inflection and restrained intensity. The divisions of the work are: "Prologue," "The Catching and the Death," "The Spilling of the Blood," "Body Present," and "Absent Soul." Only the declining matador fights at night, so to meet death at five in the afternoon is to meet it with honor, in the highest ranks of bullring aristocracy. In pliant scale the Figure of a Woman proclaims the events of the tragedy above the awesome pedal point of the Figure of Destiny's persistent declamation, "At Five in the Afternoon."

A child brought a white sheet
    AT FIVE IN THE AFTERNOON
A rush basket of slaked lime
    AT FIVE IN THE AFTERNOON
A coffin on wheels is his bed
Bones and flutes sound in his ears
The room is iridescent with agony
    AT FIVE IN THE AFTERNOON
    AYE, THAT TERRIBLE FIVE IN THE AFTERNOON
    IT WAS FIVE BY ALL THE CLOCKS
    IT WAS FIVE IN THE SHADOW OF THE AFTERNOON

This is only a fragment of the long antiphonal duet. We see Ignacio fighting the last enemy.

Up the stairs went Ignacio
With all his death upon his shoulders

We see him, with all his death upon him, remembering all his life, recalling incidents of *corrida* and *fiesta*, his feet tracing the bright patterns against the encompassing darkness. He has lain motionless on the couch, his crimson mantle covering him like a winding sheet. Now he rises to renew the fight for life, grasping at it in a fiery staccato solo, insisting upon it, testing it, proving his vitality. In blinding pain he stands upon his head, rotating his legs in air. It is over. In a symbolical passage with the Figure of Destiny, he is caught in her blue-green rope at last. He weaves his way to the coffin and disappears. There follows the mourning woman's dirge:

> The bull does not know you, nor the fig-tree
> Nor the horses, nor the ants in your own house.
> Nobody knows you. No. But I sing of you.
> I sing of a later time
> Of your elegance and your grace
> Your appetite for death and the taste of his mouth
> And the sadness lying beneath your valiant joy.

During this recitation the Figure of Ignacio appears and is seen slowly revolving on a pedestal at stage right, while the Figure of a Woman, stage left, sounds in ecstatic cadence:

> I sing his elegance in words that tremble
> And remember a sad wind through the olive trees.

The impressions of visual and aural beauty reach farther than eye can see or ear can hear, opening secret vistas on the universal mysteries. It is a dance of transfixing splendor.

From such exalted mood it is difficult at first to swing into the comedy. But *The Story of Mankind* is paired with *Lament,* and those who prefer laugh lines like it a lot better. It is no frivolous fun-making, however, for it is a sterner parable than *Race of Life.* Here we see man and his ever-ambitious if not ever-loving mate climbing from the paleolithic to the penthouse age, and promptly descending therefrom at the sign of the times printed in 120-point newspaper type, SPLIT ATOM. In the fast-paced traverse of the ages, the dancing as well as the behavior styles of each period are satirized. Beatrice Seckler created the role of the little woman, and with her physical agility and mental adroitness missed not a minute in getting at the quick of the matter. When she was otherwise engaged, Pauline Koner, a ballet-trained dancer with a flair for drama and comedy that makes her a willing ally of modern dance, played it no less satisfactorily, if differently. José Limón, who had to grow into his role, is now quite wittily the unwitting male who constantly gets prodded upward when he would much rather stay comfortably where he is.

The mobile setting was designed by Michael Czaja. It is a wooden structure of varying planes brought out in shades of gray and blue, like a lopsided extension of the Humphrey-Weidman boxes; and it is pushed around or tipped over to take on the aspect of assorted dwelling places, finally surmounting itself in the dream-house of metropolitan living. Pauline's costumes are ingenious as well as functional for rapid-fire entertainment. At the beginning the dancers are clad in plain brown maillots to indicate primeval nudity, the woman wearing ornaments of bone. They build their first shelter with a monkey-fur jacket and a pair of sticks, and much commentful byplay. For the Greek episode, white outline costumes over the maillots suggest tunic and toga, while certain platitudes of Greek culture, including dance, are taken for a ride. In the Medieval age, tall headgear tops the appearance of flowing robes by the same white-outline device, as plans for bigger and better houses continue, and man and woman make material progress while remaining essentially as before. The innate crudity of the French courtiers under the superficial elegance of their dances, the false daintiness and prudery, the finical manners of the Victorian period, with quick-change costumes to match, are likewise exposed.

Lionel Nowak's music, improved with age and revision, races along with the action to the café society era. Over the skin-fitting maillots the lady wears the fur jacket and a sophisticated air, the gentleman a top hat and a swagger. Snug in their penthouse apartment after doing the night spots, they glance at the morning tabloid. The headline sends them scurrying to the ground. The fur jacket reverts to its primitive estate, the lady and gentleman to theirs, as under its shelter they cower and fearfully scan the skies. Laugh as he may, the spectator is left with a bitter taste in the mouth and a worried expression in the heart.

The comedy is far more devastating than the tragedy. Technically, both works are an advance over anything Doris has previously done. They unveil unsuspected capabilities of the human body to move in small planes or large, in stress or at will. *The Story of Mankind* sparkles with a minutia of movement too swift for words to capture. The glowing *Lament for Ignacio Sánchez Mejías* abounds in the broad stroke, the big, sometimes startling, muscular activity. Whatever José contributed out of his background and physique, the conception belongs to Doris. She has always been able to see beyond her own selfhood and so can choreograph for others with understanding skill.

In contrast to the bold and striking *Lament,* her next ballet, *Day on Earth,* is an exquisite pastoral. The theme is the blessedness and sustaining power of work, transcending personal joys and sorrows, within or without the family unit. This unit, man and woman and child together as symbol of what is the basic and is considered the happiest human relationship, has pervaded much of her composition. In *New Dance* she idealized the love union, presenting man and woman as free co-equals in the ideal democracy. In *Theatre Piece* she cauterized the competitive and subjugative elements that flaw it, in *Red Fires* the possessive love that thwarts it; and in *Race of Life* she satirized the divided interests, the domination of one partner by another, that wreck it. In *Inquest,* she holds love of family, love of home, to the heights of sacrifice. Now, in *Day on Earth,* she rises above the instabilities and disappointments of all earthly attachments to the impersonal joy of work.

At a trial performance given at the Beaver Country Day School in Chestnut Hill, near Boston, in the spring of 1947, the radiant work theme shone through a translucency in which not all the other details were so clear. There was no program note (a clue that is dispensable only when the choreographer can say it all with movement —and a desideratum hardly attainable), and the décor was on the skimpy side. It consisted of a small chest that served as bench, and a length of rare Chinese silk that had its own part to play. The music, Aaron Copland's Piano Sonata, aroused conflicting interests at first by its own musical content, until as the dance progressed and fitted itself perfectly to it, music and movement were conjoined.

José danced the principal role with beautiful dignity of spirit and amazing technical resource, beginning with his labor in the fields, done by intimation rather than imitation. On the bare stage, against the pale backdrop, we see the brown soil of his ploughing and planting, we sense the wide space and breathe the fragrant air; we feel the deep-vigored joy of healthy activity, the strength and humble pride of achievement. So much is evoked by movement alone. Upstage (at audience right) seated on the bench, is the Woman (Letitia Ide) and at her feet, veiled under the silken cloth, like the unborn children of Maeterlinck's *Bluebird,* the Child (Melisa Nicolaides). This is a real little girl, by the way, whose natural awkwardness gives piquancy to the whole. Their pose of immobility suggests that they have not yet come into the Man's life. All three figures are simply costumed in terra cotta colors.

Before the Wife and Child emerge as living or related creatures, there is a playful duet with a Young Girl (Miriam Pandor). It is the Man's first love and not an illicit affair as one might suppose, but ends as irrevocably, so that the Man is driven to his work for solace. Following a tender interlude with the Wife and Child, the Child leaves, too, whether to go out into the world or out from the world. The feeling of loss or separation is established by an anguished sequence on the mother's part, danced with sombrous beauty, and passionate utterances of condolence mixed with suffering by the Man, who again turns to his work for comfort. When his Wife also leaves him (whether by death or divorce) work is his final consolation. In the closing tableau, the Child has returned to strike a beatific attitude on the bench, and the three grown persons lie motionless under the silken square—the birth-veil and burial cloth of man's brief day on earth.

This is a work that should not be analyzed in words, for words are crass and paltry in comparison with its delicacy of mood. It is enough that it shimmers and sings and enmeshes the spectator in its reverie, even if it does not reveal itself all at once. The main idea —the inevitableness of loss and separation, the unfailing surcease of work—was unmistakably brought out. The mother's grief at parting with her child, the torn emotions of the father, done by a running opposition leap in air, in which one part of the body pulls against another, the buoyant, assuaging work theme, harmonizing the body in all its members, spoke in the language of movement, as in the language of music, "from the heart to the heart." *Day on Earth* is lyrical, luminous. A more theatrical production would infringe upon its atmosphere. Of course it did not actually come into existence until it reached New York (at City Center on December 21, 1947), when it was duly accredited a masterpiece.

By the same token, Charles's suite of Thurber visualizations, *Fables For Our Time,* was non-existent at the preview performance given at the Jacob's Pillow Festival in the summer of 1947; but as it has since been shown and acclaimed in a Broadway week at the Mansfield Theater (in the spring of 1948), it is now an established fact. The music, by Freda Miller, composer-accompanist, calls for two pianos. At Jacob's Pillow the time-worn gray boxes served as understudies for the new décor then being readied for the New York production. A narrator, Jack Ferris, traveled or sat around the stage, adjusted props, and casually delivered lines from the text, mostly as Thurber wrote them, while Charles and his company enacted the four fables he had chosen to choreograph.

The first one, "The Unicorn in the Garden," opens delightfully with Charles as the timid Thurber male seeing the unicorn as raptly and realistically as ever Frank Fay saw the pooka. He is so enchanted he must tell his wife, the typical Thurber shrew (Saida Gerrard), but she of course will have none of such nonsense and hides her head under the bedclothes. Back in the garden he sees the unicorn again, and again approaches his wife with the wonder in his eyes. After enough of this she calls the psychiatrist, who enters with a policeman, only to turn what began as delectable fantasy into rather clumsy farce. The unicorn has disappeared. The husband is blandly noncommittal. The struggling, thrashing wife is carried off in his stead. If there is any malice in Charles's lovable Milquetoast, it is well concealed. If there is any further resemblance to *Harvey* in the plot, it can only be attributed to the impartiality of the creative idea, falling like the rain.

The second fable, "The Shrike and the Chipmunks," adds to the male and female of the species a big bad property bird, designed and made by A. Spolidore, and wafted around on a stick by the narrator. Chunky little Betty Osgood, whose comedic talents have been cultivated in Charles's company, is the spouse. She and Charles make like chipmunks, holding their arms and hands up for fore-paws and baring their teeth. While she busies herself with her housekeeping, scolding her lazy husband and warning him that the Shrike will get him ef he don't watch out, he dallies with a basket of large property acorns. His sly references to the Denishawn "bead plastique," as he extends a foot to stick the acorns between his toes, to the Spanish dance, using the acorns for castanets, and so on ad lib., are all-Weidman and no Thurber about it. In a spectacular swirl the Shrike gets them both in the end, tackling the lady chip-munk first, as expected.

In "The Owl Who Was God" the sex war is forgotten. The cynicism is directed to wider fields, as the dumb creatures gather to worship the dumbest among them, mistaking his natural air of solemnity (and a superimposed sense of timing) for wisdom. Charles, in over-sized baggy black clothes, like a sloppy rendition of a judge's robe, perches on a box that might be a branch, back to the audience, seeming to settle his feathers by quivering motions in the shoulder muscles. Two Ground Moles, seeing him thus, are impressed by the figure of austerity and call the other animals. A conference ensues. Could be—but they aren't sure. The Secretary Bird is chosen to put him to the test. Now facing front, the Owl shakes himself, blinks his eyes, and, with curious mouthal mimicry, meets the quizz pro-gram. By saying "To Whit" and "To Whoo" (the narrator omitting the h's) in exactly the right places, he passes. "He's God!" the crea-tures cry in awed (and shrill) tones. The Owl descends from his perch, and, with a walk that is truly wonderful, leads them in a ludicrous processional to thumpy music reminiscent of the death march in *The Green Table*. Each creature is characterized by gait as well as costume. The long-legged Secretary Bird strides in steps of ballet derivation; the Plymouth Rock Hen sort of clucks along; the Ground Moles creep; the French Poodle, the Hawk, Dormouse, and Red Fox all behave as implied as they follow the leader up and over a cliff to destruction. This is the fourth fable. A third, "The Little Girl and the Wolf," a low comedy skit, was fortunately dropped in favor of "The Courtship of Al and Arthur"—concerning some not very eager beavers—for the New York production.

Charles, no less than Doris, no less than Martha, has made an individual contribution to the American modern dance. And if the informal use of given names seems strange, it really is not, for it is the accepted custom. Whereas no balletomane would think of speaking of Tudor as Antony (it isn't his own name, anyway) or of Markova as Alicia, modern dance fans would not think of calling their great ones anything but Martha, Doris, and Charles.

"Martha," "Doris," "Charles," these three—in widely different ways—are the originators of the American modern dance. They are the discoverers of pre-existent movement values in the human body not discerned before. They did not invent these movements. Nor have they manufactured their techniques like so many plastics off an assembly line (any delusion of mass production in college gymnasiums to the contrary notwithstanding). They have worked from a great legacy, which they first denied, then enriched, and gradually drew upon, and they now pass on this larger legacy to a younger generation, while still contributing to it. But the American modern dance founded by them is not limited to them. There have been, as there will continue to be, other influences.

OTHER CREATIVE MODERNS

Helen Tamiris—Hanya Holm

HELEN TAMIRIS

Helen Tamiris is a creative dancer from a different background. She did not stem from Denishawn. She was not included in the Bennington circle. Warm, generous, outgoing, and high-spirited, she was the kind of girl, who, when not invited to the party, could make a party of her own. She is now the most successful modern dance choreographer in the commercial theater. The success story begins with *Up in Central Park* (1945), rises with *Show Boat* and *Annie Get Your Gun* (1946), and finds her in the spring of 1948 sitting pretty on top of *Inside U. S. A.* A longer story of struggle and determination, of semi-flops, fizzles, half-hits, and genuine triumphs precedes it. She began her concert career in 1927, as Tamiris, a stage name already then acquired. She was born Helen Becker, and did not until late in her career prefix her first name to the exotic pseudonym. Although some of her intimates call her

Tam, and others call her Helen, she is best known in the dance world by her original *nom de danse*.

Tamiris is a glamour-gal with the added attraction of intelligence. She has a penetrating mind, a wealth of ideas, and, that excellent thing in woman, a low, modulated voice. Nobody ever denied that she could dance like Terpsichore afire. But in the early days her choreography was somewhat snootily regarded. "Get a choreographer!" was a cry of the time and of the field whose pioneers started off without a standard repertory. Considering the developments in her career, and in the whole modern dance movement, it is amusing to read in an old *Dance Observer* (1934) that she was far too theatrical in style and get-up. She was no plain-jane and she had no intention of looking like one. She designed her own costumes, and probably made them as economically as any of them, but she was not averse to pinning a flower in her hair or swishing a saucy petticoat. She did many other things that were not according to the gospel of the hour, but were later quite the thing.

Her native spontaneity, buoyancy, and zest were sometimes mistaken for flamboyance. Her strong, animal vitality was sometimes referred to (but not in print) as a streak of vulgarity. Of course no girl with such an extravagant sheaf of shining curls, such deep, laughing, serious blue eyes, could escape the claws of her own sex at least. There was never a dull moment when Tamiris danced. She was a dancy dancer, all spring and aliveness. She was lively theater, even at concert pitch. But she was more than that. She was a reflective person who knew the time of day in the contemporary world. "I have always felt," she has told me, "that no artist can achieve full maturity unless he recognizes his role as a citizen, taking responsibility, not only to think, but to act."

As a *gamine*-child the small Helen was improvising dances in the streets of New York's lower East Side. She was the daughter of Russian-Jewish immigrants, growing up among poor people. It was an artistic family—one brother became a painter, another a sculptor and musician—and a careful one. At the age of eight she was sent to Irene Lewisohn's dance classes at the Henry Street Settlement (before the Neighborhood Playhouse was formed) to keep her from running wild. On the family's insistence, she reluctantly finished high school. Whereupon she got herself accepted in the Metropolitan Opera Ballet School, and was soon dancing in the *corps de ballet.* Here, under tutelage of Rosina Galli, she learned Italian ballet at its most rigid. At the end of two years, on a lend-leash from the Metropolitan, she toured South America as a sort of second *première danseuse* with the Bracale Opera Company. She returned for one more year at the Met, vowing it would be her last.

Her free spirit and strong, healthy body cried out for freer, stronger movement. She looked for it in the teaching of Michel Fokine, but his sense of freedom was not free enough for her. She tried a little diluted Duncan, but that was too bland. Meanwhile, to earn her living, she was appearing as the specialty dancer, Tamiris, in night-clubs and movie-house presentations, under John Murray Anderson. After six months in his *Music Box Revue,* she retired to spend a year and a half by herself working for a dance form that would express the life of her time in a way that was right for her. A solo program called *Dance Moods* was the result. It was presented under management of Daniel Mayer, Inc., at the Little Theater, New York, on October 9, 1927. The pianist was Louis Horst, Martha Graham's musical director, who played for, and encouraged, most of the incipient moderns of those days.

There were several dance-newsworthy aspects to this first recital, and many of the dances contained the seeds of more extensive developments. One was the use of modern American composers—Louis Gruenberg, John Powell, and George Gershwin. Another was a dance without music, *The Queen Walks in the Garden,* the first silent dance in America except the Humphrey-Denishawn *Tragica.* And a third was the serious treatment of jazz rhythms in the selection of excerpts from Gershwin's *Rhapsody in Blue,* called simply *1927.* Of the twelve pieces given, *1927, Circus Sketches* (Powell), and *Impressions of the Bull Ring* (Calleja) remained longest in the repertory. The last was, in fact, performed years later at the Radio City Rainbow Room. One little item, *Subconscious* (Debussy), was hardly noticed at the time. It is not a subject that Tamiris ever dwelt overlong upon. But its inclusion in her first program shows that it had already entered the public domain of American dance. What concerned Tamiris was just that—American dance. On this point her first program carried her from conjecture to conviction. To be an American dancer meant to dance in terms of American rhythms and going to American sources so far as possible.

Her second program, given also at the Little Theater, this time under management of the New Art Circle, on January 29, 1928, was divided into *American Moods* and *Moods Diverse*. It was again a solo program, with Louis Horst the accompanist. Conspicuous were the *Prize Fight Studies* to beaten strings; and the two spirituals—*Nobody Knows the Trouble I See* (music arranged by J. R. Johnson) and *Joshua Fit the Battle of Jericho* (arranged by Lawrence Brown)—which presaged a development that was to come near being the signature of her career. The *Twentieth Century Bacchante*, like the *Amazon* of the first program (both with music by Gruenberg), was vivid with the bold, declarative presence of the dancer. *Harmony in Athletics* (Gruenberg) was another significant item in the American section, which drew exclusively on the music of American composers. For *Moods Diverse*, the modern French school was largely drawn upon, as in *Gayety* (Schmitt); *Hypocrisy* (Satie); *Perpetual Movement* (Poulenc); and *Peasant Rhythms: Of Worship, Joy, Toil* (Stravinsky). *Portrait of a Lady* (Schmitt), and *Impressions of the Bull Ring* were repeated from the first program.

Shortly after this recital Tamiris was invited by the Mozarteum Society to dance at the Salzburg Festival. She was the first American dancer to appear there since Isadora, and the two in succession must have given the Austrians a rather exaggerated impression of the pulchritude and originality of American women. Like Isadora, Tamiris never had enough money. Her expenses were paid by the philanthropist, Otto Kahn, whom she had fortunately met through a friend of hers, Horace Liveright, the publisher. She went first to Paris, and, again like Isadora, was immediately surrounded by artists of every kind. Friends, new and old, demanded a recital, and she gave one at the Salle Rudolf Steiner on July 5, 1928. The Salzburg recital, with the Austrian composer, Felix Petyrek, her accompanist, followed on August 7, at the Stadt Theater. Great enthusiasm, much interest, much debate were stirred by both recitals, which consisted of the contents of her second New York program.

The success of the Salzburg performance brought an invitation

from the *Novembergruppe* in Berlin to give a midnight concert at
the *Gloria Palast,* a motion picture house, which she did on February 18, 1929. For this program she created two new dances, *American Serenade #1* (Sonatina for Radio) and *American Serenade #2*
(Sonatina for Radio), with music composed for them by George
Antheil, who was living in Berlin at the time. These dances did not
satisfy her. To perform for European audiences was one thing; to
create in the European atmosphere was another. Something about
the environment of old cultures overwhelmed and constrained her.
She knew then that she could never transplant herself. She belonged
in the country where she had a sense of always beginning, of contributing to a new and growing culture that was a living reality.
The tour was triumphant and stimulating. She met leading radical
artists—Picasso, Kees van Dongen, George Grosz, Palucca, and
Mary Wigman (though she did not see Wigman dance until 1931,
in the United States). She had a wonderful time, but once she had
left Europe, she did not wish she were there.

The returned traveler was greeted by an overflow audience for
her recital at the Martin Beck Theater, New York, on April 7, 1929;
and the program was repeated at the Cort Theater the following
Sunday. New dances were: a third spiritual, *Swing Low Sweet
Chariot* (arranged by J. R. Johnson); *Popular Rhythms* (W. C.
Handy); *Dance of the City,* to siren accompaniment; *Revolutionary
March* to assorted percussions; and the two *American Serenades*
created in Berlin. In the fall of the year came her first choreographic
job for Broadway. This was Michael Gold's *Fiesta,* a musical play,
presented by the Provincetown Playhouse on September 17, 1929,
at the Garrick Theater. The settings were by Cleon Throckmorton
and the direction by James Light; "Incidental Dances," the billing
read, "by Tamiris." Two subsequently prominent modern dancers
in the company were Sophia Delza, who teaches and lectures now,
and Esther Junger, now a Broadway choreographer.

As was to happen again with Tamiris, the dances received better notices than the play. The significant thing about them was that
though the big festival dance in the third act stopped the show, the
dances as a whole were integrated into it, and not separate show
pieces. John Martin, with his usual perspicacity, was quick to dis-

cern the importance of this new use of dance in theater, to theater, and dance. "The warp and woof of the play," he wrote, "are in the dancing." In October Tamiris opened the School of the American Dance. It was her first school and the beginning of her group. Her purpose was to build an indigenous American technique and a company who could use it expressively.

As soon as the school was in operation she conceived the idea of the Dance Repertory Theatre and approached Martha Graham, Doris Humphrey, and Charles Weidman with her plan. At that time each dancer, considering Humphrey-Weidman as a unit, had a separate audience of devotees who never ventured to see what the other moderns were doing. Tamiris thought that by appearing together in one theater, sometimes jointly, sometimes in individual programs, the modern dancers could develop a larger and less specialized audience, one that would come to see modern dance rather than personalities. The others agreed and the Dance Repertory Theatre was organized, with Tamiris its president and Helen Arthur, of Actor-Managers, the business manager. Mrs. W. K. Vanderbilt, Miss Anne Morgan, and Mrs. Ralph Jones headed the list of patrons. The season opened at the Maxine Elliott Theater, New York, on January 5, 1930 and continued for nine weekend recitals.

During the season Tamiris introduced her first group work and the innovation of the self-accompanied dance. This was *Triangle Dance,* for three girls and herself, each carrying a triangle and playing it as she danced. The triangles were of different sizes and timbres, and the interest was primarily in the use of them while dancing. It was later expanded into a larger group dance. In the same spirit of adventure was her solo, *Lull,* with cymbals; and the group *Wood Block* of the second Dance Repertory season. The experiment was a resort to the basic primitive in her search for the basic truths of dance. Apart from the experimental dances was the solo, *Dirge,* of the first season, a subtly and singularly evocative dance of expressivity.

In the second season Agnes de Mille joined, distinguished patrons were added, performances were given at the Craig Theater, and Tamiris prepared an ambitious work for her year-old group. *Olympus Americanus (A Twentieth Century Ballet)* called for twelve dancers. Its themes were: "Basking in the Sun," "Dance on an Ancient Theme (Priapic Ritual)," "Dance to Hermes and Aphrodite," "The Races," and "Triumphant." The music was composed for it by Aaron Copland. Tamiris, who did not then or later lean much on program notes, felt the need of one in this instance. The idea was "to weld the contemporary spirit with the classic," to relate, without narrative, "the accents of life in ancient Greece" to modern times. It was one of the first long works in modern dance, but not the first successful one. It ran forty minutes. It seemed longer. Tempus not only didn't fugit fast enough; it fidgeted instead. Naturally the response was negative. Tamiris was no group choreographer, it said in various places in fine print. But she approved of "The Races" and "Dance on an Ancient Theme," if nobody else did, and together with the "Dance to Hermes and Aphrodite" made a suite that lasted for several seasons.

The Negro Spirituals were the musts of her programs. Every new one was hailed with huzzahs. This was the thing she could really do, this was what she did best. *Crucifixion* was the new spiritual of that season; and another solo, *Dance of Exuberance* (and nobody could be moreso) also gained favor with public and press. Although Louis Horst was the musical director for both seasons, Genevieve Pitôt played the piano accompaniments for Tamiris in the second season, and this was the beginning of a long and valuable association. Miss Pitôt was soon composing the music for many of Tamiris's dances, and had her part in the formation and guidance of the group.

Unfortunately, the second season of the Dance Repertory Theatre was the last. The press had been, in the main, kindly and understanding. The public had enjoyed most the joint programs, and at these was turned away in large numbers. The box office returns had paid all expenses—just about. There had been enough success to catch the eyes of the Messrs. Shubert, who offered them a tour. The offer was turned down. Only Tamiris wanted to accept, because only Tamiris believed that all their precious individualities could remain intact while appearing in the same theater on the same program. Only Tamiris believed that the Dance Repertory Theatre could grow, and that artists and audiences could grow with it. The

American modern dance might have spared itself years of struggle for recognition if its leaders had shared her vision then. They could have had a place to dance, a possible subsidy—and the Shuberts, too.

Tamiris continued her experiments in the self-accompanied dance. In a program at the Guild Theater on November 29, 1931, she did *Mourning Ceremonial,* with drums; and at the New School for Social Research on December 18, 1932, *Gris-Gris Ceremonial,* with gourd rattles. This dance, based on primitive Negro rhythms, was revised for a group of Bahama Negro dancers who shared an engagement with her at the Lewisohn Stadium in the summer of 1933. It marked the end of the self-accompanied dances, but not of her predilection for Negro themes and rhythms. On the New School program were two new spirituals, *Go Down Moses* (arranged by J. R. Johnson), and *Git on Board Lil Chillun,* arranged by Lawrence Brown. Her interest in the themes, no doubt, was owing to her sympathy with an oppressed people. In the rhythms she found a solvent of expression. The uninhibited nature of the Negro dance, its extemporaneous air of freely expressing the feelings of the moment, would appeal to her love of the impromptu, the unpremeditated.

Not that the primitive dances are without tradition, or Tamiris's dances without form. But her dances always seemed to spring in gusts and freshets from her own essential danciness rather than to have been formulated on theory. Her rhythms were individuations of the basic, universal rhythms. There is no limit to the movement combinations that can be made, she once told me, but if they are made for effect, without impulsion, they amount to no more than beads on a string. "Dancing for technical brilliance alone loses its cords into life." Tamiris danced brilliantly, sometimes rampageously, because her cords were in life. There was little sensual smoldering about her dances. Hers was a healthy earthiness, clear as water, clean as flame. Human significance was the keynote, the vitalizing force, whether or not significant form was always the outcome. One obstruction to a more general acceptance of her early choreography may have been that she did not bow before the modern dance pedantries of the day. The tension-relaxation idol, the arbitrarily built climax, the broken surfaces in modern parlance, were largely ignored by her. Tamiris's dances spoke their own language and molded their own form. They were not highbrow or highfalutin. In the rousing thirties when modern dance was young and competitive, she turned out her share of provocative works. The *Walt Whitman Suite,* with music by Genevieve Pitôt, first performed at the Booth Theater, New York, on January 14, 1934, was very well liked. John Martin praised it as the high point of her compositions that far, and also placed her group "among the best of the dance groups." If anybody could choreograph Walt Whitman, it was the vigorous, democratic Tamiris. If anybody could dance "I Sing the Body Electric," it was the vibrantly electric she. The suite was in five parts: "Salut au Monde" (solo by Tamiris); "Song of the Open Road" (first movement), danced by Sydne Becker, Ida Soyer, Dvo Seron, Hilda Sheldon and Ida Tarvin; "I Sing the Body Electric" (Tamiris solo); "Song of the Open Road" (second movement), danced by the Misses Becker, Soyer and Tarvin; and "Halcyon Days" (Tamiris).

There followed at the Little Theater on April 15, 1934, *Toward the Light,* a cycle of five dances (three solos and two group), with special music by Henry Brant, arranged by Miss Pitôt. In this cycle Tamiris tried numbering the dances instead of naming them, in order to free them from the limitations imposed by titles. But it didn't work because it left people at a loss, not only as to how to look at the dances, but how to discuss them afterwards. Her idea had been to express her views of the social scene, at that time floodlighted by the depression, in a unified composition. At least one reviewer (E. E. in the *New York World-Telegram*) caught on, for he saw in the work a "definite preoccupation with things of the world around us and things that seem to matter." Tamiris finally gave the title "Dance of War" to No. 2 of the cycle, and the title "Work and Play" to No. 5, and by this concession kept them in her repertory for several years.

The next cycle of this period, *Cycle of Unrest,* was a manifesto of social consciousness in unmistakable terms. There were again five dances: "Protest" (Elie Siegmeister) by Tamiris; "Camaraderie"

(Siegmeister), group; "The Individual and the Mass" (Hindemith), Tamiris and group; "Affirmation" (Mosolov), Tamiris; "Conflict" (Brant), group. When first performed at the Civic Repertory Theater on January 14, 1935, it was called literal, short-breathed, after the popular formula—but it was not overlooked. Still on the social theme, *the* theme of the middle thirties, was *Harvest, 1935* in three parts: "Sycophants" (Hindemith), which is self-explanatory; "Middle Ground" (Shostakovich), a portrait of the parlor pink, employing Denishawn draperies in the modern manner; and "Maneuvers" (Hindemith—Debussy), an anti-war dance burlesquing the activities of rookies, sergeants, and brasshats. When the dancers assumed a cannon formation, discharging its members separately as cannon balls, the public was thrilled to see what it could so readily understand. But the high-minded *Dance Observer* and other critics frowned upon such obvious maneuverings. The work was performed in toto at the Venice Theater, New York, on November 2, 1935, and often served in pieces on later programs.

Momentum (Guild Theater, November 8, 1936) continued to explore the social scene. The score, consisting mainly of percussion and sound effects, was composed for it by Herbert Haufrecht. The movement themes were stated and interwoven in the action. "Unemployed," the first number, showed the group in downcast costumes hopefully faced with red, wielding long white poles, like spikes of defiance, in a modern stick dance. "Sh—Sh!" was a sound effect with movement accompaniment, the whole attesting the voice of the "Haves" trying to still the clamor of the "Have-nots." "Legion" (American, the) referred to the flag-waving patrioteers and noisome cut-ups of conventions, and "Nightriders" to the southern custom of lynching. In this grim carnival Tamiris's ebullient solo, "Diversion," a gaudy night-club dance, was particularly apt (as well as refreshing) depicting as it did the false gayety of despair. The final number, "Disclosure," was a warning processional in gas masks.

To Tamiris such danced propaganda was not incompatible with art, nor in itself reprehensible. "The validity of the modern dance is rooted in its ability to express modern problems," she has said, "and, further, to make modern audiences want to do something about them." In like spirit were her two solo comments on mental attitudes, the staccato and syncopated *Flight* (Mosolov), and the slightly balletic *Dance of Escape* (Siegmeister) of 1935. She drew freely on all her resources to say what she wanted to say; and she embraced every opportunity to enlarge them.

About this time her association with the Group Theater began. For two summers she taught dance movement to the actors, numbering among her pupils John Garfield and Franchot Tone, Cheryl Crawford and Elia Kazan. Kazan, then a dancer as well as actor, appeared in one of her large group compositions, and later she staged the incidental dances for *Gold Eagle Guy*. Her teaching was not a quickie course for turning actors into finished dancers, but a first aid to the art of acting through the fundamentals of body movement. Since the Stanislavsky principles on which the Group Theater was based include acting with the whole body instead of from the neck up, her training was quite in line. It opened new vistas on the infinite movement capabilities possible toward the delineation of character. It showed the actor how to handle the body to illumine a dramatic situation, and intensified the sense of rhythm that helps timing. Only the free, modern movement could accomplish all this, for ballet training is likely to lead to an artificial manner, the very opposite of natural acting.

The work was reciprocal. The actors studied with Tamiris, and she studied with them. She found in their adaptation of the Stanislavsky method a clarification of her own theatrical approach to dance performance and direction. She had always searched for the specific human motivation for movement and had resisted the abstract and the abstruse. The Group Theater teachings constituted a re-affirmation of what she believed in and a new incentive to its development. The inspiration spilled over into her group, which was already on a co-operative basis. She never had attempted to stamp her own personality on her dancers, but rather tried to utilize their personal qualities as the raw material of creation. Now, impressed by the Group Theater's achievements, she brought Lee Strasburg, their then leading director, to her studio, to teach them the fundamentals of acting. Their new knowledge equipped them for fuller participation in the group works.

Under booking of the Red Path Bureau, in 1936, Tamiris and a group of ten made a tour of the Middle West, which was largely virgin territory so far as modern dance was concerned. She gave a selection of dances from various periods of her career, and it is noteworthy that the audiences liked the earlier dances best. These audiences graded from the Union League Club in Chicago to a school auditorium in Hibbing, Minnesota, on the Masaba Iron Range. As was inevitable at the time, there were many college and university dates on the itinerary, and here she gave lecture-demonstrations in addition to the concert programs. The bedazzled deans and professors were astounded to hear a beautiful dancing girl get up and make sense when she spoke. Not only make sense, but speak intelligently, in a cultivated voice, of the importance and seriousness as art of something more often connected with frivolity—or worse. That dancers did not dance only with their feet, that dance could be serious enough to be taken seriously, was news.

These were busy, complicated years for the prosecuting artist, who had her finger in all sorts of pies. Not all her performances were at Broadway theaters. She appeared also in the Students Dance Recitals series, under the auspices of the Theater Union, the International Ladies Garment Workers Union, and so on. She was one of the prime organizers of the First National Dance Congress, and of the amalgamation of the New Dance League and other groups into the American Dance Association; and it is largely owing to her efforts as first president of the ADA, that dance got into the Federal Theater of the Works Project Administration. She went directly to Harry Hopkins in Washington to see that it got in, and she made more than one trip to Washington to keep it in. That the Federal Theater came to an untimely end is not her fault. That its New York dance division made a fine record before its demise is much to her credit.

A revision of *Salut au Monde* (August 5, 1936) was her first Federal Theater contribution. She developed the solo into a ballet of five episodes, using a textual adaptation of the poem by Winthrop Parkhurst and John Bovingdon, and herself writing an extensive program note, the essence of which is more tersely summed up in Whitman's own verse:

Each of us inevitable
Each of us limitless—each of us with his or her right upon the earth,
Each of us allow'd the eternal purports of the earth,
Each of us here as divinely as any is here.

Her second Federal Theater production, *How Long Brethren,* (May 6, 1937) was her first big success. It was a hit and a sell-out in its ten-week run, conjointly with Charles Weidman's *Candide* (in shortened version) at the Nora Bayes Theater, New York. It won the first of the *Dance* awards for modern group choreography. It departed from the modern conventions of the hour, for it was shamelessly theatrical and dependent on its music. But it reached and stirred a general instead of a specialized audience. It made a social comment that took.

The work was based on a selection from the modern Negro "Songs of Protest" recorded with phonograph and notebook by Lawrence Gellert, as he heard them in the fields and shanties of the South. The song structure was arranged by the indispensable Genevieve Pitôt to fit the choreographic structure, which in turn, had been phrased and accented to suit the rhythm and spirit of the songs. The Negro chorus seated at one side of the orchestra pit, left the stage free for the dancers. The episodes were: "Pickin' off de Cotton (ensemble); "Upon de Mountain" (Tamiris and ensemble); "Railroad," "Scottsboro," "Sistern an' Brethren" (all ensemble); and "Let's go to de Buryin' " (Tamiris and ensemble), an end piece that brought cheers to the throat. Even more affecting was *How Long Brethren* in a two-week run at the Forty-ninth Street Theater at the end of the year. For then the "Songs of Protest," with their note of indignation and purpose not to wait for Heaven for betterment, were preceded by four of the already famous solo spirituals to the plaintive songs of slavery, songs of resignation and hope only in Heaven. This was certainly one program wherein Tamiris's glorious dancing was not expended on inept choreography.

In the Federal Theater's *Trojan Incident,* a play with music and dance, presented at the St. James Theater, New York, on April 21, 1938, Tamiris had the speaking role of Cassandra. She interpreted the prophetess in dance movement, and also devised the group choreography. Curiously, in view of her first and later attainments in the field, one criticism was that the dances were not well integrated with the play. Wallingford Riegger had composed the score, which included chanting choruses placed in the stage boxes. Howard Bay had designed some effective settings. The production was reviewed by both dance and drama critics, and, with a great deal of pro and con writing, finally dismissed as an interesting experiment. Tamiris, always good at salvaging whatever she thought desirable, remade the *Cassandra Dance,* had it recostumed by Edythe Gilfond, and showed it in the Students Dance Recitals series the following season with more rewarding response.

Adelante (Forward) was one of the first of the big modern ballets. It was built for spectacle as well as for significance, and it had a story. Like *How Long Brethren,* which was not spectacular but was theatrical, it clearly pointed the way to better box office for modern dance via better theater. It was presented under the auspices of the Federal Theater at Daly's Theater on April 20, 1939, and ran for two weeks. It was an elaborate production lasting one hour, a dance for Spain, on a Spanish theme. Poems from modern Spain were translated by Eli Siegel and Rolfe Humphries, and additional verse was provided by Bob Whittington. The work called for a narrator and a chorus of twelve voices. The music was by Genevieve Pitôt. Sets and costumes were by Alexander Jones, lighting by Harry Peters. It was at this point that "Helen" Tamiris came in.

Adelante visualized in a series of flash-backs the thoughts of a Loyalist soldier between the shots of the enemy firing-squad and his death. It covered, in vivid stage pictures, a deal of historical background, on which, for a peasant, the soldier seemed remarkably well informed. He remembered the Renaissance, the Inquisition, the elegance and decadence of the Court, as well as personal history of love and death, marriage and war. Bill Matons was the blindfolded soldier, and Helen Tamiris the Beloved. Of the large supporting company the names of Mura Dehn, Ailes Gilmour, and Klarna Pinska have come most prominently to attention since. The order of scenes was: "In the Plaza," "Transition," "The Court (On the Balcony, In the Court)," "Love's Dance," "Chant for the Dead," "In the Church," "In the Village," "With the Generals," "Strange Encounter (Lady with the Fan, Recognition)," "Transition," and "Finale"—a march dedicated to the valor of the Spanish people. In many of these dances stylized suggestions of the Spanish idiom were embossed on the modern, as in the Court pavane, the folk dancing of the fiesta, and in Tamiris's fascinating Lady with the Fan. All were fast-moving impressions, tied into unified effect by the return to the scene of execution, and the triumphal coda of the peasants' march. This was a typical Tamiris production, bright, engaging, pleasurable, without being wholly exterior. It said clearly what it meant to say. It was not afraid of also saying it prettily. *Adelante, How Long Brethren,* and *Liberty Song* (which came a little later) are the three works Tamiris considers her best; and she looks forward to the time when she can present them again to larger audiences than before.

Not long after the closing of *Adelante,* the Federal Theater was closed by Act of Congress. This was a cruel blow to the modern dance, and Tamiris, who had been most concerned with the project, took it hardest. It was the first of a succession of blows to the new dance idea that had painfully come into being through the depression years, and had assumed a definite entity in spite of all handicaps. Now, just as it was well started and gathering momentum as a nationally known product, it was to suffer a temporary eclipse. War soon deprived it of a number of its men dancers, and made touring difficult when not impossible. Ballet had seized the popular fancy, was indeed in the ascendancy. Modern dance, having no financial backing to compete with the ballet's lavish, large-scale productions, was driven underground. Except for Martha Graham, who had somehow opened a magic door to all sorts of subsidized opportunities, the modern dancers, for the most part, took refuge in studio theaters. In these wayside shrines or temples of the concert dance, work of the highest excellence was to be seen, but not by a sufficiently large number of people.

Compulsorily, and rebelliously, Tamiris yielded to the trend. While serving as chief choreographer to the Federal Theater, she had given up her group and school in order to devote all her time to the work. It had not been easy, but it had been the happiest period of her career. The feeling of being wanted by the nation, paid for by the nation, along with other artists of the country a part of national life, the knowledge that modern dance was in the theater, where it belonged, had meant something close to fulfillment for her. The sense of shock and rejection at the abrupt shattering of her utopian ideal made the prospect of starting all over again look hopeless. But it was the only thing left to do. And she did it.

She found a large (when empty) basement in lower New York that, converted into a studio theater, became decidedly cramped when full. Here she reassembled her group and re-opened her school. She had little patience with such makeshift quarters after the space and equipment provided by the Federal Theater. She felt hampered by the lack of a stage, the inadequate lighting, limited musical accompaniment, and the necessity of going back to home-made costuming. "The nature of the first two works created in this period is significant," she has written me. "One, called *As in a Dream,* was an introverted psychological study expressed in a very obscure fashion. The other, satiric, called *Floor Show,* was con-sciously oriented to attract the attention of Broadway producers. I never felt that either work was anything but a desperate flounder-ing about. It took me another year to find myself."

Ironically, it was not *Floor Show,* which, packaged in seven numbers, made merry with night-club entertainment and shot laugh asides at various contemporaries, but the serious work, *Lib-erty Song,* that won the coveted spot, and that not in a Broadway show but in the then swank supper-club, the Rainbow Room. First presented on April 20, 1941, it was a smash hit with the studio audiences, and, as much for its intrinsic worth as for its success, al-most reconciled its creator to the sad business of giving sporadic performances in a stuffy basement. The work was so full of lusty life and love of freedom that it transcended the physical limitations of its setting. It was based on songs of the American Revolution, ar-ranged for voices, piano and percussion, by Genevieve Pitôt; and these song-dances were an outlet for Tamiris's sterling American-ism, with its foothold in tradition and liberal sense of progressive continuity. The first song, "What a court hath old England," for Tamiris and group, celebrated the revolutionary spirit on which our country was founded; the second, "My days have been so wondrous free," for Tamiris and partner, was overcast with the hues of wartime partings; "Bunker Hill," for Tamiris and small group, recalled the famous battle and its meaning for Americans today; and "Ode to the Fourth of July" was an optimistic view of national togetherness in a spirited folk dance by Tamiris and the full group.

On later programs the costumes were credited to Rhoda Rammelkamp; and Mimi Benzell (now of the Metropolitan Opera) and Leon Lishchiner were the singers. On still other programs there was a quartet of voices. Tamiris, like other modern dancers, did not fail to make alterations in choreography, costume, or accompaniment, whenever performance proved the need of them. It was the duet, "My days have been so wondrous free," that caught the eye of John Roy, the Rainbow Room director, and that ultimately took her out of the concert field. But prior to her first Rainbow Room appearance she took a flutter in the summer theater, an experience she looks back upon as a period of apprenticeship for her work in the Broadway Theater today.

The chief value of this experience was that it taught her to choreograph for a deadline, and for a cross section of the public. In the concert field she could take her time; the audiences were quick on the uptake, but too special. She appreciated the encouragement and support of the dance enthusiasts, but longed always to work for a larger public, to dance for all kinds of people. As dance director at Unity House, Forest Park, Pennsylvania, a vacation resort for members of the International Ladies Garment Workers Union, in the summer of 1941, she had to choreograph quickly for the weekly Saturday night revues and the Tuesday night dance concerts, and she had to remember that the audience was not solely dance-minded, but interested in all the other phases of the entertainment. Her own solos were probably no burden at all, for Tamiris's dancing always seemed to be a part of her.

Her goal even then was Broadway. And when the highlights of the summer's output were bunched together in a revue called *It's About Time,* and presented by Martin Blaine in New York at the Barbizon-Plaza Hotel's little theater on March 28, 1942, hopes rose high before they fell. The little show did not develop into a full-fledged Broadway production. After a second summer at Unity House, she spent a third at Green Mansions, Warrensburg, New York; and it all toted up on the profit side—of experience.

The Rainbow Room engagement opened on April 1, 1942 and ran for six weeks. Daniel Nagrin was Tamiris's partner, and the excellent Ida Soyer was featured. The program consisted of a group of Negro spirituals, the duet from *Liberty Song,* and a new duet called *Waterfront Serenade.* Mimi Benzell and Émile Renan sang the spirituals. Genevieve Pitôt was the musical director and pianist. The engagement was so successful it was repeated in the fall season, with some changes in cast and program. Daniel Nagrin had gone to war and Milton Feher took his place; Paul Creston replaced Miss Pitôt at the piano. Tamiris presented her new *Bayou Ballads,* a delightful suite of four dances based on folk songs of the Louisiana plantations: "Suzette," "When Your Potatoes Done," "Pity Poor Mlle Zizi," and "Little Carnival." Rosa Akerston and Mr. Renan were the singers. On the tide of these successes Tamiris was edging toward her goal.

Two side excursions in dancing for the good of a cause were also hugely successful, especially the first one, uncontaminated as it was by party politics. It was a patriotic endeavor to popularize meat-rationing during the war in a play, *It's Up to You,* written by Arthur Arent, directed by Elia Kazan, and presented by the United States Department of Agriculture. After the first performance, at the Skouras Academy of Music, New York, on March 31, 1943, it toured the neighborhood movie houses of Greater New York, under the joint auspices of the Skouras Theaters, the American Theater Wing, and the Food Industries, and had its final performance in Washington. With lyrics by Alfred Hayes and music by Earl Robinson, Tamiris's ballet, "Porterhouse Lucy the Black-Market Steak," was the life of the party. No other dancer in the whole modern field could lend herself with such disarming gayety and charm to this sort of social therapeutics, making the little lesson in loyalty palatable, even edible, to a vast public. On the subway circuit she found her favorite audience of just people; and among them miraculous cures must have taken place, for though the sample was irresistible, the example was moreso. Altogether "Porterhouse Lucy" made quite a splurge, even to decorating *Life* with a full-page spread.

Somewhat less popular (among "republicans and sinners" at least) was *The People's Bandwagon,* a barnstorming revue organized for the purpose of helping to elect Franklin Delano Roosevelt to the fourth term of his Presidency. The interracial cast included Mary Lou Williams, the Negro pianist; the Latin-American dance team, Orelia and Pedro; Will Geer, Lincolnian actor; and the folk singer, Woody Guthrie, among many others. Daniel Nagrin was back from soldiering to partner Tamiris in brief selections from the concert repertory and more topical material. The dances, songs, and sketches were addressed "to labor's millions," white and colored, Jew and Gentile, bond and free, not excluding white collar workers, or the occasional plutocrat who might be interested. The tour started on September 26, 1944 from Boston's gray and dignified Symphony Hall, and hit twenty-four major cities, sticking so far as possible to Dewey territory. The one-night stands weren't much fun, Tamiris told me afterwards, but the knowledge that modern dance could play a definite part in anything so important as a national election, bore her above the hardships.

Between political rallies Tamiris had two failures—in name only. That is, the musical plays flopped, but the dances she did for them sent out rapturous reports. *Marianne* opened on the road in January 1944, and died en route. Among the members of its superior dancing cast were Dorothy Bird, George Bockman, Lidija Franklin, Emy St. Just, Ida Soyer, Joseph Gifford, and Daniel Nagrin, who assisted Tamiris in the choreography. They, as well as all who saw them, loved the dances. *Stovepipe Hat* opened in Boston in May 1944 and did not live to tell its tale in New York. This musical folk play on Abraham Lincoln, in which he was symbolically represented by his hat and stick, had many enchanting qualities; but none so enchanting as the dances. Mary Anthony, Joseph Gifford, Lidija Franklin, George Bockman, and Daniel Nagrin (again assisting in the choreography) were in the cast.

Whether the *Marianne* dances were ever reincarnated, I can only guess. But from *Stovepipe Hat* the Indian ballet, led by Daniel Nagrin, was later reworked into the fabulously successful *Annie Get Your Gun.* Tamiris was working for peanuts that year. She works for peanuts no longer.

She was swept to success on what is commonly called "The Skating Ballet" in *Up in Central Park,* a musical comedy of no marked distinction in itself, that opened cold at the Century Theater, New York, on January 27, 1945. It was a period piece on the reign of Tammany Hall's Boss Tweed in the 1870's. The book was by Herbert and Dorothy Fields, music by Sigmund Romberg, costumes by Grace Houston and Ernest Schraps, and settings by Howard Bay. The charming tap dancer, Betty Bruce, had a leading role. Other dance notables were Saul Bolasni, Fred and Elaine Barry, George Bockman, and Daniel Nagrin (also choreographer's assistant). The so-called skating ballet was after the Currier & Ives print, "Central Park, Winter," and brought it to life in the most fresh and engaging manner. It was deceptively simple, for the ingenious choreography was more complicated than it appeared. The audiences, seeing attractively costumed, lilting movement that was easy on the intellect, had no idea they were looking at modern dance. But it was because it was modern dance, succinctly drawing from life, that it was so invigorating. One has only to compare this brief episode in a musical with the literal, long-drawn-out *Les Patineurs* of Frederick Ashton, presented by Ballet Theatre, to feel the difference.

"Currier & Ives" was not alone in its geniality of impact. The humorous "Up from the Gutter," "Rip Van Winkle," the wacky "Fireman's Bride" (with Betty Bruce frolicking on a fire-ladder), the folk-flavored "Maypole Dance," all had the lustihood of Tamiris's imprint. The one thing lacking was that she herself did not dance. She has not danced since she got caught up in the Broadway whirl, and has not taught since 1943. *Up in Central Park* ran for over a year in New York, spent another year on tour throughout the country, sent an overseas company to the European theater (of war), and has been filmed for Universal-International, with Tamiris staging the dances. In the release she gets a big by-line, the screen all to herself, but the dances (what is left of them) suffer, as most dances do, from movie presentation.

No less a success was the revival of *Show Boat,* with dances by Helen Tamiris, and with Pearl Primus the featured dancer. It opened at the Ziegfeld Theater, New York, on January 6, 1946, ran for over a year, and also had a long tour. Claude Marchant and Talley Beatty, former members of Katherine Dunham's company, had important roles; and for the road company, LaVerne French, another Dunham dancer, replaced Pearl Primus, thus transposing the part from feminine to masculine mode. As in *Up in Central Park,* the most spectacular dance was not the only good dance in *Show Boat.* The spot number was the tribal "Dance of the Dahomeys," but all sorts of ingratiating dancy numbers were braided into the action, in and around the songs. The primitive dances were done by the Negroes, the steppy modern dances, exempt from all reeling and writhing, by the white crew. The cast could not be called interracial like that of *The People's Bandwagon,* wherein artists were not separated according to color.

Of course what Tamiris uses on the Broadway stage is not concert dance; it is not the dance of impalpables, of imponderable weight and depth. It might be called modern dance in popular style; for, while it has strength and sinew and fiber, it collaborates with the show and with the audience in terms of light entertainment. It collaborates also with the creative dancers in a cast, as strongly evidenced in her use of the young modern, Valerie Bettis, and the bearded specialty dancer, Eric Victor, in *Inside U. S. A.* She has taken full advantage of Victor's phenomenal technique and eccentricities, and in Valerie she had almost a replica of her younger self to work with. Almost, but not quite, for there is a wide divergence in temperament. The resemblance is in stunning good looks, abundant physical energy, and prodigious dance ability. Valerie also has ideas of her own, and these no doubt were allowed to color the now famous "Haunted Heart" and "Tiger Lily."

The biggest hit of Tamiris's career (before the hit revue, *Inside U. S. A.*) was the musical, *Annie Get Your Gun,* launched at the Imperial Theater, New York, on May 16, 1946, and still holding on in the summer slump of 1948. However much of its success may be ascribed to the delectable earthiness of Ethel Merman's sharpshootin' Annie Oakley, there is a good margin for the dances. The show had everything—the Midas touch of Rodgers and Hammerstein, its producers, the tunes and verses of Irving Berlin, book by Herbert and Dorothy Fields, costumes by Lucinda Ballard, sets and lighting by Jo Mielziner, and direction by Joshua Logan. For the modern dance to keep pace with such a spectrum was in itself a triumph. The central ballet was the "Wild Horse Ceremonial Dance," led by Daniel Nagrin (who here, too, assisted in the choreography), followed by the "Adoption Dance," hilariously inducting Annie into the tribe; and there were a number of fetching songdances. For this choreography and that of *Show Boat*, Tamiris was named among the best dance directors of the 1945–46 season in *Variety's* list of bests.

In the fall of 1947 a second *Annie Get Your Gun* company was formed for Chicago and other major cities. Daniel Nagrin restaged the dances, as Tamiris was in Hollywood, and Barton Mumaw, former Shawn soloist, was the featured dancer. A London production, choreographed and directed by Tamiris, opened at the Coliseum on June 7, 1947, and became one of the shows of the year.

None of this actually meets Tamiris's conception of the ideal theater, wherein the arts of the theater are fused into a creative whole. But she recognizes the necessity of working within the medium when working for the Broadway theater, and can overlook a few sacrifices for the sake of making modern dance acceptable there. It is not a case of marrying for money, but of going where money is, for hers are not wholly monetary aims. She knows that modern dance brings a revivifying element to the commercial theater that cannot but eventuate in better theater.

Just before flying to London for her work on *Annie Get Your Gun*, and soon after its London opening, she had opportunity to work in close association with a man whose views of theater coincide with hers. Arnold Sundgaard is a writer of poetic imagination who thinks of dance and music as parts of speech, legitimate means of expressing ideas and emotions where words fail, and is not afraid to use them in unorthodox ways. Tamiris was associate director

(Anna Sokolow did the dances) of his play, *The Great Campaign,* produced by the Experimental Theater at the Princess Theater, New York, on March 30, 1947; and the choreographer for his musical play, *Promised Valley,* presented by the State of Utah in celebration of its centennial in the summer of that year.

Promised Valley opened in Salt Lake City on August 21, 1947, and ran for three and a half weeks. An outdoor theater seating 10,000 people had been constructed for the occasion, and it was filled to capacity nearly every night of the run. There was a large symphony orchestra and a chorus of one hundred voices. This was all of a vastness and a nature new to the choreographer, versed though she was in stage dancing from youth, and well accustomed to using voices (on a somewhat smaller scale) with her concert works. And when she found that she had succeeded in reaching the hearts of a Mormon audience with dances based on Mormon legend, she felt that it was another and a very special victory for modern dance. The legend, "The Cricket and the Gulls," the story of "Upper California," the duet, "Sparking on a Sunday Night," the Prologue and Epilogue that were choral ballets in themselves, were constituent, with words and music, to the basic story of the migration of the Mormon pioneers from the Eastern seaboard to Utah.

It was a thrilling project. The author, the choreographer and the musical director, Jay Blackton, were from the East. The composer, Crawford Gates, and the director, Dr. C. Lowell Lees, head of the drama department of the University of Utah, were of Salt Lake City. The singing stars, Alfred Drake and Jet MacDonald, the dance leads, Nelle Fisher and Barton Mumaw, were true New Yorkers (from all over the country); and Virginia Tanner of Salt Lake City was Tamiris's assistant and one of the dancers in the ensemble of thirty, which, auditioned by Tamiris the previous winter, had been culled from California, Colorado, and various cities and towns in Utah. Such an impressive interstate gathering for a purely state celebration was to Tamiris a foretaste of The Great American Theater. The production gave her the same kind of joy her work in the Federal Theater did.

Immediately after the completion of *Promised Valley,* she

flew to Hollywood to start the choreography for the film version of
Up in Central Park. And that was another kind of vastness, and
quite another story.

HANYA HOLM

Hanya Holm, one of the Big Four of Bennington,
has had the most far-reaching of extraneous influences on the
American modern dance. She came from Germany in 1931 to head
the New York branch of the Mary Wigman School, and from 1934
to 1940 was, with Martha Graham, Doris Humphrey, and Charles
Weidman, a leading teacher at the Bennington School of the Dance
and choreographer for its festivals. She has sent many a fine dancer
into the concert and theater fields, and in the spring of 1948 made
Broadway conspicuously on three counts. One of her star pupils,
Valerie Bettis, was the dance sensation of *Inside U. S. A.* She collaborated with José Ferrer in the direction of *The Insect Comedy* at
the New York City Center of Music and Drama, and choreographed
"The Eccentricities of Davey Crockett" for the three *Ballet Ballads*
that took Broadway by surprise.

It was quite an awakening for the New York drama critics. In
Valerie Bettis they discovered a dancer (who had been around town
for nearly ten years); and in *Ballet Ballads* they discovered dance,
although Helen Tamiris, Agnes de Mille, and others, had been
showing it to them for some time. The thing about *Ballet Ballads*
was that it was an all song-and-dance show. First presented by the
Experimental Theater at the Maxine Elliott, it made such a hit it
was removed to the Music Box for a steady run. The three ballads
were bits of theatricalized folklore done to lyrics by John La
Touche and music by Jerome Moross, in the most briefly indicative
of décors by Nat Karson, who also supplied the costumes. Mary
Hunter was the director, but each ballad had a separate choreographer. "Susanna and the Elders," a Bible story for grown-ups as

told by a revivalist, was by the former Humphrey-Weidman dancer, Katherine Litz, who danced the title role with all the sumptuous beauty of her modern style. "Willie the Weeper," perhaps the funniest, at least the rowdiest, was by the ballet dancer, Paul Godkin, who played Willie opposite Sono Osato's Cocaine Lil. This was folklore of the city pavements in blues and boogie-woogie tones (the dancers hadn't taken up bebop then). But Hanya's modern choreography for the tall tale of the American frontiersman was the most solid and imaginative of the three. Although she had been staging dance productions for years, she had been regarded primarily as the ranking educator in the American modern dance.

She had brought to the United States the dance ideas of Central Europe, the discipline, analysis, and anatomical soundness of thorough, scientific dance pedagogy. She had brought the German concept of space as a viable factor of movement. A dancer necessarily deals with space, no matter how he moves. He cannot avoid it, for dance occurs in space as well as in time. But Hanya, artistic descendant of Wigman and Laban, made more of a point of it, and so enlarged the consciousness of an element that was already there. She had brought her German background, which included training for a musical career at the Dalcroze Institute (since her childhood desire to dance was not approved by her parents), followed by years of close association with Mary Wigman. Pavlova had been her first inspiration, but an early Wigman recital was the determinator. Hanya was a member of the original Wigman group that toured Europe with high success, and was for ten years co-director and one of the chief instructors at the Wigman Institute in Dresden. She helped prepare and appeared in Mary Wigman's production of Albert Talhoff's *Totenmal,* the famous anti-war memorial, at the Dance Congress of 1930 in Munich.

This was the atmosphere the German dancer brought to the land of her adoption in 1931. In return she found a new sense of space, space in abundance, without restriction, and freedom to move in it at will. She found also a new approach to modern dance. For five years she taught as head of the New York Wigman School, and, as visiting instructor, at various schools and colleges across the country, while quietly assimilating the new rhythms of the vigorous American scene. The new impressions gradually infiltrated and perhaps fertilized the old. They did not overpower or destroy what was basic in her traditions. But out of the alembic there emerged a new Hanya, a new technique, that was not American born or American made, but was, like herself, like many others in the dance world—like a large part of our whole polygenous nation for that matter—transplanted European or hyphenated American. She still speaks with a German accent, and so does her dance.

As early as 1932 Mary Wigman on her second visit to the United States observed the difference between what was going on in American dance and what in the German, saw also what was happening to Hanya; so she was not surprised when a few years later her long-time colleague asked to be disassociated from the Wigman School, realizing that developments here justified the detachment. The separation was amicably agreed upon in 1936, and thereafter Hanya conducted the studio under her own name. She became an American citizen on September 14, 1939, and her son served in the armed forces of the United States in the late world war.

When Hanya began her work in New York she was confronted by a group of eager students who wanted to master the new form in the ten-easy-lessons way. To their advertisement-fed minds it was only natural. Such superficiality was a shock to the conscientious German teacher, and she immediately proceeded to break it down. She organized a schedule requiring daily attendance of all who expected to make dance a career. Then, systematically imparting her knowledge, she tried to supplant the careless, get-it-quick attitude with a more profound idea of the meaning and substance of dance. The response was gratifying. By penetrating to the core of each individual student she quickened their sensibilities, and she soon had classes that were both malleable and challenging. She was stimulated to new methods of technique and instruction in order to meet the needs of these strong and zealous young Americans. It took considerable readjustment on her part. But like all creative teachers, she learned and grew as she taught.

Watching a professional class of hers one afternoon in the spring of 1947, I got a close-up of pure movement, and a rousing vicarious work-out. The little blonde teacher, her honey-colored hair somewhat darkened by the passing of time, but her china-blue eyes as wide as ever, stood erect in her short black tunic, gently beating out the rhythms on a knee-high drum, and issuing her oddly philosophical directions *mezza voce*. Her assistant, Alwin Nikolais, led the class, which was swinging legs.

"Don't toss the leg. Reach into space with it. Have dignity in the leg. Don't live alone in the leg. Let the rest of the body live with it."

The class had been bending and stretching on the floor, balancing without the aid of a bar, and practicing *pliés* from what looked to me like the five ballet positions, with a sixth, progressing backward, like the fourth in reverse, added. All through the lesson I kept seeing occasional resemblances to ballet, and hearing, or so I thought, ballet terminology. Hanya assures me that this is not so, that she has never studied ballet and does not employ it in her technical system. Although outwardly some of the movements may look balletic, their very texture and base is different because they come from a different impulse, she says.

The difference lies as much in the ratiocination as in the manner, perhaps. At any rate, these techniques were done in bare feet with conscious flexure of the pedal muscles; and no ballet master would recognize either the method of instruction or the results. One felt that the soft, beguiling orders came fresh every lesson. Here again words played their inevitable part in dance. For the turned-out thigh:

"Don't frustrate the hip." For rising on the half-toe:

"To carry out verticality in the body, think high. Stay high, even when bending the knees. Be aware of what you are doing. Don't do it mechanically. Live into it." When they went from *plié* to *relevé*:

"Put mental image plus purpose into it. Each movement should be a felt and guided movement." And when they came to the pendulum swing:

"Swing gently, or swing with gusto. Decide which is your purpose. It is not just back or front swings. The leg is addressing the space behind. The leg is addressing the space in front. Each movement must be new as it is repeated."

The class understood this language, which to me was a revelation. The directions, with their illustrations by the young dancers, showed me dance notes, the makings of dance melody. It was dance without drama, without pantomime. Nobody was imitating a bluebird, nobody was denoting heartbreak. The only emotion was that begotten of movement. These were the notes; the phrases were to come later. At Bennington I had watched Hanya with one of her classes, devoting an hour to feet. The students began with flexing them, acquiring balance on them in varying positions, rising on them and leaping from them, and finally, through sequences of multiple shadings, building to a climax of thrilling turns on them. Now, in this professional class, in her caressing voice, she referred to "making fists of the feet." Then the fine points of focus were dealt with, the left arm held high as the dancers took a long step forward, body leaning to the right, face looking away from and returning to the upheld arm, "holding the same thought in the arm."

"Don't tighten the muscles. Be controlled but not tense. There must be pulse, even in steps."

Now they did *changements*. "Take the air, not with fear, but with confidence." For suspensions, "there must be buoyancy in the chest."

The class ended with special runs, leaps, and jumps, two by two diagonally across the floor. "Sweep into it." And they swept. It was most enlivening and unusual. It was movement unalloyed.

The proof of the theory was in the classroom. It used to be in the technique demonstration. Hanya could take five or six girls from her concert group and set them, in their dance dresses of the covered-up look, against a plain cyclorama or in a bare gymnasium, with brilliant effect. The brilliance was all in the movement, in the lapidary precision of attack and release, the bright linking bands of smooth legato, the glittering forays into the air. All done without showmanship; and most methodically presented. Hanya would explain each problem as it came, working through simple progressions and combinations to the rhythmic complexities. There were differentiations between movement of pulse and movement of beat (this done without accompaniment), small and large movements in the single body and in the group of bodies in space.

Space studies of direction and dimension, of planes and extensions, wove striking floor patterns and aerial designs. There were high-powered skips and leaps and twisting turns in air that rivaled the most finished ballet execution and surpassed it in communicable energy and sense of flight. Some of the solo passages were spectacular. But every dancer in that select group was a virtuoso. The heart was not caught up in any of this. Not a palpitation was stirred, no tear jerked, no laughter unloosed. Yet it was terrifically stirring, moving, and unloosening all the same. The appeal and response were entirely kinesthetic, and it was kinesthetically satisfying in the fullest sense of the word. No stage production or concert piece of Hanya's that I have seen has been half so exhilarating.

A typical demonstration program in print states the outline of her distinctive presentation, especially in regard to the space études. When you read such items as "Space shattered by explosive quality arising from inner excitement of the dancer whose body is the focal point," or "Space as scenery suggested through descriptive movement," or "Effervescent movement motivated by excitement coloring space," or "Resurgent plunging into depth," you know that here is an approach unlike any other. What seems weighty in words (Hanya's space theory is rather involved) is light and ingratiating to see.

She has never danced much in this country. She did not come as a prima donna dancer and did not strive to become one. Her solo parts have all been one of a piece with her choreography, and not star-vehicular. She took six years to acclimate herself before she made her New York debut as either choreographer or dancer. When, in 1936, she first danced before the semi-private but very professional audience at Bennington, she seemed scared and inhibited, bound to small, tight planes, quite unlike the heroic Wigman scale from which her technique derives, quite unlike the large, free elasticity of her own dancers. She was probably suffering from stagefright before that stern jury of her peers. In later performances there was discernible a freer, lyrical quality of movement, a small-scaled style of her own that befitted her diminutive stature and dresden-doll appearance. On the Bennington program, her solo, *In Quiet Space,* to percussion accompaniment by Franziska Boas, was so subdued that it was uncommunicative. She told me afterwards that rising on her toes was not just standing tiptoe, the movement of rising towered above the physical expression of it; that dance projected into space as an unspoken conversation among many people rather than as a duologue between dancer and spectator. But this solo, at the time, looked more like a self-communing monologue, and did not tower or project.

The group dance, *City Nocturne,* to music by Wallingford Riegger, satirized the jazz-spangled night life of the metropolis with bumpy, twitchy motions and much of what the late Hugh Lofting put into his fabulous story-book animal, the push-me-pull-you. It was nothing out of the ordinary. It only said a little differently what had been said before. Nor was the satirical solo, *Four Chromatic Eccentricities,* with music by the same composer, particularly original. The first set forth overflowing, undisciplined energy and emotion; the second, trying to catch the uncatchable, now frivolous, now indolent in mood; the third, the self-dramatization of self-pity without depth of feeling; and the fourth, the foolish dissipation of all one's resources, a crazily ridiculous chasing of one's own tail. There were a number of Four Somethings or Other in circulation about that time, dating from Martha Graham's *Four Insincerities* of 1929. Here then was nothing much new in the way of satire and only a little new in the way of dance.

The *Dance in Three Parts* ("A Cry Rises in the Land," "Interlude," and "New Destinies,") with music again by Riegger, was of more serious import. A cry was certainly rising in Europe and reverberating around the world, and artists were among the first to hear it. But before the cry had swelled into a world-wide scream, it was too big for any but the greatest artists to handle. Derangement of such overwhelming portent could not be formalized in dance. Divination of the engulfing tragedy to come, hope for a far tomorrow, were not enough. Yet from the Spanish Civil War on, the modern dance stage was crowded with gloomy figures groping dismally about or massing in militant formations to express the turbulent undercurrents the dancers felt more strongly than they could convey, and then gathering in a grand apotheosis of wish-fulfillment for prosperity and peace. None but the great, the seers and the prophets of irresistible urge, could infuse movement with an iota of the feeling of the pre-war period, could begin to say in dance what Picasso's *Guernica,* for example, said in paint. *Dance in Three Parts,* of course, did not refer to Spain. What it did refer to was a delicate subject for a German dancer to handle. It may have been the element of equivocation that weakened it. It was, at any rate, no more than average. These were all early essays in choreography. With lesser items, *Primitive Rhythm 1, Passing Moods, Dance Stanzas,* etc., they were performed in various schools and colleges in the environs of New York State.

Hanya's first major composition, *Trend,* produced at the Bennington Festival of 1937, introduced her to New York City dance society in December of that year. This was a non-literary epic with innovations in stagecraft. This was really something new. It had been created during the summer while she was in charge of the Workshop Group, and was presented in the Vermont State Armory. The music, for flute, oboe, bassoon, trumpet, piano and percussion, was by Wallingford Riegger, with a mechanical reproduction of Edgar Varèse's *Ionization* (courtesy of Mirko Paneyko) for the closing episode, "Resurgence." The costumes were by Betty Joiner and the setting and lighting by technicians at the School—Gerard Gentile and assistants. The program note read:

> *Trend* is a picture of man's survival when the usages of living have lost their meaning and he has fallen into routine patterns of conformity. Though in this direction of decadence lie only catastrophe and ultimate annihilation, there emerges out of the ordeal itself a recognition of the common purposes of men and the conscious unity of life.

When *Trend* arrived at Mecca Temple (now the City Center), it had been expanded and altered in some details. A new closing section, "Assurance," with the *Octandre* of Varèse for accompaniment, had been added. All the music was mechanically reproduced through Mr. Paneyko's novel electrical equipment, and the resultant noise-effect was generally considered a great advance in music for the dance. Arch Lauterer had built a world for dance forecasting the current vasty reaches of the Hollywood production number. It consisted of inclined planes and broken rhythms in multiple ramps and steps to join the upper and lower levels, with screens for wings and bare wall for backdrop, lighted to an eerie and chilling loneliness. The auditorium floor was cleared, the audience seated in the balconies, enhancing the sense of spatial immensity. The costumes, retained from Bennington, were along modern dance princess lines, nearly uniform, but for Hanya's long scarlet dress. A new program note read:

> *Trend* expresses the rhythm of our Western civilization in which social confusion overlays, but cannot eradicate, the timeless creative forces that persist beneath the surface of contemporary existence.
>
> The hectic drive of meaningless activity and strife, apathy and routine patterns of conformity, in which all the vital forces of life are debased or distorted, lead to ultimate disintegration.
>
> Out of the ordeal itself there emerges an awareness of the essential purposes of living; out of despair a renewed affirmation.

The work, danced by an augmented group led by Hanya's concert dancers, was in six parts: "Mask Motions (a) Our Daily Bread" was a piston-like group depiction of joyless, regimented labor in the industrial age and the consequent routine of commonplace living, "(b) Satiety" represented the surfeited idlers of society, bored with their own sterility. "Episodes" particularized the general doldrums in a series of solos: "The Effete," by Louise Kloepper, against a background of group inertia punctuated here and there by a swaying figure (like accidentals in music), typified neuroticism in febrile movements; "Lucre Lunacy," by Keith Coppage, was an exhibition of money madness; "From Heaven, Ltd.," by Lucretia Wilson, was a shaft at sawdust trail evangelism or freak cults; "Lest We Remember," by Elizabeth Waters, the refuge in narcosis, through drugs or less tangible mediums; and " 'he,' the Great," by Henrietta Greenhood, misplaced hero-worship in a deceptive political savior. The group section, "Cataclysm," was the struggle of all these conflicting forces, feelings and masses in movement counterpoint; "The Gates are Desolate," a half-mournful, half-hopeful solo of awakening, by Hanya; "Resurgence," the mass stirring of hope; and "Assurance (a world primal again)" hope substantiated and the will to make the world right revived. It was the age-old theme of the victory of good over evil after a prolonged engagement with whatever phases of diabolism are uppermost at the moment, that began with the tribal dances, and persists to this day in art, literature, movies, mysteries, and funny papers.

No synopsis can do justice to the musical continuity of flowing, ebbing movement, to the powerful group designs, the nuances of solo and ensemble passages, or the apt and sometimes waggish comment of Riegger's score, as in the distorted hymn tunes for "From Heaven, Ltd." It unfolded like a colossal panorama of diverse movement and music patterns. It was stupendous. It left me cold. I felt lost in the grim netherworld of excessive spatiality. The all-percussion *Ionization* sounded like a sublimated Tin Pan Alley; *Octandre* was harsh, if less violent. The dancers were so many forms and figures, not people. What the rest of the audience made of it I don't know, but an irreverent layman behind me remarked during Hanya's slow solo, "Come on, baby, you'll never get anywhere at that rate."

However, the regular dance audience gave the work a cordial reception. It ran for two nights, December 28 and 29, 1937, and was later given in excerpts elsewhere in New York and on tour. More frequent full-length repetition of *Trend,* whereby deficiencies in the beholder and in the work itself could possibly have been remedied, might have mellowed it into warmth and eventually established it as a classic of the modern repertory. It was laudable, at all events, as an intelligent departure from convention, and for the dignity and magnitude of its form. John Martin, who could not extol the work enough, awarded it his annual citation for the best choreography of the year. It was much discussed in newspapers and dance magazines, and the *Magazine of Modern Art* (March 1938) had a double-truck display of photographs, prepared for it by Barbara Morgan, with articles by Hanya ("*Trend* Grew Upon Me"), by Arch Lauterer on "Design for the Dance," and by Harrison Kerr on "Reproduced Music for the Dance." This is a work that ought to be revived.

Outside of New York Hanya's concerts were mainly under the auspices of educational or art institutions. In the 1937–38 season she made her first extensive tour, to the Middle West and as far south as Maryland, concentrating, because of the time and energy spent on *Trend,* on her unique demonstration programs. She had actually, in November 1936, made her American concert debut under the aegis of Pro-Musica in Denver, Colorado, at which time she spent an intensive week giving performances, demonstrations, lectures, classes, and radio talks throughout the state.

The Bennington Festival of 1938 brought two new works, *Dance Sonata,* to music by Harrison Kerr, and *Dance of Work and Play,* with music by Norman Lloyd. *Dance Sonata* was an experiment in using music composed before the dance but with the dance in mind. The idea was, as the title implies, to do with motor phrases what the composer does with musical phrases, to compose a sonata in movement. The movement was not to interpret the music; it was to have its own logical development. Some critics saw more repetition than development in the movement patterns, but on the whole it was an excellent example of absolute dance, affecting as pure dance and pure music can be. The four parts were: "Maestoso," by concert and apprentice groups; "Grazioso," by Hanya and a number of her polished soloists; "Andante Moderato" and "Allegro Vivace," both by the groups.

Dance of Work and Play dealt with work as "an essential part of man's being," with mutations of attitude, happy and unhappy, through growth and experience, rounding out to "a mature satisfaction in work." In each of its six parts—"Origin," "The Empty Handed," "The Driven," "The Solitary," "The Communal," and "Synthesis"—Hanya's solo statements introduced and concluded a theme worked out by the group in a combination of free movement and miming that was not always clear. In both works, the abstract and the concrete, the technical interest was paramount.

In the 1938–39 season Hanya made her first transcontinental tour. Produced on tour, at the Goodman Theater, Chicago (October 23, 1938), was her newspaper satire, *Metropolitan Daily* (music by Gregory Tucker), a great hit on the road, and the first modern dance group composition to be televised, it is said. It was done by the National Broadcasting Company. This, *Dance Sonata,* and *Dance of Work and Play,* all satisfactorily costumed by Betty Beebe, had their first New York performances at the Guild Theater, February 19, 1939. *Metropolitan Daily,* with its score interwoven of popular tunes, treated more elaborately a subject already touched upon by Trudi Schoop in *Want Ads.* Hanya presented not only the "Want Ads" (sentimental storiettes) but the "Financial Section" (stock-tables going down); "Scandal Sheet" (as may be); "Society Section" (certain ladies not averse to publicity); "Foreign News," as despatched by a conservative and a sensational reporter; "Comics," a free fantasia on the parti-colored Sunday supplement; and "Sports," wherein all-girl teams played ball as girls do and boys don't (but tennis and cheer-leading were under control), winding up with a whirlwind finish that brought down the house. Apparently nobody missed the music, theater, dance, art, and book-review columns—about all that was left out. If the humor was in the broad Teutonic vein of the Continental variety show and of the Central European choreographer in general, it was sufficiently overlaid with Hanya's Americanized point of view. The knowing New York audience rejoiced at having something from her that was unreservedly entertainment.

On the same program, *Tragic Exodus,* with music by Vivian Fine and costumes by Miss Beebe, had its first performance. This work, in which Hanya returned to her serious concern with world affairs, won the *Dance* award for the best modern dance group choreography of the year. These awards, begun in 1936 when Joseph Arnold Kaye was the modern dance critic for the magazine, and discontinued when he left some years later, were for choreography as distinguished from performance, for the purpose of upholding the principles of modern-dance composition. In this case the recognition was of the work's "uniform excellence as a dance," and because it had "emotional appeal and topical significance" without submerging the dance quality in them. Too often, Mr. Kaye remarked in his announcement, "social and political subject matter" obtruded upon the choreography with nullifying effect.

Here, of course, the subject matter was taken to be the criminal persecution of the Jews in Nazi Germany. It was before the horror camps had divulged all their hideous secrets, but what was then known to be going on was horrifying enough. The reference could have been to any of the great flood of refugees from war and persecution pouring across the map of Europe and Asia. But while the ominous boom in the percussion suggested the inescapable over-all fireworks of destruction, the singing voice (by Peter Thorne) suggested the Semitic chant or the wailing wall, and the enfilade of sorrowful figures suggested the depths of homelessness that only the Jewish exile could feel. Suggested. Reminded. Again dance could do no more than broach a disaster too big, too close for words or music or movement to compass.

In like compassionate mood was *They Too Are Exiles* (Adelphi Theater, New York, January 7, 1940), with music also by Miss Fine. The costumes were by Robert Tyler Lee. A quotation in the program note said in part: " 'They too are exiles who remain behind in homelands where free life has dwindled to a frightened whisper in the dark.' " Hanya was most cautious in dealing with these precarious subjects. Her program note stressed the point that no specific countries were represented, and that The Possessor typified a force or system and not an individual or individuals. Nevertheless she appeared as this composite tyrant wearing a semblance of the forelock (but not the mustache) and a fixed expression that registered nothing more sinister than hollow humorlessness. The Peoples, characterized by the group members, demonstrated their impartiality by indulging in folk dances of several nations, and, just to be sure, Slavic dances roped Russia in. But there was no doubt in any one's mind then which the lost nation was, which the most despicable of leaders, which the most pitiable of peoples. The sympathies were easily traceable, whether or not they were deserved.

A work that was a sensation but not a success was *The Golden Fleece, An Alchemistic Fantasy,* presented at the Mansfield Theater,

New York, March 17, 1941. It was a radical departure from Hanya's norm of movement values dominating all. Done in collaboration with Kurt Seligmann, the surrealist painter, who provided the plot and the costumes, it was outdone and undone by what turned out to be a one-man show. Hanya's wonderful dancers became so many Seligmann girls modeling his latest *couture* on the stage. They evoked gasps and gurgles, but not for admiration of rhythmic form. The grotesqueries of line and color juxtaposition were not animated by movement in kind; the movement not only did not stand up under the strain, it practically stood still. Alex North's music followed the scheme instead of increasing the general topsy-turviness as it might have done. The work brought three men into the group—Alfred Brooks, Kipp Kiernan (who executed the cellophane masks), and Gregory MacDougall. From then on Hanya's choreography included parts for men, and from time to time new men were added to what could now be called a company.

For *The Golden Fleece* Mr. Seligmann wrote a lengthy program note regarding one Nicolas Flamel, a fourteenth-century alchemist, whose prophetic dream of finding a book that would tell how to make gold from baser metals came true. Thereupon he had an allegorical fresco painted representing the seven stages in this alchemical process; and these seven stages mystically alluded to the Hermetic philosophy that would relate man, physically and spiritually, and concordantly, to the universe. Tied in with this was an interpretation of the mythological Jason as an alchemist at heart, whose quest for the Golden Fleece symbolized the stages in the making of gold. Whether any gold was actually made did not appear.

The inhabitants of this hazy never-never-land were such amusing monsters as The Inner Eye, a Cosmic Oven, Bushel of Wings, a strange Fruit-Bearing Tree, a busy Self-Grinding Mill, and the only less preposterous Mercury, Saturn, Raven-Phoenix, Sulphur, Water, and the old Serpent himself. A group of girls in gilt wigs and red tights first appeared, and then left the stage to an absurd but decorative hallucination. Figures wearing crowns of electric-light bulbs, clothes of kitchen-ware with culinary trimmings, and other extraordinary apparel, made up not only a dream walking but a rather jolly nightmare cavorting. The dream was allowed to fade into limbo after Thomas Bouchard, the artist photographer, had filmed it.

A choreographically more important *première* on the same program was *Dance of Introduction*, with music by Henry Cowell and blue-toned costumes by Liz Rytell, which also made use of the three new men. This was a formal composition in waltz measures (with balletic appurtenances—willy-nilly, they did creep in) at Hanya's own high level of solid structure, lilting movement, and abstract design. It was beautifully performed by her group.

In 1941 she began her separate seasonal career as dance director for the summer sessions at Colorado College, Colorado Springs. Her courses include technique, theory, composition, percussion playing, history, and notation. Alwin Nikolais, who is on the faculty of New York University as well as of the Hanya Holm School, has developed a system of dance notation he calls Choroscript (he describes it in an article in the old *Theatre Arts* of February 1948), and this, no doubt, is the one she uses. The season's work is climaxed by a big production at season's end.

The first of these, *From This Earth*, done in collaboration with Roy Harris, the resident composer, had its *première* at the Colorado Springs Fine Arts Center on August 7, 1941. The idea began with Western earth, the untrammeled spaces and mountain air, and the people of this earth. But as the work progressed it merged into the universal earth experience, as the sub-titles testify: "Dawn— Mother's Lullaby"; "Childhood—Children at Play"; "Love— Courtship—Marriage—Festivities"; "Work—Treadmill and Exhaustion"; "Dusk—Retrospection"; which seems to run the gamut in respect to the common man. When it was shown in New York, in the Students Dance Recitals series, on January 24, 1942, John Martin found it worth a Sunday column, but commended it with reservations. He mentioned an occasional "semi-literalism" and unfortunate costuming among the less desirable features.

Hanya is a top-notch technician, an expert craftsman of modern dance, excelling in pure dance form without associational ideas. Her choreography has originality and technical excitement. It has, or has had until recently, everything but the zing of theater. Her work at Colorado College, in collaboration with fellow artists, has been a slow crescendo toward theater. The student productions are necessarily adapted to the college atmosphere. But they can afford to be experimental and sometimes hit upon something of unusual quality.

The summer of 1942 brought, with *What So Proudly We Hail,* a dance suite based on American folk songs embraced in Mr. Harris's score, the theater dance, *Namesake.* It had a word-score for the dancers by Arch Lauterer, who can summon a village with a screen and a platform, and a period with the most economical attire. It was a dance play of nineteenth-century small-town life, a solo violinist providing the music. Along with two more new pieces, it was shown in the Students Dance Recitals and the Y. M. H. A. Dance Theatre series during the late winter of 1943. *Parable,* to music of Couperin arranged by Paul Aaron, with costumes by George Bockman, retold the story of the Wise and Foolish Virgins. *A Suite of Four Dances* had music by John Cage, of prepared-piano fame, a woman singer, and costumes by Mr. Lauterer. The third dance was an interesting duet by Robin Gregory and Paul Sweeney. The other dances were ensemble numbers in formal style. One forward glance, but nothing outstanding here.

Orestes and the Furies, the summer production of 1943, aroused major expectations but eventuated in minor rewards. The agile Paul Sweeney was miscast as Orestes, and little Hanya was about as furious a Leader of the Furies as a china shepherdess. She had devised the work in conjunction with John Coleman, who composed the score for two pianos. The stage and costume designs were by William T. Snaith. A central construction of side-steps and platform made an imposing focal point for the action. The women wore the fluted draperies of ancient Greece in modern guise, and the men wore little more than tights. The dance drama followed the *Eumenides* of Aeschylus fairly literally, without reluming the legend or bringing it any closer to our time. The work was given in the Students Dance Recitals series on January 22, 1944—the year that marked the end of Hanya's New York concert group.

Thereafter the Colorado productions did not reach New York,

but were reviewed in *Dance Observer,* the one magazine inde-fatigably devoted to modern dance. *What Dreams May Come* (Alex North) drew an analytical account (October 1944) by the distin-guished critic, George W. Beiswanger, who had seen and liked it. *Windows* (Freda Miller), according to a report by Doris Baker (November 1946), was enthusiastically greeted by a sold-out house; and for the same program Alwin Nikolais had cleverly choreo-graphed the old Aesop *Fable of the Donkey.* It is included in a book of ready-made scenarios with scores attached (choreography to be filled in) composed by Freda Miller for school and college work. Other reviews were reprinted from local newspapers. For the record, there was the *Walt Whitman Suite,* in collaboration with Roy Harris, with text sung by a chorus, of 1945; the satire, *The Gardens of Eden* (Milhaud), of the same year; and the *Dance For Four* (Riegger) of 1946.

The production of 1947 took a long step theaterward. It was a stylized and somewhat curtailed version of Karel and Josef Capek's *The Insect Comedy,* seen some years ago in New York as *The World We Live In,* and here presented under the third of its inter-changeable titles, *And So Ad Infinitum.* The work, done in col-laboration with the drama director, Reginald Lawrence, and with the assistance of Mr. Nikolais, was not wholly creative, self-existent dance theater, since it applied choreography to a pre-written play; and the figures of dance were still not people for they were insects likened to people. But the delineation of the various insects who parallel human behavior in some of its meaner aspects was accom-plished through words and movement, without recourse to masks, wings, or other literalization. The costumes, by Marion Watson, minimized realism, giving perhaps one slight clue to the insect nature. Similarly the stage set, built on the grades and tiltings that Hanya's choreography requires for its formal flow and ebb, was of a functional architecture, free of naturalism.

The stylized gesture and rhythmic movement were an auxiliary to the drama, heightening its expressivity, and the stylized speech was an auxiliary to the intensity of the movement. The two together achieved what neither alone could have achieved so well. The cast of forty was comprised of dancers who could act and actors who could dance, or who had learned to under the summer's tutelage. Most of them had lines.

The success of this production led to Hanya's direction of the actors' movement in the full-length production of *The Insect Comedy,* with a professional cast, at the New York City Center in the spring of 1948.

In "The Eccentricities of Davey Crockett," of the *Ballet Ballads,* she arrived at creative dance theater.

NEW LEADERS—
NEW DIRECTIONS

The New Dance Group—José Limón—
Anna Sokolow—Esther Junger—Sybil Shearer—
Katherine Dunham—Valerie Bettis—
Pearl Primus

THE NEW DANCE GROUP

There are no reds in modern dance today. Once there were left-wingers who, with bare feet thrust up from the ankles and fists doubled out from the wrists, outdid dancing with polemics. "Dance is a Weapon" was their battle-cry. We heard a lot about Dances of Protest in those days. The militants were anti-Nazi when more conventional people were unaware of what the Nazis were up to. They denounced the bombing of women and children in Spain; they recognized the nucleus of another world war. They thought the miners, the Negroes, and several million other people who did not cut coupons once or twice a month, were getting a tough break. Their ardor was restrained by progress (their own, not the world's) as they learned to distinguish between political diatribes and dance—long before it became dangerous to follow any but the two-party line.

Now, of course, the left wings are all tucked out of sight. Only right wings (with a liberal spread) are to be seen. And sole survivor of the Workers' Dance League, which included Red Dancers and Rebel Dancers, Theater, Needle Trades, and Office Union groups among others of similar title, is a quiet, respectable organization known as the New Dance Group. It is a non-profit corporation, maintaining a professional company and school, and charging nominal rates for tuition. Most of its classes are held after 5 p.m., because most of its clients are working girls and boys. It teaches not only all techniques of modern dance, but tap and ballet, folk and ethnic forms. Its faculty and board of directors contain the names of many of the leading dancers of their generation, and potential leaders of the next.

The New Dance Group was born in a dressing room, in a tradition of the theater, for which it then had little use; with a birthmark, caused by the depression, which was gradually effaced. A few pupils of the New York Wigman School, talking things over as they dressed, decided to band together to turn to good account for the American masses the idea of mass dances, as produced in Germany by Mary Wigman and Hanya Holm. They wanted to make dance a vehicle, not for themselves as artists, but for themselves and as many others as possible as members and communicants of the proletariat. They were revolutionaries against poverty and exploitation, against the rising evils of fascism, and also against mysticism and abstraction in the new dance. They were perhaps the first revolutionaries against the existing order of modern dance. Rule One was that to reach people it was necessary to dance on subjects that concerned them, and without ambiguity.

In February 1932 the first group and school were somewhat shakily established. That the school was more or less peripatetic and that the fee for instruction was ten cents a class, are probably closely related facts. For that sum the crusaders offered one hour of Wigman technique, one of creative work, and one of discussion. They would have no exploitation on their side. The New Dance

Group moved often but grew in size, and succeeded in its purpose. It got modern dance before more people, many people who had never heard of it before, and got more people into modern dance. It was one of many units in the larger Workers' Dance League, and many of its performances were in conjunction with these units under WDL auspices. In trade union halls and workers' cultural centers from the Bronx to Brooklyn, they danced before big audiences.

In addition to those on the workers' circuit, there were performances at the New School for Social Research, with John Martin speaking on "Trends and Future of the American Dance," at the Brooklyn Academy of Music, at the old Civic Repertory Theater, and at Mecca Temple. On June 2, 1934, in Town Hall, at a general concert by the Workers' Dance League, the New Dance Group brought forth the prize-winning *Van der Lubbe's Head*. The poem by Alfred Hayes was read in place of musical accompaniment. Masks and props were used. The reference to the Reichstag fire could not be missed. The patterns of running feet, the exciting group designs, built and sustained the mood of mounting tension. It was indeed a dance that concerned people. The prize was honorary, no doubt, but it was first. *Anti-War Cycle,* by the Theater Union Dance Group, and *Kinder, Kueche und Kirche,* by the Nature Friends Dance Group, won second and third respectively. These, *Scottsboro,* and *For Tom Mooney,* were some of the subjects that absorbed the young dance-radicals.

In the beginning, ideas were pooled. Creation often began with improvisation. Life situations, in the home, the shop, the daily struggle, the class struggle, were drawn upon for themes. The aim was to reach "people who had never had an opportunity either to dance or to attend recitals." It was non-commercial mass production, its only profits the spiritual benefits accruing to the people about whom and for whom they danced. But large-scale as the activities were, they were exclusive. The enthusiasts were snobs for the working-class. The rest of humanity might be people, might even have burdens; but the workers had all the common sorrows and worry over where their next can of beans was coming from besides. Such subjects as *Eviction, Hunger, Unemployment,* were far from phantoms. The youngsters knew the hardships whereof they danced. They studied the workers, not as specimens but as fellows.

Open forums on political, economic, and cultural questions were held, and audience comment and criticism invited. There were classes for laymen, for education or recreation. Eurythmics and percussion were added to the courses. The tumbling ideas began to be sorted out. A committee was formed to pass on them, then the originator of the idea became the director of the group for that dance. Choreography improved under this regimen and there was more choosiness about the dancers. Gradually new techniques came in. As more practiced concert dancers arrived, and artists emerged from the ranks, the New Dance Group took on a more professional tone, propaganda ceased bristling on all quills, and art began to prevail over politics.

Nadia Chilkovsky, who used to dance *Homeless Girl, Barricades, Parasite,* etc., was one of the founders; and Miriam Blecher, a Holm pupil and Graham dancer, was largely responsible for the first hit production. Jane Dudley, then a Holm pupil, joined the group in 1934, before long was directing its affairs, and became its president. Henrietta Greenhood (since her marriage called Eve Gentry), an outstanding Holm dancer, shared responsibilities and became vice-president. Nona Schurman, also of the Holm teaching, later a teacher of the Humphrey-Weidman techniques, has long been an active member. Sophie Maslow, Graham dancer, appeared as guest artist and teacher before joining. Most of the important dancers of their generation have in one way or another at some time or other been associated with the group.

There was no shortage of masculine interest in the work of the Group or the League. Charles Weidman and José Limón gave studio talks and appeared on programs in conjunction with them. William Archibald conducted an all-men's class. William Bales, who is now on the faculty, participated. And wild Bill Matons, with his Experimental Group, danced *Well Fed* (sarcastic), *Demagogue, While Waiting for Relief, Letter to a Policeman in Kansas City,* etc., with an access of energy that overshot his mark. These were all Humphrey-Weidman men. In 1935 and 1936 two notable programs of "Men in the Dance" were given by the League (the first at the Park Theater, New York, the second at the Majestic) and nearly upset the modern dance apple-cart, not because of the all-male dancing, but because the audience dared to be delighted by two ballet dancers—William Dollar and Valya Valentinoff. The pioneering in the all-male group belongs to Ted Shawn. But perhaps the seedling of the idea that ballet is not so bad after all was first sewn at these concerts.

The story of the New Dance Group is one of constant experiment, of continual branching out, of conceiving new ideas and coming to new conclusions. With its constantly changing personnel, and headquarters, its multitudinous performances, its growth has been bumpy, its life haphazardous. That it has had so much influence while growing, that it has reorganized and stabilized itself into a thriving dance center, and is still growing, is one of the modern miracles.

In the 1934–5 season the Workers' Dance League reorganized as the New Dance League, with branches in other cities, in an effort to extend its sphere of influence (still apparently not beyond the working class). In May 1936 the League, calling all dancers, staged the first National Dance Congress and Festival in the United States, at the Y. M. H. A. It lasted nearly a week and included many forms—modern, ballet, folk, and hybrid. A large number of New York dancers, or their groups, took part. There were lectures and discussion periods. The place was thronged with people and teeming with ideas. But there was nothing national about it. The active dance areas outside New York—Chicago and the Middle West, Los Angeles and the Pacific Coast—were not represented. It was a New York party, and mainly a New Dance League party. Late in 1937 the League abdicated in favor of the American Dance Association. Soon the WPA had swallowed the ADA, or much the best of it, the separate groups evaporated, and the New Dance Group stood alone.

There followed a private depression for the Group. Funds were low, student enrollment was low, moods were low. In no union was felt no strength. In 1939 Judith Delman came in on a part-time basis and began to pull things together. The studio of that period was a dingy, dilapidated affair downtown. There was no telephone, rent was paid in installments, and debt was a perpetual hangover. In the fall they edged a little farther uptown to a better studio that had a telephone but no heat after 6 p.m., the hour when working-class classes began. Miss Delman remembers typing with icicle fingers, woolen gloves on her feet, legs wrapped in a coat, while the too few pupils stripped to their nondescript practice suits and went to work in the wintry air. She stuck through everything and became the executive secretary.

By 1944 the Group was reorganized and more prosperous. They had just got settled in a large, pleasant studio, where they had spent what was to them a fortune on partitions and a stage, when the building was sold over their heads, and they had to move. While in this predicament, the busy Miss Delman listened with one ear to a sob story, heard of an appealing vacancy with the other, dashed down to a Graham concert to get the green light from Jane and Sophie, and snapped up their present bright, well-equipped quarters next day.

From the beginning, folk sources were drawn upon. Gradually the worker figurehead retreated before a more expansive sense of people and the folk superseded the proletariat. It was seen that dance cannot of itself right social wrongs, and that political spitfiring is not the best subject for dance. Such subjects cannot actually be separated from dance any more than religion, morals, sex, or other vital elements of human living can, because what the dancer is and what he thinks about everything colors, molds, and informs his work. The artist finds subtler ways than public speechifying to express what is closest to him; and these young people grew in artistry as they grew in tolerance and wisdom.

Significant of the folk trend was a program of May 1941 called "America Dances," presenting Margot Mayo and her American Square Dance Group; the Friendship Club Dancers, directed by the veteran teacher, Rosetta O'Neill, in ballroom dances of long ago; the Lindy Hoppers, a National Youth Administration unit, directed by Judith Martin; and a number of modern dancers in compositions illustrating the influence of folk and jazz on modern dance. Lee Sherman did his *Jazz Trio* with Maria Maginnis and Beatrice Seckler, and *Dubarry Was No Lady* with Beatrice; Henrietta Greenhood her *Four Walls Blues* and *The Good Neighbor* (regarding our Mexican policy); Sophie Maslow her *Mountain Shout* and *Dust Bowl Ballads;* and Jane Dudley her *Ballad of Molly Pitcher* and *Harmonica Breakdown.* The *Dust Bowl Ballads* and *Harmonica Breakdown* brought torrential applause. The audience went wild over them.

When *Dance Observer* turned impresario and presented the Dudley-Maslow-Bales Trio, supported by the New Dance Group, in a concert at the Studio Theater March 10 and 11, 1942, there could be no doubt that these three performing artists of high repute were also creative artists of importance. Jane's *Short Story,* Sophie's *Folksay,* Bill's *Es Mujer,* were greeted as Grade A stuff. The trio, formed for an occasion, became a partnership. Bags in hand and props under their arms, it being wartime, they toured the provinces from 1942 to 1946, and also gave New York concerts. There were interruptions, as when Sophie took maternal leave of absence and Frieda Flier, another Graham dancer, took her place. There was in 1947 a temporary suspension. But whatever did not or may happen, what happened during those four years left its mark on American dance. The three individual careers summarize in effect the New Dance Group's career, just as the changes in techniques and viewpoints within the Group epitomize the changes in the whole changing modern dance.

Jane Dudley

Memories of a Puritanical grandmother (from Missouri) went into Jane Dudley's matchless characterization of the Ancestress in Martha Graham's *Letter to the World,* but she was born and bred in New York. Her mother, tall, slim, dark, and fine looking as Jane herself, is a dance teacher. Jane was a pupil of Hanya Holm and a member of her demonstration group in the years 1931–5. When she joined the New Dance Group in 1934 and started her creative career, she was attracted by the social theme. She felt that here she had something truly worth dancing about, and a large audience worth dancing for because it was as concerned with social problems as she. Her interest could not have come out of an under-privileged background. Rather must it have been owing to her sensitivity to the rumblings of world upheaval and to youthful zeal for reform. The chronological list of titles in her repertory tells its own story of calming down. Jane laughs over it herself.

She began as a hot pamphleteer, banging off with *In the Life of a Worker; Time is Money* (to a poem by Sol Funaroff), a shot at the flint-hearted capitalist and his slave-driving tendencies; and *The Dream Ends,* on awakening from day-dream to rude reality; all solos, with music composed for them, given in the old Civic Repertory Theater the first year. In 1935 came *Middle Class Portraits,* a solo series of caricatures: "Swivel Chair Hero" (Honegger); "Dream World Dora" (Acron); "Aesthete" (Honegger); and "Liberal" (Prokofiev). How they used to laugh at liberals! The music was arranged by her pianist, Estelle Parnas, who composed some of the music for the first program. *Song for Soviet Youth Day* (Martinu) (comparatively inoffensive then); the popular *Songs of Protest* (compiled by Lawrence Gellert); and *Under the Swastika*: "Cult of Blood" and "Though We Be Flogged" (Alex North); all in association with the New Dance Group, carried the banner in 1937. Her first two group pieces, produced the same year, do not perhaps much matter now.

In those days Jane did not always succeed in making her points. She was a very good dancer, but naturally not the performer or choreographer she is today. Conspicuous for a rippling fluidity of muscle, she learned to master the chromatics of movement, and, after she began to work with Martha Graham in 1935, the disjointed rhythms of dissonance. She was a member of the Graham company from 1938 to 1944, and somewhere along there studied dance composition with Louis Horst. Louis teaches the craft of choreography. He teaches by rule, but not by rote. He insists that his pupils learn form thoroughly, and then tells them to forget it and create subjectively. He used to say that modern dance was moving, not stepping. In Jane's case it's true. She excels in movement. Whatever she is dancing about, it is a joy to see her move.

With the *Jazz Lyric* of 1938 it is time to sit up and take notice, for jazz is an idiom Jane cultivated with resplendent results. She had first to work off the residue of aggressive social service in an acidulous group piece, *Nursery Rhymes for Grownups,* and a few smaller items. While this branch was being pruned, new branches were cropping out. One was evinced in *The Ballad of Molly Pitcher* (1939), a solo, with words by Edwin Rolfe, turning with affectionate humor from modern revolutionary patriotism to a patriot of the revolution on which our country was founded. The music, like that of *Jazz Lyric,* was by Earl Robinson, who sat in on endless rehearsals and delivered the score at the eleventh hour.

The inspired *Harmonica Breakdown* came in 1940. This solo, with its syncopated body rhythms, its shuffles, bends, slides, and swings, was an ace stroke in comedic movement without extraneous aid. It had been simmering for six years, ever since Jane heard Sonny Terry and his band playing the *Harmonica and Washboard Breakdown.* The sheer animal spirits of the performance gave her a muscular reaction that could not help coming out in dance, though it took time (and opportunity) to put the reaction into form. Besides, what could be more proletarian than a washboard? Or more in keeping with modern dance experimentation than odd sound effects?

In the solo, *Adolescence* (Robinson), and the trio *Short Story* (Paul Creston), Jane looked over the heads of the proletariat into the hearts of people. It was two up for humanity. The woman of *Short Story* is a derelict, the kind who sits in a doorway and mutters to herself. Two tough little girls of the street appear and, all unconsciously, set up a conflict within her. She is at once drawn to them and afraid of them. They revive in her the maternal instinct, the desire to be a part of the world again. But they, oblivious, roughhouse together until one chases the other offstage. The woman, aroused, dances her longing and despair. The children return to tease her, pull at her skirt, and run away. When they come back she knocks one of them down in anger, then takes up the child to comfort her. The child resists, springs out of her lap, the two continue to taunt her, and with a parting shove, leave. The subtitle from a poem by David Wolff sets the key. "But each gets punished for his open face and turns back into himself again."

Jane's depiction of the woman's abasement, longing, and loneliness is remarkable.

Two works on the Spanish theme, done in collaboration with Sophie Maslow, are also among Jane's best works. *Women of Spain* (1938) was a duo-dance in three parts: "Caprichos" (Turina); "Evacuación" (Flamenco song); and "Salud" (Turina). It had some stunning and some stirring passages. For their joint *Spanish Suite* (1944) Jane's *Cante Flamenco* ("Dance of the enslaved in a conquered land") is a brilliant solo. The music is traditional. The movement is American modern, tinged with Spanish flavor. It spirals in a flame of passion, is percussive without *taconeo,* a dance of Spain in bare feet, by an American girl who not only feels for the Spanish people, but, contrary to the common law of modern dance as previously understood, feels a kinship between their dance and ours.

"There *are* similarities in movement," she said, and Sophie agreed, at a Trio interview we had in Boston, "and in energy, taste, and truthfulness." Neither one had studied the Spanish dance, but they had seen a great deal of it, and felt no hesitancy in appropriating what they needed from what they had observed when they had something to say about Spain—meaning of course the Spain of the Loyalists, and using the Spanish gypsy as symbol of an oppressed people.

Of Jane's later works, *American Morning* (1943), with words by David Wolff and music by Marc Blitzstein, is a forward-looking group dance; *Swing Your Lady* (Kraber) (1944), a solo, first figured on a CBS telecast by the Trio; *New World A-Comin'* (Sonny Terry) (1945) is again the bodily syncopation, the negroid dislocation and locomotion, with variations; and all blithe of spirit. *The Lonely Ones,* after the drawings by William Steig, is a psychological study of three warped characters shown in madly antic play to assorted sound effects arranged by Zoe Williams. Like *Short Story,* it pierces to the inner layers and has a strangely haunting atmosphere. It was presented in the New Dance Group's spring festival series of 1948.

Jane still has an axe to grind, but its edge, if keener, is less cutting. Her credo has been meliorated by time. She wants to dance directly about people, she says, for people.

Sophie Maslow

Sophie Maslow is a medium-sized girl of medium-brown coloring as to hair and eyes, a born New Yorker of Russian-American parentage. She went to the Neighborhood Playhouse School of the Theater (then in Grand Street) as a child, studying with Blanche Talmud and appearing in the children's Christmas productions, and later in Irene Lewisohn's orchestral dramas at the Manhattan Opera House. She went directly from the Playhouse School into Martha Graham's concert group, where she became a featured dancer, and toured the country from coast to coast. In spite of the gravitational weight and extreme distortion of the Graham technic, she is essentially a lyricist, dancing lightly, easily, in her own compositions, which are more often of locomotor pattern than of neuromuscular design. She can be as dynamic and down-graded as may be in the Graham dances. In her own she is her very different self.

Sophie danced the folk from the beginning of her individual career. Her first solo was *Themes From a Slavic People,* to music of Béla Bartók, performed in a New Dance Group concert sponsored by the *New Theater Magazine* at the Civic Repertory Theater in 1934. Her greatest work to date is the now classic *Folksay,* which made its debut at the historic *Dance Observer* concert of 1942. *Folksay* is a folk-medley based on verses from Carl Sandburg's *The People, Yes,* interspersed with American ballads. Two of the ballads, *Sweet Betsy from Pike* (a duet) and *On Top of Old Smoky* (a solo) she sometimes performs separately, to records by Burl Ives. At the *première,* Woody Guthrie and Earl Robinson played their guitars, sang, talked, and joked in their casual, homespun manner, while Sophie and members of the group danced her casual-seeming choreography. Her *Hey You, Sun, Moon, Stars* is radiantly outflung, joyous and free. The whole is simple and heart-warming and endearing.

Second only to the *Folksay* they preceded by a year are her two *Dust Bowl Ballads* to Woody Guthrie's songs, "Dusty Old Dust" and "I Ain't Got No Home in This World Any More." There is poignant sweetness and wry humor in these little solos of the migratory workers dispossessed by drought. Sophie presents them sunnyside up as reflected in a daughter of them, with youth and hope in her strong against adversity. In a costume half farm-girl plain, half peasant-gay, and with much play of an old felt hat, she pithily illumines the courageous spirit of the dust-ridden wanderers of the West.

Songfulness impresses all her dances. There is no popping of propaganda. She does not argue about racial prejudice. She makes a song of racial sympathy. Her *Two Songs About Lenin* of 1935, retrospectively called *Two Songs About a Soviet Hero* in 1947, were lovely compositions. "In January he died; in April he was born"— two inocuous statements of causes for the grief and the rejoicing of a people—were done to drum and vocal accompaniment (a Soviet-Orient folksong) in the idiom of the folk.

If popular means of the common people, Sophie says, she wants her dances to be popular. She would like to see dance have as direct an impact upon as wide an audience as the theater and movies do. She believes that "the artist is a part of and not apart from the common man." Because folk dancing grows out of the common experience of large groups of people the world over, she dances in folk terms. She makes no attempt to be authentic in step or costume, but uses the material creatively. Her dances are instinct with folk feeling, modern in form, and lean toward theatrical presentation. Anything is legitimate, she thinks, that helps to hurdle the barrier between dancer and audience, that sends the idea or mood or emotion straight into the hearts and minds of people.

The works of the Trio repertory are not intended to make a cult of Americana nor are they limited to the American genre. Two of Sophie's contributions look far beyond national borders, the one to Spain, the other to Yugoslavia. Not to put her in the red, where she does not belong, *Fragments of a Shattered Land* ("Inheritance" and "Partisan Journey") was composed when the Partisans were okay, for they were then fighting the Nazis. It had its first performance in the first New Dance Group Festival series held in Times Hall, New York, in June 1945, before World War II had ended. The accompaniment consists of Yugoslav folk songs played on an accordion, and in the solo, "Inheritance," the reading of a letter written by a dying guerrilla to his unborn child, on which the dance is based. In Boston, Bill Bales read the unfinished letter offstage while Sophie enacted in rhythmic movement the conflicting reactions of the wife and mother to the words. The lines sounded stilted and artificial over the loud speaker, and Bill's resonant voice was blurred and metallicized. The effect was distracting.

We had a talk about it next day. Sophie needed to have the actual letter read, she said, to show just why the woman was torn between grief over the loss of her husband and hope in the child to come. Otherwise the audience would see the movements of hope and sorrow without perceiving the cause of them; nor, it might be added, would they be able to feel the sad solace the words gave her. Jane suggested that the effectiveness of the voice depended a lot on the condition of the amplifying instrument. Bill thought it usually worked out better when the character spoke on stage, without a loud speaker, as he does in their trio dance, *"As Poor Richard Says—"* because then the voice was a part of the action and put less strain on the spectator. That it was a question of balance between movement and verbal tensions all agreed. The final vote was that words should be used sparingly and only when, as in "Inheritance," they supply a distinct need.

In the bright "Partisan Journey" (to a Partisan song), the trio forward-marched to dance the firm faith and brave conviction of those who fight to serve a cause. *Fragments of a Shattered Land* is utterly impersonal. It is not hinged on racial kinship, though there is probably a Slavic strain in Sophie's ancestry (as there is in the folk themes adapted), but on a feeling of kinship with the attitude of this Slavic people under stress. She admired the stand the Yugoslavs took in the war, and was impelled to express her admiration in dance.

So with her trio, *Llanto* ("We shall avenge our tears") of 1944, an expression of the renewal of courage that contrasts with Jane's *Cante Flamenco* in their *Spanish Suite*. Here the affinity is with the attitude and aims of the Spanish Loyalists. Sophie adapts the Spanish rhythms (the music is a Flamenco song) in order to identify the people. It is technically and intentionally irregular, having heel taps in heelless slippers, and hands less sinuous than the Spanish gypsy's, but, like the arm and body movements, costumes and carriage, suggesting Spain. And it is Spanish in feeling—not the feeling of coquetry and rivalry we so often find in the Spanish trio, but that of the Spanish people in their courageous resistance to oppression. It is decidedly anti-Fascist. I never heard of a modern pro-Fascist dance. Or an anti-Semitic, or for that matter, an anti-Gentile or an anti-Negro dance.

The radical American modern dance was interracial from its start. It becomes more international, with no loss of patriotism, as it becomes more liberal, as it leaves the confines of early modernism, narrow national and *class* consciousness, for the timeless, universal realm of dance, and the one world of people. To the Dudley-Maslow-Bales Trio, types of their generation, in that delightful state of young maturity when individuals look younger and feel older than they are, this world is not their oyster—it is a place to do something about. Sophie does it gently, tenderly. There may have been some sarcasm, an occasional sneer, in earlier works—as in her new *Champion,* after Ring Lardner's story of a champion heel. But mainly she dances the song of the folk, in the folk spirit, without malice—as one of them.

William Bales

To William Bales also people are best interpreted as folk, for he believes that in the life experience of people close to earth is found the nub of universal life experience. "I have tried to capture the unsophisticated quality of the peasantry," he has written me, "because I believe it is the most direct way I can communicate the simple emotions of simple people." He does it differently from either Jane or Sophie, having a different technical background and a thoroughly masculine point of view. He composes, as he dances, with forthright manly vigor, straight to the point.

Bill worked his way through the University of Pittsburgh School of Business Administration with a job on the *Pittsburgh Sun-Telegraph,* studying tap and ballet for recreation; and then worked his way through the Carnegie Tech Drama School by teaching dance at the Irene Kaufmann Settlement House. He was thus conditioned early to directness of expression. He had some ballet and Eurythmics in the drama curriculum, and his serious interest in theater dance was awakened there. It jumped into action at a physical education convention (still in Pittsburgh, his home city) when Martha Hill, head of the dance departments at Bennington College and New York University, gave a demonstration lesson. Bill got so excited at the new techniques that he tore off his shoes and stockings and dived into the class. He saw at once that modern dance would bring him closer to theater than the formal ballet; that here was what he was looking for—emotional movement, through which he could express dramatic intensities and meaning.

Martha Hill noticed the boy and watched him throughout the class. Afterwards she told him that Charles Weidman was about to conduct a scholarship session for the purpose of finding new men. Through her Bill was invited. At the end of six weeks he became a member of the Humphrey-Weidman company, where he shone among the top dancers from 1936 to 1940. Since then he has been on the faculty at Bennington, though he has done some short-term teaching at other schools and colleges, and is now one of the many teachers at the New Dance Group Studio. He has made side excursions on Broadway and as guest artist with Hanya Holm.

One of his most interesting adventures was in connection with a revival of the three-hundred-year-old Monteverdi music drama, *Il Combattimento di Tancredi e Clorinda,* when he and Nona Schurman, in the costumes of the Christian warrior and the Saracen maiden, did a stylized duet of the combat and the death scene of the heroine that contributed substantially to the revitalization of the work. The dancers worked out the choreography together and successfully co-ordinated the movement with the rhythms and content of the piece. It was produced in Olin Downes's concert series at Tanglewood (seat of the Berkshire Music Festival in Massachusetts) in July 1942, and given a New York performance in Times Hall in October of that year, as the concluding number of a recital by Yves Tinayre.

Bill's creative career began in 1940 with *Black Tambourine,* a solo, first done at Camp Tamiment, Pennsylvania, in the summer.

It was, as might be suspected, about the plight of the Negro in this country, expressing in the first part defeat, in the second, protest. The music was two Negro spirituals. There followed at Bennington College in December a group work, *Opus* $\frac{o}{1}$, (a title that seems to have a wink in it somewhere) of which nothing has since been heard. *Es Mujer* was his first major work. It is a modern ballet of primitive Mexico, to traditional music arranged by Carlos Chávez, with costumes designed by Helen Bottomly. "Es Mujer" is the Mexican way of saying "She is grown up," and the ballet is based on the ritual of initiation into womanhood. The first section shows the induction of the girl into the group of young women, her acceptance completed when her hair is put up. In the second section the single male becomes the center of interest, the girls strutting around him and displaying their charms until he selects the new girl for his bride. The last section is a celebration of the betrothal.

Es Mujer was first performed at Bennington College in August 1941, with Bill as the peasant bridegroom, Teru Osato (sister of Sono) the child-bride, and a group of eight girls the attendants. The simplicity of the work, its restrained intensity and solemn dignity, its atmosphere of primitive naïveté, and the unpretentious effectiveness of its well-wrought design won it instant recognition. Bill has been attracted to Latin-American themes by the music and by an innate sympathy with the people. He has studied their dances, music, and history. In his compositions he does not try for authenticity, but merely to say something about their lives, something that touches the lives of simple, earthy people everywhere. In *Es Mujer* it was the early assumption of adult responsibilities by girls in a primitive society.

When, in 1942, he was about to go to war and wanted to do a dance of farewell, he used a Mexican mouthpiece and native music to speak for him. Into the solo, *Adiós* ("A peon says reluctant farewell to his village"), he poured all his feeling of having to go and hating to go, but going if he must. He did not have the peon go to war. He just had him go. What the spectator sees is a Mexican youth, burdened in more ways than one under his heavy sack, pushing forward with lagging steps, every now and again stopping to look back, clinging to the familiar scene, yet trudging on, half fearfully, half hopefully, to the unknown. And this dance, which could not have been more subjective, becomes applicable to a variety of temperaments and situations. As it turned out, Bill did not go to war either, and then he felt worse than he had when he thought he was going. But if that feeling has gone into any of his dances, it has come out well disguised. What distillations of emotion make a dance, not even its author can always tell.

Bill's later solos, *Song of Experience,* and—presented at the New Dance Group Festival of 1948—*Soliloquy,* probably contain more that has happened to him than he himself remembers—or projects. Nor is every dance entirely subjective. *Field Hand,* a sequel to *Adiós* in a suite called *Peon Portraits,* certainly cannot be— not from a creative dancer; for it is intended to express "the despair that comes from work in which there is no joy and no hope and from which there is no escape." And *To a Green Mountain Boy* (Zoe Williams), one of the hits of the Trio debut, is quite objective. It conveys in one character the intrepid spirit and amusing cockiness of Ethan Allen's Vermont woodsmen.

Bill's solos are monologues in movement, little inward dramas of male experience made outward—not necessarily of personal experience, but of how a man thinks and feels about things in general. He carries them well. He is tall, broad-shouldered, dark-haired, strong-featured, and manages to look his part and *move* in it. He designs many of his costumes himself. All the music not traditional or classical is composed for his dances. He is not a lyricist. But there is poetic conception in his group work, *Sea Bourne* (Gregory Tucker), first presented in the Students Dance Recitals series on November 27, 1943.

In this modern ballet as in *Es Mujer,* Bill is virtually a solo figure. He represents an absent sailor returning to the memories of the women in his life in images of their making. To his mother and little sisters ("Three who love him"), he is a good child and a kindly big brother, always kidding. To "Two who have known him" (there are tarts in every port) he is a somewhat rougher character. To "One who is in love with him" he is somebody pretty nice. The women and girls stand gazing seaward, and as they separately visualize him he appears, summarizing his calling by steps and his relation to them by movement, with slight costume changes. First the affectionate family group (no fights), after which he removes his jacket for a bacchanale with the tarts, then, in more romantic aspect, the love duet with his girl. When he leaves, they all stand gazing seaward as before, each wrapped in contemplation of their so different versions of the same man.

The Dudley-Maslow-Bales Trio

The rest of the Trio repertory was done in collaboration. (The full individual repertories are too long to detail here.) The trio, *"As Poor Richard Says—" (A Colonial Charade),* and the duet (by Jane and Bill), *Furlough: A Board Walk Episode,* were popular with lay audiences because they were so largely pantomimic and easy of access. "We cannot afford to be too subjective, there must be some track to the audience," Jane said in defense of the pantomime. "The specific has also a place in dance," Sophie averred. Especially in theater dance is this true, they both held. When dance is closely allied to music or mood it can be allowed vaguer qualities; but when the story element enters it must be made clear.

"As Poor Richard Says—" (1943) playfully illustrates some of Ben Franklin's proverbs, with the aid of a large property Almanack opened to a lettered page and (at one time at least) a property suggestion of the old Yankee stocks. "He who lies with dogs will rise up with fleas" and the one about the field well-tilled, the house well-filled, and the wife well-willed underlay the original choreography, which was later reworked. The costumes and décor by Charlotte Trowbridge are fetching, the music by Gregory Tucker is à propos. It is pleasant light entertainment. *Furlough* (1945), with music by Robert McBride and costumes by Edythe Gilfond, is also in the lightweight class. It touches so lightly the outing of a soldier and his pick-up girl that it stays pretty much on the surface. Skilled and cheerful performances endow both pieces with more humor than they possess, for here, as elsewhere, the dancers sometimes outshine their choreographing selves.

The Trio, which with Zoe Williams, pianist-composer, record-

and-curtain fixer, and costume-zipper-upper, was actually a Quartet, did yeoman service for the hinterland in their four years of touring. They made modern dance unformidable, friendly, a language that could speak of contemporary and colloquial subjects without determined Americana or social-consciousness fisticuffs. The program glorified the folk, not as a picturesque people in native costume, but as We, the People, in whatever we had on. It was far from isolationist. It reminded the audience of people in other countries. It spoke of patriotism and love, grief, anger, courage, laughter, and other common things, so that all could understand. The dancers delighted the unsophisticated, and were delighted by their spontaneous response. In some places, where stage dancing had not been seen for eighteen years, they were hailed as marvels. In a few cities they came across an audience or a critic who had at last learned the ways of modern dance as it used to be, and was baffled anew to see it as it is, i.e., not according to formula.

The program was indeed full of obstacles for the modern purist. It opened with a *Bach Suite*—(Scherzo—Loure—Gigue), in ballet shoes, with turned out thighs and semi-courtly demeanor. It was not strict ballet, but a free adaptation, though it had enough of precision and formality to make it a courteous dance of greeting. It was not aristocratic classicism, but rather returned ballet to the people, whence much of its inspiration had come. Particularly in the Gigue, with its rocking motion of the closed feet, comparable to the Spanish jota, the Irish jig, and the British hornpipe, there was that perceptible thread of kinship which, in one step or another, can be traced throughout the national dancing of the Western world.

The Trio used ballet here because it suited their purpose. Bill had studied it first. The girls, in their early Graham period, had scorned it as they had shoes. At that time it was not considered intelligent in modern circles to study ballet. But with the European invasion and gradual acclimatization of ballet to the United States, their curiosity was aroused and they studied it to see what it was like. Now all is grist. The members of the Trio, like many of their colleagues, believe in incorporating any style or form that, adjusted to the needs of each dance, will strengthen its expressional power and elucidate its meaning. Since all dance is intrinsically related, anything goes that can be used creatively to help their dance hit home.

Ethnic Forms

In accord with this new pliability is the study and presentation of ethnic forms at the New Dance Group Studio. Through Pearl Primus and Jean Erdman, currently on the faculty and board of directors, and Hadassah, in a visiting capacity, have come strands of primitive or ancient dance cultures. Taught and learned authentically and adapted creatively, they are slowly weaving into the fabric of modern dance. Because of the relation of her work to a large section of the American citizenry largely overlooked, the Negro dancer, Pearl Primus, occupies a separate chapter.

Jean Erdman

Jean Erdman has the distinction of inadvertently conducting a cultural exchange that could be regarded as a hopeful augury. She teaches the Hawaiian hula at the Studio, and in the summer of 1939 she taught Graham techniques as guest instructor at the Kulamanu Dance School in Honolulu. Jean is the lovely little dancer who gave so much grace to the spoken and movement lines of the outer Emily in *Letter to the World,* and such felicitous humor to the speaking Fate in *Punch and The Judy.* She was born in Honolulu, went to grade school there, and studied both Japanese and Hawaiian forms with native teachers. In the United States she has studied at the Martha Graham School, the Bennington School of the Dance, and the School of American Ballet. She also studied Spanish dance with José Fernández, and has done further work in the Hawaiian dance with Huapala, its American exponent in New York. She is a graduate of Sarah Lawrence College. At the Studio she teaches fundamentals of modern movement and beginners' techniques, apart from any set school, and, in special surveys, the Spanish dance and the hula.

The classic hula is not the hula of the commercial stage and movies. It is a story-telling dance with a definite hand-language that stems from the Oriental gesture but is less complicated. To those who do not follow the signs, its swaying hips and undulating arms over a ground bass of repetitious side steps, can look monotonous, but it has more variety than at first appears. It was originally a temple dance for island deities, a dance of pagan worship done by maidens in or out of doors. Now it is a recreational dance done by both young women and young men, without the conscious sexuality of its cheap adulterations, a simple, happy alfresco form reflecting the harmony of its surroundings. Its nature rhythms and folk feeling may well supply fresh material for the American modern dance. It is actually American, being a product of a territory of the United States long stamped with American thought. The New England missionaries early laid a finger on it with their mother hubbards and hymn tunes. A gayer influence is seen in the contemporary gestures of "stepping on the gas" and "steering the wheel."

Jean's own compositions are fine-spun and tenuous, poetic of title, non-associational of idea. Her *Daughters of the Lonesome Isle,* a trio to music by John Cage, is completely unprogrammatic, yet, in its rare and delicate way, evocative. Her *Ophelia* (Cage) gives the psychosis of the character rather than the character herself. *Creature on a Journey* (Lou Harrison), with its elfin quality, is an inhabitant solely of the imagination. *"Forever and Sunsmell"* (Cage), *Changing Moment* (Harrison), and *Sea Deep* (Tucker) are other dances that provoke more than they spell out. There is a breath of out doors, a reflection of nature rhythms in much of her work (as in the solo, *Hamadryad,* offered in the 1948 festival series), as if the island memories of her childhood had come sifting through the mature intellect in attenuated form. Jean's unrealistic approach counterbalances the literalism that besets some of the young moderns when they try too hard to be intelligible.

Hadassah

Hadassah, a striking, black-haired girl, brings to the Studio the dance cultures and gorgeous costumes of the East. She was born in

Jerusalem, of an old rabbinical family and, growing up in the Palestinian melting pot, came in contact with many races. The Bokharans, Arabs, Yemenites, Hindus, Georgians, Moroccans, Chinese, and other inhabitants of the city maintained the disparate dress and customs of their mother countries, but running through their various religions, philosophies, and arts, she discerned a common vein. Her dance training began in Palestine and continued as she traveled through other parts of the Orient and, later, Europe. She has lived in Damascus, Aleppo, Constantinople, and Eskishehir; she has studied Javanese, Balinese, Japanese, and Hindu forms; and the impression of a unifying thread has remained. In teaching she uses the traditional movements, positions, gestures. In her concert dances she presents them intact, each within its own medium, but combines them freely within that medium, much as Shan-Kar did with his presentations. No native dance can be set forth in its entirety on the American stage. It must always be abridged, transcribed.

In her treatment of the Jewish theme Hadassah comes nearer to actual creativity, to composition in the modern sense. What the archaic Hebrew dance was like, whether there is an authentic Jewish dance, is a question. It is not an ethnic form, since it emerges from the orthodox liturgy of the synagogue, the domestic ceremonials of a people who worship God. It is Oriental and European and American, for it is colored by the culture surrounding the Jews wherever they have lived. Thus the folk dance known as the "Horra," a circle dance with a weaving back-and-forth step, done at Jewish weddings, and now considered the national dance of Palestine, is of European origin and has its counterpart under different names in the folk dances of many nations.

There are several exponents of the Hebraic dance in the United States, and notable among them is Benjamin Zemach. His Chassidic dances are based on the innovations of Baal Shem, which included an ecstatic movement of the arms and hands intended to inject a note of joy into the ritual. Hadassah, who has been in this country since 1940, and part of the time associated with Zemach, has only recently begun to show her work from Hebraic sources. Her beautiful *Shuvi Nafshi (Return, Oh my Soul),* an interpretation of Psalm 116 to a cantoral sung by Lebele Waldman, was first performed at the Y. M. H. A. on February 12, 1947. *Shir Hatemony*, to a Yemenite song sung by Moshe Nathanson, was first done at a Jewish Dance Festival held at Hunter College on December 13, 1947. The Jewish theme is not new to the American modern dance. Many members of the New Dance Group and others have built dances on the subject, often, but not always, in its contemporary aspect. Hadassah clothes it with the biblical traditions of her homeland. But her impressions crystallized and she learned to work creatively in the United States—where also she learned a few other things. A distinctly Americanized dance in her repertory is the *Broadway Hindu* to Raymond Scott's *Powerhouse*, first performed at Camp Tamiment in the summer of 1943. This must be attributed to the influence of Jack Cole, with whom she has worked in the past.

Jack Cole was first to swing the Hindu dance on Broadway. He began his career as J. Ewing Cole, an obstreperous member of Shawn's original men's group who had also studied with Ruth St. Denis at the New York Denishawn School. From that start he became an avid researcher in Orientalism. He was at the same time enamored of Baudelaire's *Les Fleurs de Mal*. Out of the spirit of perversity that grew in him he conceived the idea of dancing Hindu to American jazz, which he developed with great success in Broadway shows and night-clubs, enchanting the cognoscenti of those circles by indicating a favorite four-letter word with Oriental fingers, and other impish tricks. He handled Harlem themes with the same smart sophistication, and became altogether the rage. He had long since ceased parting his name in the middle, and taken the sturdier name of Jack. He had some Humphrey-Weidman training, having slept on their studio floor in his vagabond days. He is a superlative dancer, an inventive choreographer, and has in recent years been one of the leading lights of Hollywood, where any flagrant violations of the Production Code can easily be dissembled, especially in dance. Now the Broadway Hindu is an established idiom, but none of Jack Cole's followers is as wickedly clever as he.

Two other American Orientalists have had their influence on the young native Oriental—Ruth St. Denis and La Meri. Soon after her arrival in New York, Hadassah appeared on a program at the studio the two had launched together, which is now known as the Ethnologic Dance Center and is directed by La Meri alone. La Meri, whose pseudonym is a derivative of her maiden name, Russell Meriwether Hughes, was born in Kentucky, but lived mostly in Texas, and from the Mexican and other Latin-American dances she saw in childhood was inspired to devote her life to the study of Spanish, Oriental, and other ethnologic forms. She spent years in world travel, both as touring dancer and scholar, and considers India the matrix of the dance. She is essentially an educator, teaching and presenting the authentic forms in authentic costume, but of recent years she has been composing freely within those forms. Her translations of the ballets, *Swan Lake* and *Scheherazade* into the Hindu idiom, to their original scores, have been novel and entertaining accomplishments. Her *Bach-Bharata Suite,* which adapts the classic Hindu movement to the classic Western music in an abstract dance of singular beauty, is even more interesting, for in it can be discerned certain basic movements that faintly approximate the movements of modern dance. La Meri is not a modern dancer, but her explorations within her chosen field may yet indirectly sway some of the new directions the modern dance will take.

As a matter of fact, there has always been an Oriental undercurrent in modern dance, beginning with the occidentalized Orientalism of Ruth St. Denis. Oriental feeling underlies Mary Wigman's work and sometimes Martha Graham's. Doris Humphrey and Charles Weidman, early conditioned to Oriental dance, could not wholly escape what was bred into them. It comes out in subtle ways —in Doris's eloquent hands, in Charles's comically wriggling fingers. It is not so strange that the younger generations should revert to these only half-forgotten types.

Festival and School

The lovely and gifted Hadassah was the highlight of the New Dance Group's Festival Series at the Mansfield Theater, New York, in the late spring of 1948. She offered in addition to her *Shuvi Nafshi,* a new *Fable* created in the Hindu idiom with spoken text written by herself. There were six performances in five days and a great deal of ground to cover by eight ambitious choreographers. It was like an overcrowded art gallery. Not all the new works could be properly appreciated among so many. Some that looked disappointing need a second chance before they can be fairly judged. But the creative spirit, the broad range of interests embraced in the roving imaginations, and the large number of excellent dancers affiliated with the Group, bore witness to a state of spiritual and material prosperity.

In the fall of 1947 the Studio had an enrollment of over 850 adult students and 250 children. The staff is large and flexible. The artists teach when not on tour, and sometimes by request. The curriculum, apart from the basic schedule, is regulated by a non-commercial law of supply and demand. When people ask for a ballroom class, ballroom is added. And so it is with tap.

Tap is nothing to look down one's nose about. It may be a dance of city folk, springing from the sidewalk and transferred to the stage. Its origin is as earthy as any folk dance. It is a distant relative of the primitive Negro dance done in bare feet, the American Indian dance in moccasins. Its toe-and-heel step can be seen in the Spanish dance and the Russian dance, with weight, balance, and accent altered by different kinds of boots. Jitterbug, too, is earthborn and tap-related; and if some phases of modern dance aren't called jitterbug they ought to be.

It would not be surprising to see these once lowly forms creeping increasingly into modern dance composition with no more thought of condescension than the dressier folk and ethnic forms, for they also are dances of people. And the New Dance Group Studio is a center of the people's dance. It has gone a long way past the purpose of its founders. In enlarging its own scope it has extended the horizon of the American modern dance and endowed it with new openings for development. It is proving dance to be something more gracious and more powerful than a weapon.

JOSÉ LIMÓN

The Mexican-born José Limón stands pre-eminent today as the leading male dancer in the American modern dance. With his Aztec-Hispanic features, his dark eyes and straight black hair, the virile strength of his broad shoulders, he is virtually typecast in the role of Ignacio Sánchez Mejías, though he is probably much taller than the average bullfighter. When, at the work's New York *première,* he danced the role in the venerable Belasco Theater on a night in January 1947, he was both within tradition and against it. The old house exuded memories. The place was redolent of theater feeling. Blended into the aura of the past were the dancer's own memories—the flash of the *torero's* cape, all the panoply of the bullring—intangibly threading his characterization. And mingled with these effluences were the thoughts and responses of the special New York audience, keyed to the new theater dance.

Not only because he looked the part, and by the heritage in his veins impregnated it, or because every surrounding circumstance helped to fructify it, did José give a performance worthy of the theater's great traditions, while breaking away from most of them. By his own energy of spirit and skill of execution he created drama without rhetoric in a dance of Spain that contained no formal Spanish dance; a dance about a bullfighter that exhibited no *veronicas* or other feats of the bullring, at least made no more than oblique reference to them. By modern movement alone, by some movements that had never been done on the stage before, he communicated the ambience of Spain, the emotions of the dying *espada;* he transmuted the outer into the inner event.

This creative performance was given in a work not created by himself, thereby smashing an established precedent and freeing a whole generation of modern dancers from the onus of choreographing every work they dance. The theory used to be that subjective movement could not be devised by one person for another except in group works (the group members being held negligible until each in time became a choreographer). Opposition had been feeble until José broke the spell that bound every reputable modern dancer, choreographically gifted or not, to the allied but separate art of dance-making. He proved that one could dance creatively in a work he had not himself composed, provided it was a good work; that the important thing for a dancer is to dance, and not to choreograph unless he is impelled and equipped to do so.

Doris Humphrey's *Lament for Ignacio Sánchez Mejías* and *The Story of Mankind,* also on the Belasco program, were not the first works she choreographed or directed for José. The practice began in the Studio Theater before the war, and was revived during the latter part of his army service when he organized his initial trio, preparatory to returning to civilian life. Trained in the Humphrey-Weidman technique, he was habituated to appearing in the Humphrey-Weidman works. His first appearance in a Humphrey work was concealed from public view, for he was holding up one of the central boxes, crouched inside of it, throughout the long *Dances of Women.* Even in this position he could appreciate the delicate foliations of movement, the tender little pats on the palm, like small leaves falling, the sounds and sights of growing things she poured into that early work. Increasingly he found consonance in her dances, was happy to have a part in them, and grew in respect and admiration for them. So when the time came for him to begin over again it was natural for him to turn to her whom he knew to be a greater choreographer than himself, whom he sets apart as the master choreographer of modern dance, the one who has most to give and says best the best there is to say.

This does not mean that he has surrendered his prerogative to choreograph when he chooses. Although essentially a performing artist, he enjoys composing, and always has something of his own to work on. He explores movement, develops new movement values, and in pupils and partners finds fresh material for experiment. He has a long list of compositions to his credit, dating from late in 1930 when he designed, to the *Étude in D flat major* of Scriabin, a duet to dance with Letitia Ide at studio and other "little" recitals. His first composition to be performed publicly and repeatedly was the solo, *Two Preludes,* to music by Reginald de Koven, done in the spring of 1931.

José is a worker. He is and has had to be. As a young student he had to work hard for the balance and co-ordination he has long since attained. He had to work mightily on and for his role ın *Lament*. He looks sᴏ right in it, as if it were made for him (which it was), that one could easily imagine he just fell into it. The role was composed with him as the prototype, but the movements were not limited to his capabilities. They were evolved out of the mood of the work, a mood not wholly elegiac, and he had to stretch beyond his powers, or rather, perhaps, bring out latent powers, to be able to do them. The staccato passages call for the utmost in adroitness and dexterity. Yet slow, sustained movements are more difficult to perform—and as for rotating his legs in air while standing on his head—well, altogether it is an exhausting role. Having given a consummate performance of it, José next had to pay for the privilege with a year of intensive teaching.

The Belasco concert was sold out, but the thousands of dollars that came in through the box office did not meet the thousands that went out for expenses. It was acclaimed in all quarters, barring one or two dissenting voices, as of Rosalyn Krokover in *Musical Courier* and an initialed picker-to-pieces in *Dance Observer*. There were pictorial displays in *House and Garden* as well as in *PM, Dance,* and other periodicals. The enthusiastic after-publicity could not be turned to account by repeating the performance while dancers and public were still warm with it, because of the *bête noir* of modern dance—lack of funds. The glory had to be allowed to fade, the artistic success to peter out, and the artist hailed by John Martin as "the greatest American male dancer in his field" and by Walter Terry, dance critic of the *New York Herald Tribune,* as "without peer in his generation of men dancers," had to settle down to work at non-union hours on a non-profit basis.

The situation, like others in modern dance, cries for a Ministry of Fine Arts, the nearest approach to which ever reached in the United States was the various art programs under the Works Progress Administration of the depression years. Depression is the constant of the artist who lives on the wrong side of the dollar sign by refusal to compromise, who is neither sufficiently conventional nor sufficiently sensational to capture the fancy of public or private patrons. Teaching is his only means of support. That may be the reason why every modern dancer, from the least to the greatest, teaches to some extent. Teaching is a part of being a modern dancer. It can be beneficial to the artist, unless he is driven to such excesses of teaching that his creative energies are drained.

So José, tall-dark-and-handsomer than any movie star (and without aid of celluloid), an infinitely more vivid personality, and a real artist to boot, must plug along between concerts, receiving nowhere near the opportunities or the rewards he deserves, until some miracle occurs, as yet it may, to change his luck. José is no glamour boy, be it understood, even if the young women who flock to his classes do set him upon a pedestal, and not solely as a figure of dance. He is a man, and no longer a very young man. His sensitive, modeled face looks worn since he left the army, and he is acquiring the lightly silvered temples that are so much more interesting in a man than in a woman. The magnificence of his presence comes as much from the munificence of his nature as from physical endowments. His bigness is not wholly a matter of stature. It is composed of modesty, humility, generosity, cheerfulness, a warm, outgoing disposition, and is augmented by the cultural wealth of his background. Because he is a splendid human being he imparts splendor to the dance of humanbeingness. He became a dancer by fortuity. He started out to be a painter and got sidetracked on the way.

Spanish dancing was part of the scenery when José was a boy in Mexico. He loved it, but had no desire to become a dancer. He played bullfight with other boys, and watched the refulgent *torero* drive by in his victoria, adoring him, never dreaming of becoming anything so unapproachable, even by proxy. He was at home in the land of the serape and the huarache, imbibing the native essences, both Indian and Spanish. When he was about seven, the family, fleeing a revolution, went to Arizona to live. Soon afterwards they moved to Los Angeles, where José went through high school. He spent an unfinished year at the University of California at Los Angeles, for, having decided by then to be a painter, he found academic education dull and pointless for him. He loved to play the organ (his father was a musician), and played Bach by the hour. But painting was to be his life-work. He was sure of it. He was talented and his work showed promise. Then he went to New York to pursue his art studies, and suddenly the desire to paint was gone.

This was a blow and a mystery at first. Later he realized what the trouble was. Everybody was painting French. The studios were filled with imitation Cézannes, Gauguins, Matisses, and Van Goghs. He himself was enamored of El Greco. He would stand for hours, just as he had played Bach for hours, before a painting at the Metropolitan Museum, worshipping the strange, elongated lines, the mystic atmosphere, until it dawned upon him that he was in danger of spending the rest of his life "either trying to paint like El Greco or trying not to paint like El Greco," as he once told me in an interview. What ensued was a revulsion from all derivative work, and scant hope that with his idol blocking the way he would ever do anything creative.

In this lost state, not knowing how to fill the emptiness, he wandered into a dance concert by Kreutzberg and Georgi. He was so enthralled that he resolved at once to become a dancer. A mutual acquaintance led him directly to the Humphrey-Weidman door. He was in, but not on. He was a slow study and gave no sign of genius. His big frame was unwieldy, too strong for elasticity, he had no sense of balance, a poor sense of direction, and was all but bowled over by the most elementary aspects of dance. But he had found what he wanted. He found living movement that, for him, transcended painted or sounded movement. He found movement that came alive in himself. He could not get over the wonder of it.

This was in 1928, actually the first year of the independent Humphrey-Weidman company. José practically grew up with the company, after an interim in California. He made his unofficial debut as one of four boys in Charles Weidman's *Javanese Impressions* at the Guild Theater, New York, in the late fall of that year. Then family affairs took him home and he did not return until March 1930, when his uninterrupted studies began. In April he appeared in the Humphrey-Weidman dances for Norman Bel Geddes's *Lysistrata*. From that time on he continued to study, to improve, and became the outstanding featured dancer in the Humphrey-Weidman productions.

From 1931 to 1937, with a few by-passes into musical comedy and revue, José's compositions consisted of trios and duets, danced with Letitia Ide, Ernestine Henoch, Eleanor King, singly or in combination, and, in Boston and vicinity with Pauline Chellis (complementary partners all); and solos, as the *Danza* (Prokofiev) and *Canción y Danza* (Mompou) of 1933, and the *Pièces froides* (Satie) of 1935, in which year he did the dances for Jerome Kern's popular musical, *Roberta*. In 1937, José, Anna Sokolow, and Esther Junger received the first fellowships to be awarded by the Bennington School of the Dance, and for that summer's festival he prepared his first group work, *Danza de la Muerte*. It was alerted, like so many dances of those days, to the Spanish Civil War. Between the ensemble numbers, "Sarabande for the Dead" and "Sarabande for the Living" (with music by Henry Clark), was an interlude of three satiric solos by José (with music by Norman Lloyd). "Hoch!" was for generals, "Viva" for landlords, and "Ave" for church, as "personified causes of the destruction in Spain." More in movement than in content, the work was tinged with originality. It marked José's departure from pre-existent music as well as into larger form.

In 1939, when the entire Bennington School moved to Mills College, California, for the summer, he presented his *Danzas Mexicanas*, a suite of solos, to music by Lionel Nowak, which later became popular at the Humphrey-Weidman Studio Theater. As in any dance of Spanish or Latin-American flavor, José looked so eminently right in his costumes, moved so much as if in his native air, that it is a question whether personality, suitability, choreography, or just dynamic dancing was the cause of the work's success. It was probably the combination. The costumes bore out the sub-titles—"Indio, Conquistador, Peon, Caballero, and Revolucionario"—offered chronologically, like a five-word history of the country.

José delineated his gallery of Mexican types pictorially and effectively. There was imperious pride with an undercurrent of brutality for the Spanish conqueror, romantic dash and elegance, with the same undertone of cruelty, for the gentleman land-grabber or owner; all in José's large-scaled muscular style of unusual extensions and arabesques. But in the two types closest to earth, the primitive and the enslaved Indian, he came closest to warm and earthy characterization; and as the far-visaged, mildly savage revolutionist of mixed race he was something more than pictorial. The planes and contours of José's face are a shade more Indian than Spanish. His sympathies are less with the grandee than with the people. In the subjective dance, things can often be subjectively accounted for. The work was well-made within its frame, and grew with performance. It was a distinctive contribution to the American dance.

If *War Lyrics* (in its first state) was half as fascinating in performance as it is on paper, it was most impressive. This, José's second venture in group form, was produced at the Mills College summer session of 1940, with May O'Donnell and ten girls of the workshop group. The girls were used as a chorus, in dance interludes between duets by May and José, and as declaimers of the verse, either in unison or divided ensemble passages. The first score was done by Esther Williamson. When the work reached the New York Y. M. H. A. in 1942, it was reduced to a suite of three duets called *Three Women*, was shorn of verse, had a new score by Ray Green, and failed of its effect.

A copy of the first work-sheet shows the painstaking care that went into the original production; how the clean-boned if somewhat uneven poem (written for the dance by William Archibald) was measured for timing, phrasing, and accent; how movement and lighting directions were detailed; and how musical possibilities were considered. José designed the costumes: simple, long dark blue dresses for the choric dancers, a gray stage uniform for himself, and characteristic attire for the three women impersonated by May. In the first scene, "The Wife," she speeds her husband off to war in a gray gingham blouse and long black skirt, to verse ending bitterly:

> You,
> the wife with need of glory,
> give your husband to the dead.

The work-sheet calls for angry, changing lights, and double forte in the last line, reinforced by the drums. The chorus moves and makes tableaux in the background.

In the next scene, "The Prostitute," she is a honky-tonk blonde in a short tight skirt and revealing low-necked bodice. The small platform that served as bed in the marital scene is here a dance floor. The music is "lascivious blues" and the lighting a "vulgar orange spot." The soldier forgets his troubles for a while to the measured tread of the verse beginning:

> And you, the blond in the back-room bar,
> let your drinking glass be filled—
> drink the red wine that he's spilt—
> Your wet flesh giving
> the last of living
> to the man
> who is here
> to be killed.

In the third scene, "The Nurse," she is a sculptured gray angel of mercy attending the soldier as he lies dying. "Cold blue lights over entire stage, no shadows" gives the atmosphere of a deserted battlefield. On the platform, now a rise in the terrain, José has a stylized death, the nurse tenderly holding him as if putting him to sleep (the music is a lullaby) while Lee Sherman and two girls do slow falls, and the group turns in legato motion.

> He feels the pain
> But must not cry
> Bind them together (repeat)

The chorus chants separate lines antiphonally, "Bind them together" in unison, to "give the effect of a chorus of fates."

War Lyrics, which began with a Prologue:

> The women take the blow and bow
> Bow low, bow deep—

the lighting sardonically "to be over entire stage as though for a gay folk dance," with variations on the "Taps" theme sounding in the music, closed with an Epilogue in pale diffused light, fading toward the end. There were changes in tempo from the main funeral dirge theme, each spoken line underscored by the pound of heavy footsteps, and pantomimic dancing downstage.

It is done—
Dig deep—
It is done—
   Dig deep—
Dig deep, dig deep.

Variations of the "Taps" theme were sounded, but there was no accompaniment for the closing phrase, which began (with another sardonic touch) to a bacchanale rhythm:

But thank no god—
no living god—
no supernatural
mystic god—
no high
all mighty
gracious god—
that you
are here
to
dig—

With this work began the partnership of the Humphrey-Weidman-trained José Limón and the Graham-trained May O'Donnell. Together they devised three new duos and with a program including *Three Women* toured the Pacific Coast for eighteen months. All the music was by Ray Green, May's husband. Claire Falkenstein did the décor and costumes for the three new dances, which were designed for entertainment and left two beautiful dancers sadly in need if not then in search of a choreographer.

The opening number was quite aptly *Curtain Raiser,* a set of five short pieces in gay theater mood, naturally very well done. Then came *This Story is Legend,* based on Hernán de Soto's discovery of the Mississippi, with spoken text from William Carlos Williams's *In the American Grain.* May was the virgin continent and later, in a tremendous blue veil, the river. José was of course the explorer, and between them they made rather a sex-drama of the great discovery. May was voluptuous, enticing, elusive, José the tortured pursuing male, until the blue veil engulfed him and

the wanton river danced his elegy. This was evidently not intended
to be funny.

But the end-piece, *Three Inventories on Casey Jones,* bound-
ing from the ballad into flights of child-like (or childish) fantasy,
went determinedly in for broad comedy. It had a painted set in the
manner of a child's drawing. May's bolt-and-rivet trimmed bodice,
if not her bright red ankle-length tutu, identified her as the triple-
threat Locomotive—"Choo-Choo, Sick Engine, Streamliner." José,
in red shirt and bold blue-and-white striped overalls, wore the cap
of the Engineer. He carried an oil can, which, with a temporary
lapse of taste, he used suggestively. He had not then learned to distinguish between honest sex and talking dirty in dance.

A lot of good dancing was wasted on this program. It was received as "theater magic" in some places on the West Coast, but
silence was the answer in New York. It had two performances there,
one at the Y. M. H. A. and one at the Studio Theater. *Dance Observer* was more tolerant than enthusiastic about it. May eventually
went back to Martha Graham, José to Doris Humphrey. Both partners were too perceptive as artists to be content with such banalities.

José married Pauline Lawrence in California in the fall of
1942, and came East in time to prepare his solo *Chaconne* for the
all-Bach program at the Studio Theater. This program, which
opened on December 27, 1942, was scheduled for three Sunday
nights and ran to sold-out houses for eleven. José composed and
danced his role in the spirit of the music, that is, of Bach's *Chaconne
in D minor* for unaccompanied violin. More than that, he composed and danced it in the spirit of the chaconne as he knew it—a
dance form that according to the program note originated in
Mexico (when it was called New Spain) as a "robust and raucous
dance," was refined and formalized at the court of Old Spain, and
later spread to other courts of Europe. It was because the chaconne
had an especial meaning for him as a dance form issuing from his
native land as well as a musical form developed by the composer
he most loved, that he made it so persuasively pure dance not de-
void of feeling. It is such dances as this that have helped to gain him
his reputation for magnificence.

During this interval he was *premier danseur* (quaint title for a modern) in the New Opera Company's production of *Rosalinda,* an Americanized version of Johann Strauss's *Die Fledermaus,* which did him no particular good or ill. There followed at the Studio Theater in 1943 several fine-grained works, either by him or Doris Humphrey, in which he appeared. There was her *Song of the West* and *El Salón Mexico,* to Aaron Copland's score, designed for him and Florence Lessing (as guest artist) with a background group of six girls. In this Mexican "Roseland Ballroom," or cheap amusement hall, the Latin lover woos his dream-girl, a sultry beauty in white, and emotional cross-currents well up and pattern themselves within and around the tense and yearning duo-dance of courtship. The whole is woven of the songs and dances of the people (no Humphrey dance leaves people out) into a stinging art dance.

José's hearty *Western Folk Suite,* danced by him and Maria Maginnis, consisted of a "Reel," to music by Norman Cazden (after a song by Woody Guthrie); "Ballad," ("The Ballad of Charlie Rutlage," to music of Charles Ives); and "Caper" (later "Pop Goes the Weasel") to an arrangement of the air by Esther Williamson. This was good lively dancing, unstereotyped in the use of folk themes, though José is built in too heroic a mold for capering, and the neatly packaged words from the wings got mussed in delivery. As a dancer, José is happiest when he is miserable, in somber dark velvet mood or roles of solemn grandeur.

In April 1943, just as he had got well started on the road of individual achievement, he was inducted into the Army of the United States. He trained at Camp Lee, Virginia, and in almost no time at all was preparing a new dance for a show. This was *We Speak for Ourselves,* to a prose-poem written for him by Lynn Riggs, and presented as the feature of a soldier-revue, *Fun for the Birds,* staged by the Special Service Office for a war bond rally in Richmond. A pre-war dancer, Private Diane Roberts of the WAC, was his partner, and there was a dance chorus of twelve infantrymen. The Narrator was Corporal Richard Kendricks, a New York actor in civilian life. The costumes were the official fatigue and battle dress.

The dance-poem was published, with an outdoor rehearsal

picture, in *Theatre Arts* of December 1943. It expressed the sentiments of the rookie who was in the army now but hadn't got used to it yet—to the uniform and the shoes, the crowded, too intimate barracks, the KP and latrine duties, the drill and unquestioning taking of orders, to the whole abhorrent idea of war and killing— but was ready to carry on and do his best because as a man he must. It was of course a natural for the soldier performers and the soldier and kin-to-soldier audience. Private Limón adapted modern dance to military formations and details that struck the common chord. A nostalgic interlude touched upon the soldier's longing for home, with all the dear particulars of house and tree and yard, all the "little unimportant things" magnified by distance; the devotion of father and mother, the love of the one girl, hauntingly, heartbreakingly, by separation enhanced. The ending was a resolute forward charge by soloist and chorus into the fight. It was one *pièce d'occasion* that rang true.

All his army life José worked, practicing when he could, to counteract the effect of military training on his dancing muscles. Fortunately in some respects, less so in others, he was placed in the Special Services, where he had an opportunity to exercise a portion of his talents directing and appearing in entertainment units and camp shows. Nevertheless, army life is army life, no matter how much modified, and orders is orders, whether one likes them or not. Serious dance was regarded with less favor than bumps, grinds, quivers, pratt falls, and what José describes as "the rest of the blatant vocabulary" of burlesque. It is not surprising, then, that toward the end of his service, when he was stationed near New York, he inaugurated his trio with Beatrice Seckler and Dorothy Bird, and began serious work with them under Doris Humphrey's direction.

What is surprising is that when he left the army, nearly as jittery as a battle-fatigued veteran, he went to a ballet teacher, Nennette Charisse, to be put in shape. At that time, he has told me, going to class was the only security he knew. Whether it was the exactitude of a codified system or the precision of the steps that he needed to ease him from military precision into the free movement of modern dance, he got into alignment after twenty lessons, and that was all he required of ballet. The turning to it, however, is significant of both a trend and a tradition.

Modern dance has never been as completely divorced from ballet as it thinks it is. The founders had it. The young dancers want it. Some of them feel cheated because they did not have it earlier. "Martha and Doris had ballet training," they say, "why shouldn't we?" They unblushingly put bars in their studios and go to work, and think of themselves as no less modern because of it. Others hedge and refuse to call what is obviously balletic by name. José has a good explanation of what happens to the ballet step when done by the bare, unrestricted foot of modern dance. A class of his had been crossing the floor with agitated torso over one foot modern and one in the classic (or classic-derived) *relevé*. "It is really very different," he said when questioned. "The modern *relevé* is not so mechanical, there is more pulsation in it; it is more supple, more *human,* there is more a sense of breathing in the foot." It is a *relevé* all the same, and, consciously or not, it has to be done by *human* succession movement in the foot, even in ballet shoes.

José teaches to the top of his class and at the top of his bent. In an old sweater and trunks in the classroom he is nearly as spectacular as he is in costume on the stage. Where the more temperate teacher addresses the middle of the class, he streaks ahead, letting the proficient pupils catch up with him if they can, and the poor ones lag behind if they must. The process is not so callous as it sounds. Teaching modern is a different proposition from what it was twenty years ago. When José was a beginner so was the American modern dance. Techniques had not developed as they have today and everybody went more slowly. Now, when techniques are more complicated, the pupils are more ready for them. With the spread of modern dance instruction in schools and colleges, the girls (there are still more girls than boys) come into an intermediate or master class well prepared for advanced work. Besides, the country is overflowing with talented youth, in dance, as in music, art, and theater.

The class I watched was at the Duncanbury School of Arts in

Boston, where José came once a week to teach during the 1946–47–48 seasons. Some of the established New England teachers held back, but a few husky Amazons from the West could take anything he gave them. He was using the third movement of a Bach Toccata (he always teaches to Bach) with many intricate steps in it, the body bending forward to one side, sharply accented and changing position while arms and legs were engaged in several rhythms simultaneously. The sequence was from one of his own compositions. I asked him later how he could teach a group of girls steps and movements that originated in his own body. He seemed to think he got around it by slanting the work to the female body. What actually took place was that he danced it male and the girls danced it female—it being impossible for them to do otherwise.

When at the end of the 1948 season he presented six of his advanced girls in a lecture demonstration, I realized his importance as a teacher. The girls had choreographed their own pieces, using words, using established music, or improvised music, or no music. They did things I had never seen done before. They opened a new door on the infinite movement possibilities in modern dance. Teaching that so releases the creative imagination is a great work in itself.

But to go back a bit. When José, with his army haircut and army nerves, finally left the Brooklyn Army Base in 1945, he had already prepared a trio program, and, in a two-week furlough, toured to Chicago and St. Louis with it. As has been said, the dark and wiry Humphrey-Weidman-trained Beatrice Seckler and the blonde and luscious Dorothy Bird (of the Graham training to which he so easily accommodates himself) were his partners. His first work of this period was the *Vivaldi Concerto,* to Bach's piano transcription of Vivaldi's *Concerto in D minor,* which, with new partners, is given on his current programs. It is a dance of abstract design, having a coolly formal Fugue, a sober, unsentimental Adagio, and a spirited Finale. The girls wear gowns of courtly grace and José's well-formed thighs are noble in brown tights. There are interesting technical devices, such as double lifts in the Finale, and also some rather trying convolutions, reminiscent of Balanchine, in the slow movement. There is something about a formal trio of two girls and one man that follows an ancient pattern in Balanchine ballet.

Eden Tree, of the trio program, was said in the program note to follow "an ancient pattern in human experience." In this ancient and perennial pattern, Beatrice was the faithful Wife, Dorothy the seductive Lilith. José, ever the apex of the trio, was here the apex of the triangle. "Idyll," "Discord," "Invocation," "Enchantment," "The Return," were the chapters in the little story with a happy ending, which had slight dramatic impact but was pleasing for movement that curved and flowed and did not stab the air. The music was arranged from a score by Carl Engel, but José composed the accompaniment for "Invocation" and "Enchantment." The trio dispersed when Dorothy went into a Broadway musical, and in the summer of 1946, amid a somewhat larger ensemble, José stood forth in full stature in the great works of Doris Humphrey. He composed two other pieces that year, the solo *Danza,* to music by J. Arcadio, first performed at Jacob's Pillow, and *Masquerade,* a solo in three parts—"Carte Blanche," "Secret Formula," and "Gordian Knot"—given on tour and not heard of since.

José composed his third large group work in 1947, while teaching a summer session at the Duncanbury School. It was choreographed to Lukas Foss's Biblical cantata, *Song of Songs,* and presented, with Miriam Pandor as partner, in an all-Limón program at the Hatch Memorial Shell on the Charles River Esplanade in Boston on two evenings in August. This was a student production. It was not covered by the newspapers, and caused no great stir. Although Boston is singularly impervious to modern dance, it is said that approximately 5000 persons attended the second performance (admission free).

On December 21, 1947 José and his company gave a program at the New York City Center. The new work was Doris Humphrey's *Day on Earth.* It brings out in José a tender radiance and earthy sweetness not called forth by either the *Lament* or *The Story of Mankind.* It is indeed a beautiful work, and critics and public found it so. Soon afterwards the company played a one-week engagement at the Mansfield Theater, dancing the *Lament* as a curtain raiser for the revival of Marc Blitzstein's *The Cradle Will Rock*. From there Meg Mundy went on to her sensational success in Sartre's *The Respectful Prostitute*. The company again scattered after winning the highest praise and all sorts of glowing publicity. "Every time we give a New York program," Pauline Lawrence Limón has written me, "we have to pull the company together from shows, husbands, children, hospitals, etc., and begin all over again."

It is not any of it good enough for a dancer of José's quality. If Ballet Theatre were as wide awake as it ought to be, it would present him as guest artist with his own ensemble in *Lament for Ignacio Sánchez Mejías* and *The Story of Mankind* (for a starter) and have reason to be everlastingly grateful for its courage. And it would do this quickly, before some more enterprising company snaps him up.

But if the way of the modern dancer is hard, it is not fruitless. Struggle has made José stronger. Out of all that has happened to him, in dance and out, he emerges a puissant individual artist. His long association with Charles Weidman may have grounded him in masculine technique; it did not transform him into a Weidman comedian. There is none of the visual onomatopoeia or the quick-darting evanescence of his former teacher in anything he does— not only because Charles is inimitable, but because José is not imitative; and also because he lacks the instinctive comic sense. A sense of humor in real life, yes. But on the stage he wears jocosity more with rue than with blitheness. His romantic mien is against it, besides.

Although he is so far at his dancingest in Doris Humphrey's works, and thrives within her radius, he is no mere reflection of her style. It is the saving grace of irony and the tragic undertone of *Story of Mankind* that fit that role to him. It is the exalted tragedy and poetic majesty of *Lament* that brings out all his best. It is the wide range of his own technical expansion, the depth of the motivating impulses within himself, that charge him for his potent radioactivity in American dance.

ANNA SOKOLOW

Anna Sokolow was a rich little poor girl, blessed with humor and imagination. Her career began in the children's professional company at the Neighborhood Playhouse when it was still in Grand Street, wended through the concert field and a couple of foreign countries, and is now in theater again—with concert asides. Early in 1947 she staged for the Elmer Rice–Kurt Weill *Street Scene* the short and snappy jitterbug duet that brought down the house. It was brilliantly done by Sheila Bond and Danny Daniels. More than that, it was composed out of full consciousness of its invironment. It did not forward the plot action one mite, but it added more than a mite of atmosphere to it. In the fall of the year she was teaching movement as an element of acting at Stage for Action, numbering among her distinguished pupils Elia Kazan, the director of the hour. She had done theater work before, having staged the dances for the Federal Theater's *Sing for your Supper*, for the Theater Guild's *Valley Forge,* and the *Noah* starring Pierre Fresnay. But this was a rediscovery, an enlarged sense of theater as a means of reaching people.

Anna is a people's dancer. In the early days, the days of the Dance Unit and the New Dance League, her left wing was always showing. It was indeed protuberant. Everything she did was riffled with caustic wit and satiric jab, not in plea for the proletariat alone, but for people (provided they were underdogs) everywhere. Now maturity, experience, a new war, have moderated her attitude.

There have been several turning points in Anna's career. The first was in 1930, when Martha Graham came to the Neighborhood Playhouse to teach. Anna had taken the cultural courses, studied music, painting, stage design, acting, and what she looks back upon as a more or less Duncanesque type of dancing. When she joined Martha's classes, and eventually her group, "it was like being inspired seven days a week." She was in Louis Horst's first composition class, and in time returned to her alma mater to conduct classes of her own. She was a prominent member of the Martha Graham concert group until 1938, and never forgot what she learned there. But she is not a typical Graham dancer. For one thing, the motivation of her dances is sociological rather than psychological or psychiatric. For another, she is creative, and could not content herself with being a carbon copy (not that Martha would wish it—she always fosters individuality). By 1932 she was going the rounds of the workers' clubs and trade union organizations with her Dance Unit, touring as far West as Chicago and Detroit.

Whether or not it was a second turning point, it was an encounter of surprises, when Anna spent five months in Soviet Russia in 1934. The Russians looked upon her revolutionary modern dance, bristling with social themes, as so much calisthenics. They objected to her name because it was too Russian. They got around that difficulty by putting it on the billboards in English lettering, though they would have preferred it to be Anne Smith or Jones, apparently entertaining the same idea we have at home that foreign talent is more exciting and better box-office than domestic. At that time the revolutionary Russians, making radical departures from tradition in government, economics, even drama, were reverently preserving the established traditions in their theater dance. Anna decided that it was because it had not long been possible to see the aristocratic ballet in shirt-sleeves, so to speak, and that after the workers had had enough of it, the ballet would then progress to new developments.

The joker is that she herself came to love ballet, to study it, teach it, and rationalize her use of it, not on account of Russia, but because of its inevasibility in the United States. Before she had left Martha's group she felt the need of knowing ballet, and went to Margaret Curtis at the Metropolitan Opera Ballet School. Ballet, she reasons, has always been nourished by folk forms; like all dance, like all the arts, it draws its life from the people. The lively peasant dances gave a new spurt to the formal dance of the courtiers. So it has ever been, and will be. As people move, so are they. As they are affects their dance. Ergo, ballet, stemming from the people, ties right in with modern dance.

Anna had already established a repertory and a following when she gave her debut program at the Guild Theater (under the auspices of the *New Masses*) on November 14, 1937. Only the octave-leaping *Opening Dance* (Shebhalin), a group number, and the very pertinent solo, *Slaughter of the Innocents* (Alex North) were new. The audience, keyed up by news of the bombardment of Barcelona, received this dance of sorrowing motherhood with a kind of joy, as if she had eased their hearts by saying for them what they felt and giving their feelings the dignity of form. For it was a dance and not a philippic. There were Spanish rhythms in it and the plaintive cry of the guitar. It was a dance for the Spanish people, and if somewhat overwrought, it could hardly be otherwise just then.

War is Beautiful (North), with the Dance Unit augmented to ten girls and five boys, was a mocking indictment of the glorified lust for war in Fascist Italy. It was based on excerpts from a poem by Filippo Tommaso Marinetti, and was presented in five parts: (1) "War is beautiful . . ." rushed with the frightened steps of women, helpless against the preparations; (2) ". . . because it fuses in Strength, Harmony and Kindness" impersonated the false idealization of these qualities in a gruesome trio of graces; (3) ". . . because it realizes the long dreamed of metalization of the human body" posed the soldier ranks, opening, closing, struggling, falling, against smooth passages in another group commending the holocaust with the repeated statement, "How beautiful!" (4) ". . . because it symphonizes pauses choked by silence, the perfumes and odors of putrefaction, and creates the spiral smoke of burning villages," recalled the gloating of Mussolini's son Bruno over the entrancing view from his plane, while the women's running steps were re-employed in distorted form to signify the actual suffering under the so-pleasing picture; and (5) ". . . because it serves the greatness of our great Fascist Italy" crashed the foregoing themes together in a modern dance of death, demolishing all the decencies under pretence of preserving and exalting them. It was, perhaps, a little heavy going. But it was done in terms of movement, not clumsy realism. Anna always managed to be more the artist than the agitator. The urgency of her message never displaced her from the realm of dance.

Other dances on this program, some of which had already

been nominated minor masterpieces, were the group work, *Strange American Funeral* (Elie Siegmeister), based on Michael Gold's poem of a steel worker "Caught in a flood of molten ore—whose flesh and blood turned to steel," the words, sung by the baritone, Mordecai Bauman, somewhat intrusive in their complexity; and the following solos: *Case History Number* . . . (Wallingford Riegger), a study in juvenile delinquency by the poverty route, showing a youth, bored and restless in his grim environment, releasing stifled energies in the petty offenses that lead to felony, and culminating in a tense crouch of fear against the backdrop; the devastating *Four Little Salon Pieces* ("Debut, Élan, Reverie and Entr'acte") (Shostakovich), putting the hated debutante in her place; and the bright *Ballad in a Popular Style* (North), a lyrical jazz journey to whistling accompaniment.

In the summer of 1937 Anna had shared the first Bennington Fellowships with Esther Junger and José Limón, and prepared for the Bennington Festival the group work, *Façade—Esposizione Italiana* (North), an exposition or exposé of fascism that could be called a sequel to *War is Beautiful*. Anna, symbolizing the people (good, of course) was the Citizen, silently, but not inactively, observing the bad, bellicose ones proceed to heap ruin on all their heads. "Spectacle" illustrated the pomp and pageantry of Mussolini's nefarious régime (funny, nobody has thought it necessary to make a dance about his ignominious end); "Belle Arte" the pride in nationalistic culture; "Giovanezza" vainglory in athletic skills as ingredient to martial glory; "Prix Femina" maternal awards for woman, breeder of soldiers, sacrificing her wedding ring *en masse* to war; and "Phantasmagoria" the nice mess all this got the simple Italian people into. It was, like its companion piece, a little heavy going choreographically.

But Anna herself, with her beautiful inward composure and gracile strength, was a pleasure to watch. Always the dancer, she projects unerringly in her own performance, whatever is going on around her. Her pale, oval face, framed in straight, mousy hair brushed severely off her forehead, her finely chiseled little body, express the calm, not of passivity, but of the complete self-contain-ment that can break into controlled dance activity at will. She is at once lyrical without softness, dynamic without violence, restrained but not tame.

Like José Limón, Anna has appeared and taught in Boston without making much of a dent in the civic consciousness. José (via his New York successes) is gradually gaining recognition. He will yet become the fashionable thing to see. In Anna's case, there was no social cachet in seeing her dances of social significance, and unless she gets a display in *Life* or a profile in the *New Yorker,* there is not likely to be. She made her first appearance in Boston with the New Dance League in 1936, when none but the faithful if not happy few were the wiser. She did a humorous trio, *Death of Tradition,* with Jane Dudley and Sophie Maslow (equally under-rated), her *Ballad in a Popular Style,* and *Histrionics* (Hindemith), a parody on styles in acting. The slippers of her Hamletesque costume were, in relation to modern dance, the most revolutionary thing about it. The costumes of that period were generally the rather dismal regulation outfit. Modern dance had not been to charm school or consulted the beautician.

A few years later the Contemporary Dance Group, Boston branch of the New Dance League, brought Anna on once a week to teach. For four seasons, with some interruptions, she made the weekly trip from New York, to teach a small class of working girls at night. She gave an occasional lecture-demonstration, as at the Y. W. C. A., an occasional college program, at Tufts, Wheaton, and Wellesley, and did her best to develop a group and promote dance interest in Boston. To no avail. The members of the Contemporary Dance Group, all working girls, made sacrifices to bring her. But the time came when they could afford the expense no longer, and the Group eventually disbanded.

In 1939 something happened to Anna that changed the entire course of her career. She was invited by the Fine Arts Department of the Mexican government to give a season of concerts at the *Palacio de Bellas Artes,* and has been living half in and half out of Mexico ever since. Just before she left she gave a concert in Boston's Jordan Hall (sponsored by the Contemporary Dance Group and the American League for Peace and Democracy) that showed an already changing artist, still concerned with social problems, but now also turning to her own racial heritage for inspiration. New that season was the solo dance poem, *The Exile,* to Palestinian folk music arranged by Alex North, and a script written for the dance by Sol Funaroff, spoken and sung by Mordecai Bauman. The verse was spare and simple, the dance strong and clear. The first part, "I had a garden . . . ," was a tender reminiscence of ancient Jewry, the flowering of Judaic culture, Oriental, almost Biblical, in atmosphere. The second part, "The beast is in the garden . . . ," was turbulent with the age-old story of persecution climaxed in the destroying beast of Hitlerism.

By poetic indirection Anna takes the line of direct action. At least of her solos this is true. Some of her group passages are cloudy compared with the direct drive of her solo work. Groups are expensive, especially on tour, and that is one reason we so often see a cluster where a crowd is indicated. They are variable, hard to get and to keep. They must earn a living and are often otherwise engaged when most needed. It is a problem that confronts all the young choreographers, who thus remain superior soloists, unable to fulfill their promise in group·works. Anna did not have a group worthy of her in Boston, where she did *Façade* with eight ineffectual girls. But Boston (the same faithful few) saw an improvement in costuming (Rose Bank the designer), a hint of décor in the ascending levels. It heard in the score by Alex North, her pianist-composer (and whilom husband), music co-operatively written for her dance. It was partially prepared for the changes that were to come.

The Mexican reaction to Anna's ideological dances was very different from Russia's. The public responded to them at once. Themselves a dramatic people, they reveled in the dramaturgy of her work. The social theme was recognized and appreciated. Artists like Rivera and Orozco, long practiced in projecting the theme in paint, were astonished to find that the same thing could be done through dancing. Such use of dance was new to them. Anna, supported by her own group, gave twenty-six concerts in Mexico City between April 4 and May 15, 1939. At the close of the series she was invited to train a Mexican group and give performances with them. The American group went home, and Anna founded the first modern dance group in Mexico.

The native girls, trained in Spanish dance and ballet, fell easily into modern movement, perhaps atavistically linked to it by the basic movements in the primitive dancing of their ancestry. Anna returned the compliment by composing a dance for them in Spanish style mixed with simple ballet, *Visión Fantástica* (after Goya), with music by Padre Antonio Soler, dedicated to the memory of Silvestre Revueltas. At the end of the first six months she was invited to come back the following season, and for several years, the Mexican group, *La Paloma Azul,* gave performances under her direction. She and her painter husband, Ignacio Aguirre, now spend the summer half of the year in Mexico and the winter half in New York. In 1948 she was invited by Carlos Chávez to conduct a new group in Mexico City.

To the American girl of Russian parentage, Mexico opened up a whole new avenue of culture. It was through Carlos Mérida, then head of the dance division of the Department of Fine Arts, that she was first invited. Once there, she met other painters, many Spanish refugees, artists in other mediums, among them the writers José Bergamin and Constancia de la Mora, the composers Rodolfo Halffter, Carlos Chávez, and the late Silvestre Revueltas. Such illustrious good-neighborliness was bound to flavor her work, though not to best effect at once.

Visión Fantástica was not a success in New York. The flavor had not been assimilated. When in 1941 she presented it in revised form, under the title *Caprichosas,* naming the sections after the etchings from which the dances were derived—"The Little Bullfighter," "Blind Man's Buff," "The Hazing of the Effigy," "The Flirtation"—it remained an alien work. In 1942 she brought back *Lament for the Death of a Bullfighter* from her suite, *Homage to García Lorca,* and *Songs for Children,* based on the García Lorca poems, both with music by Revueltas. The *Lament,* in an approximation of the matador's attire, was an individual interpretation but lacked the force of compulsory expression. Of the song cycle, "Mother, I want to be made of silver," tremulous with childhood fantasy, touched closest the core of poetry.

As a dance it was no match for Anna's own childhood song, *Mama Beautiful,* to a poem by Mike Quinn and music by Alex North. In this colloquial lyric of the tenements, the small Anna, in her little-girl dress, limns through her movement-responses to the verse the gallantry of the mother who tries to make her child see butterflies where cockroaches are, and brownies in place of rats, against the ingrained toughness of the child, already hardened by contact with the streets. "Ma said it was a butterfly— She can't fool me." The reader of the verse was Arno Tanney, again a baritone.

Apart from the Mexican products, in which she had not yet found herself, this was a changing Anna. The social comment was sweeter. She did not look so fighting mad about it. The acerb harangues of *Mill Doors, Speaker, Inquisition* ("Provocateur and Vigilante") were far in the past. Her Russian memento, the *Suite of Soviet Songs* (Adonian) (in which, in Boston, she was assisted by members of the nonprofessional Contemporary Dance Group), was in the main healthy and happy with folk feeling. There was a new esprit in her costumes (still by Rose Bank), a new lightness of mood and manner in her dancing (lifted by ballet techniques), a new outlook, an expanded internationalism, in her Mexican subjects. But the best was yet to be.

It came in the spring of 1946 with the most beautiful concert of her career, a program of new dances she showed in Boston before New York. She had mastered her Mexican material, found what there was for her alone to use, and how to use it. She had looked deep into Jewish traditions and found what there was for her to say about them. It was a solo program, presented with the artistry of a song recital, Anna, like a lieder-singer, projecting each number with jewel clarity, creating and sustaining a mood. Choicest were the dulcet little figures of the madonna in *Mexican Retablo,* and the shy and hesitant Jewish maiden in *The Bride.*

"Our Lady" of the paisano, as depicted in native paintings, stands on her pedestal with fixed outward arms, moving with stiff gestures like an animated doll, gently, metronomically tapping one foot to the native air. She is half musical toy, half holy image, until in one unbelievable moment she bends toward the worshipper in an attitude of infinite tenderness, and becomes a living image of love. The dance, with its slow rhythmic movement and metrical tapping, its effluvium of compassion, holds the spectator, like the peasant, in a spell.

The Bride, derived from orthodox Jewish wedding customs, to traditional music, is in its way as exquisite. For décor there is a suggestion of the wedding canopy, the ritualistic Chuppah. The girl, in her simple white dress and headdress, waits with timidity and wonder at the brink of her marriage to an unknown groom, only a little comforted by her mother's assurances (soprano voice offstage), wistful in the midst of the elaborate ceremonials, not sure whether to be sad or glad. Anna invests both figures, the Catholic virgin no less than the young Jewess, with propulsive feeling, and, in her own small person, endows them with delicacy and grace.

The second part of *Mexican Retablo* dramatizes an emotional attitude toward the Virgin, in dark, impassioned contrast to the serene luster of "Our Lady." Anna is a shawled and anguished supplicant kneeling before the image (now of course invisible), appealing for the life of the man she loves. The dance, done altogether on the knees, is not particularly Mexican, or unusual. *Danza,* to music of Rodolfo Halffter, in gay, native-type dress and pattern, is a bright adaptation of Mexican rhythms, the artist now in full possession of her medium.

Of the other new Jewish dances, *Kaddish* ("Prayer for the Dead"), to music of Ravel, was most strongly racial in its deep, wailing tones of voice and movement. The three *Images from the Old Testament* had not then been developed to capacity, though they may have been in later New York programs. "Rose of Sharon" (Hemsi), "Miriam" (Engel), and "Pastoral" (Folk) were but dimly evocative compared with "Our Lady" and *The Bride.* But *The Exile* was more evocative than ever, the balletic opening dance, *Two Preludes* (Bach), was radiant in its free and happy sufficiency, and the recital as a whole crowned Anna with a new and shining loveliness. Save for the slightly cynical *Mama Beautiful,* there was no reference to social, or at least economic, problems. The sharp and bitter irony of former days was gone.

Like her great predecessors from Isadora on, Anna has a tremendous sense of responsibility toward the dancers of the future.

It is not enough to be a good dancer yourself, she says, you must help others to be good dancers. It was amusing to watch her, one night at the Contemporary Dance Group studio, dressed in the black wool tights and soft slippers of ballet practice, teaching a modern dance class in leotards and bare feet, attaching weight to ballet techniques and instilling lightness into modern movements. She felt no conflict in combining the two forms, she said, because all movement is organic. Both methods require the controlled and centered body common to all good dancing. The five foot positions are the perfect base for action. You can use a person with a well turned-out thigh in modern work, whereas you cannot use a person with a turned-in thigh in either ballet or modern.

She believes that the young dance student should begin with the classics, as the young music student does; then, with the trained extremities of ballet and the free torso of modern dance, he can do anything. In fact, she thinks young dancers should learn all techniques, be open to every kind of dancing. There should be no isolationism in dance, but a reciprocal exchange among all forms.

She taught in picturesque phrases, and the New York accent.

"Puncture the air!" she cried, for reaching into space on the upstroke of a movement, instead of bobbing up and down in space.

"Don't lead with your chin!" (when running).

"Don't squirm!" (contractions).

"Don't overreach yourself!" (elevation).

"Push from under, Under, UNDER. The movement becomes arbitrary when done without musical flow, flabby when done without feeling."

She taught as if the future of dance depended upon it. As, in part, it does.

ESTHER JUNGER

From the beginning of her career Esther Junger has moved in an orbit of her own, flashing comet-wise in a recital, starring in a musical show, taking a speaking part in a serious one, always maintaining a solid reputation for artistry if not a fixed place in the modern system. In the year 1947 her trajectory streaked from circus to poetic drama to night club. She directed the dances and pageants for Ringling Brothers–Barnum and Bailey in the early spring, staged the dances for Robinson Jeffers's *Dear Judas* in the early fall, and then rehearsed a straight ballet on toe (to music by Raymond Scott) for Billy Rose's Diamond Horseshoe until the end of the year—ready to swing into her 1948 circuit with the circus again. The circus was an adventure in space and size, and in presenting dance to a four-sided audience, as in primitive times. The drama dances, straight modern, to group singing of Bach chorales arranged by Lehman Engel, were superior to the play, which was not well received and did not last long. As for the night club, well, Esther had been there before, having staged a modern dance show for the Diamond Horseshoe in 1945.

Esther made a triumphal entrance into the concert field at the Guild Theater on November 23, 1930. Her first major work, *Go Down, Death,* from James Weldon Johnson's *God's Trombones,* was an immediate success. The poet himself read the lines, and Esther danced in a neo-primitive style to which she later largely adhered. It was a solo program. *Woman in Yellow,* to Ravel's *Bolero* (before it had become hackneyed), and *Inertia,* to music by Maurice Lawner, a slow-motion study in sustained movement, also contributed to her success. The new dancer with the plain, piquant little face and the beautiful plastic body under marvelous control, danced like nobody's business and like nobody else.

After a season at the Dance Center, appearing in the modernized versions of *Petrouchka* and *El Amor Brujo* by Gluck-Sandor and Felicia Sorel, she gave another recital at the Guild Theater on February 28, 1932. She repeated *Go Down, Death,* with Richard B. Harrison, the beloved "God" of *The Green Pastures,* reading the poem, and added several new solos. There was *Wide Open Plains* (Debussy), in broad, fluent movement, a space-covering departure from the then prevalent axial base, and its foil, *Closed-In Cities* (Kathryn Philbrick), in the tight, restricted movements expected. Both were criticized as rather literal at the time. There was the satirical *Soap Box* (Philbrick) in three parts: "Politician," "Lady

Reformer," and "Revolutionist"; also the apparently irresistible
Scriabin, *Toward the Light,* and *Conscience* to drums only. So far
the dancer excelled the choreographer.

During these years she was seen with comparative regularity
(for her) in the Y. M. H. A., Students Dance Recitals, and Brooklyn
Museum series, in John Martin's lecture recitals at the New School
for Social Research, and in intimate recitals, as at the famous Studio
61, Carnegie Hall. In 1934 she was star dancer in *Life Begins at 8:40*
at the Winter Garden for nearly the whole year, and in 1935 she
was star dancer in the Theater Guild's *Parade* during its brief existence. In both shows she was supported by a group for whom she
did the choreography.

Parade tried out in Boston, to the dismay of the proper Bostonians, whose subscriptions to the Guild plays are a part of their
social whirl. Dowagers stalked empurpled up the aisles. The politely
infuriated Apley gentlemen tore their tickets into bits. The management had quite a time. For this, in the days when Communism
could be mentioned without danger of burning at the stake (but
was nevertheless frowned upon by our best people), was a Com-
munist show. Worse than that, it was facetious about it. It dared
to have fun pretending to telephone Joe Stalin for orders, speaking
to and of him in colloquial camaraderie. It also had its serious
moments, along the lines of "we want bread but we want roses,
too."

In all the furor the most unorthodox thing about it was overlooked. That was the dance movement, modern and no compromise. Esther was not concerned with the comedy of Communism,
or at that time, with theater. She was strictly giving a recital in a
revue. Even the chorus she had trained merged into the scenery
for her, as she danced in a straight-cut silver cloth tunic to the
duet, "Life Could Be So Beautiful" (if there were only money
enough to live on), her solo theme and variations. The dance was
wonderfully vital and varied, but stood absolutely alone. It emitted
no sense of monetary problems or yearning for financial betterment, unless the silver garment and gleaming tiara could be taken
as symbolical of the desired improvement. In the more dramatic
but less effective ballet, "Sugar Cane," as a leader of a revolt among

the workers, in jerky-striped costume, she had to play to the other dancers, and, attacked by a vicious overseer, go in for mimetic action. But here, as in the even more pantomimic musical number, "Tabloid Reds" (costume to match), she remained a being apart, a dancer of striking singularity.

She had not then become accustomed to adjusting herself to a group or to the special requirements of a Broadway show, in which she must perforce dance to subjects and music not of her own choosing, in costumes not designed by herself. She *had* insisted on having her costumes simplified to allow freedom of movement, but she couldn't have it all her own way. However, she did not dance in *Parade* with any glint of social consciousness in her eye. Whatever her beliefs, she does not believe in mixing art and propaganda, and there are no overt remonstrances against the social order in her repertory. In composition, she starts with a fairly bare outline and lets the dance fill itself in as it grows by performance. The dance thus takes on only the movements and gestures necessary to it. "If you begin the other way around," she said in an interview we had at the time, "your dance is overburdened with detail that has eventually to be deleted."

Esther was born in New York, on the East Side, of Austrian parentage. Her father was a singer, the first to record the singing voice for the then Victor Talking Machine Company, she says. She was a sickly child, unable to go to school until she was nine. But she was early conscious of movement. She remembers with what formality she conducted a burial ritual for a dead bird in the back yard, her playmates serving as mourning chorus. She was, paradoxically, fond of movement and averse to dancing, or to the interpretive dancing to which the children of that period were exposed. What it really amounts to is, no doubt, that she preferred muscular tension to stepping. She trained in physical education, studiously avoiding the dance classes while reveling in the exercises and the classes in anatomy, physiology, and kinesiology—with the curious outcome at commencement of a surprise solo called *Fugitive,* indulging in high dramatics to Rachmaninoff's *C# minor Prelude.*

Strengthened in body and alert in mind, she became a teacher of physical education in a New York high school, and injected so much dance into her course that it was more popular than any other. It was her own concept of dance, a growing concept, for which she could then find no suitable guide. Unmoved, except for a glimmer of latent possibilities, she saw Isadora late in her career. Untouched, she studied briefly at the New York Denishawn School. When, in 1925, she saw Bird Larson in a lecture demonstration, she was convinced that dance and movement could be combined to suit her purpose. She studied with the newfound teacher at the Neighborhood Playhouse for over two years, appearing with her in her only two recitals there.

Bird Larson was an individualist, an innovator, and a forerunner of modern dance, who died untimely in 1927, leaving a legacy of movement values that Esther has been among the few to expound and the chief to represent professionally. She too began her career in physical education. She was a teacher at Barnard College, taught corrective gymnastics at Teachers College, Columbia University, and spent a year at the New York Orthopedic Dispensary and Hospital—all of which gave her a sound anatomical foundation for her dance. The forward flowing movement from the base of the spine, the changing movement center in the torso, the pelvic rotations seen in modern dance, were independently worked out by her, without distortion. She was concerned with "natural rhythmic expression." She experimented with silent dancing, with dances to speech and song, to percussion alone, with religious dances. Before Ted Shawn or Ruth St. Denis performed their rituals and religious dances at St. Mark's-in-the-Bouwerie, she composed religious dance rituals for the famous church that nearly became infamous by harboring them.

After Bird Larson's death, Esther, with ten other Larson pupils, calling themselves the New World Dancers, gave a concert at the old Gallo Theater, presenting most of Miss Larson's dances and some of their own. It is, perhaps, not without reason that Esther's *Go Down, Death,* with the poet reading the lines, was first performed there. The group dissolved, as such groups usually do, and Esther, working alone, eventually developed her own theory of movement from the Larson base. Before her debut at the Guild

Theater, she took part in Irene Lewisohn's orchestral dance dramas, and in the Provincetown Playhouse production, *Fiesta.*

The most startlingly novel dance of Esther's career was the *Animal Ritual* given at a Guild Theater recital in November 1935. It was inspired by passages from Frazer's *The Golden Bough,* and used animal movements to suggest the atmosphere created by animal presence. Interlaced through its unique muscular patterns was an odd percussion accompaniment devised by the dancer herself and played by R. Sybil Ross. The costume was derived partly from Gauguin's paintings and partly from primitive drawings; that is, the skirt, like a sarong without the drape, was after Gauguin, and the upper section, leaving the midriff bare in stretching, but with a high neck, and sleeves, was after tribal dress. The colors were brown and rose with red and white accents, all most unusual, and of the dancer's own design. In those days, and in the main, Esther designed her costumes, which were strikingly original but simple, and, like the music (either pre-composed or composed for her), subservient to her dance.

Her movement theory is (and it does not sound so very different from Hanya Holm's) that the body must be used as a complete unit, that a displacement in any one part calls for compensatory action in other parts, that the center shifts but is always there. There is more to it than this, but this is what pertains just now. In her animal themes the center continually shifted, but legs, arms, torso, and head, when separately animated, were never separate. The movement was not naturalistic, but fabricated from nature into a free fantasia.

John Martin pronounced *Animal Ritual* one of the three best solos ever done by a concert dancer in this or any country. On the other hand, Henry Gilfond in *Dance Observer* thought *Archaic Figure* ("Untouched by Time and Times") (Philbrick) had more content, and Joseph Arnold Kaye in *The American Dancer* selected *Variations on a Tango* (Zuera) for top rating, as "an illustration in good dance terms of the seductiveness, the exhilaration, the vulgarity, the insolence and captivating rhythm of the genuine tango." Thus critics in their little nests do not agree. New also on this program were *Negro Themes* (Alexander Tansman), done in the man-

Jane Dudley in NEW WORLD A-COMIN'

Jane Dudley, Nina Caiserman, Phyllis Kahn, in SHORT STORY

Jean Erdman in OPHELIA

Jean Erdman in CREATURE ON A JOURNEY

Hadassah in SHUVI NAFSHI

and in
BROADWAY HINDU

THE LONELY ONES: *Jane Dudley, William Bales, Sophie Maslow*

José Limón (at Mills College) in DANZAS MEXICANAS

Letitia Ide and José Limón in LAMENT FOR IGNACIO SÁNCHEZ MEJÍAS

Anna Sokolow

Esther Junger
in Animal Ritual

Sybil Shearer

RARA TONGA:
Roger Ohardieno,
Katherine Dunham,
Tommy Gomez

Katherine Dunham and Archie Savage in CARNIVAL OF RHYTHM

Valerie Bettis in THE DESPERATE HEART

Valerie Bettis (completing a complicated ascent)

Pearl Primus in HARD TIME BLUES

Alphonse Cimber (drummer), Pearl Primus, Joseph Nash

Lester Horton

Scenes from Lester Horton's Dance Theater

SALOME *Above: Bella Lewitzky with unnamed dancer*
Below: with Carl Ratcliff

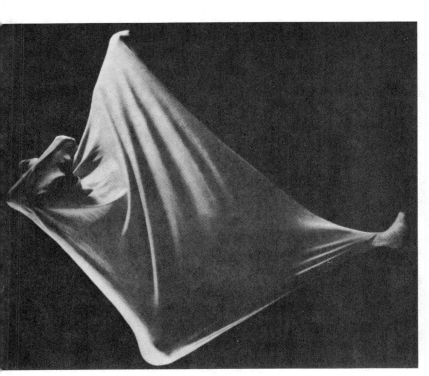

Ruth Page in The Expanding Universe

CBS Television

*Pauline Koner
and Robert Pagent in
It's a Date*

*Pauline Koner,
Bernard William,
Olga Lunick,
Forrest Bonshire
in Summertime*

ner of a Covarrubias painting; *Festival* (Jerome Moross), a study in rhythmic counterpoint with stylization of a celebration and its excitations, avoiding the ordinary bacchanalian approach; and *Untimely*: "Sentimentality" (Poulenc); "Pomposity" (A. Tcherepnin); and "Preciousness" (Casella); which, more after the order of the day, scooped up a handful of attributes to satirize in dance.

In February 1936 Esther appeared at Radio City Music Hall in her own solo, to music composed for it by Lehman Engel, and in November of that year introduced a new solo, *Dance for Tomorrow* (Moross) at a concert in the Y. M. H. A. Dance Theatre series. This dance, unprogrammatic in spite of its title, and done with large extensions and fluid torso, won by the verve of its movement values alone, and she long retained it in her repertory. There was in her work none of the studied equalization of movement—so much to the right, so much to the left—that monotonizes some dances. Hers was the asymmetrical twist.

In the summer of 1937 Esther shared with Anna Sokolow and José Limón the first Bennington Fellowships, and created her first major group work for the Festival. *Festive Rites,* to music by Morris Mamorsky, was in three sections: "Processional," "Betrothal," and "Recessional." The underlying feeling was earthy and folk, the rhythms primitive, or, modern-dance primitive. The "Betrothal" solo became a recital number. At Bennington also she did *Dance to the People* (Moross), and the impressionistic *Ravage* (Harvey Pollins), both solos. In the late fall she was one of the representatives of America Dancing at the Dance International's Rainbow Room performances.

Whether owing to the dominant background of physical education or to the early aversion to dance, Esther's reputation was built on uncommon, elastic movement rather than on uncommon expressivity. *Dance to the People,* which had its first New York showing in the Y. M. H. A. series, March 1939, was distinguished for this large, broad, rather graceful movement, exciting in itself without carrying any particular thought of or to the people. By that time her interest in Negro themes and rhythms had led her into jazz, and from then on she did a great deal in the jazz idiom. On this Y program was *Torch Song,* to music of George Gershwin, and

Mr. Bach Goes to Town, to Alec Templeton's celebrated piece, the latter compounding the early court dance and jazz with highly diverting effect.

The following March, again at the Y. M. H. A., she gave an interpretation of James Weldon Johnson's *Judgment Day,* to music by Harvey Brown and spoken text from the poem. A dramatic dance with amusing interludes of dice-rolling and other sins not of the Negro flesh alone, it displayed her aptitude for mimicry (and sometimes for mugging). Pauline Koner, as guest artist, appeared in it with her. They did together the scene to "Oh-o-o, sinner, where will you stand, In that Great Day when God's agoin' to rain down fire?", which began with shooting craps and ended with hymn-singing. The dancers were well matched in suppleness and comedic flair.

Pauline Koner is a beautiful dancer, with a wide travel background in Russia and the Middle East, a varied repertory, particolored by these experiences, the most attractive costumes, designed by herself, and a sense of the world picture. She uses modern dance techniques effortlessly, is in fact, generally considered a modern dancer, though she has until recently lacked the rough-hewn element of pure modernism. She is, at any rate, creative, and progressive. Since partnering José Limón in Doris Humphrey's *The Story of Mankind,* she has gone further and asked Doris to choreograph a work for her. The solo, *Voice in the Wilderness,* to music by Lukas Foss, includes a part for baritone who assists in the action as well as in the accompaniment. Pauline has often sung or spoken while dancing, in her own solos.

On their joint program, she and Esther performed together a trifle in tutus called *Cinema Ballerinas* that went out for laughs and hit below standard. In later years, Pauline did a ballet satire, in which she played both partners, that was far more suasive and entertaining. But this was Esther's program and it was reaching toward theater. *Negro Sketches* ("Barren Fields" and "Off to the City") to music of Duke Ellington, showed a girl in the cotton fields lured by the whistles of passing trains and finally obeying their call. *Scene: A Drawing Room* (Trude Rittman) served "The

Ingenue," "The Tragedienne," "A Wench," and "A Timid Soul," with sauce of satire.

An appearance as soloist and choreographer in the musical, *'Tis of Thee,* at the Maxine Elliott Theater (1940) gave Esther further opportunity to work a modern dance group into a Broadway show. Her first group work in the New York concert field was *Rhapsody, U. S. A.* (Alex North), using three girls and three boys. It was a syncopated square dance, in all jazz movements, but based primarily on the patterns of American square dancing, and again the juxtaposition of contrary folk forms made its comic effect. *Primitive Rituals* and *Lupe,* of South American savor, with the rumba as musical and movement motif, both with music by Alex North, were also in group-and-soloist form. But none of these group works had the originality or impact of her earlier and more outstanding solos.

Esther is attracted to the color theme, and to novelty most of the time. But once she was attracted to a Milton Berle show. The events leading up to the tragedy went this way. In the 1942 season she had taken a speaking part in *Black Narcissus,* that of Ayah, a Hindu woman, basing her visual interpretation on dance movement. It was an interesting experiment that like most out-of-the-run things did not run long. In 1945 she took over the choreography and special staging for *Dark of the Moon* in preparation for its year on Broadway.

This was a charming folk play when first presented at the Cambridge Summer Theater in all its frank and pristine innocence. When it had its pre-Broadway tryout in Boston, it was considerably coarsened for its destination and had lost much of its charm; but the movement in it looked very much as before. Certainly Richard Hart, the Witch Boy, with his stark, wild-mountain stances, moved as well in one production as the other, and that was most impressively. The witch girls were a silly lot of Hollywood temptresses in both cases. Esther gave them a little more to do, disporting them around hollow logs, slithering them over craggy places, and put a pleasing country dance in the first act.

The "Legend with Music" was bereft of its intrinsic quality,

but it established Esther as a theater choreographer, and prepared
her for the really big-time—for *Spring in Brazil,* starring Milton
Berle—which also tried out in Boston. She staged a tribal dance
for the first scene and other native dances sprinkled through, as
well as a Negro ballet that, gagging on the comedian's gags, I was
unable to stay to see. She had former Dunham dancers Roger
Ohardieno, Talley Beatty, and LaVerne French among others to
work with, but whatever she did with them, it was artistically a
waste. However, no harm done to Esther. She ascended from there
to the Diamond Horseshoe, and thence to the circus, as related.

An American modern with a will and a way all her own, she
has taught that will and that way to a portion of the younger generation. She has spoken on the radio and given television shows.
She has reached a large, if irregular public, is reaching a new public
now. A quiet, demure little person with a lot going on inside that
she does not tell the world, she is a modern dancer with a difference, a different difference from all the rest.

SYBIL SHEARER

Sybil Shearer is a perfectionist who likes to believe
that perfection is humanly attainable. The temptation is to call her
Supersonic Sybil, so rarefied is the wave frequency through which
her dances are signaled to the human eye. But the atmosphere is
spiritual rather than technological. The altitudinal dances come
from love of Nature, love of God, whom she is not afraid to speak
of out loud as a friend of hers. On a less transcendental plane are
her dances of sardonic pity for mortals, particularizing in womankind. She has no desire "to dance for the millions." The small, at-
tuned audience is all she asks. She prefers an intimate theater but
a large stage, for her short solos are space-absorbing. When she
tours she carries her own cyclorama. Her lighting designer, Helen
Balfour Morrison, travels with her. Together they inspect the stage
and incidental properties to be sure that all is well. Then Sybil must

have a three-hour rehearsal on stage the day before performance. The program is planned for perfection, and, having taken every precaution, the artist expects nothing less.

A sample program will serve to illustrate the scope and caliber of her work. She and Mrs. Morrison were in Boston, in the early spring of 1947, looking for the perfect dancing place. No satisfactory hall or theater was available. They scouted around in nearby towns until they found a beautiful new auditorium with good sight lines, an ample stage, and everything as it should be. This was Denworth Hall at Bradford Junior College, a girls' school in Haverhill. The school, informed by a modern dance teacher, was delighted to present the renowned young modern dancer. Sybil was delighted with the opportunity. It is unimaginable that money, or the thought of it, entered the transaction.

But, alas, the human equation entered in, and the program missed perfection on several counts. For one thing, Sybil had not brought her own pianist. For another, the party from Boston, having lost their way on the long drive up, bustled in after the first three numbers were over; thus, according to Sybil's calculations, beginning the program in the wrong place. Its theme had been stated in the opening numbers. *In the Field* (Villa-Lobos) was in the vein of a prayerful fertility rite, as if invoking in its rhythms of sowing and planting, a blessing on the dissemination of ideas to follow. The principle of those ideas, of the performance, was declared by *In the Light* (Beethoven). Then, after these devotions to Nature and to God, the first downward dip to mortal frailty in *O Lost!* (Chopin), the lost one, in blue dress and blue-latticed slippers, fumbling, perhaps, toward the light. A further descent came with *In a Vacuum* (Mussorgsky), and that is where we came in.

At that time Sybil was running her programs through without interruption of curtain calls or intermission, regarding the comedy dances as intermissions in the perfect whole. *In a Vacuum*, a tragicomedy, was, therefore, half an intermission. The auditorium was filled with silken girls, whose bright faces and shining hair (of assorted natural colors) lit up the semi-darkness. They laughed in their well-bred manner at the comedy, while the few older women silently felt the "tragi." It was a tight, neurotic dance. The nervous tremors of lowered hands and crazily lifted feet met in an enclosing circle of light; the body angled toward these extremities, which seemed to be in a state of transposed tic; and the minute patterns of restless futility were incessantly repeated, until the spectator was all but drawn into the weird circle of meaningless motion. The drab and dowdy costume, the unkempt hair, added to the manic-depressive effect.

Sybil apparently uses no make-up. This absence of artificial bloom in an age of the universal lipstick and pancake complexion, heightens by its very ghastliness the intensity of the frustrated-female dances. Equally by remoteness from current realism, it imparts an ethereal aspect to her dances of lofty sentiment. Neither beauty parlor nor fashion magazine comes within her frame of reference. She does not groom her abundant reddish-brown hair as she might. She designs and cuts her own costumes, working them out with Mrs. Morrison as to color and lighting, in unrelenting faithfulness to the dance. She has her own notions about music, picking what she wants from the established repertory, separating it from its context, and putting it to her own uses. The question for her is, what is the right combination of sounds for my dance; not what the music says, but what the dance says.

The next number, *Pastoral* (Corelli), continuing the main theme of the program, shot up again, to out-of-doors in spring. Here all was gentle, slow, the arms wide and free, the movement soft and caressing. The design was formal, the feeling of life and growth, of birth's seedling of death, faintly seeping through. Very faintly. To be honest, Sybil told me afterwards. I simply relaxed in the easy, flowing movement, the serenity of spirit, glad of a respite from the fidgets. But not for long. There followed two more uncomfortable comedy pieces, cryptic of title, if not of impact. Whether because of a certain reptilian fascination, or of a greater power of projection, these disturbed dances hovering on the verge of nervous break-down cut into consciousness with a knife-edged keenness that the broad, sustained, peaceful dances lack.

One Blocking's Worth Two in the Bush (Ted Fiorito) is in intentionally fussy hair-do and evening dress, including long black gloves that play a busy part in the action. Phrases of stylized ballroom dancing are continually halted by the dancer's stopping to flick a stubborn speck of lint from one of the gloves—most unfortunate for the invisible partner and trying for the spectator—who becomes as concerned with getting the speck removed as the character herself. After an inordinate expenditure of energy without reward, she lightly blows the speck away, and everybody is relieved. The girls laughed gleefully at the exaggerated picture of a familiar experience, but for some of us there were distressing overtones. Sybil's humor is less riant than astringent.

African Skrontch by Mail (Moorehouse) done like the preceding number to popular music, brought the dancer before the curtain to say that the dance was to be about learning jitterbug by correspondence course. The appearance must have been due to an omission in the printed program, as Sybil does not customarily address her audience, even when dancing. The props are a hard wooden chair, a cheap phonograph on a small table, and an endlessly long strip of paper representing the chart of steps, which the dancer spreads over the floor and keeps getting tangled up in. Tightly drawn hair, nondescript short skirt, and sweater not after Lana Turner, define a spinster in bobby-socks, pathetically eager to acquire the accomplishments of a younger generation. She starts the record and contorts herself to its dreary blare, now consulting the chart, now entangled in it, and not succeeding very well in mastering the explosive jerks of arms and legs or bodily ejaculations. The healthy ebullience of a young dance-hall crowd is missing. Without companions there is no fizz in it. An atmosphere of terrible loneliness invades the bare room. Again the dance is only outwardly funny.

Sybil regards these so-called comedies as interludes of audience relaxation from her dances on a higher level, valleys among the hills of her program. From the valleys the hills look higher, so when she comes to *"O, Sleeper of the Land of Shadows, Wake, Expand!"*, from William Blake, to a Bach chorale, she is atop a very high hill indeed. On this occasion the altitude was heightened by the fact that she was able to dance it to organ for the first time. Also for the first time (at this recital) she looked lovely in an angelic blue robe (no harp attached) and softly arranged hair. She seemed to rise and expand with reverential feeling from her base of perfect poise. But there was a flaw here, I learned at lunch-for-three next day. The costume and lighting designed for piano were too brilliant for organ, Mrs. Morrison said; and Sybil agreed. In case of organ, the color would have to be changed to a rich red, and the lighting directed from above (as through a stained-glass window, perhaps). In every case, lighting and costume must harmonize with the musical instrument used, and all must harmonize with the purpose of the dance.

The rest of the program kept to the hilltops save for one declivity into tragedy. In *No Peace on Earth* (Scriabin) the stooped figure of an old woman wrapped in the gray of sackcloth and ashes, painfully crawls across the stage, her hands clasping and unclasping in commingled agony and prayer. It is very short, and poignant, for it is a concentrate of misery. Sybil can use her hands with Oriental fluency. She can do anything with her body. She can liquefy it to the point of dissolution, or coil it taut as a steel spring, only to let go in lashes of energy. She can practically turn herself inside out with convulsive movements, or flow with the placidity of a sunlit stream. From the molecular to the largest muscular area, every fiber, tendon, and tissue is hers to command. The news should be withheld no longer—she is a remarkable dancer.

But she has soared above the battle. She prefers her dances of fulfillment to those of frustration, which she calls negative dances. Since art helps to make up the deficit in human affairs, the smoothness of spiritual peace has less need of expression than the rugged grandeur of the human struggle (the essence of modern dance); and that may be why her dances of exaltation, so sincerely felt, are not more compelling. For climax to her Haverhill recital the end-piece was *Let the Heavens Open that the Earth May Shine* (Vivaldi-Bach), and it must be admitted that the celestial radiance of the title is not matched by the dance. The music is from the concerto used by José Limón, but quite differently applied. The costume consists allusively of spangled black jersey tights under a diaphanous pale blue sheath that is discarded midway in the dance. The first part is all legato movement and reposeful mood. After the sheath drops, the movement turns staccato, with much activity of extended

arms and hands. The religious conviction is there—the peace of
meditation, the active joy in the Lord—but it remains Sybil's private hymn of praise.

The entire program was offered with an air of ritual, divided
between the sacred and secular though it was. It was planned for
its young audience as well as for perfection. Sybil always considers
her audience—or nearly always. She forgot it temporarily when, in
the winter of 1948, she gave a recital in Boston's New England
Mutual Hall, which has a flat floor. Mrs. Morrison's changing color
harmonies and intensities, like a subtler rendition of the color performance at Radio City Music Hall, did not have that equipment's
carrying power; and Sybil, who became disjointed by other people's
heads from the rear seats, could be seen only in outline from the
rear. There were mishaps, too, as when they both forgot to "hold"
the electrician in their' thought, and he made a mistake in lighting.

In general Sybil does better than that. She looks out for her
audience. She weighs its cultural potential, knowing that those on
an advanced cultural plane are able to "reach" higher. She believes that the artist controls the audience, and, by sensing its tem-
per, can make it respond. She realizes that it is difficult for laymen
to adjust themselves to modern dance and tries to make it easier
for them. Her lecture-demonstration is tantamount to a complete
course in modern dance, from kindergarten to college, she says.
It gives her audience a chance to grow through the program, so
that by the end the responsive ones are "reaching."

Sybil is herself a reacher, and a delver, too. Up to the ideal,
deep to the source. She carries her dances around inside, sometimes
for years, before they fully develop. When the time of parturition
overtakes her, be it in subway or railway station, Pullman car or
city street, it is necessary for her to yield at once. Sometimes it is
a single phrase, sometimes a rush of phrases. They do not lie near
the surface. They are the result of "digging till you come to the
most alive moment." In that moment they must be recorded in
mind by actual movement. It was four years before *Pastoral,* a
culmination of felt springtimes merged with remembered music,
took its final form. A spring day in the country opened it to life.

Another dance, *Is it Night?,* was conceived during the dreadful

August week the first atom bomb was dropped on Hiroshima. Sybil was probably sharing the universal feeling that the end of the world was at hand, for, again in the country, she watched a strange sunset cloud against a luminous blue-green sky, shaping itself in the mushroom formation caused by the bomb. It was telepathic, it was psychic, it was awesome. The portentous shape, the violent contrast of pink sunset and blue-green atmosphere, stamped themselves in, and a new dance dimly began. It lay dormant until the following March, when, at Karl Priebe's one-man show in New York, she noticed that his paintings were all in this same blue-green tonality. Then, a little later, she observed that one of the backdrops in *Carousel* was also in blue-green. This was enough. Her suspicion was confirmed that the chemistry of the world had been changed from the "Shocking Pink" of the war years to this all-pervading blue-green—by the atom bomb. If this seems a bit mystic, wait: I can explain everything. Sybil is of Scotch-Irish ancestry.

The impressions fluttered in embryo, and gradually approached dance. The warning came in the subway, en route to the Brooklyn Museum of Art. Just as she reached her destination the dance was at the point of emergence. Her mind paced with the burden. If only I could get this into form, she thought. Failing a more secluded spot, she took the one she was in, a corridor of the museum. "The whole thing tumbled out like mad. I got the movement, feeling, quality—it all came in a flash." So, whatever passersby may have fancied, one more dance was registered and preserved.

But each time is different, she says. You can't force anything. Often a composition grows by small pieces. A short time before the blue-green episode she had done a problem in pink and gray. She was looking for the right music, or combination of sounds (she no longer uses percussion) for the colors of the dance. A high-school girl, an ardent pianist, who happened to be in the studio, started improvising as she watched, and spontaneously produced the syncopated music of her age, which was just the ticket. Sybil has fun when things snap into place like that. It was one of the rare occasions she leaned on an especially written score. The girl's mother wrote down the notes and had them recorded; then Sybil's own pianist adapted the music to her dance.

In the Cool of the Garden, which, as the title implies, is a lyrical celebration of the garden at dusk, is, like *Pastoral,* one of Sybil's favorites. She has always loved to dance and compose out-of-doors. She grew up in the country air and scene, on her parents' estate in Nyack, New York, (and later on Long Island), and usually spends the summers at her mother's country place in Lyons, near Lake Ontario. There she has a studio and does a great deal of composing. When she was a child she used to make up little dances while her mother played the piano. She was sent to dancing school at the country-club, but she was the smallest one in the class and very bashful. Rosetta O'Neill was the teacher; the dances the slide, slide, heel and toe of polite ballroom, and the bird-butterfly-bee type of the period. In those days children were encouraged to circle around freely to music, and that was natural dancing, or to impersonate flowers and winged creatures, and that was interpretive. The process did not then inspire Sybil to become a dancer.

As she grew older she dabbled in painting and sketching, Nature, as always, her theme. Her father, a business man whose nearest approach to art was gardening, hoped she would be a commercial artist. Sybil, then as now, could not abide anything savoring of commerce. She could not bear to be circumscribed, to feel bound by regularity or routine. Manifestly, she was not good material for the business world or for college. But she went to Skidmore College and was duly graduated—to please her father—majoring in English literature and world history to please herself.

All her growing years Sybil was carrying little unborn dances without knowing what to do with them. Ballet did not attract her. She was disappointed in Colonel W. de Basil's newly organized Ballet Russe de Monte Carlo because she could find in it nothing comparable to the great spirit of Pavlova. Then she read John Martin's first book, *The Modern Dance,* a compilation of lectures given at the New School for Social Research, and everything was clarified. The sentence, "Modern dance is a point of view rather than a technique," was a guiding beacon. This was it. She would be a modern dancer. She hied to Bennington and studied with each of the Big Four.

When she was ready to select a teacher for the winter season, she characteristically avoided following the crowd. "Everybody was going all out for Martha," so Sybil was not interested. She liked Hanya Holm's mobile teaching, but decided on Doris Humphrey. "Doris worked for quality," she said. "She was not dogmatic. Her pupils were urged to dance, not just do exercises. The idea was the important thing." As has been recounted, Sybil was a member of the Humphrey-Weidman company during its peak years (the middle thirties) when every member was an artist. Inevitably she came under Charles Weidman's direction also, and this may have nurtured her mordant comedy sense. She made her first public appearance as a choreographer in a suite of five solos, on a program with several other dancers at the New School in this period.

At Bennington Sybil had taken a course on the Dramatic Basis of Movement, an experimental dance-drama workshop inaugurated and conducted by Louise (Mrs. John) Martin. In these classes the student drew upon sensory memory to indicate by movement and gesture the presence of imaginary objects and his relation to them. If the rest of the class guessed what was intended, the student had done pretty well. When the action suggested walking into the sea up to the neck, fighting a fire, frolicking in the snow, setting tables or making beds, it was easy. When a whole room had to be evoked, its doors, windows, and furnishings established by the act of dusting, it was more difficult. And when a make-believe egg was hidden in the make-believe room, it became complicated indeed. There were exercises in mood—fear, annoyance, surprise, and so on— digging to the roots of expression. From these pantomimic fragments the significant movement was abstracted, and, by deletion, augmentation, accent, and rhythmic formalization, developed into a dance theme or a dance.

This training stood Sybil in good stead when, in 1938, she and Eleanor King, William Bales, George Bockman, and Kenneth Bostock, all Humphrey-Weidman dancers, banded with Fe Alf, Louise Allen, Elizabeth Coleman, Alice Dudley, and William Miller, of other concert groups, to organize the Theater Dance

Company. Sybil continued to work with Mrs. Martin, who coached the group, and had some lessons with Maria Ouspenskaya. The company made a brilliant start on a little theater scale, giving concerts at the Y. M. H. A. and elsewhere around New York. It lasted two years, about as long as any dance collective of this kind seems to last.

Sybil made her solo debut in Carnegie Chamber Music Hall, New York, on October 21, 1941, and was promptly saluted as a gifted, unusual dancer. Whereupon she packed up and went to Chicago to live. She chose Chicago because the openness of the West appealed to her, and it offered raw material. Chicagoans, she felt, didn't have preconceived ideas of what dance should be. They were not too intellectual to be told anything. In other words they had not become "cast." By "cast" Sybil means that an individual or group is no longer growing and becoming, but is crystallized (one might say sot in his or its ways) instead. She teaches, or has taught, at Roosevelt College part of the time; and returns to New York for an annual recital when everything can be suitably arranged.

One specialty of hers she calls "liquid acting." It is based on emotional sequences rather than on pure dance form. In this medium she has composed a suite to a set of maxims. For "You Can't Have Your Cake" the dancer, at first tentative about going after what she wants, finally goes all out, and then decides it wasn't worth it. "As the Twig is Bent" shows a slum child hitching and twitching from sullenness under abuse to potential criminality. "Spreading like Wildfire" might be a rumor, anything, in quick, agitated movements covering space. "Time and Tide" embodies the thought of recurrence. What seems to be the end is a beginning. But nothing too literal. The maxims are merely clues to the individual meaning of each and continuity of the whole, which is a Prologue to a longer work not yet completed.

While in Boston, at the Duncanbury School of Arts, Sybil gave a demonstration of liquid acting in two sketches from life. With an old broom-handle for prop, she portrayed an old-time "darky," wobbling along with the aid of a cane, whom Mrs. Morrison had photographed in the South. At the word, "Come on, Sam, and have your picture taken," the Negro straightens up, assumes a more assertive carriage, and walks proudly over to the photographer. The second sketch was of a famous artist entering a hotel lobby in search of Mrs. Morrison, who was to make a photographic portrait of him. Sybil, in man's coat and scarf, strides in, head aslant, her body twisted into a question mark. This is really liquid acting, and not pantomime, for the whole body engages in the characterization.

Mrs. Morrison lighted Sybil's first Chicago concert, and they have collaborated ever since. They felt at once a "synchronization of the spirit." Light is their common theme. After the concert they began a photographic suite of Sybil in varying degrees and kinds of light, which took them a year and a half to finish. Its title is *The Inheritance,* with the sub-title, or motto, "Man may desert the light, but the light never deserts man." It is a pictorial treatise on their philosophy of light, issuing from their "reaction to God," from being "tuned in on the universe." Art comes out of the universe, Mrs. Morrison says, through the artist, in the spontaneity of reflection. The suite opens with a portrait of Sybil in the rain. Mrs. Morrison, who composes portraits in lights as well as in photographs (and both very handsomely), made this additional portrait of Sybil in verse:

> She weeps for the rain,
> She weeps for the disappointed heart,
> And she bears all life's sorrows:
> Yet, suddenly borne on a vapory breeze
> An echo comes from the long-gone leaves,
> And she hears the sound of music
> Tolling song of brief surcease
> From the ruptured, haunted world of grief.

God does not use footlights, Mrs. Morrison says, and she never likes to interfere with God, so she does not use footlights either. She follows but does not copy Nature, finding infinite variety in God's lighting effects, and color schemes. Lighting from above has a different quality than lighting from the East or West, for example, and a shiny coal black has a different quality from a warm, penetrating black. White, of course, is supreme and separate in its spiritual connotations. Since God is everywhere, is life, it all comes out of life.

Sybil concurs in this philosophy, which, construed from our desultory conversation, seems to have a somewhat pantheistic tinge.

Sybil confines herself at present to solo composition. She cannot work with a group she does not know well, or with people in whom she has no interest and who have no interest in her. When she does have a group, all its members must believe in what she believes in, must feel that she is going in the right direction, and want to go her way. They must be willing to work as a unit, to become a living whole. When she has gathered about her enough people who answer that description, she will be able to choreograph for them. Until then, she awaits the perfect group.

KATHERINE DUNHAM

Katherine Dunham came dashing on to Broadway in a one-night Sunday stand that lasted for thirteen consecutive Sundays. *Tropics and "Le Jazz Hot"* opened at the Windsor Theater on February 18, 1940, and had New York agog. Who *was* this brilliant new dancer from Chicago? Well, she had just staged the "Bertha the Sewing-Machine Girl" number for the current second edition of *Pins and Needles.* Before that she had staged the dances for the Chicago productions of *Run Little Chillun* and *The Emperor Jones.* And now she was flying back and forth between concerts to Chicago, where she was working on the dances for a swing version of *H.M.S. Pinafore.* Oh, show business! No, not exactly. She is actually an anthropologist, with a Ph.B and an M.A from the University of Chicago. A scholar, then? Yes, and between degrees she spent a year and a half in the West Indies studying the native dances, on a Rosenwald Fellowship, two of them, in fact. She writes articles for learned periodicals, and for *Esquire* (which doesn't confess to lady writers in print) under the *nom de plume* of K. Dunn. Oh, I see, she puts anthropology on stage, and writes about it, too. Well, something a little more than that. She's a dancer, you know.

Because Katherine was a dancer and had already mastered the shoulder dance of Damballa, in the plains, she was once mistaken for a native, in the voodoo ceremonies in the Haitian hills. She had more difficulty with the social set of Port-au-Prince, who, outwardly at least, looked askance at the *vaudun* carryings-on; but she got around the high-class Haitians by giving them a "nice" concert in a "nice" rose-sprigged chiffon dress, and was thereafter socially accepted. In Trinidad she inadvertently stopped one voodoo show by the click of her concealed camera, and was lucky to escape unscathed for her temerity in making pictures of the secret rituals. But she continued to make records when she could, with notebook, camera, and recording machine, and later used them to train her group and teach her classes. She lived in tiny villages, in remote settlements, spending some time in Martinique and other small islands of the Lesser Antilles, as well as in Jamaica, Haiti, and Trinidad.

Only a small part of all this went into her first revue, which was subtitled "From Haiti to Harlem." The press made casual reference to high temperature in both places, without undue excitement. The only American-naïve number, *Bre'r Rabbit an de Tah Baby* (after the Joel Chandler Harris stories), which had been well liked in Chicago, was dropped for lack of interest or critical acclaim in New York. From this she preserved the lively *Plantation Dances* as a separate number. The rest of the program consisted of primitive rhythms and modern jazz, with snatches of song and speech. Talley Beatty, Archie Savage, and LaVerne French were outstanding members of this first small group.

Katherine's next New York appearance was as the seductive Georgia Browne in *Cabin in the Sky,* starring Ethel Waters. Then she went on to Hollywood to do *Star Spangled Rhythm, Stormy Weather,* and the really superior Technicolor short of her own dances, *Carnival of Rhythm.* From Los Angeles she made a successful tour of the West Coast, dancing in night spots, and with the Los Angeles Philharmonic and San Francisco Symphony Orchestras, along the way. Her ambition was to maintain a permanent company and establish a permanent school in New York. It was a wise and worldly anthropologist who put on the next Dunham show there, under the aegis of S. Hurok, always astute in presenting American artists on the upgrade. Her company of dancers, singers, and musicians now counted thirty. It came, of course, well heralded.

When *Tropical Revue* opened at the Martin Beck Theater on September 19, 1943, it sent the critics thumbing through their thesauruses for synonyms of "torrid." The pelvic girdles, and there were many of them, did indeed seem to be made of melted lastex. The brown beauty who could address a Yale graduate class on anthropology in horn-rimmed spectacles, now wore a pearl in her navel. According to the reports, the dancers bumped and wriggled, the drummers slapped and thumped (their drums), and the risqué and raucous vaudeville quieted down only when the singers— Bobby Capo and the Leonard Ware Trio—sang. As a matter of fact, much of the so-called "sizzling" was in the eye of the beholder, spanked on by the publicity department.

"You have to go at night to get the atmosphere," Mr. Hurok said happily, all in the spirit of the thing, as he kindly provided me with a pair of seats. It was a skilled company, highly trained in muscular energies, not exclusively below the belt. Most of the dancers were more exciting than the star. She looked lovely in the Melanesian *Rara Tonga,* adorned with open lotus flowers (and the pearl); she executed the curious and difficult narration in rhythms with utmost finesse. She could shimmy with the best of them; her *Florida Swamp Shimmy* with Roger Ohardieno, a big bruiser of a man, was sultry, sinister, and expertly done. Her *Woman With a Cigar* was evidently supposed to be coarse. But somehow in everything she did she seemed too refined for her milieu. Torrid, indeed! An antonym would be more suitable. This was just a very good looking American girl playing primitive.

Some of the others made up for it—Lucille Ellis, the most abandoned of the rotators, nearly shook herself into a pulp. Pretty Lavinia Williams and Syvilla Fort, now the supervising director of the school, were less excessive. Claude Marchant, with the spring of a panther, sinuous Tommy Gomez, air-borne LaVerne French, stood out individually. Handsome Vanoye Aikens, smooth Lenwood Morris, in small type then, were later to make their presences felt. There were other good dancers; and several charming Latin American numbers, aromatic with dialect, ejaculations, and bits of song. The Brazilian *Bahiana* (Don Alfonso); *Choro,* a nineteenth century Brazilian quadrille (Gogliano); the half dance, half sketch, *Callata* ("Sh—sh, Be Quiet"), with music by Candido Vincenty, one of the drummers, and the light-footed, light-hearted *Plantation Dances* were innocent gambols compared to burlesque types like the *Street Scene in Haiti,* with Lucille Ellis rolling her eyes and hips at a pair of drummers (not traveling salesmen but the effect the same) who were part of the act, on stage.

The *chef d'oeuvre* was a solemn concert piece in a jungle setting, called *Rites de Passage,* adapted from puberty and fertility rituals of anonymous primitives. The music, derived from a Haitian theme, was by Paquita Anderson, with percussion by Goucho, another of the drummers. The work was of a *longueur* that was tiring, but of an integrity that commanded respect. It was performed with dignity by principals and company. Taken seriously, it was a religious ceremonial concerning important periods of transition in human experience. But one irreverent scrivener seized with glee upon the fertility ritual as associated with marriage OR mating; and altogether the outward physicality of the work contributed to the sexational build-up that led to the show's success. *Tropical Revue* prolonged its original two-week engagement at the Martin Beck, moving, when it had to make way for another customer on November 13, to the Forrest. On December 4 it started on tour, and opened at the Boston Opera House on January 17, 1944.

Now whatever else may be said of Bostonians, proper and improper, we *can* read. We can even read the New York papers, and find out ahead of time what's what in the arts so that we will know what we ought to think of them when they come to us. This incredible fact is not altogether believed by certain New York managers and press agents. Gerald Goode, then chief publicity representative for S. Hurok (and K. Dunham) was taking no chances. He placed lure-advertisements in the local papers, and sent out lurid flyers quoting all the hottest remarks about the approaching heat-wave. Boston was prepared for the worst, but did not stay away. The show went on, nobody in the audience fainted, though a few rather angry looking persons left early. Next morning came the great todo. The Censor had not approved. The Censor had ordered out, not the silly vaudeville bits, not the occasional leer or calculated animality, but the solemn, sacred *Rites de Passage*. *Tropical Revue* ran a week in Boston with its serious feature deleted and all the rest left in. Whether sold for sex or for art en route, the show toured the country without further censorship—other than that bestowed by regional racial prejudice.

A calmer spirit prevailed when a second edition of *Tropical Revue* opened a week's engagement at the Boston Opera House on December 4, 1944. The advance publicity had been modified and thereby created a less sex-conscious attitude in the public mind. Also, the general performance tone had been raised, though the fluid pelvic girdle was as much in evidence as before. In New York, too, when the Dunham company played a more extensive season at the Century Theater, opening December 26, press and public became acclimated to the so-called tropical atmosphere, and accepted the undulating rhythms, not as a sign of moral undulant fever, but as sincere native expression. African movement is pelvic movement, natural and un-selfconscious. It becomes erotic on the stages of civilization, where the translator is faced with the onerous task of moderating it to meet a different set of tastes and standards, without too drastically sacrificing its essence.

In an interview we had at the time, Katherine assured me that she had no desire to make hers a sexy show; that she was interested in dance and what it said of and to people; that it was her interest in dance as a valid expression of what was fundamental in human nature that had led her to the study of ethnology and anthropology, and not the other way around. She was not even making a point of the Negro dance. She had simply gone to primitive sources to try to find the key to the universal rhythms. Lithe and slender in her tight, leopard-cloth slacks, gentle of voice and manner, she was poised and charming, and very keen in her observations. It was difficult to realize that not many generations ago her ancestors had left Africa in slaveships. A shadow came into her fine, clear eyes when she reminded me, then a strange light, as she spoke of the mesmerism of the drums, the mass hypnosis of the voodoo rituals.

On this theme was the new West Indian ballet, *L'Ag'Ya*, derived from the traditional rhythmic fighting-match of that name.

banned but secretly performed on the island of Martinique. Katherine had lived there, in the little fishing village of Vauclin at the foot of Mont Pelée, for several months, and the ballet was compounded of her impressions and the story of love and jealousy she had made up to fit them. She had first prepared it for the Federal Theater in Chicago, but had revised it for the tour. John Pratt, the stage designer (and Katherine's husband), had dressed it beautifully, and given it sketchy but evocative settings. In addition to the drums, outcries, and patois of the people, was the special music by Robert Sanders. Katherine was Loulouse, the beloved, Vanoye Aikens, Alcide, the lover. Claude Marchant was the vengeful Julot (in shades of snaky green) and Roger Ohardieno the Zombie King.

The ballet opens on a morning market scene, thronged with fishermen, vendors, and townspeople. Loulouse and Alcide have a tender love duet in waltz time, which infuriates the repulsed Julot, who, after rhythmically venting his wrath, goes off to obtain the *cambois,* or love-charm, from the Zombie King. In the Zombie Lair sits Roi Zombie in an old-fashioned rocking-chair on a raised platform, like any comfortable suburbanite on his front porch smoking a pipe. A black overcoat partially covers his straw skirt, and straw blades fringe his tall silk hat. Witch-like creatures cackle at either side of him, and, stalking around the premises on stilts, or lying flat on the ground, are the awesome zombies, swathed in tissue-thin black. The scene is as amusing as it is eerie. It shows the play of the primitive imagination in adapting the clothes of civilization to its own superstitious beliefs. Julot, trembling before the massive, bare-legged stances of the Zombie King, endures the terror to secure the *cambois,* and leaves.

The final scene is bright with the full white embroidered skirts and variegated striped basques and headdresses of the women, and matching white-and-stripe effects for the men. It is rich in native dances, opening with the "Mazouk," or Creole Mazurka, as formal and stately as a court dance. Then the drums sound and accelerate, cries of "Beguine, Beguine" fill the air, and the crowd roars into the wild native dance, all thought of courtly decorum evaporated. The revelry is brought to a sudden halt as Julot enters, swinging the mystic love-charm, which, without let or hindrance, he directly applies to the lovers' heads. Alcide manages to wrench himself away from its sphere of influence, but Loulouse gradually succumbs. As she sinks deeper and deeper under the spell, in the "Majumba" or love dance of old Africa, she removes her outer garments piece by piece, standing (or half swooning) at last in a very decorative long underslip. Alcide can bear it no longer. He rushes to challenge Julot to the Ag'Ya, and the climax of the ballet (ending in the hero's death) begins.

This is an extraordinary fighting dance or dance fight, similar to the French *savate* in its dexterous use of the feet. It is done entirely in rhythm, to singing and drumming accompaniment. After each attack the fighters balance into the rhythm again, and the fray is likely to continue until one of them falls dead. The Ag'Ya is indeed done in deadly earnest, even when there is no more personal reason for the fight than there is for the average wrestling match. It is because of the fatalities that so often ensue that it is forbidden by the government.

The natives of Martinique, Katherine told me, love to dress up in Empire costume and put on the airs of the old régime. They'll be sitting around sipping lemonade as pretty as you please, but as soon as they hear the call of the drums they revert to type. The drums are a tie to the pagan customs, customs that prevail in the islands for all the colonial overlay. The hereditary beliefs give vitality to the dancing, and the dancing gives validity to the ballet. This is not the modern dance of Martha Graham or Doris Humphrey. It is, in its re-creative use of movement born of emotional impulsion, modern dance none the less. It speaks of Negro psychology, of psychokinesia, of an ancient witchcraft that is not, in its reliance on hypnotic suggestion, so far removed from certain brands of modern necromancy.

Like many members of the younger generation, Katherine is an eclectic modern, drawing on all forms within her experience. In the *Cuban Slave Lament, Havana Promenade,* and *Moorish Bolero,* standard numbers on her programs, are leg extensions and body tensions, whirls and half-turns, leaps, jumps, and torso accents that are more than midway between the primitive and modern. Other movements, throughout the repertory, are balletic or in folk vein;

and in the *Rara Tonga* of the South Pacific are the horizontal neck movements, the sinuous shoulders, arms, and fingers of the Oriental dance. Jazz, swing, and boogie woogie of course come under the modern Negro-rhythms.

Another new dance of the second *Tropical Revue* was *Flaming Youth 1927*, with music by "Brad" Gowans, trumpeter of the Dixieland Band that sometimes appears in her shows. This is a depressing sketch, set in a cheap speakeasy of the period, the women in the shapeless knee-length dresses once considered smart, the men in collegiate clothes, dancing the Charleston, the Black Bottom, the Mooch, and the Fishtail between plays in the sex game. The city ballroom dances, Katherine believes, grew out of seeds from the West Indies. She is sure the Charleston originated in some remote religious ceremony in Africa and filtered into the Western world through the slave traffic, for she remembers seeing kindred steps and gestures in the island rituals and in the church society at home.

Katherine traces her ancestry to Madagascar. She grew up and went to school in Joliet, Illinois. Her father, a business man, and her mother, a school teacher, were devout Methodists; and one of their small daughter's first acts of shock to them was to stage a cabaret in the church. (The act righted itself by raising money for the church fund.) At home musicals Katherine played the piano while her father and brother plucked their mandolins. Albert, who later became a member of the faculty of Howard University, was educated at the University of Chicago and got his Master's degree at Harvard. When Katherine arrived at the University of Chicago, she found that the study of anthropology brought out the relation of a people's dance to their character and history, and therefore decided to major in it. But it was always dance first with her. She had had some lessons in her home town with a pupil of Margaret H'Doubler, in the pre-modern interpretive style.

In Chicago she went to Ludmila Speranzeva, a character dancer who had studied with both Preobrajenska and Mary Wigman, and had come to the United States with the original *Chauve Souris*. In Chicago also she studied with Mark Turbyfill, a gifted, eccentric poet and dancer, who sometimes appeared in Ruth Page's ballets. Katherine had her first top role in Ruth Page's West Indian ballet,

La Guiablesse. She had her first dance school in an abandoned store. A daughter of Julius Rosenwald saw her there in a recital, and soon afterwards Katherine was dancing before the Rosenwald Committee to show them the kind of research she wanted to do. The choice of a dance career was another shock to her parents, but once started nothing could hold her back. She was invited to direct a large group of young Negroes in a production at the Century of Progress Exhibition, and this taste of direction took her into the professional theater. She was never a concert dancer. The girl who could wind up her *Tropical Revue* by taking a half dozen or more curtain calls in as many different costumes, had the theatrical instinct from childhood.

In the fall of 1945, Katherine was presented by George Stanton in a musical play, *Carib Song*, that exercised all her talents. She starred in it, did the choreography, and staged it together with Mary Hunter. It was a handsome production, having scenery and lighting by Jo Mielziner, and costumes by Motley. The book and lyrics were by William Archibald, who was born in Trinidad, the scene of the play. The music was by Baldwin Bergersen. On its way to New York, *Carib Song* tried out in Boston, opening at the Shubert Theater on September 2, 1945. As usual, there was a good deal of anxious tinkering to make the play worthy of Broadway, where it was heartlessly sniffed at, and out, by the drama critics, with parodies of "I ain't like" as an example of the stilted dialect of the piece.

In Boston, before the tinkering, it was a delight. The first act mounted from a slow-paced wake to the climax of the Shango (voodoo ritual), wherein Tommy Gomez, as the Boy Possessed by a Snake, had the audience almost seeing what they were almost believing. Avon Long, as a wandering Fisherman with a love-cast in his eye, who had earlier stopped the show with his own inimitable kind of dance and song, in Calypso style, here declared his love; and the Woman (Katherine), who had only just acquired a husband but had a bit of a look for the Fisherman, too, didn't say Yes and didn't say No. The second act built through a succession of charming folk scenes to the final retribution for guilty love (offstage), the Woman's body borne in a wonderful processional down the mountainside.

The tragic mood of impending destiny was offset here and there by the playful interlude. The whole, through the means of choreographic pageantry and song, climbed to the crises and down to the dénouement, in the vein of poetic drama.

It is true that Katherine's sweet singing and speaking voice was too well-bred, her dancing and acting too constrained, for the semi-primitive role; that the dialect, in its effort to be intelligible, lost its savor and became artificial. But the piece was pervasively atmospheric, and at times moving. The Shango ritual, in its serious intensity, was more alarmingly realistic than the slightly ludicrous Zombie scene of *L'Ag'Ya*. These are Katherine's two best works (the Shango ritual is offered on current programs). They speak dance volumes on Inside the West Indies. They give more than a tourist-eye view of what goes on behind the front curtain of palm trees and mist-hung mountain cones and jet bodies diving for thoughtlessly flung coins in the aqua foreground.

Katherine has spread her knowledge of Caribbean culture and people in other ways. Her album of Afro-Caribbean Songs and Rhythms, produced by Decca, is an aural record of her experiences, not all of which has been heard in her shows. Her first book, *Journey to Accompong,* brought out by Holt in 1946, takes the reader into the forbidden territory of the Koromantee dances, among the Maroons of Jamaica. Having trained in field techniques with Melville J. Herskovits at Northwestern University, she went as a field worker—and lived among the people as a friend. The text, in the casual form of day-by-day notes and comments, imparts the feeling of actuality, of being there. In September 1945 the Dunham School of Dance and Theater was opened in the heart of New York's theater district. Anthropology and philosophy, sociology and languages (chiefly dialects) are among the subjects taught. Tap, ballet, folk, and primitive dance, as well as the eclectic Dunham technique, percussion, eukinetics, and body training for actors, are included in the curriculum. Although professional training is emphasized, there are classes for amateurs and for children. The school is strictly interracial.

In 1947 Katherine gathered her best dances and a few new ones into an omnibus collection. She called it *Bal Nègre,* and the New

York critics called it the best revue of her career; but when it went on tour the management thought it safer to call it simply *New Tropical Revue*. After a thrilling conquest of Mexico, and a pause in Hollywood to make some stunning dances for *Casbah* (left in large chunks on the cutting-room floor), the new show made the port of Boston in April 1948. The company was in fine form, but Katherine was tour-tired and dance-tired. Why any mature, integrated person, his mental and physical house in order, should want to get up and dance, she didn't know. Primitive dance was functional because it had a purpose—preparing for war, propitiating gods, warding off evil spirits, etc.—anything else was exhibitionism. The scholar in horn-rimmed spectacles was fighting the girl with the pearl. Or it may have been the hour, which was breakfast for her, and lunch for me. Or that a summer engagement at the Prince of Wales Theater, London, loomed just ahead. "It will be a fine thing for the company," she said in a resigned voice.

The *New Tropical Revue* was not so very different from the others. It featured *L'Ag'Ya* and *Shango*. It rearranged and re-titled some of the familiar pieces. Katherine wore more gorgeous costumes and danced less than ever. She walked across one scene in a vastly circumferential skirt of appliquéd quilted patchwork; and her lovely Loulouse had a new white dress of equal hem-mileage, bordered with a wonderful collage of flowers. In the new piece, *La Comparsa,* an encounter with three men à la Josephine Baker at the *Folies Bergère,* her black costume was lit with multi-colored stars.

As *A Caribbean Rhapsody* in London, the show (and it *is* a good show) was ecstatically received. *The Times* of London, and *The Observer,* gave it brief but positive praise. The *Dancing Times* was almost reverential before the scholarly background, the theatrical presentation. No mention was made of sex; and apparently no one suspected the presence of modern dance.

VALERIE BETTIS

Valerie Bettis is a big, handsome girl from Texas, who was walking like a million dollars and dancing like a billion before she ever stepped foot in *Inside U. S. A.*—the Broadway revue that put her on the drama critics' map. *The Desperate Heart (fecit)* came before "Haunted Heart," and "Tiger Lily" (a true daughter of the Felidæ) is the kind of character one would expect a proud, petulant, imperious, and temperamental young woman to depict. There is a lot to her besides glamorous looks and high voltage. She is a creative dancer, if a better dancer than choreographer. Her movements are sharply defined, deep-breathed, buoyant, free. She cuts wide-swathed, swinging arcs in space, or gashes jagged holes in it like a stylized streak of lightning. Or she can compact herself into knots of neuroticism. Her range is as broad as her native state. But while the body is young the heart and mind are young with it. Her own dances are mainly concerned with youth and love and young married life, themes of perpetual interest to young and perpetually young women. When she is older, and identifies herself more with humanity than with a segment of it, she may have larger things to say. As it is, she dances and composes out of a large technical background.

The young dancers today, she feels, are going on from an evolved technique. They do not have to build a new system. That has been done. They are the heirs of a great tradition, a fuller tradition than any other dancers have had before them. It includes modern dance in all its variety, and all other forms, to adapt as they choose. The wealth of movement is immeasurable. The free dance has no established vocabulary; it cannot be departmentalized into categories. As in the science of mathematics, which is not limited to the numeration table but permits infinite combinations of numerals, so the technical figures of dance hold within themselves infinite possibilities of combination and progress. Let the young dancer train to the nth degree, body, mind, and soul, Valerie says, and out of the rich resources of the whole person and the whole dance will come new expressive movement.

Valerie began with ballet, which she learned and felt in phrases rather than steps. Her first teacher, Rowena Smith, in her home city, Houston, taught a ballet type of dance in that spirit. The child who saw dance in everything was simply going to dancing school, not ballet class. She took it easy, too, as she did her piano lessons, until, just in her teens, she began to *want* to dance. Then she really worked. A six-week course by Tina Flade (from the Wigman School) had stimulated her. A performance by Myra Kinch in Los Angeles further stimulated her, and she subsequently visited different dancers on the West Coast to sample their wares. Finally, after a year at the University of Texas, where she decided that formal education was not for her, she went to New York and studied with Hanya Holm. Here she found ballet again (she said "ballet," positively), but again free, not academic. "Ballet is dance, after all, and not a dead language." It was a rediscovery, a deeper understanding of the ballet premise, in which was no conflict with modern dance.

Valerie charged into Hanya's classes like a Texan colt, to be broken and tamed. She had enormous drive and danced all over the place until she was gentled (but not too much so) by the finesse and exactitude of Hanya's teaching. She had her first part in the New York production of *Trend* (hers is the distinction of not being a Bennington trainee). In Hanya's classes and company for the next three years she became increasingly conspicuous for her beautiful, free movement. At the end of that time she left to spend a year by herself, working out her own dance on the basis of movement first. She tried to get to the essence of movement, using some of Hanya's theories, but bending them to her purpose. In November 1941 she gave her first solo recital, in Carnegie Chamber Music Hall, New York. All the music was by Bernardo Segall, a Brazilian composer (later her husband). All the costumes were designed by herself.

The dances were not epoch-making, but there was balance, control, velocity, breadth of phrasing, and individuality in the dancing; and some of the pieces, re-worked or re-evaluated, lived to dance another day. The silent dance, *Theme and Variations*—"Rhythmic pulse must be externalized to satisfy the eye in dances without music"—was retained in the repertory. The first section of *Triptych* ("Heritage," "Environment," "Destiny") was likewise preserved and warmed over. *City Streets* ("Broadway," "Avenue A," "Park Avenue") and *Country Lane* were other items heralding the brave new dancer coming up.

During the summer of 1942, while teaching at the Perry-Mansfield School of the Theater in Steamboat Springs, Colorado, she composed her first group work, *Study* (Segall) dedicated to those "who have suffered the monstrous oppression of the Axis, but whose spirit lives to inspire the free." The same summer, as guest artist at the Colorado Springs Fine Arts Center, she did *Southern Impressions,* two dances set to an arrangement of spirituals. Then, on December 6 of that year, on a program with Sybil Shearer and Erick Hawkins at the New York Y. M. H. A. Dance Center, she presented her first notable composition, *And the Earth Shall Bear Again,* a solo to music by John Cage. This little ritual of fruitage, done from a basis of low levels but with variety of plane and dynamics, and with fine feeling throughout, won her her first spurs as a modern dancer and choreographer to be counted in. Thereafter she gave concerts regularly in the Y. M. H. A. and the Students Dance Recitals series.

With the solo, *The Desperate Heart,* Valerie's place as a creative dancer of quality was assured. It was first presented March 24, 25 and 26, 1943, at the Humphrey-Weidman Studio Theater, on a program with Virginia Hall Johnson, Erick Hawkins, and Pearl Lang, in a series sponsored by the *Dance Observer.* It soon resounded in all quarters and became virtually a must on every Bettis program. It won John Martin's critical award of the year, and was mostly praised everywhere, though one dissident ballet critic saw in it a repressed maidenhood that was not there. The work's great drawing power was partly due to the poem written for it by John Malcolm Brinnin, and read at the first performance by Horton Foote. The poem is part of the dance and is the property of the dancer, and is here reproduced with her permission.

THE DESPERATE HEART

It was darkness, and a great hurry of silence then.
Only the cold stone hung in the breast and, backward
and forward, no answer.
The wooden roof of the world seemed close, easy to touch,
perhaps to break,
But the hard hands were full of stones.
Brightness was backward, and the bright look of love
Trapped in its only time, time past, now and forever,

The voice was love's voice then, the darkness saying
"My dear, my dear," the darkness saying, "My dear, my dear"
In the great hurry of silence . . . . .

But shadows die in a dark place, the fading past, the last
        pathetic day.
Stops in the air, and through these dreamy doors in dreamy
        sequences
The pictures of an afternoon return, the lamentations of
        a street,
The accent of a single voice among all voices loveliest . . .
And the heart, the desperate heart like a box of roses
Burns in the luminous dark . . .

It was all a long, long time ago . . . .
That century of the awkward heart and the hands quick as
        wings.
It was another time, far from here, farther than seeing,
Farther than hearing on widest wind, nor written, even, on
        sand.
It was all a long, long time ago.
Time enough for a life? a death?

It is darkness, and a great hurry of silence now.
Only the cold stone hangs in the breast and, backward or
        forward, no answer.
The wooden roof of the world seems close, easy to touch,
        perhaps to break,
But the hard hands were full of stones.
Brightness was backward, and the bright look of love
Trapped in its only time, time past, now and forever,
The voice is anonymous now, the darkness saying,
"My dear, my dear," the darkness saying, "My dear, my dear'
In the great hurry of silence . . . . .

    When properly spoken, the words glimmer through the action,
like the music (composed for the piece by Bernardo Segall), bridg-
ing transitional passages and heightening the intensity of the whole.

Valerie, in a soft dove-colored gown with a cut-out crimson heart as part of the bodice, moves eloquently, taking no gesture out of stock, to ply the fragile inflections of mood between melancholy and the bright, clear moments of remembered happiness, The movement, with its plaintive intervals and rare high notes, carries the air. It is like a haunting melody to the accompaniment of words and music. The solo is, as she describes it, poetic drama within the heart. And in it she succeeded in doing just what she wanted to do—a long dance for the solo figure, deeply emotional, changeful, and with the modulations of feeling amplified by words. When composing it, she talked it over with the poet, who felt the inner dynamics, and, working independently, wrote the poem for the dance after the dance was done.

Following this triumph came *Daisy Lee,* a dance play written for several voices and soloist by Horton Foote. It was first presented on a program with Pearl Primus in the Y. M. H. A. Dance Theatre series, January 23, 1944. At the original performance, which was generally acclaimed for its novelty and persuasiveness, the voices were disembodied, as in radio technique. They represented from offstage "the imaginings of the tortured mind" of the protagonist, whose marriage to Charley, a drunkard and a gambler, had been a failure. In a revised version at the Y. M. H. A. in the spring of 1947, the voices materialized into human forms flitting by as in a reverie—Mother, Sis, Charley, and two town gossips—their lines still coming from the wings. The costumes, by Saul Bolasni (artist and dancer) were late nineteenth century.

Valerie, writhing on, off, and around a piano stool, had a few lines of her own. The hysterical goings-on emphasized her resemblance to Tallulah Bankhead, even to the voice, though she has not yet the register, gamut, or years of that stormy actress. But she ties herself up into bundles of nerves as Tallulah could never do, in a long movement soliloquy of half-angry, half-remorseful post-mortem (for Charley is a passed-on inebriate) while trying to recall the piano tune that lurks like a secret message between them. The other characters sketch in the exposition of connubial unhappiness, which Daisy tries to cover up with protestations of love. As a solo with prose accompaniment, mingled with Mr. Segall's incidental music, the piece is more imaginative than it is in full physical regalia. New also on the 1944 program was *Caprice* (Segall), a portrait of a flame-skirted, finger-snapping, bitchy girl at a party.

On March 5, 1944 Valerie was presented in the Y. M. H. A. Dance Theatre series for the first time alone with group, and presented her first group work to be performed in New York. This was —*And Dreams Intrude*—(a retake of a dance drama she had done in a second summer at Perry-Mansfield) with *simpática* music as usual by Mr. Segall. It was, in the main, a distinguished company of young moderns. Valerie and Welland Lathrop were the lovers; Nona Schurman, Nina Fonaroff, and Maria Maginnis the "in love with love"; and Miriam Pandor, Mary Elizabeth Broussard, Janet Polk, and Joan Frederickson, the "denied of love." The work was less distinguished. In April came "An Evening of the Theater" by the American Actors Company (some of whose members had supplied the voices at the first performance of *Daisy Lee*), with Valerie doing the choreography for Arnold Sundgaard's one-act play, *Virginia Overture,* and *Hi Song,* a trio set to folk tunes; and in September, her first bout with musical comedy.

It, not Valerie, was knocked out in the second round, for David Wolper's *Glad to See You* deservedly flopped in Boston. She staged the dances and danced in it during the brief tryout, and learned a good lesson on how not to behave in musicals. She had one solo, to a sort of baby torch song, "Guess I'll Hang My Tears Out to Dry," in which she was supposed to express the emotions of the singer. The singer, being a Hollywood starlet (name of Jane Withers) had no emotions to sing of, so the dancer's tragic declensions were wasted. The effort, however, was not. Valerie knew how to treat a Broadway show the next time she met one.

Valerie made her Broadway debut as a concert artist with group at the Adelphi Theater on May 13, 1945. But the group works missed the impact of the new solo, *Theatrics,* with music by Paul Benet (later performances had music by Mr. Segall) and costumes by Saul Bolasni, which became a popular item of her repertory. Semi-circus tights and bodice set off her powerful, shapely figure and magnify the sense of physical presence, always inescapable with her, though not as in this solo with similarity to an expensive burlesque queen. Donning numerous accessories, she good-humoredly ridicules the exhibitionistic performer in four different veins: "Bravura," "Sentimentale," "Lento," and "Finale." Kleig-lights placed around the stage point up the idea of display. A tall stool holds the purple and fuschia cape, the yellow scarf, large white square, and sets of plumes with which she goes into her acts—a performer of florid gesture, well pleased with herself and her admirable legs, skilled in high jumps and splits. She prepares herself with attendant flourishes, changing her headdress for each act, not failing to make good use of her lovely, natural blonde hair.

It was again a solo, the *Suite (Five Abstractions in Space)*, to music from Arnold Schönberg, that advanced her another peg in the esteem of New York dance audiences. As with the more facile *Theatrics,* there were aspersions of narcissism or a dangerous near-ness to it in a few reviews. But on the whole the clarity of design and virtuosity of performance were appraised at their true value. Valerie changes, and changes things, like every growing artist. Here the costume seemed to be a problem. One outfit, credited to Mr. Bolasni, gray and green "pedal pushers" with a fancy top, was un-duly fussy. The simple slack suit or dark slacks and light blouse worn on other occasions helped to define the linear patterns and dynamic volume more advantageously. *Suite* combines modern and modified ballet techniques, and its extensions and progressions are tremendously interesting. It has unity and form and style, and is one of the best examples of pure dance on the young modern market.

After composing three ensemble dances for CBS Television shows in February, March, and April, Valerie came out with the superior trio dance, *Yerma,* based, but wordlessly, on the play by García Lorca, in a Barbizon-Plaza Theater program on June 25, 1946. "The dance does not attempt to follow the action of the play," the program note read, "but is concerned only with the main theme, the unfruitful marriage of Juan and Yerma." It is in five sections performed without pause: "Marriage Ritual," "Dance of a Woman With Child," "Conflict of Juan and Yerma," "Lamentation of Yerma," "Conclusion." The three characters were danced by Val-erie, Duncan Noble, and Helen Waggoner. At a Y. M. H. A. concert on May 4, 1947, Doris Goodwin had the role of the Woman With Child. The music is by Leo Smit, a young composer whose musical style, like Mr. Segall's, comports with Valerie's movement style. It calls for flute, trumpet, bassoon, and piano, though under some circumstances a piano has to suffice.

The costumes (by Valerie) are the plainest of peasant clothes, low-keyed, like much of the lighting. The atmosphere is of people close to earth, enfolded in the functions of physical being. We feel the wife's disappointment and longing, the husband's increasing disaffection for her, aggravated by the happiness of the woman with child, fulfilled in her pregnancy, the bitterness that arises between the husband and wife because of their deprivation, and, in a superb solo, Yerma's desolation over the marriage empty of its promise. The movement is stylized, the action clear in its portrayal of the passage of changing emotions through the characters.

It was a dance feeling and not a literary feeling that led Valerie to compose *Yerma*, she told me. She saw it as a work of primitive formalism in stylized poetic movement, not on a romantic level, but on an earthy, primitive level. "The soil is between your toes all the time," she said. The fact that Yerma is barren is not so important to her as the movement that ensues from the feeling of being barren, of longing hopelessly for a child. There is no plot, no explaining, no immediacy but the feeling beneath. And that pretty well summarizes Valerie's general approach to dance. New also on the Barbizon-Plaza program were *Toccata for Three,* done for other dancers than herself, and her solo, *Rondel for a Young Girl,* both having music by Leo Smit and costumes by Saul Bolasni, and both lightsome, locomotive, refreshing.

In the summer of 1946 Valerie and her husband made a Latin-American tour, spent mostly in Brazil. They went to many little places, smaller than dots on a map, some of which had seen no stage dancing before, and others that had seen none since Pavlova. In Trujillo City, in the Dominican Republic, she danced in a tiny theater with a clay floor, on a stage so broken down and full of splinters that she had to wear shoes in every dance. There were no lights, so two natives, all but naked, rigged up a pair of lamps and covered them with colored paper. The audience remained throughout, in spite of the violent tremors of an earthquake. She never did find out whether they liked or understood her dancing, but deemed it a tribute that they were held in the theater while the rest of the city was running around like crazy.

The opera-house stages in South America, as in parts of Europe, slant down to the footlights, and for a dancer accustomed to the more level stages of North America, it is "dancing on the side of a hill." In Belem, at the mouth of the Amazon, she had her first experience with this sloping stage. The lights flickered for lack of juice, and the audience was so still and undemonstrative that she was sure the whole thing was a flop. Next morning she was surprised by a large group of smiling people bearing flowers, come to pay their respects. Conditioned by American movies, they had only just recovered from the shock of seeing a person in real life on the stage, and dancing. Valerie, in her turn, had a shock when they danced for her in imitation-movie instead of native style. With the missionary zeal of the young, she tried to impress upon them the importance of doing their own dances, and was rewarded by a small boy who got up and improvised for her.

When the travelers reached Recife, they began to find a more intelligent and articulate reaction, though the people there had never seen a modern dancer before. In the cultural centers of São Paulo and Rio de Janeiro, where only European moderns had preceded her, Valerie received the most intelligent criticisms she had ever read, and her concerts were the most exciting she had ever given. She had been advised before leaving, to just look pretty and do light dances, and she was very glad she had not followed the advice. "The Brazilian goes to a dance concert as he goes to a music concert . . . he expects serious works and a serious artist. The people judge for themselves what is good and what is bad, and luckily for me they loved all of my most serious works and the ones that I too think are best."

At home again in the early fall, she did the choreography and staged the musical numbers for *Beggar's Holiday,* a modernization of John Gay's *The Beggar's Opera,* with score by Duke Ellington and book and lyrics by John LaTouche. The interracial cast was stunningly and sexily costumed (by Walter Florell), for the ladies were gangsters' molls, and the gentlemen, though no dopes, were dopesters and worse. The show was attractively set by Oliver Smith, and had a fairly successful run in New York. The dances were a vast improvement over the *Glad to See You* melee. Although ballet to the managerial and public minds, they were definitely in the modern idiom, with jazz and jive intonations, and some balletic leanings. In view of her aptitude for welding the two supposedly irreconcilable forms, she was looked to as the mediator between them, when the Ballet Russe de Monte Carlo announced a new modern ballet by Valerie Bettis for the 1947 spring season. This was to be a royal welding. This was going to be good.

The commissioned ballet was produced at the New York City Center on March 4, before a capacity audience. *Virginia Sampler,* in one act, was said in the program note to be a "theater sampler of early Virginia, at a time when there were still frontiers, and people from beyond were a natural cause for excitement. . ." It was indeed almost as stationary as a piece of needlework; and it boasted one cause for excitement. Charles Elson's dull-toned backcloth of distant, low-rolling hills, with a few far-spaced housetops and a church steeple showing through the foliage, gave pallid background to the settlement. His multi-hued period costumes were more attractive. Inside them were: the Young Girl (Marie-Jeanne), her Mother (Patricia Wilde), the Eligible Young Bachelor (Frederic Franklin), the Frontiersman (Leon Danielian), a General, four Couriers, a Child, some walk-ons, and, bursting in on the star's late entrance, an Unidentified Lady on Horseback (Valerie as guest artist, minus, of course, the horse).

In her flamboyant red riding habit, with the wide-ranging swings and swirls, sudden suspensions and abrupt transitions of her intense and vivid style, she looked so tremendously alive that she made all the others look like lay figures. The music, by Leo Smit, was as unreasonably nervous and jumpy as her highstrung ladyship. It jerked and jarred along with her vampish deportment, as she proceeded to bait the Bachelor and the Frontiersman away from the Young Girl, disrupt the emotional content of the entire community, and, mission completed, make an exit as gusty as her entrance—the General submissively trotting after.

The impression was that Valerie had composed the work with her modern self very much in mind, sprinkling just enough ballet techniques around to give the others something to do. But, as she told me later, that is not what she was working for at all. She chose the title (a wag in the audience had dubbed it "Virginia Creeper") to indicate the "gauche-classic-naïve" mood of the piece. The movements had come out of her own style. The trouble was that while she felt the phrases as movement, not thinking of them as steps, the regular members of the company, trained in the classic ballet, interpreted them as steps because they were unable to think in terms of movement. What she did not say but what one can surmise is that she was not allowed sufficient rehearsals. In any event, the ballet served rather to divorce the adversative forms than to bring them into practical relationship, much to the gloating of those who opposed the union, and to the disappointment of those who approved it.

Before *Inside U. S. A.* at least, Valerie considered teaching an important aspect of her work. Her aim was to impart an inclusive technique and feeling for dance that would liberate the young dancer from restriction to one form or method, so that he would be able to dance in any group or company. Some choreographers use dance to express ideas, she said, and others use ideas to express dance. The latter are the dancers who want to dance but have nothing of their own to say. They are the necessary interpreters, and as such they should not be limited to one choreographer.

This regard for the uncreative dancer, or fine dancer without the compositional urge, is prevalent among the younger generation moderns, as is also the desire to embrace and adapt other forms originally considered outside the realm of modern dance. A further desideratum seen by Valerie and shared by her young colleagues, is the establishment of a large repertory company, in which everybody, choreographers and dancers alike, will have a chance. Q. E. D.

PEARL PRIMUS

Pearl Primus, the youngest of the four-star moderns, flared into a dancer overnight and literally leaped into fame. Since her first appearance at a Y. M. H. A. Audition Winners' Concert in February 1943, she has become better known to the lay public than many of her older colleagues. That appearance led to a long engagement at the New York night club, Café Society Downtown, then a two-week concert season with a large company at the Belasco Theater, another Broadway engagement at the Roxy with a larger company, and repeated performances in the Y. M. H. A. and Students Dance Recitals series, always to sold-out houses. In the fall of 1946, Ruth Page, ballet director of the Chicago Opera Company, invited her to play the Witch Doctor in *The Emperor Jones*. Early in 1947, the young woman who had intended to minister to her race as a physician, received the Newspaper Guild's Page One Award for her interpretation of Negro culture through the dance, interrupting her first transcontinental tour to attend the annual Page One Ball at the Waldorf-Astoria as an honored guest.

In the spring of 1948 she received a Rosenwald Fellowship for nine months research in Africa. She had applied for the Fellowship in order to keep her group together to do a ballet on James Weldon Johnson's "Go Down, Death" from *God's Trombones*. But it was not granted for that, nor at all until the president of the organization happened to see her perform some of her African dances at a concert in Nashville, Tennessee. When he learned that she had never been to Africa, he felt that steps should be taken at once, that the Rosenwald Foundation owed it to themselves and to the world to send her to study the authentic forms at their source. This fulfills the young scholar's ambition to compare and contrast for herself the types she has been studying (she had intended to get to Africa somehow, anyway) and to finish her thesis for the doctorate she is working for at Columbia University. Like Katherine Dunham, Pearl is an anthropologist.

Her primitive dances came out of books, reinforced by racial memory and a deep respect and love for the traditions of African culture. Her modern dances come out of modern racial problems. It is through her knowledge of modern movement that she is able to give the basically allied primitive movement artistic form, retaining the native flavor while shortening and clarifying the dances. It is as a modern dancer that she is able to give impact to the contemporary theme—when that theme concerns her. When she tries to go outside the felt experience and create an abstract dance in modern style, as in *Trio,* with its regulation Statement, Counterstatement, and Conflict, she produces an exercise rather than a composition of any real urgency. She can toss off a humorous number like *Study in Nothing,* a solo dialogue with piano, or the duo, *Mischievous Interlude,* with its unexpected curlicue at the end, or a happy little *Folk Song,* irrespective of race, because humor and folk feeling are universal.

But there is no good in trying to separate her from race, and no reason for it. As an artist ambassador of her race, she has something that no white dancer can give, something it is immensely important for her to give. She is intensely Negro. Her skin gleams dark against the silver bracelets and dangling ear-rings she loves to wear. Her hair is a bush of black, which she delights in tying up in rutilant kerchiefs. Her big brown eyes, with their expanse of whites, look out from jungle distances. Her person recalls the far land of her remote ancestry. Her voice bespeaks the composed, college-bred American girl of today.

She presents the African, Caribbean, and American Negro rhythms with excellent stagecraft, but with less showmanship than Katherine Dunham, though she is a more powerful dancer. She does not glamourize her material, does not overstress the native pelvic movement, instinctively avoids personal contact with her audience. She does not over-refine her art as some Negro artists, inhibited by the stigma of racial inferiority, are wont to do. With dignity and pride (and perhaps some idealization) she sets forth the ancestral customs, the hopes, aims, and struggles, the inherent grandeur of her people. There is only occasional dullness in all this dignity. The performance is rife with rhythmic excitements and emotional undercurrents, except where she dwells too dotingly on tradition. Her stocky body, now copper, now bronze in the changing lights, is extraordinarily supple for its build. The manifold muscular activity in the shoulders, the pulsations of the diaphragm, are something straight out of Africa; but the element of trained athleticism in her co-ordination, speed, and skill, is strictly North American.

The primitive dances, done with fervor and reverence, and presented as "Dark Rhythms," do not all have a beginning, a middle, and an end. Some of them drift and fade from view, giving an illusion of continuity. They are not, and could not be, authentic replicas of the tribal dances that last from six to eight days and nights. They are choreographic compositions derived from the tribal dances, lasting from three to seven minutes. Within that small frame (her ensemble and group works are longer) Pearl is careful not to breach the spirit of a single movement or gesture.

The modern "Dances of Protest" have form, originality, communicable content. They are quick with plaints against oppression, as well they may be. They reveal the aspirations of the advanced. They present her race in favorable aspects. A progressive step, and a novelty in the Negro arts (save journalism and literature) would be for her to use the modern dance as a means of racial criticism, pointing out the flaws of character and attitude that help to hold back the race, as other moderns have exposed the white man's evils in dances of social criticism. She would thus enlarge not only the general understanding of her people, but her people's understanding of themselves.

Over a late and long Sunday breakfast following her first Boston concert, Pearl told me how she became a dancer in spite of herself. She was born in Trinidad, but as her family came to the United States when she was three, and she has not since visited the West Indies, her knowledge of the Islands comes through hearsay. Her mother, whom she describes as tall and lovely, with an English accent, was such a beautiful social dancer that she was called the Queen. Her grandfather was one of the great voodoo drummers, so popular he was given the name "Lassido," a term of endearment. It was not until Pearl became a dancer that her relatives began remembering for her. Now they all look back to the old folklore, dancing out the steps and movements, telling her why this was done this way and that the other. She has had a few lessons and made a few appearances with Belle Rosette. Otherwise her Caribbean background has been handed down to her within the circle of family and friends. It was in her blood, but it did not come out in dancing until she had trained for quite another career.

She was educated at Hunter High School and Hunter College, New York, graduating with a B.A. in biology and pre-medical sciences. For a time she took health education courses at New York University, and returned to Hunter for her M.A. in psychology. She expected to achieve an M.D. rather than the Ph.D. she is now working for, but the training was all turned to good account. The biology, pre-medical, and health courses gave her an understanding of the body; the psychology, of the mind; and the anthropology, of mankind. At college she was a track and field star, played badminton, tennis, hockey, la crosse, was indeed, an all-round athlete and sports lover. Even as a child at Sunday School picnics, she invariably won at racing.

When Pearl left Hunter, where no issue was made of color, she was shocked at the racial prejudice that confronted her. What she had heard about only vaguely became real enough when she tried to get a job as a laboratory technician and none was open to her. She tried and tried for jobs, any job, going constantly down the scale, till at last she landed one as a vegetable picker. And all the time she was working for her master's degree, she had a string of jobs, in factories, in shipyards, as welder, burner, riveter (it was wartime then), and in several other places and capacities. In 1941 she was employed in the wardrobe department of the National Youth Administration, and when they needed an extra for their part in the "America Dances" production, they took her on because there was nobody else around. She was very bad at first. She had had a little clog and folk dancing at Hunter High, a little modern dance at Hunter College, but her feeling for movement had not been awakened. Suddenly she felt a change of heart. It happened overnight. She gave her performance everything she had, and the audience singled her out for applause.

From that moment Pearl loved movement; but just as she got interested, the NYA Dance Group came to an end. Then she heard of an audition for a working scholarship at the New Dance Group, and it meant working. It meant two hours of washing floors, cleaning toilets, and other menial labors, for two hours of instruction. Nothing daunted, she was one of thirty-seven dancers trying out, and one of the few to make it. She had no idea what to do at the audition, so, doing what came naturally, took a flying leap. The qualities of spontaneity, speed, and power were instantly recognized. Her first class baffled her completely. When she found the girls stretching and limbering, she wondered what it was all about. "Aren't you going to warm up?" they asked her. "Who, me?" she replied, "I don't need to warm up, I'm warm enough." She was hot with anticipation and did not know that dancers warm up their muscles before using them.

Later she studied at the Martha Graham School, the Y. M. H. A. School, and with Charles Weidman. But in the early days, at the New Dance Group (where she now teaches in addition to having a studio of her own), dancing was an aside to working for her master's and working for a living. Part of the time she posed as a photographer's and artist's model. The photography was all right. It didn't take long and she could wear clothes. The going got tougher when one artist asked her to pose in the nude. She did it, though, and came out none the worse. "It was not the stillness I minded, but the nudity." She learned the value of stillness, and how to make good use of it, preparing her lessons mentally or creating little dances for the fun of it, "never dreaming I'd want to become a professional dancer."

She was then engaged in research on primitive dances, an outgrowth of her student work, and also a balm for the wounds inflicted by racial discrimination. It gave her confidence and courage to learn of African culture; it gave her a sense of background, of belonging to an aristocracy of the spirit; for the Africans were a proud and honorable people, a rich and happy people, before the white man went in and exploited them, she said. She visited libraries and museums, consulting all the pictures available, taking two or three lines from one book and half a line from another, slowly piecing together a dance. She had to watch, in adapting her source material, to keep each tribe and each dance of each tribe separate.

When a dance was finished she checked it with her African friends, many of them students at Columbia, who were not dancers but knew the traditions so thoroughly they could detect the slightest error. Then she checked the rhythms with the two native drummers—Norman Coker, a doctor and dancer, too, who came from Africa with Asadata Dafora, and knows all the intricacies; and for the West Indian dances, the Haitian, Alphonse Cimber, equally versed in Caribbean ways. They corrected and instructed her in the fine details, like keeping the fingers closed or open, the niceties of rolling shoulders, or skimming across the stage on the flat of one foot. Now Pearl could write a book—and may—or give a lecture—and does.

Her first dance, *African Ceremonial,* was made after the first six months of research. Its point of origin is the Belgian Congo. The legend is that once a year the priest appeared before the people and, standing on a high rock, sacred and remote, performed the fertility ritual until he fell, received the ministrations of special attendants, and vanished. Pearl recreated the legend, compacted it, preserving the virility of the movement while modifying the pelvic rotation. "It should have more drums," she said. "What you heard on one drum would in Africa have been played on three. One man would give the steady beat, the deep rhythm, boom, boom, boom, and the others would carry the more complicated rhythms in the treble. The smaller the drum the more treble it is, and treble notes, being shorter, can complicate more readily."

Pearl was a switchboard operator when the opportunity to present *African Ceremonial* arose. A fellow clerk who had seen her practicing techniques at odd moments, told her about the auditions at the Y. M. H. A. Jane Dudley fitted her into one of her costumes, and with the primitive and a dance to the spiritual, "Hear de Lans a-Cryin'," (and still with no intention of becoming a professional) she won her chance to appear in the subsequent "Five Dancers" concert on a joint program with Nona Schurman, Iris Mabry, Julia Levien, and Gertrude Prokosch. On that memorable

Sunday afternoon she repeated the *Ceremonial* and gave her first performances of the modern solos, *Strange Fruit* (a man has just been lynched), *Rock Daniel* (a lesson in jazz), and *Hard Time Blues,* all of which became famous.

Strange Fruit is based on the poem by Lewis Allen. It does not follow the verse or its rhythms, though until recently the poem was spoken by a narrator. In Boston, Pearl omitted the recited words for the first time, because she had nobody to speak them properly, and found that the dance went better without them. With no sound but the brush of her garment, the swish and thud of her bare feet and fists, the dancer hugs the earth, beating it, flinging herself upon it, groveling in it, twisting her sinuous body into fantastic shapes across it, now fleeing, now facing in timid fascination the invisible sacrificial tree which is the focus of the dance.

The spectator knows at once that this is a woman's reaction to a lynching after it is over. What woman he does not know. Pearl says it is not one beloved of the victim, but one of the lynch mob who had been screaming and shouting in animal fury with the rest. Then, the act accomplished and the satisfied mob departed, this one, drained of the poison, stays behind, realizing with grief and terror what has been done. It comes through to different people in different ways—the right way for modern dance. It is noteworthy that here she identifies herself with a white person, and has the acumen to see, even in a lynch mob, the possibility of remorse.

Hard Time Blues, to a record by Josh White, is phenomenal for its excursions into space and stopovers on top of it. Pearl takes a running jump, lands in an upper corner and sits there, unconcernedly paddling the air with her legs. She does it repeatedly, from one side of the stage, then the other, apparently unaware of the involuntary gasps from the audience. The feat looks something like the broad jump of the athlete, but the take-off is different, she tells me, and the legs are kicked out less horizontally. The dance is a protest against sharecropping. For me it was exultant with mastery over the law of gravitation, and the poor sharecroppers were forgotten. "Going up in the air does not always express joy," she explained. "It can mean sorrow, anger, anything; it all depends on the shape the body takes in the air." So what appeared to be a triumphant assault was evidently a projection of defiance or desperation.

At all events, the dances had their first audience cheering, and in a Sunday article John Martin did some cheering, too. As a result of three eloquent paragraphs, Pearl wrote him asking if he thought she should become a dancer, and with his encouragement made the decision that has by so much enriched the American dance. The next step was into the night life where jaded sophisticates get a kick out of innocence. As later in young Susan Reed, with her zither and sweet folk-singing, then in Pearl Primus, with her freshness and exuberance, her speed and elevation, here was a new thrill for them. In this foreign atmosphere, Pearl remained unspoiled and unspoilable. She was not even tempted to smoke a cigarette, and continued to drink milk in preference to cocktails. It was a better job than scrubbing floors or answering a telephone, and it gave her more time for study, research, and composition.

Magic is discounted by most educated Negroes today, she says. They feel she is going back to superstitions they have outgrown and that it is a mistake to dwell upon them. She feels that she is showing the beauty and dignity of the African traditions, which should be preserved as a record of racial culture and as a part of the American Negro's background. It *is* a muscular culture, she admitted, mainly a singing and dancing culture, but not wholly a physical thing since it expresses the deepest and sincerest beliefs of a people. In a land whose villages may at any time be raided by animals or an enemy tribe, where raging storms may blow the huts away, or where nomadic tribes must fight for subsistence and fend off beasts of prey, it is natural that physical prowess should be highly esteemed. Something of this she declares in her *Dance of Strength,* in which the warrior beats his muscles to display power, a custom common in the Sierra Leone region.

From more benign territory comes her *Dance of Beauty,* celebrating the Watusi tribe, who live peacefully in the hills of the Belgian Congo and grow to be seven feet tall, or, with some assistance, taller. Their heads are bound from babyhood to give length to the cranium. They wear long robes and high headdresses. The women, not unlike their sisters under the skin, are willing to undergo a little discomfort for the sake of fashion. They bear twenty pounds of iron on each foot to train themselves to move in the correct stately manner. "These are the elegant people of the earth," Pearl cried in jubilant voice. (She is a short girl.) But the dance, even when done *con amore* by Pearl herself, is inclined to be static with stateliness, and does less justice to the people than her ecstatic description of them. Trouble, like sin, makes art more exciting.

The Negro Speaks of Rivers, to the poem by Langston Hughes and music by Sarah Malament, is one of Pearl's best. It is beautiful with undulating rhythms over deep-flowing currents of movement that wind into whirlpool spins. She pivots on one knee or circles the stationary bent leg with the free leg, leaning her body in a long slant away from the traveling foot. The pale soles flash, the brown toes clutch and grasp, the dark fingers spread wide, the whole body sings:

> I've known rivers ancient as the world
> And older than the flow of human blood in human veins . . .
> My soul has grown deep like the rivers.

Her chaste intensity and passionate imagination carry to a sweeping finish. She has no hesitancy in assuming the male as she does the white identity. In *Shouters of Sobo,* to a Trinidadian chant, she is again the priest, with loquacious body and swinging bell summoning the people to the forest rites. *Te Moana,* a study in African rhythms, *Myth,* a Melanesian Pygmalion and Galatea, symbolical of creation, *Caribbean Conga,* and *Afro-Haitian Play Dance,* often done by her supporting dancers, are full of changing rhythms, including the syncopation that fathered jazz.

Pearl is not choreographically limited to the solo or small ensemble. She expanded *African Ceremonial* into a group ritual for the Roxy show. She re-staged, in Helen Tamiris's absence, the Dahomey tribal dance which she originally led, as well as the white group dances for the touring *Show Boat,* which, by the way, she considers at least two decades behind the Negro times. She cannot approve of artistic segregation. She believes the Negro artist should be accepted as an American artist, allowed to speak as one human being to another, regardless of race. She cannot forget the wrongs done her race, yesterday and today. In her own people is the inevitable common denominator of humanbeingness for her. From that denominator she goes out to all people. Her solo, *Motherless Child* (to the sung spiritual), with its querulous search for comfort, is dedicated to all the lonely ones in the world. *Chamber of Tears* ("No, there is no music. Only a beating in my breast . . . even like the ticking of a clock"), to a poem written by herself, is, though it could hardly exclude racial suffering, an incantation of world sorrow.

In the summer of 1944 she visited the Deep South, where "the Spanish moss hangs like a crape over everything, is a fungus that creeps through everybody," to see what she could see of Negro dancing there. It was all in the little rickety old churches, to which the workers go after the long day in the fields (time and a half overtime without extra pay) for recreation. They have no hills to hide their dances in as the West Indians do, so satisfy their atavistic longings under the sanction of the church. The religion in both places is a superficial coating of Christianity over the inbred pagan superstitions, and the movement can be traced straight to African origins.

Now, as in plantation days, the preacher is the core of Negro society. He is the witch doctor of the South. His voice supplies the deep rhythm of the drums. He hardly bothers to articulate but goes on, after a few words, with a wordless drum-beat intonation that incites the people to frenzy. He himself dances. Pearl saw one preacher doing a perfect modern back-bend to the floor. The people go wild, half in the belief that the spirit of the Lord possesses them, half in surrender to barbaric impulses. They tremble all over. Tears stream down their faces. They spring into the air, shooting their arms up as they go, and, at the peak of the jump, begin to curve them down close to the body, hands meeting in a stab at the breast with the descent. The ascent is not of joy but of anguish over their sins (an un-African activity) in African movement.

The people are confused by the conflicting symbols. The sign of the cross looks to them like a simplification of a similar gesture which in Africa is symbolical of calling down help from a specific

power. They are bewildered by the act of kneeling, for their ancestral blood tells them one never kneels to the gods, one dances and
sings to them. (Pearl has expressed something of this conflict in her
Santo.) Then there are snake-like undulations on the floor, in worship of Damballa, until the crawling bodies actually take on the
semblance of snakes to the self-hypnotized participants. It is mass
mesmerism and you can't help being drawn in, Pearl says. More
than once she found herself on the mourners' bench without knowing how she got there; and the people did look like snakes.

She visited sixty-seven of these shabby little churches, as well
as open-air revivals and "spur home" prayer meetings, in Georgia,
Alabama, and South Carolina. Not daring to take notes ("It would
have meant death"), she took part in the services instead. She lived
with the sharecroppers and tried to work in the fields with them,
but on their frugal diet could not stand the long hours of unremit-
ting toil. Her imagination had gone ahead of her in her attempt
to put the lot of the sharecropper into *Hard Time Blues,* and so far,
this and other early compositions that came out of books and out
of hearsay, are her best. The Southern experience saddened and
deadened her for a while. Facts are harder than fantasy. But the
fact that the Negro remains a physical person, an ignorant, superstitious person where he is still suppressed, given the lowliest and
cheapest kind of labor, denied his rights as a free man (and it is
not only in the South), is the very stuff of the fantasy that quickens
and reveals.

In the late fall of 1947, Pearl was starred and ill-starred in a
badly managed Negro musical called *Calypso* in Boston and *Caribbean Carnival* in New York. She was utterly miserable in it, and all
but buried alive. Her ballet, *Zinge,* was too concert for its surroundings. The group action, though pierced with the outcries that are
as much a part of native dancing as the drums, was not as rousing
as the informal passages she had choreographed for the production.
Her devotion to authenticity kept her standing on a tree-stump,
immobile except for sporadic gestures in the arms, until a last-
minute stomping dance of violent muscularity that was soon over.
Rookoombay replaced *Zinge* in New York to no better effect. At the
last Boston matinee the star, who had done less dancing than any-

body, was seen punctuating the finale curtain with a series of high jumps like exclamation points. She might as well have been a trained seal. Fortunately the show closed in short order and Pearl's contractual chains were broken.

She was overflowing with creative ideas, her big work, *Go Down, Death,* still in the future. Squatted on my living-room floor in dungarees and one of her brother's flannel shirts, she told me about it. Her round face radiated the celestial glories, her strong, stubby hands embraced the skies, as she quoted the verses about Death's downward ride "past suns and moons and stars," and then, with Sister Caroline in his arms, "up beyond the evening star, out beyond the morning star . . . On to the Great White Throne." The Preacher was to remain unseen, so that the audience could create him. She knew exactly what she wanted to do. She had been studying choreography with Doris Humphrey, and it had opened a whole new world of movement to her. She had learned how to explore a phrase and extract every possible variant of it before letting it go. Doris counselled her not to be too held by tradition, but to make a freer translation of the primitive into the modern, in her own way.

"Doris says I can make this a wonderful thing if I really create the movement."

But Pearl was also studying ballet—"to give the figure of Death a feeling of lift."

MODERN DANCE ON
THE WEST COAST

Lester Horton—Eleanor King

LESTER HORTON

New York is not the whole of the American modern dance, though modern dance is less popular or progressive anywhere else. The New York moderns are the standard-bearers, and probably years ahead of the rest of the country, as they believe. But there are many active sub-centers across the continent, and any number of modern dancers who maintain a good technical level without rising creatively far above it. Their work is useful in perpetuating modern dance, even if their compositions offer nothing to push it forward. The name of these *et als* is legion, and they are by no means all on one level. Among the solid reputations are always a few with wings, and, straying on the borders of daring, a genius or two making ready.

Coincident with the development of modern dance in the East

has been its development on the West Coast. Lester Horton, its foremost exponent there, has been head man since 1928, when he went to Los Angeles to direct a group of American Indians in a festival, and stayed to organize, train, and present a modern dance group in modern works. It is true, as he admits, that he was somewhat influenced by the leading moderns in the East. Long before they began arriving on their transcontinental tours, he followed their careers in print, and his admiration of them and their creative output predisposed him to the sincerest form of flattery. On the other hand, he came of a different background, began with a different point of view, and educed a different system of techniques and terminology. In the general conceptual exchange there is as much reason to suppose that the Eastern dancers picked up an idea or so from him as that he did all the borrowing.

In any event, he produced a work titled *Chronicle,* compiled of episodes from American history, before Martha Graham had begun to rehearse her abstract, anti-war *Chronicle;* and had in rehearsal a work on various religious manifestations in American culture, titled *American Document,* before Martha Graham's *American Document* of historical context was produced. Although his *American Document* had been announced, and was again unlike that particular Graham work in content, he dropped it after two numbers were finished, not only because of the title, but because her *American Provincials* and Doris Humphrey's *The Shakers* appeared to have said definitively what he had intended to say.

A man of the theater from the beginning, he used props, masks, mobile architectural units and objects, before Martha Graham had adopted functional décor for her theater pieces; always considering the relation of the object to the person, so that none was used but those organically involved in the action. The geometric solids in some of his productions bore a strong resemblance to the Humphrey-Weidman blocks. But again the motivation was different, likewise the outcome. They were arranged to catch lights and cast shadows in an angular refraction that made for pictorial background, as well as to serve the dance in practical ways.

Thus without plagiarism artists in different parts of a country or of the world work simultaneously along similar lines. There is some interrelation of influences, but each leader works primarily alone, and all work from the heritage of what has gone before. The modern dance is not a personal property but an open field. The motor laws governing expressive body movement were established long before they were perceived and adapted by the creative modern dancer. The individual application of these laws cannot help but vary, and the process of individual discovery must inevitably continue.

In the very years the three creative revolutionists in the East were making their discoveries, Lester Horton, in his native Indianapolis, was making discoveries of his own—not so much as a rebel as a researcher in primitive forms. His interest in the American Indians had begun at the age of five with an enchanted view of them at the circus. It was also in his blood, since one of his great-great grandmothers was a full-blooded Algonquin and there was another Indian strain even farther back in his English-Irish-German ancestral mixture. In high school he studied zoölogy to prepare for a course in herpetology because snakes were symbols in Indian folklore; and after graduating he studied design to help him in herpetology. The snake designs led him to the tribal dances, and they, curiously enough, led him to ballet. He wanted to learn something about dancing and ballet was closest at hand.

He studied with Madame Theo Hewes, and made his debut as a dancer in her company *circa* 1926. The youth was not satisfied with the rather fancy formalism of Italian ballet, and when he heard of the greater freedom in Russian ballet, went to Chicago to see what Adolph Bolm was doing. But this was not the kind of freedom he was looking for. Back in his home city, while still in his teens, he became art director of the Indianapolis Theater Guild. During this tenure of office he managed to attend any Indian ceremonial within negotiable distance, and so got to the source of traditions among the Eastern tribes. He lived among the Indians, danced with them, learned their lore, and came home to create dances and costumes on the authentic base. He performed the dances as solos, and still was not satisfied, for Indian dancing is group dancing, the solo figure only momentarily detached from the group.

With the opportunity to stage the American Indian dances in Los Angeles, his career was definitely begun. From there he studied the Indian dances of the Southwest and Mexico, of the Northwest and the Plains, always as a subject of artistic rather than of ethnological importance, as material to be creatively presented. The native American dance became for him the fundament of the American modern dance, and his best and most original work has been on aboriginal themes, in movement most closely allied to the primitive. In Los Angeles, too, he was able to observe other racial strains—the Latin American, the Chinese and Japanese—noting the dissimilarities in carriage and behavior, and the similarities common to all races. He studied with Michio Ito for a time. These impressions came also into his work.

In all the diversity of Indian material the universal thread of kinship persists. Among the tribesmen of the Western plains can be found rhythms not unlike those of the Dalcroze system, an approach to the canon form in music, and social dancing, apart from the religious ceremonials, that can be compared with our square dancing. The religious symbol of the Hopi snake dance has a counterpart in the Damballa of Haitian voodoo. The Indian medicine-man, like the African witch-doctor, is the customary master of ceremonies. Some of the Pueblo dances are linked to the ancient Aztecs; and some ceremonials are as elaborate and as carefully rehearsed as the theatrical ballet. The basic steps among all primitives have a recognizable affinity, the variations being mainly in the body movements. Songs, outcries, hand-claps and body slaps are a part of primitive dance, as of many folk forms. The drums in great variety, the gourd rattles, are also basic. In the Indian flute and reed whistles primitive versions of our woodwind appear. The multifarious brilliance of the American Indian's native dress is well known.

This then was the lavish treasury the young Horton had to draw upon. *Hiawatha, Takwish the Star-Maker, Pueblo Ceremonial, Rain Quest,* and *The Painted Desert* are among the early pageants and dance dramas he staged. He staged them for all they were worth in spectacularity, with native instruments, costumes, masks (or their artistic approximation), and sometimes native

dancers. His knowledge of theater, of design, and of lighting imple-
mented his effects. He strove for economy of movement—an outstanding trait of Indian dancing. In *The Painted Desert,* given at
the Shrine Auditorium, Los Angeles, in 1934, he largely evaded
the regulation steps—the hop, drag, and jump—and went in for
rhythmic movement. But some of the critics found it repetitious,
saying he used the same movements for different ideas. The music
was by Homer Grunn, who had not composed a ballet since Shawn's
Xochitl. With its cast of one hundred in war dances, sun-worship
rituals, fire, rain, and rainbow dances of the Southwest Indians, it
was the sort of big-scale production (shades of Hollywood) the
young Horton liked to do.

Voodoo, set in a forest of wide-spaced black trees on a rise of
ground at midnight, in black shrouds and green masks, accompanied by huge bongo drums, was a Haitian dance after W. B.
Seabrook's *Magic Island.* Its four parts were: "Emergence," "Exor-
cismal," "Sacred Circle," and "Ceremonial." Already Horton was
playing his dancers over many levels, but again it was more spectacle
than movement. In *The Eastern Way, Chinese Fantasy, Oriental
Motifs,* and other items, he slid easily from the American and West
Indian into the Asiatic primitive, all in gorgeous costumes, with
native masks and musical instruments. In times he acquired a
superb collection of these racial artifacts.

The official Lester Horton Dance Group was organized in
1934, and from then on the work became more modern, less stupendous. The group was co-operative, democratic. The dancers
made costumes and décor, worked on everything together. The
director invited ideas, gave assignments to be worked out individually, and generally avoided setting the stamp of his personal
style upon the group members. Although highly praised when he
did dance, he did not dance a great deal. His interest was mainly
in group development and group production. The over-all picture
from the press book (1929–41) he has so kindly lent me, is one of
constant change, of works revised, retitled, recast continually, of
music rewritten or composers shifted in midstream. The man was
apparently never satisfied, and always saw room for improvement.
The newspaper clippings draft a record of critical rebuffs (more at

first than later), of adjectival ecstasies and adverbial scorn. Lighting, costumes, stagecraft in general, were pronounced excellent or superior. There was more color and variety in them than in the movement, it seems.

This dim view may be partially ascribable to the usual resistance to the unfamiliar, and partially to the fact that modern dance, then in an experimental stage everywhere, was rather moreso in the West. Horton was feeling his way through movement progress. Movement was the main problem. Material was plentiful. He did not have to look to the American Far East for that. He covered a wide range of subjects. He was as capable of sophisticated satire as of the primitive-naïve. He did not fear the phallic, even the androgynous reference. He had all manner of things to say and saw all manner of ways of saying them. He had to find the way that was right for him.

According to the early pictures, Lester was a serious lad with a mop of curly dark hair and a dedicated gleam in his eye. When I talked with him in Boston in the winter of 1946, the hair had somehow grown shorter and straighter (and a little lighter around the temples), the brown eyes wore a subdued twinkle, and the mature man, tall, slim, cool, and self-contained, was easy and affable. He had flown East to stage the dances for *Shootin' Star,* a musical play on the life of Billy the Kid, that did not survive its tryout. The play was denatured *"Oklahoma!"* but the dances had individual robustness. There was not a pistol packin' papa in them and there was no Big Ballet—a rare departure then. He was not too perturbed by the failure. "In show business," he said philosophically, "you have to be realistic." More seriously he said that his interest in Americana was not regional, not a matter of local color only, but of America as part of the world.

He had had rather tough luck in the East. Two years before he had brought on a few of his dancers to be featured in a Broadway *Folies Bergère* with dire results; and in 1945 he had tried to organize a modern dance company under the aegis of William Katzell without success. He was working against war time. Military training had superseded dance training and men dancers were scarce. But at the time of our talk his mind was plunging ahead to greener pastures. He was going back to reorganize his group and establish a permanent dance theater and school. "If we don't find a suitable place, we'll build one," he declared. He and three of his former associates—Bella Lewitzky, Newell Reynolds, and William Bowne—did find suitable quarters and also built and re-built for over a year before they were ready to launch the new project.

Dance Theater opened in Los Angeles on May 22, 1948, and ran a series of performances on Saturday evenings throughout the summer. The program contained two new works, both with music by Judith Hamilton. *Totem Incantation,* based on initiation rites of the North Coast Indians, had a small cast, and costumes and décor by William Bowne. *The Beloved,* a duet for Bella Lewitzky and Herman Boden, "on a theme of divisive suspicion ending in violence," or, more bluntly, murder, had words by Solomon (Song of) and costumes by the choreographer, who also did the costumes and accompaniment for the revival of *Salome,* with Bella Lewitzky in the title role. The productions were received by some reviewers with the faintly derisive witticisms of the baffled, and by one of them as if Lester Horton and his company were newcomers to the field. Dorathi Bock Pierre in *Dance* gave them cordial welcome but was disappointed to find that they had begun just where they had left off. Constantine, whose excellent photographs were reproduced in *Dance* and *Dance News,* praised Dance Theater and its works in both papers.

Salome is an early production that has gone through many reincarnations. It first appeared at the Little Theater of the Verdugos, in the Verdugo woods outside Hollywood, as a "verbal ballet." Then it became a "choreodrama," with music by Constance Boynton, in which the Dance of the Seven Veils was done without a single veil but with a fairly stripped torso. When Bella Lewitzky joined the group she endowed the title role with the magnetic sensuality it had been waiting for. A small girl, with heavy dark hair and big dark eyes, a dancer of quality from the outset, she was well adapted to the barbaric exoticism of the piece. *Salome* was later done with a new sound accompaniment by Bertha Miller English, new costumes by Jaron de St. Germaine, and settings by William Bowne. At one point in its career it was called (by a mistaken reviewer) a kinetic pantomime. But that did not last. Throughout its mutations *Salome,* "a study in the pathology of decadence," remained a choreodrama at heart, and was so presented in its latest revision.

Many of the early programs were divided between a section of short pieces and one ballet. Of course the young choreographer had to have his try at Ravel's *Bolero.* With his designer's eye he clothed it in bold gypsy colors, which, under the lighting, increased in intensity with the music, as the formations repeated the insistent theme with variations. The whole was in modern movement in the spirit of a gypsy festival. Then there was *Whirling Symbol,* after Mary Wigman's *Monotony Whirl,* and Lester's satirical solo suite, *Escape from Reality*: "The Ivory Tower," "Escape into the Exotic," "Refuge in Piety." His solo, *Lament,* touched upon Hebrew themes, it was said. It seems to have been clad in a winding-sheet something like that of Martha Graham's *Lamentation.* First steps in any art are apt to be derivative.

A more original work was *Mound Builders,* with music composed for it by Sidney Cutner, first performed at the Figueroa Playhouse, Los Angeles, in November 1934. This was a Mexican cycle, beginning with the ancient Aztecs and ending with modern revolution. The order of subtitles was changed at subsequent performances, and some of the episodes were later performed separately. A comprehensive list from one program gives the order: "Part One, The Plumed Serpent: Dance for the Sun; Dance for the Earth; Dance for the Maguey; Dirge: Part Two, Post-Conquest: The Black Madonna, Pastoral, Tehuantepec; Dance of the Revolution; Dance for Zapata; Dance into Solidarity." Under the mantle of its color wound the serious social theme. In contrasting mood was *Art Patrons* (Cutner), presented at the Figueroa Playhouse the following year. It lampooned various species of dilettante—Yearners, Seekers, "The Last of a Tired Convention"—and the Censor among them. Like the somewhat earlier interpretation of George Gershwin's *An American in Paris,* it was a jollification of human foibles, part pantomime, part modern movement.

The more modern the movement became the less it was un-

derstood. Serious dances sometimes evoked giggles, and in general
the home-grown company was not regarded with the veneration
bestowed upon the imported article. Critics (mostly music) often
referred to the Horton group as the California Ballet, and were
surprised to find that what they did was not "toe-dancing," but a
"stylized" form which to them lacked variety and had little meaning for laymen. One bright boy, like the London critic who said
of Shawn's men's dances that they were "all the same dance in
different pairs of pants," said of Horton, "you've seen him once
you've seen him all." Certain critics, however, were more discern-
ing. W. E. Oliver, in the *Los Angeles Herald Express,* saw "the
dramatic opposition between sinew, muscles and inertia," and
realized that the young dancers were trying "to express the emotional surges in our times by the unique avenue of kinesthetic
feeling." But he added, "Whatever names the Horton Group puts
at the head of their dance numbers, it is still dancing, and its content is far from being as expressive as definite ideas."

There were dancers of many nationalities in the changing
early groups. One was an Indian girl, Kuuks Walks-Alone; another,
Kita Van Cleve, was of Javanese birth. Joy Montaya was a French
dancer from the Vieux Carré Theater in New Orleans. A Los
Angeles socialite, Madame Herminia Yberri de Ruffo, took the
leading role in at least one performance of *Bolero.* Elizabeth
Talbot-Martin was an actress and costume designer as well as
dancer. Thelma Babitz later became a member of Martha Graham's
group. Eleanor Brooks ranked second only to Bella Lewitzky, who
was always top girl of the company. Among the men, William
Bowne has a record as dancer, percussionist, technician, stage designer, and librettist.

It is from the Horton Group that James Mitchell came out of
the West to win his spurs on Broadway in *Bloomer Girl, Billion
Dollar Baby,* and *Brigadoon.* Such was his fame in the latter, a
speaking-dancing role, that he was boomeranged back to Hollywood on a long-term picture contract for straight acting roles.
Myron Spaeth, another sturdy Horton dancer, appeared in Orson
Welles's extravaganza, *Around the World.* Horton training was

good training. The group was known for its technical skills, co-ordination, flexibility, and power. As W. E. Oliver once said of them, they ran "an extraordinary gamut of technique."

Along about the middle thirties the latent social theme came into prominence. Several concerts were given under the auspices of the New Dance League, of which the Horton Group had become the Southern California branch. During this period Isabel Morse Jones of the *Los Angeles Times* wrote: "It is not the intention of these young dancers to entertain. They have a message." She did not say they'd better give it to Western Union, but that they failed to convey it, except to those in the audience who were *convinced beforehand.*

She could not have meant *The Mine* (Cutner), which was based on Horton's own observational experience in the mining country at the time of an explosion. His impressions of the poverty of the environment he put into a duet, "The Dependents." The second part, "Women Waiting," was so well conceived and so well done that it was often given separately on other programs. It showed a group of women waiting for news of their men after the disaster. The movement consisted mainly of a slow, rhythmic swaying, a keening of the torso on an all but stationary base, that by its very restraint accentuated the feeling of helpless, inarticulate anguish, so that, one imagines, each of the huddled women stood solitary in her anxiety and grief, yet linked by the bond of sympathy to her sisters. For the third part, "Strike," Horton was not an eye-witness but a wishful thinker, visualizing the sole retaliation of the exploited in united action.

Other characteristic titles of the period were *Prelude to Militancy; Dictator; Two Dances for a Leader, Ode and Homage; Pasaremos!* ("We will pass," the slogan of Loyalist Spain); and *Departure from the Land,* a duet on the dust-bowl exodus, done before *The Grapes of Wrath* was published. This work, with music by Gerhardt Dorn, had for background a symbolic farmhouse made of a few strips of wood, and the beaten farmers filing by, against which the figures of a dust-exiled farmer and his wife dramatized the lost feeling of homelessness. It was largely pantomimic, but some critics considered it too short for its content, so there could not have been any waste motion.

While Horton was under the Eastern modern spell, some of his costumes were likened to graveclothes (by Alfred Frankenstein in the *San Francisco Chronicle*), and the company verged for a time on the brink of the abstract-intellectual that turns dance into a doleful guessing-game. With a notable adaptation of *Lysistrata,* he led his flock away from that morass back to its starting point of theater spectacle. In this comedy of ancient Greece he developed the anti-war theme comprehensibly and entertainingly. The work was a fresh interpretation of the Aristophanes classic in stylized modern movement, not hiding the essential sex element under a bushel, but not being salacious about it, either. It was another work to undergo many metamorphoses.

For the first version the music was by Dane Rudhyar and Sidney Cutner, then composer-accompanists with the group. A later version, titled *A Noble Comedy,* a choreodrama in one act, had music by Simon Abel. The prevailing color scheme was a deep pink and warm yellow suffusion. Horton was often the costume designer and always the choreographer. In this instance Bella Lewitzky had assisted him, and Eleanor Brooks had the leading role. *A Noble Comedy* and other good works helped to win friends and influence people. As the Horton Dance Group grew in prestige, its concerts became big events in the community. They were attended by the movie great and the movie intelligentsia, by society and by people.

A big event indeed, and one of Horton's greatest achievements, was his staging of Stravinsky's *Rite of Spring,* presented on August 5, 1937 as a ballet-under-the-stars in the gigantic Hollywood Bowl. It was scaled and toned accordingly, with massive formations and clanging technicolor effects. Bella Lewitzky danced the Chosen One, Renaldo Alarcón the Seer. William Bowne did the costumes, and Dorathi Bock Pierre wrote extensive program notes. The ballet, performed without pause, followed the original argument but gave it a universal rather than an exclusively Russian interpretation. The idea was the consecration of spring among all primitives, and the choreography was based on authentic movements restyled in modern dance terms. It was vividly projected, frankly if abstractly erotic, and a controversial subject for months afterwards.

It started off in a bit of a tizzy when Efrem Kurtz, who was scheduled to conduct, declined at the last moment on an excuse of insufficient rehearsals, and the assistant conductor of the Los Angeles Philharmonic, Henry Svedrofsky, took over. There were other disturbances. Some spectators, looking for toes and tutus, asked for their money back. Others, titillated or annoyed without knowing why, just sat and tittered in embarrassment. But that was nothing to the heated discussions that ensued. The work was idealized by the pros, ridiculed by the cons. The movement was said to resemble cave drawings. Its realism, forthrightness, and stark ugliness were said to be right for the music. The movement was said to be wrong for anything. It was detested for being bizarre, grotesque, monotonous, given to modern dance stereotypes; and adored for being simple, original, exciting, and, in its closing section, a consummation of religious ecstasy. The work was, in short, a success.

Two works of epic proportion and compact title mark the same period. *Chronicle* was a super-epic. It was, minus the rape-seduction-and-boudoir accessories, a dance equivalent of the modern historical novel that later flooded the country, though it was less romantic and more socially aware. When first presented at the Pasadena Playhouse on January 17, 1937, it took half an evening to perform and was only half done. Its two parts, "Colonial Theme" and "Expansion," carried through to the Reconstruction era following the Civil War. The closing number, "Incitation," depicting the Ku Klux Klan in flame-red robes with white hoods persecuting a veiled victim in earth-brown, was so inciting it lifted the audience out of their seats. The costumes were by Horton and Bowne. The score (by Sidney Cutner), for two pianos, flute, trumpet, percussion, and voice, blended with the dynamics and emotional content of the work.

Chronicle was of the de-bunking school, emphasizing the social injustices rather than the patriotic ideals running through our history. It began, not with the noble Pilgrim Fathers landing on New England's stern and rockbound coast, but with the aggression of

the first economic imperialists. It considered, not the heroism of
the early settlers, as taught to every budding American, but the
oppression of indentured servants and bond-slaves by rich and
powerful landowners; not the fight for freedom of faith, but the
religious bigotry, hypocrisy, and fanaticism underlying things like
the Salem witch-trials. It scrutinized certain aspects of the American
Revolution without rose-colored glasses. Thus ended the first
lesson.

The second took a more cheerful view of "the awakening of
the new self-ruling Americans to the potentialities of their land"
(not without a little land-grabbing and money-grubbing to boot),
the push toward new frontiers, up to the expurgative catastrophe
of the War between the States. One of the sunnier numbers, "Agrar-
ian Possession," showed a pioneer man and woman establishing
their home "amid the congratulatory celebration of their fellows"
—the very subject, though handled differently, of Martha Graham's
much later *Appalachian Spring*. Dance and musical themes were
interwoven. For the Revolutionary days, the dancing was in the
style of minuets and sarabandes; for the Western expansion, folk
themes were done in counterpoint. One number, "Pastoral," was
in fugato form.

After the Pasadena preview, Sam Bennett, a local critic, hailed
the Horton Dance Group as a relief from the banalities of ballet-
russe, and said that *Chronicle* placed Lester Horton among the
ranking moderns, confessing ruefully: "The true blue kinestheti-
cians pounded and 'bravoed' for excellencies in this number I
couldn't grasp." With switches of subtitle, expanded program
notes, and other alterations, the work was presented at the Philharmonic Auditorium, Los Angeles, the following year. There, and
thereafter, audiences applauded it with both hands and feet—and
not only because the bang-up "Incitation," like the noisy finale of
a symphony, was sure to bring down the house. There seems to be
no record that *Chronicle* ever proceeded beyond the Reconstruction. But "Incitation" was often performed separately, and everywhere with howling success.

Conquest was created during the summer of 1938 at Mills
College, California, when Horton gave an intensive course there

and directed the workshop production. The music, for percussion, flute, piano, and rhythm gadgets, was by Lou Harrison, on the faculty at the time. Dorothy Gillanders, one of the dancers, designed the costumes. Merce Cunningham was also in the cast, and, praiseworthily as usual, Bella Lewitzky, who, judging from her pictures can do anything—all varieties of leaps, lifts, leans and bends—and what Horton in his technique demonstrations calls "dimensional springs." The setting was an architectural abstraction of cubes and blocks, the movement an abstraction or stylization of tribal steps and movements, and the theme was an abstraction of the universal social struggle, embodied in the Mexican legend of Quetzalcoatl.

A mask symbolically indicated the white god who had brought culture to the people and then inadvertently betrayed them by partaking of a magic brew that deprived him of his powers. His departure and promise to return were covered in the Prologue. In "Conquest (Race, Pillage)" the Aztecs welcomed the golden-bearded conquistadors, believing them to be descendants of Quetzal-coatl returning in his place—a fatal mistake, ending in bondage. "Inquisition (Mortmain, Auto da Fe, Trial and Serfdom)" was an episode of torture and intimidation, using the dancing body to suggest the torture wheel. "Mestizaje (Clash of Cultures)" showed the vain attempt to fuse the Mexican and Spanish ways of life, with a prophetic figure rising out of the melee to carry the strength of rebellion into "Tierra y Libertad," a dance of attainment. The work was later condensed and submitted under the latter title, and as *Tierra y Libertad* became a popular item of the repertory. It was noted for its sculptural mass effects, similar to Horton's earlier Indian productions, as well as for its dialectic.

Last on the pre-war concert list is the jaunty and quiddative *Something to Please Everybody,* with music by Lou Harrison, introduced in the 1939–40 season. Presented in the guise of a variety show, with an M. C. presiding over a loud speaker, it made cogent comment in passing. Like the little shop on the Côte d'Azur, it offered "Du Tout un Peu"; but the merchandise changed, with subtitles and context, at practically every performance. Taking a program at the Wilshire-Ebell Theater, Los Angeles, on November

15, 1940, for sample, there was satire on the story-ballet, on sexy night-club shows, on escapism, surrealism, and on the romantic duet. There were serious intervals and primitive rhythms, and the festal grab-bag was brought to a jovial finale by a group mixture of jitterbug syncopation and modern dance.

Among the serious numbers, "Tragedy," a duet by Eleanor Brooks and Bella Lewitzky, spoke, in its yellow arm bands and hints of the Chassidic theme, of racial persecution; and the Lewitzky solo, "Madrigal Doloroso," in Flamenco style, with interludes of speech, and four men seated in the background beating manual and pedal accompaniment, was in memory of Loyalist Spain. On later programs "Tragedy—1942" extended sympathy to China, the primitive rhythms were done (before war made its inroads) by a vigorous male sextet, and there was an authentic Indian Hoop Dance, as well as such notions as "Boogi Bali Woogi," jiving the Bali-Javanese movements, and the Dali-esque "Paranoiac Incident with a Cello and the Divided Pair."

The best of Horton's works, or those that can be reduced in scale, will no doubt be revived (and revised) for the new Dance Theater—which apparently has the old race to run all over again. California, birthplace of Isadora, the matrix of modern dance, and first home of Denishawn, its fostering parent, is still backward in its responses to modern dance. But Horton is well known and has a following. He is a careful workman, a fine teacher, an artist and a theatrician. In the 1947 season he presented a new ballet, *Barrel House,* with the Los Angeles Philharmonic, and completely remade it after its first performance. One can have faith in an artist who remains so humble and dissatisfied.

Since way back to *The Phantom of the Opera* and before, he has been staging dances and musical numbers, off and on, for the films. He recently did the choreography for the film-fantasy, *Atlantis,* with Milada Mladova and Maria Montez the principal dancers. For this story of the lost continent, adapted from Benoit's *Atlantide,* his ethnologic research went into the Berber country of North Africa, a land where the men wear the veils, and all wear as many garments as they can get on at one time. How he adapted his material to the needs of the narrative and of the camera eye, as well as to his ballet-trained dancers, he has told in the July 1947 issue of *Dance*. He wrote a number of articles on the American Indian Dance for the magazine when it was *The American Dancer*. He is a great hand with the camera himself, having recorded many of his dances in 16mm. Kodachrome film, which he plans to blow up in public screenings.

The Dance Theater building is a reconditioned store with a trussed roof, adjacent to a parking lot. The studio is the convertible type, having the open floor for classwork and rehearsal that becomes the dancing arena when seats are arranged around it. The school teaches stage deportment as a part of dance and dance as a part of theater. Art and dance history give cultural background, and composition now includes courses in film and television choreography. Since Lester is no longer dancing, his personal style is less than ever reflected in his company. But he is still head man, the choreographer and integrating director of all Dance Theater productions.

ELEANOR KING

Eleanor King is a transplanted Easterner, a former Humphrey-Weidman dancer now settled in Seattle with her own studio and company and her own approach to dance. She took to the West the concept of modern dance based on Doris Humphrey's principles of sequential form, of labile flow between the extremes of stasis, which still base her work today. She found there a vast, unspoiled territory rich in ethnic forms—the American Indian, the Oriental—and the new impressions, both geographical and racial, have colored her later work. She went to the West because she had fallen in love with it; and also because she thought that modern dance should be decentralized, that it was becoming inbred by being centered too much in New York.

She met the typical New York reaction when on December 28, 1947, she gave at the Y. M. H. A. her first New York concert in two years, two days after the Big Snow. Cocooned in her sister's parka and other impedimenta, she had pushed her costume cases up Lexington Avenue from the subway station on a sled, having come in from her parents' home in Brooklyn. She was rewarded by an audience of not over one hundred and fifty people, and of course no newspaper critics. The few dance magazine critics in attendance implied, or said outright, that she needed to come to New York more often to refurbish her dance style. The program, given in conjunction with Mary-Averett Sealye, who has her own way of moving to spoken poetry, repeated popular solos by request. A week later Eleanor presented with the Choreographers' Workshop at the Studio Theater, a new group work, *She,* which was pronounced much more advanced. Apparently the artist *had* grown, even while separated from the New York stimulus.

Of the solo program, *Roads to Hell* ("Pride," "Sloth," "Envy," "Wrath"), with music by Genevieve Pitôt, her accompanist on this occasion, had been created in 1941; and Thomas Bouchard, the artist-photographer, who will not for love or money film anything he does not believe in, gave it his endorsement by making a motion picture of it while she was in town. The common down-slipping paths to torment are removed from commonplaceness by a remote, medieval atmosphere, their essence abstracted by distortion and dramatization. In "Envy" the serpent insinuation of that unenviable state is neatly done. In "Wrath" the green-eyed monster becomes the red dragon of rage, making a stormy climax to the suite, which begins with the less rabid and half humorously portrayed evils of "Pride" and "Sloth."

The opalescent *Moon Dances* ("Sick Moon, Night"; and "Moonspot") to Arnold Schönberg's *Pierrot Lunaire,* danced in palest filmy yellow, are delicate and imaginative, with eerie overtones, not only of lunar magic, but of the moon's especial significance to women. And these, created in 1944, Bouchard had previously thought well enough of to film, as he had the lyrical, low-planed *Song of Earth* (Eugene Goossens), which dates to 1935.

An interesting feature of this snow-ridden recital was that José Limón, attending as a friend, was asked to pinch-hit for the absent critic, Anatole Chujoy, editor of *Dance News,* and turned out a far from routine or partial review. Of the somewhat obvious

Peace—An Allegory (Scarlatti) (1936), he said that the Y audience did not get its "subtle irony" at all. The goddess is shown "in the midst of her many tribulations . . . pathetic and gallant, pleading and scornful by turns. When the gentle refrain she plays on an imaginary lyre is drowned out by the sounds of war, she flees in disgust and terror." *To the West* (Roy Harris, piano sonata) (1943), was, according to his report, hampered by a recorded version of the music, and by the inadequacy of the solo figure to cope with the inference of magnificent distances and scenery. Seattle critics, however, have found it full of the feeling of freedom and expansion the West has meant to her.

She, of the following Sunday, was also hampered by a recorded version of the music (Leonard Bernstein's "Jeremiah" Symphony), and by a rather inept group of four girls and four boys. But it proved to be most unusual in treatment, if not in theme. It is a ritual of womankind, half primitive, half urban (or suburban). In the first episode, "The Mothers Create," the slow, brutal process of childbirth is depicted even more relentlessly than in Antony Tudor's ballet, *Undertow.* In "The Mothers Possess," doting motherhood, encumbering its offspring with necklaces of millstones, is as unrelentingly bared. The third episode, "The Adults Conflict," carries on the sex war, no holds barred, and no sex the winnah. It is distinguished by virile, masculine movement for the men, but is not otherwise distinguished. The work, also filmed by Bouchard, was presented at the Seattle Repertory Playhouse on May 25, 1948 with a new score by the composer-pianist, Lockrem Johnson. *Tempest on Olympus* (Purcell), composed in Seattle in 1947, was a comedy about Jove and his ménage that did not quite come off.

Eleanor is small, fair-haired, pretty in an interesting un-Hollywoodian way, what schoolgirls call cute. Her eyes are sea-changing blue, panes of a complex nature. She has the actor's rather than the dancer's voice. She was the kind of child who wrote and produced little plays and acted in them, too; and she uses her three-fold talent to present concert dances with theater feeling, independent of theatrical appurtenances. The costumes, mostly designed and made by herself, are simple. One set for a group piece was cut out of an ex-army parachute. And one, for *Roads to Hell,* was likened by Doris Hering in *Dance,* to "the nearest of kin to a mothproof garment bag."

There seems to be a lot of Scotch-Irish ancestry in the American modern dance, and Eleanor, too, has enough of that mixture mingled with French to offset the German and English strains. She was born in Middletown, Pennsylvania, but was graduated from high school in Brooklyn, New York. She won the Jane Cowl medal for an essay on *Romeo and Juliet* at the time. She took a few months course in journalism at New York University; then studied at Clare Tree Major's School of the Theater, where she had her first dance lessons under Priscilla Robineau, who encouraged her to go to Denishawn.

Doris Humphrey and Charles Weidman were in charge of the New York Denishawn School when Eleanor entered in 1927; and she left with them and became a charter member of the Humphrey-Weidman company, appearing in all their productions, both concert and stage. She had, among other important roles, those of Cunegonde in *Candide,* Electra in *Orestes,* and the one originally danced by Louis XIV in Molière's *School for Husbands.* In 1931, she and José Limón, Letitia Ide, and Ernestine Henoch formed the Little Group (within the Humphrey-Weidman group), and here her choreographies began. *Dances for Saturday, Sunday, Monday* was a trio to Peter Warlock's *Capriol Suite,* done in 1932. In 1934 she did a solo *Antique Suite:* "Minuetto" (Stravinsky's *Pulcinella*); "Gagliarda" (Galilei-Respighi); and "Siciliana" (Ignoto-Respighi). Then in 1935 came the solos, *Mother of Tears* (Reutter) and *Song of Earth.* That was the end of her Humphrey-Weidman period, for she became interested in summer theater work, and teaching movement to actors.

Icaro was her first major composition. It was produced in the Sculpture Court of the Brooklyn Museum of Art (then a weekly Dance Center) on April 10, 1937, before a non-paying audience of four thousand people. It was a long dance drama based on the verse drama by Lauro de Bosis, who wrote of the flight that failed in Crete in 1500 B.C., and afterwards flew over Rome, in like protest against tyranny, to his own destruction. The music, for piano, trumpet, and percussion, was composed for it by David Diamond, with Franziska Boas assisting in the percussion. The cast called for eight principals. Jack Cole had the title role. Alice Dudley, Katherine Litz, Ada Korvin, William Bales, Kenneth Bostock, William Miller, and George Bockman, who did the costumes, were the others. There were in addition two choruses of dancers, and three readers to intone the verses.

Eleanor, who did not dance in it, had worked on it for a year. She had met the poet, and was attracted to the poem for its relevance to the times. But in her dance she used the Italian words for their melodic sound rather than their meaning. She infused the modern movement with adaptations of the free dance of ancient Greece. The key was minor and the mood foreboding in the first section, which dealt with the flight of Icarus on the wings invented by Daedalus as a means of escape from despotism, and his tragic fall into the sea; the second, "a paean for heroes," invoked "glory to him who dares." The work was performed on a somewhat smaller scale by the Theater Dance Company, of which Eleanor was cofounder and active member; and ten years later, on May 11, 1947, it appeared in slightly altered form at the Seattle Repertory Playhouse, under the title *Icarus*. *Icaro*, which received *Dance's* Honorable Mention in 1937, placed its creator in the front rank. It led to her appointment as one of the Bennington Fellows (with Louise Kloepper and Marian Van Tuyl) of 1938.

For the Bennington Festival, Eleanor composed *Ode to Freedom* for ten dancers and soloist, to a Revolutionary hymn arranged by John Coleman for voice and piano, with costumes by Betty Joiner. It was patently a *pièce d'occasion*. The admixture of song and art dance is more difficult than that of song and folk dance, and when the words are unintelligible, as they usually are, they make for confusion unless they are used solely as sound effects. More satisfactory was the vivacious *American Folk Suite* ("Hornpipe," "Bonja Song," and "Hoe Down"), to music adapted from traditional sources, with costumes by George Bockman. It was, with its folk spirit and light, skipping measures in groups of five and three, a novelty for Bennington at the time; but only the "Bonja Song" was new.

During the short happy life of the Theater Dance Company, Eleanor studied ballet with Margaret Sande, then Patricia Bowman's understudy at the Radio City Music Hall. She found it good for polish but limited in expressional values; and though she uses it for practice she has very little use for it in composition. The techniques of ballet and modern dance do not coalesce, she thinks. One or the other is bound to be stressed and the result is a hybrid form. Still she did learn it and does use it (if only in the studio), as do most modern dancers nowadays.

She rounded out her experience by dancing in Jack Cole's Ballet Intime at the Radio City Rainbow Room, making a few night-club and vaudeville appearances in New York, Boston, and Washington; and continued her summer theater work, teaching and staging dances. She had done about everything but circus when in a circus locale, before a circus-sized audience, she mimed Arturo Giovanitti's poem, *L'Italia* at Madison Square Garden, New York (February 1942), in a Red Cross benefit sponsored by the Italian-American Labor party. With all her theatrical background, she has no interest in the commercial theater or motion pictures. She never made a Broadway debut.

Her first solo recital was given at the Humphrey-Weidman Studio Theater on May 26, 1941. The chief works (and later staples of her repertory) were *Roads to Hell* and *Characters of the Annunciation,* the latter to Hindemith's *Mathis der Maler,* in broad, sustained movement. Portia Mansfield liked it well enough to photograph a good part of the "Gabriel Dance" and most of the "Dance of Mary" in color. The program included *Saint and a Devil,* without music, and *Song for Heaven,* to Bach's chorale, "Rejoice, Beloved Christians." The religious theme (not always to be taken too seriously) reappeared the following year in *Beasts and Saints,* a fable based on Helen Waddell's translations from Fourth Century Latin, with music arranged for baritone recitative and piano by Dora Richman, and a cast consisting of a Lion, a Donkey, an Abbot, and a group of Monks. It was shown in preview, with an unprogrammatic group dance to Bach's Brandenburg Concerto No. 2 in F major, at the Studio Theater in June 1942—the year Eleanor's Westward trek began.

She had had her first thrilled glimpse of the West when she went to Colorado in the summer of 1936 to teach at the Perry-Mansfield School of the Theater. In the summer of 1942 she taught in Michigan, and in the winter season in Minnesota. By the summer of 1943 she had reached the Cornish School of Art, Music and Drama in Seattle, and stayed for the regular school year. When that was over she decided to open a studio of her own. She had been giving recitals and technique demonstrations all around—in Oregon, British Columbia, and other parts of Washington—mostly at schools and colleges, where she also staged productions, and her work had been very favorably received.

Like *To the West, Who Walk Alone* (1945) was a product of her new environment. Done to Alban Berg's Violin Concerto, it is a solo study in solitude, imparting the same creepy chill her *Moon Dances* do. In quiet costume and lighting, making eloquent use of arms and hands, it stands simply on its merits as a communication of feeling, the feeling of solitariness one may have in a crowded room or street as well as in forced confinement, the aloneness the recluse seeks as much as the gregarious person fears (perhaps the special isolation of the artist or leader, too), the realization that we are each, whether we like it or not, abysmally alone. The solo suite to Bach's Partita No. 6 (Toccata, Courante, Sarabande and Gigue) of the same year, has the coolth of abstraction without the chill of loneliness. And *Lonesome Train Blues* (1946), a skipping and stepping dance to a record of Sonny Terry's, treats a different kind of lonesomeness altogether.

The intense and sharply focused *Spirit Dance* (1945) came of Eleanor's observation of the Northwest Indians. It is, characteristically, more a psychological étude than a literal or exterior reproduction, though the Indian dress with its deer-hoof rattles and cedar-bark arm band, and the drum accompaniment, are authentic. It derives from the midwinter religious celebrations held at La Conner reservation, when the Indians dance under seizure of the spirit. Each dances separately, each dances differently, on a counter-clockwise base. There are sobs and moans, spasmodic outcries, a tortured rubbing of face and hands as the spirit enters, followed by transports of ecstasy that make their own wild patternings. Eleanor puts into modern dance form the contrasting movements of struggle between the conscious and the unconscious.

As in the voodoo rites of the West Indies, mass hypnotism prevails; and the coating of Christianity (in the Northwest a mixture of Catholicism and Protestantism) superimposed on the ancestral paganism results in little more than a fetish-use of the outward symbols. And, just as human sacrifices are said to be a part of the Negro ceremonies, cannibalism is said to be practiced among certain Indian tribes. Naturally in both cases the native dances are prohibited and done in secret—as in the back hills of the islands, so in the remote fastnesses of the north.

At La Conner, Treaty Day (January 21) begins a short open season for the tribal dances, which though minus the extreme manifestations are violent enough. These and other festivals occurring around the Easter season, Eleanor visited with the anthropologist, Dr. Erna Gunther, and described in the *Dance Observer* of November 1945. It is noteworthy that some of the younger set are inclined to jitterbug or introduce new ideas like imitating a locomotive (much to the displeasure of their elders), and others disapprove of the spirit dances, feeling that they have outgrown them. The dance of the Northwest Indians, Eleanor told me, is Dionysiac, individual, while that of the Pueblo Indians is Apollonian, social, reposeful.

She draws the Greek comparison because she has never lost interest in the Grecian theme and still composes on it. She follows Isadora's ideal of dance as the tragic chorus, and believes the voice is an aid to its realization. She hallows individualism, as most creative dancers do, teaching composition by suggesting the outline and letting the pupils fill in. Her work has impressed Seattle audiences and critics, who recognize modern dance as something that glances from the creative imagination to the receptive, something no more mystifying than an iridescent bubble, though quite as elusive and as much fun to try and capture.

One unpretentious reviewer, Joe Miller of the *Seattle Post Intelligencer,* said it this way: "While I didn't understand much of it, I nevertheless liked it. Thing that put the show across, for this layman's money, was the theatrical quality of Miss King's group. They put on a colorful, crowd-pleasing show that looked good— even to dopes like me who didn't exactly get the arty part of it."

In the summer of 1948, Eleanor gave in her own Dance Theater a second season of "One World in Dance." This is a series of weekly performances exhibiting the dance resources of the West Coast— and beyond. In the 1947 season seventy-one dancers, artist and folk, representing thirteen ethnic groups, appeared. There were American Indian dances of the Coast (including Vancouver Island) and of the Plains; Peruvian, Colombian, Ecuadorian, Scottish, Swedish, Mexican, and Philippine dances; examples of the sixteenth- and seventeenth-century classic Japanese and of the nineteenth-century classic Hawaiian dance, as well as of contemporary American Negro and Palestinian forms. The enterprise sums up her attitude toward creative dancing. "There are no barriers between types of dance," she says. "Any style, any period, any idea can be used, if used with taste and imagination. The idea creates the form, the scope is absolutely unlimited."

STRANGE SUBSIDIES

It is generally lamented that modern dance has never been subsidized as ballet has. The fact is that modern dance *has* been subsidized, in uncommon ways, almost since before it began. The support has been subjective rather than institutional, for though effected largely through some kind of organization, the incentive has been individual. The Guggenheim and Rosenwald awards, the Federal Theater, in New York the dance series at the New School for Social Research and the Brooklyn Museum, the First National Dance Congress at the Y. M. H. A. and the Dance International at Radio City, all originated in individual instigation. Nor should the Elizabeth Sprague Coolidge Foundation in Washington and the Alice M. Ditson Fund at Columbia University, which commissioned many of Martha Graham's later productions, or the private group of theater people who backed her first week on Broadway, be overlooked. But these are among the more transitory subventions.

Of long-term projects the Neighborhood Playhouse stands

first among pre-natal influences. Antedating the California Denishawn School by a few months, it was established in 1915 by the
Lewisohn sisters, Alice and Irene, together with Helen Arthur and
Agnes Morgan. It was a little theater in Grand Street, lower New
York, that had developed out of the work of the Henry Street Settlement founded by Lillian D. Wald soon after Jane Addams started
the settlement-house movement in Chicago. It drew upon the
neighborhood children and young people for its casts and classes,
since the work was both theatrical and educational. It was experimental in nature and international in scope. Its ideal was a synthesis of the arts in theater form. Alice Lewisohn was inclined to
drama and Irene to dance, each directing her own department.
The result was that there were often words in the dance productions and dance movement in the dramatic. Music, lighting, costume, and décor were carefully blended into the whole. They were
the work of artists who later became famous in their fields.

Irene Lewisohn had studied the Delsarte system with Genevieve Stebbins, and had observed a great deal of native dancing
during her travels in the Orient. Her appulse was creative, tinc-
tured somewhat perhaps by the prevailing Duncan and Denishawn
ideas. She was a woman of broad culture, having a knowledgeable
taste in music, as in all the arts. The first dance productions, choreographed by her and performed by her Festival Dancers, were based
on Hebrew rituals, accompanied by a spoken or chanted text in
Hebrew from the Psalms or the Prophets. In that opening season
(1915–16) ballets by composers then hardly known in this country
were produced under her direction. Stravinsky's *Petrouchka,* Ravel's *Ma Mère l'Oye,* Debussy's *Boîte à Joujoux,* and Prokofiev's
Chout were distinct novelties at the time.

Russian Wedding, with its familiar folk steps, was a favorite
with the Russian-Jewish girls of the East Side. The Rossini-Respighi
ballet, *La Boutique fantasque,* had Paula Trueman (the actress) as
the French doll, and Gluck-Sandor (co-founder with Felicia Sorel
of the later Dance Center) in another leading role. In the 1916–17
season the first dance drama, *Kairn of Koridwen,* from Celtic
sources, was introduced, and the music for a chamber orchestra in

an unusual combination of instruments (precursor of Martha Graham's musical usage today) was by Charles T. Griffes.

All through the twenties the international medley went on. In the Spanish section was *The Royal Fandango,* by the Cuban composer, Gustavo Morales, with Irene Lewisohn as the Lady with the Fan (a lady who reappears in Helen Tamiris's *Adelante),* and Danton Walker (who afterwards thought better, or worse, of it and became a columnist) as the Prince. Spanish dancing there was also in the Quintero Brothers' play, *Fortunato,* choreographed by Irene for the Festival Dancers, to Andalusian songs arranged by Griffes in collaboration with Laura Elliot. Robert Edmond Jones and Aline Bernstein were among the stage designers of these early years.

In the Oriental section was the Japanese Noh drama, *Tamura,* with Michio Ito in the title role, and masks brought from Japan by Irene; the *Arab Fantasia,* based on her observations in Arabia, having native dances climaxed by whirling dervishes, and music by Anis Fuleihan, played largely on native instruments, including grain in the percussion, and chants and songs in Arabic. There was the traditional Burmese *Pwe',* with music composed for it by Henry Eicheim, again using native instruments, some of them played on stage. The Chinese opera-fantasy, *Kuan Yin,* was sung in Chinese, with native instruments played in a little gallery above the stage; and nearer home was Haydn's opera-bouffe, *The Apothecary,* with English text spoken to harpsichord accompaniment.

In the modern American wing was a stage version of Walt Whitman's *Salut au Monde,* by Alice and Irene, with music by Griffes, completed (as to scoring) after his death, by Edmond Rickett. In five scenes of mime and dancing, the words were spoken by Ian MacLaren as the poet, and the whole was greeted as an exalted rendition of the poem. Most modern was Irene's dance satire, *Sooner and Later,* an excursion into the past, present, and future of man. The first part showed the natural man in songs and dances of primitive peoples; the second dealt with the driven men and women of the machine age, re-creating themselves in the image and likeness of the machine; and the third foretold a brittle race in processed form, like its pleasures, making witty use of Thomas

Wilfred's clavilux, an instrument for projecting dissolving chords and arpeggios of color upon a screen. The music was composed for the piece by Emerson Whithorne.

In 1927 the Neighborhood Playhouse was reorganized, with Irene Lewisohn in charge. In 1928 she began her celebrated "orchestral dramas" at the Manhattan Opera House and at Mecca Temple, where Ernest Bloch's *Israel,* Richard Strauss's *Ein Heldenleben,* symphonic works by Bartók and Borodin, and lighter, impressionistic things like Charles Martin Loeffler's *A Pagan Poem,* Debussy's *Nuages,* and Griffes's *The White Peacock,* had notable productions; and, commissioned for the Coolidge Chamber Music Festival at the Library of Congress in Washington, Bloch's String Quartet and a Bach Toccata and Fugue. In many of these Martha Graham, Doris Humphrey, Charles Weidman, Felicia Sorel, Gluck-Sandor, Benjamin Zemach, and others had leading parts; and most of the young dancers of the day appeared in them at one time or another.

The Neighborhood Playhouse School of the Theatre (holding its first summer session in 1948) has moved farther uptown. There are no more Lewisohn productions. But the basic studies of choric speech and movement, carried on for years by Martha Graham, of music and movement, inaugurated by Louis Horst, go on, mostly for the benefit of people who do not pay high income taxes.

JOSEPH MANN AND THE STUDENTS DANCE RECITALS SERIES

A like continuous subsidy has been provided in the work of Joseph Mann, manager of the Students Dance Recitals Series that used to be given of a Saturday night at the old Washington Irving High School in lower New York, and in the 1942–43 season removed to the new Central High School of Needle Trades in midtown. Mr. Mann, a big, genial Irishman, is a practicing musician and music-lover whose sidelong eye for dance has been instrumental in bringing and keeping it before the public since 1925; and in presenting "proven" dancers, not only without extra expense to themselves, but with payment for services rendered. This was a great boon to modern dancers in their early struggles, and still is.

The Dance Recitals Series is an offshoot of the Peoples Symphony Orchestra, founded in 1900 by Franz X. Arens, its first conductor, and financed by wealthy philanthropists. The concerts were organized "to bring the best music to students and workers at minimum prices," and run on a subscription basis. Those were the good old days when Gadski, Nordica, and artists of similar stature, could be heard for ten cents admission in Carnegie Hall. Mr. Mann, in his modest little office in Union Square, has programs and flyers on file to attest it. At one of these early concerts, he told me, Nina Morgana had replaced Alice Nielsen, and Caruso, who was in the audience, got up and sang a number without accompaniment, just to express his delight at being there. When some ingrate later grudged the great tenor his informal behavior, Mr. Arens retorted, "What do you expect for ten cents, anyway?" Mr. Arens, artistic administrator of the Peoples Symphony in those years, also introduced the first chamber music series and the first piano recital series in the city. In 1914 his son, Egmont, succeeded him, and Mr. Mann became the concert manager.

In those years eight to ten concerts a season were offered on each course, and the last concert of the season was a dance performance, optional to subscribers. Dance was more of a rarity then, and the public, then as now, less interested in dance than in music. Noticing through the seasons that the dance concerts were the least popular, Mr. Mann finally suggested that they be dropped from the music courses. But not dropped altogether. The dancers were having a hard time, he told the directors, and ought to have some place to perform. Why not organize a separate course of dance programs, to which those who were really interested could come? So eager was he to get the series started that he volunteered to work on it without pay in order to keep down the deficit. There was some question of applying to dance funds contributed for music. Egmont Arens got around that problem by raising a new fund, and Mr. Mann was so successful with his end of the scheme that he earned the stipend attached.

The next obstacle was the dancers, who had to be persuaded

to appear on the same program with other dancers when necessary. Mr. Mann argued that even joint appearances would help to push dancing in general, help to build bigger audiences for their other concerts and bigger classes for their schools—and won. After much sweat, if not blood and tears, the initial series of six dance concerts was launched. In the pre-series days, Ruth St. Denis and Ted Shawn, Isadora and her six Duncan Dancers, had appeared with the Peoples Symphony, and the Lewisohn sisters had come up with some of their productions; somewhat later Martha Graham danced on the chamber music course, and Doris Humphrey, Charles Weidman, and Tamiris on various courses. For years the four leading moderns (and later Hanya Holm) were the mainstay of the series.

In making a place for dance, Mr. Mann helped to make a place for modern dance. His idea was to present all kinds of dancing, each the best of its kind. Let the public see for itself and decide; subscribers wouldn't lose much if they were disappointed in one or two concerts, and they could always follow their favorites uptown, was his theory. But the public did shy away from modern dance at first. It took about eight years for the new dance firmly to catch on, and it was the persistence of the manager plus the quality of the dancers that did it. Together they developed the fine audiences for modern dance that the series in time came to draw. Today houses are sold out and people turned away at all dance concerts, modern or otherwise.

The Students Dance Recitals Series is a people's affair, and people heartily enter into it. They do not hesitate to express their opinions or make suggestions by mail, telegraph, or telephone. An impecunious young student will come into the office in the spring and put down his little quarter deposit, confident that his season ticket will be held for him until he can resume installments when he returns to school in the fall. There is a twenty percent turnover in the audience each year, as students graduate and leave town and new students take their places. Teachers, libraries, welfare organizations, the municipal board of education, all help to promote the courses (both music and dance), which are primarily for students, professional people, and other near-indigents, though anybody (with or without a bank balance) may subscribe.

The number of concerts on a series is determined by the current income. Thus, eight concerts may be announced, and if more contributions than have been counted on come in, nine will be given. In 1932 the dance series went up to twelve, the highest number ever reached. The organization loses about $1200 a year on dance recitals alone, and $2400 on all courses. The deficit is taken care of by income from the principle and by donations. The principle, which has never been touched, was endowed by Anna Louise Carey, a prominent mezzo-soprano of her time, whose coach the elder Arens was. Daniel Guggenheim and James Speyer were among the first contributors to the fund.

The auditorium at the Central High School is very modern in its granolithic structure and extensive murals, very commodious, but its seating capacity of about fifteen hundred is no greater than that of the old frame auditorium in the Washington Irving High School. The advantage is in the well slanted floor and excellent sight lines unobstructed by pillar or post. But the stage is smaller and the acoustics not good. The music courses are still given in the old school. Dancers at the Central High have some difficulty in working out their accompaniments, but in spite of the musical handicap the setting is becoming to them. The dance events at nominal fees (from $4.80 to $6.00 including tax for nine concerts in the 1946–47 season) have every aspect of prosperity. Even the ushers (who are students) are paid; and the dancers receive from $300 to $1000 according to standing.

When William Kolodney wanted to start his Sunday afternoon Dance Theatre Series at the Y. M. H. A., he went first to consult Mr. Mann to see if he felt there would be any undue competition. Mr. Mann, who has good business sense as well as a generous disposition, thought not. There was full co-operation from the beginning. Artists would often take a Saturday night engagement in the Students Series and appear the next afternoon in the Theatre Series. This was economical management for them, and helped to take care of the overflow, as single seats were more readily obtainable at the Y. The co-operation has been profitable all around, bringing in more people to both series.

WILLIAM KOLODNEY AND THE
Y. M. H. A. DANCE THEATRE SERIES

In the New York dance world there is only one Y, and the Young Men's Hebrew Association at the corner of Lexington Avenue and Ninety-Second Street is it. Since 1946 it has been known as the Young Men's and Young Women's Hebrew Association. Since 1935, when William Kolodney became the Director of Educational Activities there, it has been the busiest dance center in the city. Dance is not the only activity at the Y, nor is dance Mr. Kolodney's principal preoccupation. But dance, and mainly modern dance, has been consistently promulgated by him. The reasons are summed up in his definition, "Modern dance is the poetry of the dance field, as chamber music is the poetry of the music field," and also explained by it, for he is a poet at heart.

He gave up writing in his youth (he is only at young middle-age now) because he felt that he was not good enough at it. Poetry and theater are his chief personal interests; people and their reaction to art his general concern. He was not so much interested in dance as art, he assured me, as in dance as an art people treated as religion. That's what got him about modern dance. He is a small man, with a blue-eyed sensitive face and a gentle voice. And he is a busy man. Yet he talked with me for an unhurried hour across the huge flat desk in his capacious office, saying some surprising things.

His dance experience began with Isadora at the Neighborhood Playhouse. Then he read her autobiography and later *The Art of the Dance*. While he was Director of Education at the Pittsburgh Y. M. and Y. W. H. A., he went to Cleveland to see Martha Graham. In her he found the same attitude of dedication he had found in Isadora (and her books). In the audience he felt the same devout, enveloping aura one feels in a church or synagogue. He had thought that the religious ethos of art as it existed in the medieval age could never be recaptured in our scientific age. But here it was, bearing living witness to the fact that high art could fill a deep need for a certain number of people.

"You find the same hushed atmosphere of rapt religious attention at a chamber music concert that you find at a modern dance recital," he said. When later he saw Fokine and Fokina, and much later, the ballet companies, he came to the conclusion that there was the same kind of difference between people who follow modern dance and people who follow ballet there is between those who follow chamber music and those who follow the soloist personality in music.

The fine arts cannot have mass appeal, Mr. Kolodney believes, and the attempt to popularize them, at least in their more subtle forms, is a mistake. You cannot eliminate effort from the appreciation of modern dance, chamber music, or poetry, he says. And he is right. The true artist never finishes a sentence. You finish it. And if you haven't got it in you, or are unwilling to make the effort to finish it, the sentence remains incomplete for you. Mr. Kolodney realized that the masses did not have the rest of the sentence in them. On the other hand, he was opposed to art as cult. In organizing the dance recital series he knew he must bridge the gulf between the cult and the market place. For himself the theater was not entertainment but a purveyor of ideas, possibly a vitamin complex for the intellect and emotions, a provocateur to keener awareness of life. Well then, let those who found that nourishment or emotional release, that provocative agency in modern dance, be given the opportunity. Let the modern dancers have a place wherein to say what they had to say in their chosen form, and let those who could and would, respond. These were the mental processes that led to the Dance Center and the Dance Theatre Subscription Series.

The next step was to overcome the opposition of the governing board, who promptly turned down Mr. Kolodney's plans. That the general public would never come so far uptown, never would come to see modern dance anyway, and that non-Jews positively would not come, they were sure. He finally induced the president, Frank Weil, and the executive director, Jack Nadel, to take a chance. If the chance had failed, the whole program would have been sunk. But it did not fail. Fortified by okays from these members of the board (and Mr. Mann), Mr. Kolodney asked John Martin's advice on how to go about inaugurating the series. At his suggestion a preliminary meeting was held with Martha Graham, Doris Humphrey, Charles Weidman, and Hanya Holm, and, with John Martin as chairman, a committee was formed to arrange a collective technique demonstration by these artists in the Theresa L. Kaufmann Auditorium, admission free.

All the public had to do was to send in their names and addresses for the tickets, and thus supply the Dance Center's first mailing list. The turn-out for the technique demonstration convinced the governing board that the idea was sound. Through the mailing list subscriptions were sold for the entire series, and at the first Sunday afternoon concert a long queue of latecomers extended well around the corner. The Dance Theatre Series was in. This was in 1936, the year the Y housed the First National Dance Congress, and the four leading dancers who helped inaugurate the series conducted classes there during that year.

A Dance Teachers' Advisory Committee was formed to direct the dance activities. Mary O'Donnell, head of the dance department at Teachers College, Columbia University, the first chairman, was later succeeded by Louis Horst. Mr. Kolodney, Doris Humphrey, Martha Hill, and, for slightly right of center, Muriel Stuart of the School of American Ballet and Anita Zahn, exponent of Duncan dancing, were members in the 1947–48 season, when the subscription series was suspended, though separate concerts and classes went on. The Committee auditioned young dancers for the annual Audition Winners' Concert, which did so much to foster new talent in the modern dance field; and arranged the various supplementary concerts and symposiums of college dance groups in the Kaufmann Auditorium, the dance forums and critics' panels in the halls and lounges, and classes in techniques and composition in the numerous studios. Classes are not so much for making professional dancers, though this can happen, Mr. Kolodney told me, as for making more intelligently understanding audiences.

The Dance Theatre Subscription Series presented known dancers, who were exempted from the usual recital costs and received half the gross proceeds besides. The other half was applied to the cost of running the recital. As the series gained in popularity the established artists received a set fee. There were three types of audience—first the large, dependable nucleus, composed of people who followed modern dance in general; then the smaller, floating audience fluctuating according to the importance of the name presented; and finally the family audience, consisting of friends and relatives of the performing artist, predominating at concerts by the young unknowns.

Although the big-name dancers were the drawing-cards of the Series, the Dance Center was primarily a debut place, the aim being to afford young dancers an occasion for casting off. The work has not been restricted entirely to modern dance but has included other creative dancers. It was there that the wonderful Carmalita Maracci, who does devastating things with the Spanish dance and the Italian ballet, made her debut. Paul Draper, after some coaxing, because he felt that his particular combination of tap dancing with classical and popular music might not go well with modern dance audiences, gave his first full-length recital there. Ensembles like Lincoln Kirstein's Ballet Caravan and a group headed by Agnes de Mille were other debutantes. They were given the use of the auditorium, and California artists like Maracci were paid their transportation.

The Y. M. and Y. W. H. A. is operated by the Federation of Jewish Philanthropic Societies, which makes up the deficit incurred by the purely nominal fees charged for instruction and entertainment in all departments. In the dance budget the annual deficit (up to 1947–48) seldom amounted to more than $350 on twenty-five performances. If the costs were apportioned to include the expense of maintaining the auditorium—lighting, air conditioning, janitorial services, replacements, and office administration—the deficit would be more, say about $100 a performance. The faculty and membership are interracial and nonsectarian. In classes and courses, no point is made of race, color, or creed. Mr. Kolodney has counted the number of O'Neills and O'Reillys in the list of subscribers, and even discounting the Smiths (you can't tell about them, he says, for Smith is a favorite among Jews who simplify their names by changing them), he finds that at least fifty percent are non-Jewish. They're not all Irish, either.

When Mr. Kolodney assumed the direction of educational activities, there were afternoon music classes for children first and adults second, night classes in English for the foreign born, classes in Hebrew and Jewish History of the Bible, and lectures on miscellaneous subjects. The auditorium was dark most of the time. He has kept it lighted ever since, for the activities in the arts and learning are manifold. It is an excellent theater for dance, seating about eight hundred and fifty people, having a good stage, good sight lines and acoustics. Without that theater, and William Kolodney, the modern dance would not be where it is today.

JOHN MARTIN,
THE FIRST AMERICAN DANCE CRITIC

Like the newspaper for which he writes, John Martin is practically an institution in himself. He went to the *New York Times* as a space writer on dance in 1927 and became a staff critic in 1928. In addition to four books and many magazine articles, he has written approximately twenty-five hundred words a week for twenty years, and in all that time has missed only one Sunday column. At first he felt it was important to keep the column going for fear if it were dropped it never would be missed, and later he found it imperative to do so because there was always so much going on. In recent years the column has often had to be given over largely to coming events. But some of his best analytical writing has appeared in it, and to read it is a must among dancers and dance followers. He is, of course, the most frequently quoted dance critic inside the U. S. A. His words of approval and honorary awards are worn like medals. When the medal shows a reverse side, John Martin is not such a good critic. Dancers love him for praise, of which there is never quite enough, and hate him for blame, of which any is too much. But all enjoy a clever panning—of some other dancer.

He does not officially cover concerts off the regular beat, but he goes to everything; and when some outstanding debut is made or concert given out of bounds, has been known to devote a Sunday column to the artist. His impersonal criticism and personal counsel have helped young dancers to make decisions and helped to start new projects. In writings, lectures (before dance got so busy in New York, across the country), in discussions, conferences, chairmanships, classes, and so on, his has been the sovereign influence (outside of the dancers themselves) on the development of American dance.

The founder of dance criticism as a separate vocation in American journalism came into the field on the tidal wave of the American modern dance. It was a challenge to him, nipping his interest sufficiently to compensate in a measure for leaving the theater, where his heart was, always has been, and, he says, always will be. Martha Graham tore up his first review of her, threw it into the waste-basket and declared, "Nobody can say such things about me!" He did, though, and continued to say what he felt to be true, including some very fine things, about her and the other moderns. But his view has not been circumscribed within the American or the modern dance scene.

He was a staunch champion of Mary Wigman, of La Argentina and Argentinita, and other great artists from foreign shores. He was quick to recognize the special qualities of such creative tap dancers as Ray Bolger and Paul Draper. Since the rebirth of ballet in 1933, he has done as much to encourage and chastise that form as he has done for other forms. And when musical comedy took up the higher dancing, he lent his abilities as mentor, guide, and friend to that crossbred art. No dance event in New York is complete without the presence of the tall and lean and tawny-haired dance critic of the *New York Times*. But look out for the engine! The fire in his hair gives warning. Under the faintly British voice and courteous manner is a core of hardness. He is of fighting Irish and stalwart English stock—born in old Kentucky.

As a high-school boy in his native Louisville, the young John spent most of his time in the theater. He carried a spear in *Kismet*, was a chorus boy on occasion, and a choir boy in the Episcopal church. His mother and sister had beautiful singing voices (he didn't say *he* had), and between home and the visiting opera companies he learned the operatic repertory. The family loved music and theater. There was no opposition there. He studied stage dancing (ballet, tap, waltz clog, etc.) in preparation for his prospective career. Louisville had two good theaters then, and the road companies came for split weeks, making four shows a week; and either as spectator or super, it was a case of Johnny on the spot. When the family moved to New Orleans, the same program of split weeks and road shows kept him happy. His professional career began, not on the stage but on the *Dramatic Mirror,* a reporting job that brought him (just out of the Army) to New York in 1918; and, with him working his way down, he says, to editorship, lasted three years. It was followed by an abruptly terminated job on a confectionery trade paper.

Out in Cincinnati, as press agent for Stuart Walker's company, John met Louise—Hettie Louise Mick, actress and puppeteer— who became his wife. After a year or so with Stuart Walker (and somewhere in here a brief spell with the Wisconsin Players), they moved on to Maurice Browne's Little Theatre in Chicago, and then again to Swarthmore, Pennsylvania, with the Swarthmore Chatauqua. John had been invited to take over and make over the dramatic department, to inject new life and new ideas into the plays and vaudeville acts that went out from there. He was in charge of productions, and as there were eight or more of them going at one time, it was fairly complicated. He soon found, too, that the Chatauqua set-up didn't really want new life and was terrified of new ideas. So after one season (about six months of trial and error), he packed up his ideas in his old kit bag and left; Louise, who had previously gone out with one of the companies, leaving with him.

These ideas, which both of them entertained, were tied up with the Stanislavsky method of acting. They wanted to find a way to adapt it to the American mentality. The next move brought them to New York to study with Richard Boleslavsky and also with Maria Ouspenskaya, a former member of the Moscow Art Theatre. Thereupon ensued a period of starving for an ideal, a period full of odd jobs, odd meals, aches in the heart and pains in the neck. There was one interim of a steady job (for John) as executive secretary of the Laboratory Theatre, which meant running the outfit, teaching, and playing parts, for a pittance, in an atmosphere of constant experiment that never jelled. A gap of two years repeating the odd job, odd meal pattern—as press agent, in a casting office, teaching acting in dramatic schools, staging amateur shows for girls' schools, and getting hungrier and hungrier the while—and then the descent into the maelstrom. John Martin became famous, not as the stage director he wanted to be, but as the first American dance critic, for a time the only, and at all times the top.

Dance (and dance interest) increased mightily in the United States after he began writing about it. Restive as he has been out of the theater, routine as he can be when he is off the beam (he loves to say that he hates dance), he has shone, and very often sparkled, in print. And he has never really left the theater. It is partly because he took it with him and it colored everything he wrote that modern dance (which he helped to mold) became a theater art; an art that he believes (without claiming credit for his part in it) has helped to change the whole idea of theater. The three strongest contributors to vital, creative theater in our age, he says, have been Maurice Browne's Little Theatre, the Moscow Art Theatre, and the Modern Dance. He is the author, by the way, of a play that he insists upon directing himself—a stumbling-block that may turn into a step-ladder. And they say he keeps a naughty novel he has written in an old trunk.

At New York's New School for Social Research John put in ten years of pioneering work on behalf of modern dance. From 1930 to 1940 he conducted a series of lecture-recitals there that did much to clarify the subject for those who attended, and possibly for the dancers as well. He would introduce the artist, explain the technical approach, and the dancer or group would illustrate it. Most of the leading moderns and many of the lesser ones participated at one time or another in these demonstrations. The series began with four or five sessions in a basement studio and rose with appreciation to the ground-floor auditorium, stretching out to ten or twelve weeks. The financial basis was co-operative, artist and speaker to share what was left over after expenses were deducted from the intake. Only nothing was ever left over.

During the later years of his connection with the New School, he conducted seminars in dance criticism (as he did also at the Bennington School of the Dance). The examination consisted of covering a recital and turning in a review within one hour after the performance, as professional critics on morning papers have to do—and it is no fun. About ten hardy souls would take the test, and some of them would pass it. But no eminent critics from these courses have yet been heard from.

As a lecturer John Martin found widely varying degrees of receptivity across the land. In some communities, "only an astrologer could bring out more nuts." At his first lecture in Boston (a semi-private affair at Pauline Chellis's studio in the middle thirties) he was approached afterwards by an elocution teacher who said in enunciative tones, "Mr. Martin, I should like to discuss your lecture from the point of view of SPEECH." The poor man, who had been talking about MODERN DANCE, humorously but informatively withal, swallowed a grimace, smiled bravely under his trim moustache, and handled the lady with his usual respect for the amenities. In college towns and cities, barring the anomalous incident, the response to a modern dance lecture (he later talked on ballet, too) was compensating. The support of modern dance then lacking in the entertainment world was freely given in the academic. Without the educational centers, moderns would often have been, and might still be, dancing in a vacuum.

THE BENNINGTON STORY

Modern dance had entered the schools and colleges through the door of physical education. It was welcomed for its possibilities as American gymnastics, an improvement over the conglomeration of Swedish, German, and Danish gymnastics then in use. In the late twenties, as news of the new dance got around, dance-minded gym teachers from all over the country began taking vacation courses at the New York studios of Doris Humphrey and Charles Weidman and of Martha Graham. The techniques were different, and, it must be added, more easily adaptable in the Humphrey-Weidman studio. Although rhythmic and artistic, the work was, in the teacher-students' estimation, fundamentally and functionally gymnastic, utilitarian.

Their training in the Normal schools of physical education had included the theories of Delsarte and Dalcroze, modified ballet, folk forms, and the free, pre-modern interpretive dance stemming from Isadora. That is, what was done in bare feet was interpretive, what in ballet shoes, aesthetic. They knew little of choreography, but did ready-made dances such as "At Dawn," "The Brook," "To a Wild Rose," and endless Scarf Dances, until slowly through the twenties a new type of program developed, which offered the pupils opportunity to compose dances of mood and emotion for themselves. The dances were romantic, loose in form, and led to considerable rhythmized emoting around the campuses.

This was the background of the majority of physical education teachers, who taught dance along with field hockey and basket ball, and other sports, exercises, and athletics of the full course, when they began to look into modern dance. They appropriated it as advanced calisthenics, as a logical successor to the interpretive dance, and because it was more assimilable and practicable for educative purposes than ballet, modified or classic. In the early days of modern dance infiltration in the colleges, the point of view was preponderantly that of evolved gymnastics, and choreography was mainly a combination of movement techniques with little or no imagination in the use of space, and without expression. But it was a time of ferment and change.

Analagous to and contemporary with the revolution in American dance was the revolution in American education. Through John Dewey and other progressive educators the idea of creativity had come in. In the early twenties, Margaret H'Doubler had introduced pre-modern dance into the curriculum at the University of Wisconsin, which, in 1926, offered the first dance major. Her approach to dance was philosophical, analytical, creative. Many modern dance educators received their early training in her summer courses at Wisconsin.

Pre-eminent among these was Martha Hill, head of the physical education department at New York University and of dance at Bennington College. Although her work was primarily in physical education and she is now a professor in the subject, she was well prepared in dance. She studied with Anna Duncan, she studied Dalcroze Eurythmics, ballet, music, and art, and in 1930 and 1931 was a member of Martha Graham's concert group. Out of this background, and with her native taste and insight, she did much to steer dance in physical education away from mere gymnastics into a creative activity. She helped to develop an entirely new point of view toward the educational dance.

The whole problem of dance in education was brought to focus by the Bennington School of the Dance at Bennington College, Bennington, Vermont, which opened in the summer of 1934, and with some changes and one interruption, continued for eight seasons. It was the first college summer school in the United States to be devoted to modern dance, and it stimulated and altered modern dance teaching throughout the country. As in the case of other benefactions, its organization was due to individual vision and initiative.

Mary Josephine Shelly, then administrative director of student activities at the University of Chicago, conceived the plan of utilizing the beautiful Bennington grounds and buildings for a specialized summer school; Robert D. Leigh, founder and first president of the new progressive college, co-operatively approved it; and Martha Hill, head of the dance department, co-conferred and co-operated in putting it in motion. True to form, John Martin was on the advisory board. Modern dance was chosen as the most far-reaching and least served of the arts, for specialization. Martha Hill's classes in techniques and composition gave the solid groundwork, and the leading moderns—Martha Graham, Doris Humphrey, Charles Weidman, and Hanya Holm—were called in for two-week sessions each. Mary Jo Shelly took on the administrative duties. The school started with an enrollment of about one hundred pupils (that in 1936 went up to one hundred and sixty), and thereafter had a waiting list on its hands.

The majority of the students at Bennington were associated with physical education, and wore skirts. Trousers came in with Charles Weidman's workshop production of *Quest* in 1936, when twelve men students were added. There were a few artist dancers on their way to professional careers, a number of young people not yet decided what they were going to do. They came from nearly every state in the Union, and from parts of Canada. They ranged in ages from the middle and latter teens to an acknowledged thirty-nine. They lived in the charming white colonial houses around the open greensward on a spacious hill, ate in the Commons Building, where supply shop and assembly rooms were, browsed in the lovely old red building that houses the college library, sometimes practiced or just sunned themselves in the high, sweet air. But it was no country-club existence. They worked. With the formation of the workshop groups and final festival performances, beginning with Martha Graham's *Panorama* in 1935, they worked harder, for advanced pupils had a chance of getting into the productions.

The study program increased in intensiveness as it expanded in scope. The faculty, student body, and audiences increased in distinction as in number. Key people came to teach, to study, to watch. In all the comings and goings, the two gifted and attractive co-founders were the central twin-rock of stability. Mary Jo Shelly, cool and unruffled, smooth and soignée in Abercrombie-and-Fitch-type sports clothes or graceful Valentina-like evening gowns, held the pulse of the place; and if she had occasion to deal with any dispositional pyrotechnics, the fact was kept well out of hearing. Martha Hill, dressed with equally expensive simplicity, and equally imperturbable, was the backbone of law and order in the pedagogical department.

Bennington had its flaws, apart from the normal amount of enmities, rival factions, and other personal entanglements. It was a fairly close corporation, a little complacent, a little cliquish, a little snobbish. Its seal was tantamount to a stencil. The Bennington Pattern, like a stock pattern in chinaware, stamped all but the creative student. The pattern ensued from a jumble of impressions that had to be sorted out, but it was clear Bennington in the end. There, and in large educational classes long afterwards, one saw wholesale reflections of the masters. From Louis Horst's courses in choreography came repeated exercises in the pre-classic, the ABA, and the theme-and-variation forms. In Martha Hill's composition classes the student learned how to combine techniques into formal design with regard for their logical development and intrinsic meaning—but they were inevitably Bennington techniques.

In the main, however, Bennington served its students well. If choreographers (like poets) cannot be made, and are much too occupied with creating forms to study them, choreographic form (like poetic form) can be studied with great benefit by those who are not of the creative elect. The student-teachers went back to their own classes with a new conception of choreography, a new idea of dance form. From the artists and their productions they learned the difference between dance meaning and dramatic meaning in movement. In the music courses under Louis Horst and Norman Lloyd, and later other resident composers, in the courses on stagecraft, including Arch Lauterer's special course in stage design, and in many other courses added from year to year, all in relation to modern dance, they got a grasp of the subject as art that did much to remove it from the realm of calisthenics in the education field.

Through these teacher-students the Bennington idea permeated other educational institutions throughout the country. It was a spur to action, to a more imaginative, if still somewhat imitative application of modern dance study. The workshop group became a commonplace of the educational dance. Dance pupils in physical education classes were encouraged to choreograph, under the teacher's direction, and their choreographies were presented at the season's end. There might be about fifteen dancers in a class of one hundred and fifty, and one of the fifteen might be an artist. Whatever the ratio, a random spark sometimes flared up and caught fire, and something of charm, or perhaps of weightier quality, was the result. Whatever else happened, there were more intelligent practitioners and observers of modern dance every year.

That the process is self-perpetuating owes much to Bennington, and also to the general awakening in those centers of learning that provided the audiences for viatic moderns during the early years. Today dance is recognized as an integrating cultural factor in a liberal education, and it is hardly more remarkable to major in dance than to major in history or literature. Dance, and modern dance, is gradually spreading into the public schools. For its recreational values, its physical and emotional release, as well as for its sharpening of skills and co-ordination, rhythmic movement, apart from the spiritual values of dance as art, deserves its place in education.

In some ways the Bennington years were the most important years in the whole history of the American modern dance. Bennington made possible the first full-length, large-scale productions, by supplying the plant and equipment. It provided the artist with a place to live, to dance, to work, and material in large groups to work with. The impress of the festival performances had a lasting effect, not only on those who saw them, but on those who took part in them. In addition to the stir of experiment, the salvos of excitement, the miracles of attainment, shared by audiences and performers, the workshop participants had the inspiration of artist leadership, the experience of being one of a composite selfhood, bigger than personal selfhood, that was diversified by the size, personality, and facility of each dancer. In the modern dance group, individuality is at once sacrificed and retained. The flow of rhythm through bodies of different proportions and breath-control, of feeling through different temperaments, imparts individuality to and within the group, while subducting any tendency to starshine. It is a very different thing from the uniformity and precision (when and if) of the classical *corps de ballet*.

Up to 1938, when each of the Big Four conducted professional classes during the six-week session, and each prepared a new production for the festival, Bennington was an expanding school of dance, but basically unaltered. In the summer of 1939 the school moved in a body to Mills College, Oakland, California, and was never the same again. For outward sign, the women all came back wearing California sports clothes and flowers in their updone hair. More seriously, the Bennington School of the Dance was changed, but changed, to the Bennington School of the Arts.

At Mills, Rosalind Cassidy, head of the dance department, and a frequent guest at Bennington, was the hostess. But as in Vermont, Mary Jo Shelly ran the show and the Big Four conducted the big courses. Martha Hill, with her then assistant, Bessie Schönberg (translator of Curt Sachs's *World History of the Dance*), continued the regular classes in techniques, and Arch Lauterer his classes in stage design. On the supplementary staff were José Limón, Louise Kloepper, Katherine Manning, and Pauline Lawrence. Although there was no festival there were performances, and a good time was had by all.

In the transferred music department of Bennington-at-Mills was one of the most interesting people on the faculty—Franziska Boas, daughter of the late illustrious anthropologist, Franz Boas. She is a modern dance teacher, trained first with Bird Larson and later with Hanya Holm, and an innovative percussionist of extraordinarily adventurous ideas. She is also a beautiful woman, with a darkly grave, modeled face, and a melodious contralto voice. In a talk I had with her at Bennington one summer, she spoke of how percussion (and not necessarily drums) could carry the inner line of thought, like the unspoken currents behind a conversation, while the dancer or dancers expressed the spoken thought. Sound, she said, creates an actual substance to dance in; and she creates the most unusual musical sounds from most unusual combinations of non-musical instruments. But it would take a chapter, or more, to describe her work. She has long since conducted a summer school of her own.

The Bennington 1940 model included new courses in drama, design, and music, and four festival performances each in drama, music, and dance. Chamber music concerts were given in an old coach house (a recent acquisition, with other property), which had been reconverted into a concert and recreation hall. Drama and dance events were held in the college theater, and the crowning events were the first performances of Martha Graham's *El Penitente* and *Letter to the World*. There were, as before, smaller events through the season. The 1941 program followed the 1940 model, with wind-up productions of Martha Graham's revised *Letter,* her new *Punch and The Judy,* and Doris Humphrey's new *Decade.* In 1942 there was no festival and not much school, though the work was, if feebly carried on.

By the summer of 1943, Mary Jo Shelly was a lieutenant in the WAVE, stationed at Washington, in charge of physical education and drill for Navy women throughout the country, and the school was **no more.** At Bennington College, Martha Graham and her retinue were in residence during July, working on *Deaths and Entrances*, which had an un-dress rehearsal there. All further dance events were under the college auspices. The Bennington School of the Dance rather dissipated itself in the Bennington School of the Arts. The glory faded in the latter years, and not wholly because of war.

In the summer of 1948 the newly organized New York University–Connecticut College School of the Dance at New London, Connecticut, picked up where the best of Bennington had left off. Martha Hill was chairman of the administrative board, of which Mary Josephine Shelly was a member. William Bales, Jane Dudley, Sophie Maslow, were added to the faculty and festival, which included José Limón. Of the old guard, only the names of Hanya Holm—in her eighth season at Colorado College—and Charles Weidman, who had planned to transform his favorite farm into a summer school—were missing. Martha Graham prepared *Wilderness Stair* and Doris Humphrey *Corybantic* for the big ten-day festival, which had new productions by the younger dancers, and was billed as An American Dance Festival.

At the summer-long Jacob's Pillow Dance Festival in Massachusetts, with Ted Shawn back as artistic director, Myra Kinch was head of the modern dance department. The year before, under management of Arthur Mahoney and Thalia Mara, the promising newcomer, Iris Mabry, had the job. American Dance is an old story at Jacob's Pillow, but the American modern dance (in contradistinction to the Central European) slipped into the curriculum by inadvertence in the summer of 1946, when Margarete Wallman was unable to cross the Atlantic in time for her scheduled classes, and José Limón was invited at the last moment to teach. His were the first American modern dance concerts to be given there. Valerie Bettis had appeared that year and the year before in solo recitals. Modern dance, though represented on the weekly programs in 1948, is only a part of the polygenic dance at Shawn's place. And at Mills College, Colorado College, and the Perry-Mansfield School, it is only one among other art activities in the summer sessions. The Bennington School of the Dance was single in its devotion to the American modern dance.

ESPECIALLY *DANCE OBSERVER*

Among modern dancers' sternest critics and best of friends, the little monthly magazine, *Dance Observer,* must not go unsung. It was founded in 1933 by Louis Horst as the organ of modern dance, or, as some people said, of Martha Graham, since she alone was, and is, sacrosanct in its pages. Like so many things connected with the modern movement, it was, and is, done all for love. It is not only non-profit making, but non-salary paying. Its editors and contributors work and write for it because they believe in it and because they want to. The personnel of the editorial board, headed by Louis Horst, the mainspring and mainstay, changes frequently. Henry Gilfond, Gervase Butler, Lois Balcom, Elizabeth McCausland, and Robert Sabin are among those who have served long and well. Until ballet seized the public fancy, *Dance Observer* rarely divided its allegiance. Now all forms come under brief review. There are also longer, analytical articles. An important feature is the regular account of work in the colleges and universities. Outside of the dancing moderns, the circulation is pretty much limited to the college crowd, mostly by subscription, and for a meager sum.

As *Dance Observer* began to notice other forms, other dance magazines began to notice modern dance. *The American Dancer,* founded in 1927, largely as a trade paper for the commercial dancing schools, began this departure in the middle thirties, and in 1937 ran a series by John Martin on the subject. The younger and snappier *Dance,* which came along in 1935, ran a "Modern Dance Lexicon," compiled by Paul Love, through several issues in 1938, and in 1939 an illustrated series on "Modern Dance Elementals," by Alida Ward. In 1942 the two magazines merged under the general title of *Dance,* with modern dance a normal part of its coverage, including special articles.

The same year, the first dance newspaper, *Dance News,* issued monthly, was started by Anatole Chujoy and put to sale on the newsstands; and the highbrow and somewhat precious *Dance Index* was brought into being by Lincoln Kirstein, Paul Magriel, and

Baird Hastings, on a subscription basis. Both periodicals are edited by ballet loyalists. The newspaper, as such, was bound to unbend to the inclusion of modern dance. The elegant brochure, with its scholarly monographs, its choice reproductions of old prints and new paintings, was bound to the academic ballet. But it has made two gestures toward modern dance. The January 1947 number was an illustrated monograph on "The Recent Theater of Martha Graham," by Robert Horan; and the April-May 1948 issue, a catalogue of souvenir programs, included those of modern dancers.

Out on the West Coast the valuable little *Educational Dance* (much aware of the modern school) continued for several years before the war; and in New York the charming little *Folk Dancer,** adorably decorated, was edited, written, and practically hand-made by Michael Herman until late in 1947.

Today as a matter of course modern dance finds place in the popular magazines—glossies, slicks, and pulps. It gets superficial treatment in the text for the most part, letting the pix tell the story. It is a case of following the fashion.

Only the faithful pioneers in promotion, those who knew modern dance when, and did what they could about it, count here.

* Publication resumed 1948.

HUMANIZING BALLET AND
MUSICOMEDY DANCING

Ballet is so popular today that every woman in the fashion advertisements stands in (something like) fourth position, with an off one daring to take third. The custom began with the longer skirts, when the merchants were not sure their style-*putsch* would go over, and by placing the feet so and the body on a slant could thus equivocate on length. The advertisements also feature ballet slippers, ballet exercises, and ballerina skirts for ordinary females, all, of course, looking marvelous in them. But ballet has come closer than clothes to people since it has been democratized by modern dance. And so, by the same token, has musical comedy dancing.

The princes and princesses of the classic ballet have been succeeded by a handyman in dungarees, three footloose sailors on shore leave, a plain little cowgirl who gets her man, a middle-class young woman suffering from an inferiority complex, people of the common herd. Murder, lust, homosexuality are set upon the ballet stage, not too realistically, but with truthfulness to what happens to human beings. Musical comedy dances have sprouted ideas. They are less frequently ground out by dancesmiths, like so many catchy tunes. They are instead created by choreographers, who can fasten their meaning upon an audience without burdening it with too much thinking. The substance of modern dance is reduced on the musical comedy stage, but not to a minimum. Its influence has re-vitalized the theatrical dance and the commercial theater.

This is not to disparage the beauty, the intangible communi-cation of abstract dance, or the aristocratic classic dance, which has its place in tradition and the continuance of tradition, if not in a discussion of modern dance. Nor can such a discussion include the works of the eminent choreographer, George Balanchine, who has done so much in ballet and musical comedy, sometimes brilliantly and sometimes to infinite tedium. Balanchine is not apparently con-cerned with human values. He does not use movement, but *pas* and *enchaînements*. He is a Euclidean choreographer, winding his unit-automatons into seemingly inextricable entanglements of arms and legs; and when he does try to be romantic or nostalgic (by way of being human, perhaps), it is like trying to impinge a kiss or a mem-ory on a theorem. Clever as he can be in his mathematical, neo-classic inventions, advancing the academic ballet as he may be with his maneuvers, he is mainly a technical engineer of mannerly show pieces, leaving out the heart and soul of the matter.

ANTONY TUDOR

The English choreographer, Antony Tudor, is the antithesis of Balanchine, though he, too, never departs from taste or manners, and works within the ballet medium. He is an intuitive modern, translating life movements into dance movements, directly from their source. His lifts are charged with feeling. They are ir-regular, unlike any other lifts in ballet, but they *are* ballet. When the discarded mistress leaps to the shoulder of her lover in *Jardin aux Lilas,** all the fury of the cast-off woman, her sadness at loss of love, her lingering desire to hold her lover, are felt at once; and when he firmly removes her from the embrace, it is a renewal of rejection. In the same ballet, the fleeting handclasps of the younger pair, the furtive glances of longing as they incline toward each other in passing, and similar impulsive gestures, intensify the heartbreak of the piece. *Jardin aux Lilas* was produced in London, and Tudor brought it, with several other ballets, to Ballet Theatre for its initial season at the Center Theater, New York, in 1940. It was his first success in the United States.

His *Dark Elegies** of that season (also produced in England) was all but overlooked. This ballet comes more definitely near the modern idiom. It is instinct with human feeling expressed in movements just over the borderline, movements derived from no school of modernism, but from the basic emotion itself. Set to Mahler's *Kindertotenlieder,* it transmutes the personal sorrow of the songs into communal grief. The mourners in peasant dress, in stark cold landscape setting, are seated in a ceremonial circle, and every now and then one among them rises to break into a separate litany of woe. We often hear cries of anguish in music. In this ballet we *see* a scream, or that is the intention of the wide-flung legs in one of the variations. The work, which ends in a calm processional of resignation, has Biblical simplicity and repose. It is a beautiful ballet. According to American modern standards, the formal patterns are too symmetrical, there is not enough accent in the torso, the rhythms are not sufficiently harsh. According to strict ballet standards, it does not quite belong. It is given infrequently, but when it is, it is reverentially rehearsed, and the dancers selected to take part in it regard it as a solemn ritual.

Tudor's *Pillar of Fire,** his first major ballet composed in the United States, and still considered his greatest work, is completely balletic (with Tudor touches), yet it has many of the advantages, and one of the limitations, of modern dance. During Ballet Theatre's New

---

* Fully described in *The Borzoi Book of Ballets,* by Grace Robert.

York spring season at the Metropolitan Opera House in 1948, it could not be performed until Nora Kaye, who created the role of the neurotic Hagar, returned from sick-leave. Nora Kaye and Hugh Laing, her partner in Tudor ballets, are great Tudor dancers, or, great dramatic dancers who are at their best in Tudor roles, and Tudor's works lean heavily upon them. Nora Kaye's Hagar is a modern classic of interpretation, and the ballet is unimaginable without her.

The role is modulated between tensions and relaxations. Hagar's movements of frustration and remorse are closed in, arms lax or tense at sides. When she is at last united with the man she loves, her movements open, expand, she wears her joy like a halo, and rises on her points in an apotheosis of ecstasy. The vicious young man (Laing) to whom she gives herself in a moment of despair, makes his improper proposal with a rude pelvic thrust unmistakable in meaning. If the censors understood it as they do the bumps and grinds of burlesque, it, and certain other passages, would have been expunged long ago.

Motives are motions in this ballet, and thoughts are gestures, the slightest of which is laden with characterization and comment. The malicious brattishness of the younger sister, the struggle between disapproval and sympathy in the old-maidish older one, the smug virginity of the two Maiden Ladies Out Walking, bowing stiffly from their waists and looking down their noses at the unhappy heroine, are made transparently clear; nor is there any ambiguity about the difference in moral status between the Lovers-in-Innocence and the Lovers-in-Experience.

Most good choreographers are good dancers first. Tudor is not much of a performing technician, but he holds within himself every character he conceives, and ably manifests them for his cast in rehearsal. He is tall and erect, of imposing presence. In his own roles he sometimes bears himself like a lay figure strayed from a shop window. Yet by some subtle emanation he can endow a scene with eloquence. As the Friend in *Pillar of Fire,* his straight back and bended knee exude humility and compassion while he begs Hagar's forgiveness for his thoughtless neglect of her, and offers her his own in faith and understanding. His inflammable Tybalt in *Romeo and Juliet* * is alive with hateful kicks and pugnacious gestures.

Tudor (the choreographer) can rifle the emotions with a *rond de jambe,* a step that, like the butterfly on Whistler's etchings, amounts to an insigne in his work. It varies in key with the mood it is expressing, just as his other steps and poses do. A Tudor arabesque may be watchful, alert, for the harried Caroline in *Jardin aux Lilas,* or, weighted and depressed with Hagar's tribulation. Like grace notes of feeling are the little human touches—the dropping of a handkerchief, and the swift flight of retrospect on the breath of its perfume when it is picked up, in the high comedy, *Dim Lustre;* * and also in this ballet, the telepathic fingering of his tie by The Gentleman With Her when The Lady With Him wanders off in thought to another man in another tie at another time.

In *Undertow,** Tudor's single ballet so far to have a score composed for it, each character is identified by gait and behavior as well as by costume and make-up, and (after one has had time to figure them out) by the names from classic mythology so ironically bestowed upon them. This ballet of sex-murder in a city slum was mystifying at its *première.* The shock of its subject matter hid the design of its form. But gradually there came to view significant parallelisms and guideposts in the action. Volupia, the harlot, the first woman The Transgressor sees in the city, stands approximately where and as his mother had stood when she repelled him in the Prologue. The quiver of murderous desire tenses in The Transgressor's hands long before he actually attempts to choke Ate after her disreputable play with the street boys. The tension mounts in these rhythmic repetitions and resemblances to the climax, and the death sequence is a recapitulation in choreographic structure of the birth sequence.

There is more psychoanalysis in *Undertow* than some of this world dreams of. The ballet shows not only how sex criminals can be made, but how the callousness of women can drive a sensitive youth to perverted love. This is plumbing pretty deep. It may be revolting but it is salutary in the end. For its expressive choreographic

---

* Fully described in *The Borzoi Book of Ballets,* by Grace Robert.

form, its strongly substantiating music by William Schuman, its dark, oppressive setting by Raymond Breinen, and for the pity and terror it stirs in the human heart, it is a great ballet.

Tudor has always been arbitrary in his choice of music. He takes what he likes regardless of the composer's plan. Chausson's *Poème,* Schönberg's *Verklärte Nacht,* have served him admirably, though they should not have. His latest ballet, *Shadow of the Wind,* produced by Ballet Theatre on April 14, 1948, is set to Mahler's symphonic song cycle, *Das Lied von der Erde.* It seems to be without psychology or story, following the Oriental pattern of beauty for beauty's sake, after the Chinese poems of Li Po, which base the German translations. The ballet has, indeed, a beautiful production by Jo Mielziner, and an augmented orchestra for Mahler's great song of humanity, which needs no visualization, and is better played unadorned. It lasts one hour, too long for mere decoration.

No choreographer likes to be typed, and that may account for Tudor's departure here from his own traditions. But he changes things, like all the rest of them. Therein lies the hope that the poetic title of his new ballet will ultimately be verified. In the musical comedy field, Tudor made two rather dismal tries, and failed. His "Success Story" in *Hollywood Pinafore* was painfully obvious, if temporarily popular. His dances for *The Day Before Spring* rehashed motifs from his great ballets with belittling effect.

AGNES DE MILLE

The life of humanized ballet for the wider public began with *Rodeo,** and of meaningful musicomedy dancing with *Oklahoma!* Of all that has gone before and come after, these fabulous dance successes of Agnes de Mille's set the mark by planting it right in the hearts of people. *Rodeo,* which had its *première* by the Ballet Russe de Monte Carlo at the Metropolitan Opera House, New York, on October 16, 1942, was stormed with nineteen curtain

* Fully described in *The Borzoi Book of Ballets,* by Grace Robert.

calls (and an obbligato of yells) and Agnes de Mille, the Cowgirl, and Frederic Franklin, the Champion Roper, received them in a long, congratulatory hug. The ballet is so strong in human and dance values, borne out by Aaron Copland's wonderful score and Oliver Smith's atmospheric settings, that it has since withstood inferior casting and slipshod supervision, and still not lost its appeal. Why? Because the choreographer gathered up an armful of young people off the ranches she had known in the West, and placed them by proxy on the stage.

She told a human interest story in dance, movement, and gesture—movements, not only of riding a bucking broncho, but of the emotions of the rider; gestures, not only of roping and showing off, flirting, or meditating alone in the twilight hour, but of what is going on under the surface motions; dance steps, not only of country-dancing, but of disappointment or glee. When, in the first scene, the little Cowgirl slides one leg forward to slip into a fall, you know she is forlorn, so forlorn she has gone limp with it. The movement repeated is a leitmotif of her unhappy state. When, in the last scene, she has changed her cowboy clothes for a cotton dress and been accepted in the community, her dance steps cannot contain themselves and spill over in improvisation. The other characters move as veraciously from human impulses. The natural voices of the caller and other dancers, the clapping of hands, in the square dance, add an audible link to life.

Rodeo is a ballet of the folk, in common parlance, in common dress. It is simple and clear, and far warmer than its predecessor, *Billy the Kid,** which had its *première* in Chicago by the Ballet Caravan in 1938, and is now the property of Ballet Theatre. *Billy,* by the estimable Eugene Loring, is considered the first important American ballet. It is based on frontier life at the time of the notorious two-gun killer, William Bonney. The score is by Aaron Copland, and scenery and costumes by Jared French. Loring abstracts human gesture imaginatively, deals movement ideas out for the spectator to finish, but his characters, apart from the title figure, are types rather than people, his plot action complex, and the dancing, for the most part, keeps its distance in the realm of the

---

* Fully described in *The Borzoi Book of Ballets,* by Grace Robert.

academic school. It is a fine ballet, but it presents the Wild West formally and in fancy dress. Balletomanes like it and think *Rodeo* is indebted to it. Balletophiles like both, without arraignment of either. Plain people love *Rodeo*.

Oklahoma! (still on the Western theme) opened in Boston under the even more banal title of *Away We Go.* It was a hit, nevertheless, except for the few who felt that the poetry of Lynn Rigg's play, *Green Grow the Lilacs,* from which the musical was concocted, had got lost in the shake-up. The poetic effluvium was found in the central ballet that told without saying it of the conflict in Laurie's mind over her sweetheart, Curley, and the evil Jud. The big ballet, or dream sequence carrying forward the story, afterwards became a public nuisance in the hands of copycats, till managers ran a mile from them. But it was that ballet, the first really expressive ballet-ballet in a musical, and the clever incidental dances, that made the show, and saved the redoubtable Theater Guild to boot.

Agnes de Mille is a free-lance choreographer, disclaiming any affiliation with modern dance, although she has played around its edges since the days of the Dance Repertory Theatre. She uses ballet with expression marks that bring it close to modern style. She believes, as many others do, that the ballet-trained body can do anything, and it is no effort to her to adapt modern movements from observation, or devise them from expressional need. She is acute, adroit, and endlessly inventive. Many of her later and larger works were pre-sketched in her recital repertory.

What underlies her best work is folk feeling, a genuine feeling for the folk. Even her sophisticated *Tally-Ho!* shows the courtiers as just folk under their varnished manners. Every bow and headshake in that ballet has a background of scholarly research, amplified by the gifts of humor, musicality, and creative intelligence. It is a very human ballet, with all sorts of foibles teetering around on points and nodding from silly heads, and more than one touch of the barnyard—as when the Prince, a roué, pursues the Young Wife across the stage, spreading his arms like the wings of a ruffled cock. It is because she did not wish to be typed in Americana that she did this ballet of an eighteenth century garden of love—laid in France, of course.

Her latest ballet, *Fall River Legend,* based on a nineteenth century American murder-mystery, changes an historic whodunit into a shedunit for the purposes of psychological melodrama. The case, commemorated with levity in the jingle

> Lizzie Borden took an axe
> And gave her mother forty whacks
> When she saw what she had done
> She gave her father forty-one

was never proved. It is treated seriously, and with some poetic license, by the choreographer. She presents The Accused as the convicted, standing before the gallows on the arm of her Pastor, and, after exploring the background of suppression and abuse that might make for justifiable parenticide, returns her there. The mental flashbacks move through Oliver Smith's skeletal sets of a prim New England home, to Morton Gould's underlining score, over the bitter girlhood experiences—loss of a loved mother, her replacement by an unloving stepmother, thwarted romance, and the alienated affections of her father—that culminate in her crime, and reconcile her to the penalty.

The role provides a diapason of moodful movement and neurotic gesture, not danced for all its organ resonance until Nora Kaye was able to pull out the stops. It was composed for her, but created by Alicia Alonso at the *première* during Ballet Theatre's spring season at the Metropolitan (April 22, 1948), and danced at another performance by Dania Krupska, on whom it had been modeled. When Nora Kaye stepped in, the whole cast reacted to her performance as to a magnet, and the ballet was galvanized into a better work than it had at first appeared to be. Agnes, though accused (but not convicted) of following in Tudor's steps, had planned to do the ballet long before *Undertow* was produced.

Since *Oklahoma!* De Mille has had a long line of musical successes, each different from the last. She projects emotion through formal design, believing that content without form is as void as form without content. But, she says, the content makes the form. Her "Civil War" ballet in *Bloomer Girl* was packed with the anxiety of women parting and parted from their men. In *Carousel,* the ballet of tortured adolescence ends in a startling sob. Her pithy incidental dances are clean-cut and shapely. She uses the free torso as to the modern dance born, and the shod or the bare foot with equal expressivity. Her Scottish dances for *Brigadoon* were beautifully designed from authentic material. The sharp picks of his pointed feet by the leading dancer in the "Sword Dance" tell how it is with the dour and irascible Scot who loses at love, as much as they do of his dexterity. In the idyllic barefoot ballet of girls preparing for her wedding, the bride-to-be speaks in a little stuttering step of the hesitancy and doubt mixed with glad anticipation she feels on her nuptial eve.

Not everybody likes everything Agnes de Mille does. She can lapse occasionally. She choreographed and directed the Rodgers and Hammerstein *Allegro* of the 1947–48 season with signal unity of effect, but the dances, despite their *espièglerie,* were not her best. They were duly expository, and still rather shallow and run-of-the-show. The musical was a modern morality play, tracing the life of a young doctor from babyhood to manhood, with a neo-Greek chorus speaking and singing its comment in the vernacular. It was heartily disliked as an inspirational tract, and as heartily approved for the same reason. Its pretentiousness may have been one difficulty. Another was the music, the bane of most musicals. Songs at their dittiest aren't always at wittiest, and when they are sentimental they last forever. Verse after verse repeats one idea, if any. Besides, you seem to have heard it all before. Amid these arid stretches, the dancing, with its instantaneity of impact, is a lifesaver. It hits you where you live and takes you along with it, no questions asked, no answers needed. The marriage between such music and such dancing can only be of convenience, and the wonder is that the dancing so often surmounts its handicap.

RUTH PAGE

Another smart free-lance is Ruth Page, of Chicago and the rest of the world. Small, dark, chic, and debonair, bright as a brand-new dime, she keeps the New York censors busy. Her latest ballet to upset the town was *Billy Sunday,* with music by Remi Gassman, and a word-score from the revivalist's sermon on Temptation by J. Ray Hunt. Words are not new to ballet, but so many and such rough words are; and to hear the English Frederic Franklin, in a baseball outfit, deliver them with American pep, is something; to hear the prima ballerina, Alexandra Danilova, bedizened as Mrs. Potiphar in a sequined short tutu and feather boa, attempting to seduce Joseph (Franklin in Shriner regalia) with a Russian accent, is something more.

According to Billy's sermon, there is only one sin and it doesn't pay, and he drags in the unrewarding affairs of Joseph and Potiphar's Wife, David and Uriah the Hittite's Wife, and Samson and Delilah (in prostitute-pink) to prove it. There are also the Five Foolish Virgins gotten up like Mack Sennett Bathing Beauties, and a group of Philistines in Ku Klux Klan attire. The costumes are by Paul DuPont, and the set, suggesting one of Billy's temporary tabernacles of the sawdust trail, by Herbert Andrews. This rowdy modern ballet is anything but classical, and not very choreographical, but it is fun. It was produced at City Center by the Ballet Russe de Monte Carlo early in 1948.

The same company, encountering the same censor-trouble, produced *Frankie and Johnny,* a balletization of the old ballad, at the same place, early in 1945. It was first done by Ruth Page and her partner, Bentley Stone, for the Federal Theater in Chicago in 1938, and the spice had not lost its savor when it reached Boston in the spring of 1946. The first night the action sprawled rather awkwardly, especially in the succession of gentlemen-callers running up and down Nellie Bly's front stoop with appalling frequency and astonishing rapidity. As this and other raw irrelevancies were dropped, the choreography became more compact, the anecdote showed through in an ingenious combination of jerky and jazzy, humorously contortional, violently acrobatic and mildly modern movements.

Ruthanna Boris, who has studied modern dance, following Miss Page in the better half of the title role, gave a serio-comic interpretation that took it out of the cartoon-caricature class.

Franklin as the other half, Nikita Talin as the Bartender, used their bodies well in the modern manner mingled with plastique. Three Salvation Army lassies, stationed at one side of the proscenium, chanted the verses intermittently. Here again we have audible words, lively music (by Jerome Moross), telltale scenery (by Clive Rickabaugh) and costumes (by Paul DuPont), and exaggerated human movement, in a ballet that is good fun, if not precisely good form.

Chicago, the home of Ruth Page's productions, never raises an eyebrow over any of them. Ruth thinks nothing of sticking a pair of Lesbians in a corner, or of giving a fictionalized Kinsey Report on the deleterious intrusion of homosexuality on married life. Such was the theme of *The Bells,* presented by the Ballet Russe de Monte Carlo at City Center in September, 1946, and at the Boston Opera House the following April. But neither Boston or New York batted an eyelash. They looked upon the ballet as so much not very good choreography, and overlooked its meaning.

The Bells transcribes the romantic poem of Edgar Allan Poe into a poetic problem-ballet without words. The silver bells are betokened by a bride in the first flush of happiness, the golden bells by the young wife still happy though married, the brazen bells sound the alarum of mischief brewing, and the iron bells state what it is. They state it definitely in unison passages for a male group representing the Ghouls ("They are neither men nor women— they are Ghouls") led by their King, who, after a fight as fierce as ballet design permits, carries off the husband in triumph. Whereupon Isamu Noguchi's flat white church-and-steeple collapses like the House of Usher. His *outré,* bell-hung costumes have furnished silent clangors and tintinnabulations, but no bell rings in Darius Milhaud's score.

All three ballets are better than they appear to be at City Center, where any ballet, especially when done up in the economy package of under-rehearsal, is likely to have a cut-rate look. They are original and have something to say. The flaw is that the ideas are keener than the choreography. The fact is that the choreographer takes a slightly more literatesque than balletesque view of her chosen art. She grew up eating words, not her own, but of the poems she read with her father at breakfast. She loves words, and has a whole repertory of solo dances to modern poetry, which she recites effectively while dancing. Every poem she reads goes to her feet and soon involves the rest of her body. She sees solos in words, and scenarios in everything.

While in Boston in the spring of 1948, she visited the Gardner Museum, Mrs. Jack Gardner's Italian Palace in the Fenway, and she hadn't prowled around ten minutes before she was plotting a ballet on "The Fascinating Mrs. Jack." She had the Boston Brahmins, who suffered the erratic society leader without exactly counting her in, gathered for a soirée in the Tapestry Room, and their hostess introducing an Isadora figure, bare-legged, gauze-clad, ungirded of loin, to shock the daylights out of them. Ruth was at the time reviving for the Ballet Russe de Monte Carlo her ten-year old ballet, *Love Song,* (of poetic group phraseology delicately tinged with modernity, apart from the wan romanticizing over lost love in the ballerina role). She spent her spare time at Fenway Court, bought the official biography of Mrs. Gardner, and in less than a fortnight after her return to Chicago had drafted the full scenario, with further plot complications, and directions for music, costume, and stage design. Everything was done but the choreography, soon to be worked out on herself and then on other dancers in her company.

Ruth Page is a pioneer in Ballet Americana, combining ballet with modern techniques when serviceable. Her tours with Harald Kreutzberg, in the United States and the Orient, have inclined her to the Central European brand of modernism; but she is always dashing to New York, and, during the Bennington years, kept track of what was going on there. Hers is the acute Americanism and chronic cosmopolitanism of the seasoned traveler, the ranging mind of the wide reader. One of her early ballets, *La Guiablesse,* with music by William Grant Still, was choreographed on a Martinique legend after reading Lafcadio Hearn.

The Expanding Universe, title of one of her dances, indicates that the sky is not the limit with the irrepressible Ruth. She has not done so much for Broadway as for ballet. But her ballets and incidental dances for the operetta, *Music in My Heart,* were the best of that sorry falsification of Tchaikovsky's love life. There was a big ballet satirizing the Italian style favored in Leningrad when it was St. Petersburg, a *grand pas de deux* in the style of Papa Petipa, and, characteristically, a "Danse Arabe" that was censored out after the first performance.

JEROME ROBBINS AND MICHAEL KIDD

The youngcomers, Jerome Robbins and Michael Kidd, thoroughly awake to their time of day, have contributed conspicuously to modern ballet and modern musical comedy. Both have studied the modern as well as the classic dance, and, as dancers in Ballet Theatre, have come under Tudor's influence. These impressions have streamed through their works and brought out the human values, in their own youthful and colloquial terms. Robbins was a shy and retiring though excellent character dancer, already getting a lot of notice, when on April 18, 1944, his *Fancy Free* * burst on the stage of the Metropolitan Opera House and rocketed him into sudden, spectacular fame.

It was a case of perfect if unplanned timing. There was a war on. Men in uniform were dear to the American public, which could not help taking to a collective heart already wide open to receive them, the three sailors on shore leave who came just as they were to the ballet stage, and behaved just as expected, even to chewing gum and not having enough girls to go round. There was more to it than that, of course. There was wonderful dancing, with radiations of humor and tenderness, aided and abetted by Leonard Bernstein's descriptive score, and a corner bar set by Oliver Smith that put everything and everybody in its place. Robbins had choreographed the three solos that kindled the audience into roars of enthusiasm on the personality of each dancer, and thus given the sailors distinct individuality.

* Fully described in *The Borzoi Book of Ballets,* by Grace Robert.

The first one, danced by Harold Lang, showed the extrovert in a brilliant ballet variation with such plebeian garnitures as the pause for a glass of beer; the second, by John Kriza, combined ballet and jazz in a subtle evocation of sentimental naïveté; the third, by Robbins himself, revealed the intense one, the introvert, in modern movement with rumba embellishments and frequent How'm-I-doin' glances at the two girls they are all out to get. The way the three danced over the counter and stools of the bar could be traced directly to Martha Graham's use of functional décor and to the scenic mobility of the Humphrey-Weidman blocks.

Humor, warm and friendly, was the seed of Jerry's first success, and it developed in his later works, sometimes into a fine plant, sometimes into a rank weed. His ballet, *Interplay* (1945), is full of healthy laughter. It puts four boys and four girls in gay practice clothes, through technical paces that make an abstract design, faceted with the high spirits of vigorous American youth. They swing the classic steps hot, they swing them sweet, they punctuate them with zippy fragments of American sports, or quiet interludes of love-making. They are hearty young Americans having a communicably good time.

In *Facsimile* (1946) the humor becomes sardonic, baring the psyches of a trio of spoiled sophisticates in a Daliesque setting as barren as their own hearts and minds. Here the love-making is less innocent. The Woman (Nora Kaye) is alternately bored with it or so surfeited she goes hysterical and cries "Stop! Stop!" in the middle of it. In the end her two cavaliers (Hugh Laing and John Kriza) walk off in disgust, leaving her in contemplation of her own emptiness. The movement, classically based, reflects both the Tudor gesture and the Balanchine convolution, which is something of a feat.

Fancy Free was expanded, and unavoidably diluted, in the musical, *On the Town,* in which the sailors were multiplied and the dancing diminished. Robbins did create one funny new scene, in the Museum of Natural History, bringing primeval man and his mate out of their show-cases, to grope and grunt about the stage. His success in the musicomedy field has not been too good for him. The highly touted "Mack Sennett" or as it was later more discreetly labelled, the "Chase" Ballet in *High Button Shoes,* was really, when analyzed as dance, just so much rag-tag and bobtail. And for his long awaited, semi-autobiographical *Look Ma, I'm Dancin'*, he plagiarized this (his own) farce-fantasy into a coarse and cluttered extravaganza called "Mademoiselle Marie," a burlesque-boudoir ballet, in which was a great deal of stripping off of pants and display of striped underwear, and more tearing on and off stage than dancing.

For "The Ballet" (in this production) he served a warmed-over *Interplay* in less compendious form and less attractive costumes. The great public does not know the difference, he may figure, but there are always some people who do, including himself. His "Pajama Ballet," a sleep-walking scene in a Pullman, based on walks and lifts, was smarter, secreting a sly notation in the back line, where, among a stageful of boys with girls on their shoulders, he placed one boy with another boy on his. The opening "Gotta Dance" was a slick patchwork of all kinds of dancing. But none of it was Robbins at his best save the luminous little *pas de deux* rehearsal from *Swan Lake*. Mama, Look at Jerry, and make him work.

Michael Kidd's first ballet, *On Stage!*, had its *première* by Ballet Theatre at the Boston Opera House on October 4, 1945. Like the lady with the lorgnette, who didn't think the young people in *Fancy Free* were quite the right sort of young people to have in a ballet, one conservative dance teacher felt that "Okay" and "That's swell" weren't quite the right words to issue from a ballet, if one must have such unconventional things as words. Nevertheless, *On Stage!* went to the spot with most of the audience, for it is a balletina lifted from life. The backstage atmosphere, with the boys and girls lounging about smoking cigarettes, or jitterbugging behind the ballet master's back, their squeals and chatter, his directions, bore the impress of genuine experience. The little story of the Girl in Pink who is too shy to go through her audition, but with the help of the Handyman gets into the company all the same, is simple and human. Likewise the manner of telling it. And here again the Humphrey-Weidman boxes come in. The rehearsal of the ballet within the ballet is played on a large packing case, and the action spreads over many levels, and with props.

On Stage! was made by heart while Michael and his wife, Mary

Heater, were making their loft studio in Hell's Kitchen by hand. They had scavenged junk piles for the plumbing, and carried off rusty beams from abandoned buildings. Michael always had a hammer in his pocket and was heavenly-at-home on a ladder. Short, dark, quick of speech and step, he could always stop for comedy tricks, like balancing a folded newspaper on the end of his nose. One day, when he was cavorting around the studio with a broom, Mary said, "You ought to put yourself in a ballet." So together they devised the short-short story that would set the Handyman in his work-clothes, broom, hammer, ladder, tricks and all, against a ballet background. They were in the Ballet Caravan at the time. Before they could get their ballet produced they had joined Ballet Theatre, and Antony Tudor's *Dim Lustre,* with its dim-outs for remembrances, came along. Their ballet had dim-outs for day-dreams, and they were afraid everybody would think they had taken the idea from Tudor. But *On Stage!* passed on its own merits when it was finally produced, except for the strict balleticians, who likened its playful incidents to musical comedy gags.

Michael's first Broadway assignment was staging the dances for *Finian's Rainbow,* a fantasy on an interracial theme. With charming alacrity he weaves his white and Negro dancers through the plot and right across the color line. The all-movement part of the mute girl, danced during the first of the run by Anita Alvarez (a former Graham dancer), is especially well worked out, but all the dances are fresh and engaging. In the spring of 1948 he did the dances for a tumbling, collegiate, not to say extremely sophomoric piece called *Hold It,* with less success. That the dances were the best of it was easy.

Good as it is for modern dance to be in the commercial theater and for the commercial theater to have modern dance in it, modern dance can preserve its integrity only in its own theater. It is in itself dramatic enough to satisfy the dramatic dancer. Its pure creativity cannot yield to compromise. But these are the sacred precincts of the great. There are creative dancers of quality who find a satisfactory outlet (and intake) in the theater, and the theater is thereby blessed. By all means let them follow the uproad so long as it does not lead to the downgrade. Broadway success is dangerous, but less dangerous for those who know how to take it. It is bad for the ballet dancer who considers it a boost to get a speaking part in a musical show, or, with his or her dancer's voice, aspires to legitimate drama. Nobody expects to dance professionally without training. Why should a dancer expect to speak or sing professionally without it?

If modern dance does not improve the voice, it does liberate the torso and free the extremities for something more vivifying than mere flinging about. Because of it, dancing on the musical comedy stage is no longer a thing of arms and legs, or of legs only, but of the whole being. The old-fashioned dances went in one eye and out the other. The new dances have more staying power. Modern dance does not always tell its real name on Broadway, but it's there.

IN PROCESSED FORM

Radio, Video, and Movio

Late in 1947 a new Graham mystery filled the air. Who was Miss Hush? She was a dancer. Her initials were M. G. She spoke on the radio once a week, throwing out clues to her identity in verse. A Texan housewife, Mrs. Ruth Subbie of Fort Worth, miraculously guessed it, and thereby won around $20,000 worth of washing machines, electric refrigerators, electronic blankets, Venetian blinds, a television set, a trailer, and other gadgetry of the good life, besides a trip to Honolulu, and about $5000 increase in income tax. Whatever additional benefits accrued from the contest went to the March of Dimes. Mrs. Subbie wept, for joy, it was said, though it might have been worry over the large assortment of hardware coming her way. This is one woman! This is three million women! This is America! In February 1948, Miss Martha Hush Graham gave the most brilliant Broadway season of her career, without amassing much more than expenses, if that. There were rumors of her starring in a film version of her life, to be called, with great significance, *Miss Hush*. They ebbed away with the excitement over Mrs. Subbie's fortune, which failed to include tickets to a Graham concert, or a book on Martha Graham.

So much for the air waves, where modern dance can take its place among the soap operas and be Hooper-rated, all in a good cause. The contact is not very close. You do not feel modern dance by your cozy radio-side. You do not hear modern dance. You sometimes hear its audible partner, in suites made from its most celebrated scores. You occasionally hear about it, in instructive talks by its leading dancers and lecturers. Turn on the radio and *what* d'ya hear? Certainly nothing kinesthetic bending your ear.

Then there is Television, called Video by its addicts, a department of public works being pushed for all or more than it is worth in 1948. The *coup* of the year was the televised broadcast of Toscanini's modeled face and mobile hands, conducting the NBC orchestra. The instruments and the players were also shown. And I believe you could hear the music if you weren't too busy looking. On such triumphs national merchandising waits. Whatever locked-in-goodness Video may hold for the future is more likely to come out in advertising than in art. You can probably learn a lot about Crunchies if you have one of these private kinetoscopes (there isn't much scope yet) in your front parlor. You can see a pitcher curve a baseball, a scrap of prizefight, or a fragment of slalom on a patch of mountain snow. The great white hope of the brave new world is still in a nubilous state. According to some of its promoters, it expects to conquer space and time, to sublimate the theater arts, to put its sister arts out of commission. But as these noble works have got to be paid for, and by not wholly disinterested backers, the noble sentiments are not likely to be less commercialized than those of Mother's Day.

Some people think that dance is a natural for television. It may be for little dances. But how can great dance be scaled to televisibility? How can the dance of volume be performed in a two-by-four set (literally ten feet square, but growing), with converging floor lines and backdrop painted to give an illusion of space that isn't there? Long shots have to be used sparingly. Where is the group work of sweep and power? Modern dance is not essentially a solo form, so close-ups are undesirable. It cannot be confined to the verticality the television studio is said to require, because it is multi-dimensional. It has breadth as well as height, and depth in several senses. One of them is meaning, which, in the family living-room, might be tabu. No psychological research or pathological clinics can be held in the House of the Future, where the Video Nook or Reception Wall will supplant the fireplace, and entertainment must be made safe for children—who will have to hang their Christmas stockings on knobs. In the age of television, modern dance will be video dance, as easy to take and as empty of nourishment as processed foods. There is one advantage—in the boasted continuity. Look, no cuts! No retakes! No plot interference! It is something to see a screen dance through from start to finish.

By now most modern dancers, and many others, have appeared on the new wonder-machine. One of the early venturers in the medium was Tashamira, of Jugoslavian origin, a specialist in Balkan folk dances, who studied with Laban, Dalcroze, and an exponent of Russian ballet, and uses all forms creatively. In 1931 she telecast for CBS *The Crystal,* adapted to the then even more limited space in movements of hands, head, and torso only. Her *Impressions of Negro Spirituals,* over WNBT–NBC, did not need much adaptation since it was again in the upper body, and not space-roaming. In recent years, Sophie Maslow's *Folksay* has come through well, they say. Martha Graham, who has so far appeared once, came to the conclusion that what was needed was "not televised dance, but dance designed for television." She is not the one to come down from her great work to make a toy of dance. The new pioneering belongs to the new generations.

PAULINE KONER AND KITTY DONER

Among those in the forefront of tele-dance activity are Pauline Koner and Kitty Doner, who have done a great deal of experimenting in the field, and written extensively for *Tele-screen,* the first and possibly the only magazine devoted to the subject. In 1945 they introduced a series of Choreotone Ballets for CBS, especially choreographed and cameragraphed (the new art brings new contributions to semantics) for the specific demands of television. Only a few dancers were used, the whole body could be seen (in miniature), and, with suitably simple décor and costumes, the dances were so pleasing that people asked for more. A new series was issued the following year. *It's a Date, Grandma's Sofa, Park Bench, Frisco Blues* were some of the titles, clearly on the lighter side. From various articles it seems that the camera is co-choreographer, that trick shots and angles are as important as the dancing, which, perhaps, has to be tricked up a little, too. In the tectonics of television, the stresses must all be upright.There is no space for flying buttresses, or dancers, and it depends on the choreotonic artist how much for flights of imagination. One thing is sure, there cannot be much digging below the pictorial surface. If the development of television parallels that of radio, a Humphrey or a Graham production will be a greater novelty on the telescreen than a Mahler symphony on the air.

People who are fond of having concert or commercial voices carolling in the home at the push of a button, will also think it an asset to have concert or commercial movement on tap as part of the domestic scene. For those to whom music and dance are events, to put your shoes on for and go half way to meet, radio, turned on or left running like so much wasted water, and television, turned into a suburban party, are to be classified among the household pests. Happily, the canned arts are good for shut-ins, who for unhappy reasons are unable to obtain fresh products for themselves. To those who like their music live and their dance living, and can have them so, and prefer a good book at home, they are a blight on the pursuit of happiness. Television, like radio, can be made useful for study, analysis, cultural information, current news, or idle recreation. Sat around and watched in slippers, or served with refreshments, exclaimed over and chatted about socially, the subject descends to the level of its surroundings. This is not the milieu for modern dance. Out of experimentation a new dance form may emerge, as expressive of its time as any that has gone before. It will still be the artificial Nightingale. Let it reign for those who want it, so long as the real Nightingale is not banished.

Of the mass magic of movies there is more to be said. For one thing, excepting the imposition of home travelogues, you have to get out of your own four walls to see them. You sit among large numbers of other people, popcorn crackling around you, and on holidays ice-cream cones dripping over you, one with humanity, immersed in the communal deliverance from care. On the screen you see people live like the ladies and gentlemen you would be if you could, in grander houses, and with much nicer furniture than your own. And wearing far finer clothes. You may not yearn to behave as all of them do, but who wouldn't look like a movie star? Of course there are character actors and extras, with straggly hair and unpressed garments, and other signs of the dishevelment of human living, by way of keeping in touch with the lower grades of life. There is also dancing—mostly in blobs and blurts—for the story keeps getting in the way of it. Lovers must kiss at the proper moment, whether the dance sequence is finished or not.

WALT DISNEY, JACK COLE, EUGENE LORING

Dance in Hollywood has advanced from the Busby Berkeley formula of circular bouquets made of lovely flower-like girls. Walt Disney, whose Silly Symphonies were dance symphonies from the beginning, modeled his "Rite of Spring" number in *Fantasia,* the best of that overblown production, on modern dance. His prehistoric animals, in their stark, primordial setting, all moved as if they had been studying with Bennington's Big Four, or, more likely, with Lester Horton. As nobody could say exactly how a dinosaur or a pterodactyl walked, nobody could gainsay him. At any rate, the slow, ponderous pace, the movement differentiated according to the size and contour and imagined nature of each animal, the dignity of their march to doom, made a ritual of mammoths, that, given a score composed for it, and a title without Stravinsky's connotations, might have been a masterpiece. But modern dance is still the exception in the commercial picture. When it gets in it is more or less smuggled in and regarded as "stylized" dancing. It is not as modern dancers (which, basically, they are not) that Jack Cole in *Tonight and Every Night,* and Eugene Loring in *Yolanda and the Thief,* accomplished their work of manumission. The dances they designed and directed surmounted the obstacles of both plot and color in ballets of free, space-covering mobility unmarred by plot intrusion. They were, in fact, a part of the plot action.

Here, though, as in other pictured dances, Hollywood's space consciousness runs wild with freedom. It sometimes ranges such vasty vistas that the scene becomes as desolate as the prospect of an eternity one is not prepared to meet. The endless ramps and limitless gardens make lost wanderers of the dancers, and emit the swampy miasma of a long, depressing dream. There is as much too much space in the motion picture as there is too little in television. As for garish cinema color, it usually blurs the edges of a dance into a fuzzy kaleidoscope. It is too lush for dance. *Ziegfeld Follies,* for example, began and ended in pink, with a smoky-blue "Limehouse Blues" number between, and the effect was that of having eaten a large box of sugar bonbons, all pink, unrelieved by a raisin filling. The most satisfactory color dance film to date is Katherine Dunham's *Carnival of Rhythm.*

GENE KELLY

For modern dance values in the commercial movie, the prize goes to Gene Kelly, the hoofer of Broadway's *Pal Joey* and *The Time of Your Life,* who does not dance with his feet only. His "Shadow Dance" in *Cover Girl* was manufactured within its medium creatively. Technically, the dance colloquy with his alter ego, or conscience—himself reflected progressively in the windows of a city street, but moving differently the length of the passage—depended on the dolly shot and double exposure. Dancically, the expression of inner conflict depended on his free, widely varied movement of arms and body on the base of his skilfully tapping feet. Such a combination of dance and motion picture technique makes for creative dance cinematography, prefiguring the cine-dance, which, like the *ciné-poème* and the tele-dance, is evolved out of its own mechanisms. In *Anchors Aweigh,* a lesser picture, Kelly's duo with an animated cartoon mouse in the fantasy, "The King Who Wouldn't Dance," was also creative in the cinema sense. It was light, infectiously rhythmic dancing, done in Kelly's free, individual style, with the mouse a diminutive counterpart—again impossible without the cinematic machinery. As an actor in *The Pirate,* a dish of treacle in Technicolor, Kelly still shone as a dancer, but less creatively.

The appeal of the movies is movement. We live, therefore we move. And we like to watch other creatures move, as if in confirmation of our inborn feeling that movement means life. The movies present movement images, designs from life, that sometimes interpret life. They convey mental states and reactions. A fine picture like *Naked City* can hold us by its fluidity of movement (and mental comment) alone, apart from the story. The movies at their best use movement with something approaching the intelligence and expressivity of modern dance. At that rare level, the movement images become movement imagery—in a mechanized representation of life. For cinematic movement imagery of poetic truthfulness to life in dance, we must generally look to the non-commercial field.

THOMAS BOUCHARD

In this field the creative photographer Thomas Bouchard has done most for modern dance. His film records of complete dances, and they are all too few, are of inestimable value as history as well as art, and so are his portrait studies of dance movement. As an art student in Paris, contemporary with Soutine and other painters then little known, he learned the fundamentals which, in the United States, he applied to photography. As an artist susceptible to movement, it was natural that his work in America should gravitate to modern dance. His best photographs vibrate between deep, luminous blacks and glowing lights in supple intermediate tones. They are marvels of design and chiaroscuro. Some of his most unusual compositions are too dark for reproduction; others come out flat and uninteresting. But in the main he cuts to the quick of modern movement and illumines it in his presentation. Others have come and gone in modern dance favor, but none has equalled his special quality.

One of his earliest motion picture experiments was a sound short of John Bovingdon's *Underground Printer*. He has filmed some of Martha Graham's dances, though he does not list any of them in his completed works. His first major dance film, made in 1938, was Doris Humphrey's *The Shakers,* silent, in black and white, running nineteen minutes. Then he did Hanya Holm's *The Golden Fleece* in color, also silent, running twenty-seven minutes. Her *Ozark Set,* to Elie Siegmeister's score, is edited with music, in black and white, and about twelve minutes long. Bouchard was a Bennington character and went out to Mills College with the outfit. There he started shooting José Limón's *Danzas Mexicanas* in black and white, and in 1947 was still hoping to get it finished and to film the *Vivaldi Concerto* in color. His dance films are not made in a hurry. They are all in 16 mm. size and have been shown in leading art museums, schools, and colleges throughout the country.

Other notable artist photographers are Barbara Morgan, whose brilliant "portraits of energy" are consummated in Martha Graham's work; and Gerda Peterich, who did "dynamic portraits" of Doris Humphrey, Sophie Maslow, and others, before she left the dance field. The exciting, whirlwind Gjon Mili photographs action without particularizing in modern movement. John Lindquist, of Boston, photographs all kinds of dancers as they come to Jacob's

Pillow in the summer. Richard Tucker, in Boston and New York, used to snap stage action from the prompter's box before it was forbidden, and still follows the shows (and the dancers) with his camera. There are hosts of good photographers who are amenable to modern dance but whose work is not confined to it.

MAYA DEREN

If in dance photography Bouchard goes furthest in nuantial penetration without becoming inaccessible, Maya Deren goes further, into the subconscious, to an extreme of inaccessibility. Her one real dance film is the three-minute short, *A Study in Choreography for Camera.* It is, as she defines it, "a duet between space and a dancer," and its strangeness is enhanced by silence. The dancer is the Dunham-trained Talley Beatty, an excellent dancer without the aid of a camera. Under its *sorcellerie,* his leaps become phenomenal, a sort of universal wish fulfillment to navigate the air. The absence of aural rhythm gives it the haunting unreality of dream, a dream to remember and understand. The dancer, seen in slow motion, lands on his feet every time. And so do we.

The other three films are very, very ultra. They are not dance films, but phantasmagorias of frustration, done in terms of movement imagery that often resembles modern dance at its most baffling. In *Meshes of the Afternoon,* a shrouded figure in black with a mirror for countenance (seldom disclosed) actually looks and walks like Martha Graham, back view, and is as darkly foreboding and tantalizing as some Graham dances. The action roves over a deserted house and garden, again in that awful soundlessness. The sufferer (Miss Deren herself) keeps chasing the mysterious woman in black, and never catches up with her. Perhaps she is only expressing the frustration one can feel at the first performance of a Graham work.

At Land shows the girl, still Miss Deren (and comely), still frustrated, this time to find the dry land as slippery and furrowy as the waves of the sea, and the sea firmer than terra firma. She has a bad time, too, pursuing people and things ineffectually, and running across a chess game reminiscent of *Deaths and Entrances.* Is this a Graham complex? The race question enters *Ritual in Transfigured Time* with a remarkable use of blacks and whites, and scenes suddenly frozen into tableaux, and as suddenly breaking into freak action again. The heroine, who has been slighted at a party, ends, by reverse negative, as a wonderfully photogenic black-faced, white-frilled bride. Here as in the other pictures, all is highly imaginative, and all is silent as the grave.

Miss Deren screened these *avant-garde* (16 mm.) films at Boston's Institute of Modern Art, which lately repudiated the "Modern" and now calls itself the Institute of Contemporary Art. She spoke before the screening, explaining or trying to explain her ideas in that precious patter to be heard only in art galleries, so that her lecture was about as remote as her pictures. One item did channel to the mind. Her next experiment was to be with sound. She would portray the idea associations flickering through the thoughts of a woman by an open window, in the audible cross-currents from within the room and from the street without. She was carrying forward her audio-visual researches into the subconscious on a Guggenheim Fellowship. She is a mettlesome pioneer in the processed forms.

Agnes de Mille once said that in Western civilization the sixteenth and seventeenth centuries represented the age of words; the eighteenth and nineteenth the age of music; and the twentieth century the age of movement. If in the next fifty years we can preserve the three together, and put them up in cans and boxes, the twenty-first century will bring a millennium of mechanized art.

But we have fifty years to go, and, the split atom permitting, that long to enjoy living movement.

BIBLIOGRAPHY

ARMITAGE, MERLE (editor): *Martha Graham,* miscellaneous essays, illustrated. Los Angeles: Merle Armitage; 1937.

ARMITAGE, MERLE (editor): *Modern Dance,* miscellaneous essays compiled by Virginia Stewart, illustrated. New York: E. Weyhe; 1935.

DUNCAN, IRMA: *The Technique of Isadora Duncan,* illustrated. New York: Kamin Publishers; 1937.

DUNCAN, ISADORA: *The Art of the Dance,* miscellaneous essays, illustrated. New York: Theatre Arts, Inc.; 1928.

DUNCAN, ISADORA: *My Life.* New York: Boni and Liveright; 1927.

GENTHE, ARNOLD: *Isadora Duncan, Twenty-four Studies* (photographs). New York & London: Mitchell Kennerley; 1929.

GENTHE, ARNOLD: *The Book of the Dance,* miscellaneous photographs. Boston: International Publishers; 1920.

H'DOUBLER, MARGARET N.: *The Dance and Its Place in Education.* New York: Harcourt, Brace and Company; 1925.

H'DOUBLER, MARGARET N.: *Dance, A Creative Art Experience,* illustrated. New York: F. S. Crofts and Company; 1940.

HORST, LOUIS: *Pre-Classic Dance Forms,* illustrated. New York: The Dance Observer; 1937.

355

Magriel, Paul, (editor): *Isadora Duncan* (Reprints from *Dance Index*, illustrated). New York: Henry Holt and Company; 1947.

Martin, John: *America Dancing*, illustrated. New York: Dodge Publishing Company; 1936.

Martin, John: *Introduction to the Dance*, illustrated. New York: W. W. Norton & Company, Inc.; 1939.

Martin, John: *The Dance*, "the story of the dance told in pictures and text." New York: Tudor Publishing Company; 1946.

Martin, John: *The Modern Dance* (lectures given at the New School for Social Research). New York: A. S. Barnes and Company, Incorporated; 1933.

Morgan, Barbara: *Martha Graham, Sixteen Dances in Photographs*. New York: Duell, Sloan and Pearce; 1941.

Radir, Ruth: *Modern Dance for the Youth of America*. New York: A. S. Barnes and Company, Incorporated; 1944.

Selden, Elizabeth: *Elements of the Free Dance*. New York: A. S. Barnes and Company, Incorporated; 1930.

Selden, Elizabeth: *The Dancer's Quest*, illustrated. Berkeley: University of California Press; 1935.

Shawn, Ted: *Dance We Must* (lectures given at the George Peabody College for Teachers, Nashville, Tennessee). Privately printed; 1940.

St. Denis, Ruth: *An Unfinished Life*, illustrated. New York and London: Harper & Brothers Publishers; 1939.

Terry, Walter: *Invitation to Dance*. New York: A. S. Barnes & Company, Incorporated; 1942.

Trowbridge, Charlotte: *Dance Drawings of Martha Graham*. New York: The Dance Observer; 1945.

Wigman, Mary: *Deutsche Tanzkunst* (in German, illustrated). Dresden, Germany: Carl Reisner, Publisher; 1935.

GENERAL INDEX

See also specific Index of Dances, page xv

INDEX OF DANCES

A NOTE ON THE TYPE

THE TEXT OF THIS BOOK was set on the Linotype in Baskerville. Linotype Baskerville is a facsimile cutting from type cast from the original matrices of a face designed by John Baskerville. The original face was the forerunner of the "modern" group of type faces.

John Baskerville (1706–75), of Birmingham, England, a writing-master, with a special renown for cutting inscriptions in stone, began experimenting about 1750 with punch-cutting and making typographical material. It was not until 1757 that he published his first work, a Virgil in royal quarto, with great-primer letters. This was followed by his famous editions of Milton, the Bible, the Book of Common Prayer, and several Latin classic authors. His types, at first criticized as unnecessarily slender, delicate, and feminine, in time were recognized as both distinct and elegant, and his types as well as his printing were greatly admired. Four years after his death Baskerville's widow sold all his punches and matrices to the Société Littéraire-typographique, which used some of the types for the sumptuous Kehl edition of Voltaire's works in seventy volumes.

The original edition of this book was composed, printed, and bound by Kingsport Press, Inc., Kingsport, Tenn., and was designed by Harry Ford.